Your Internet Consultant: The FAQs of Life Online

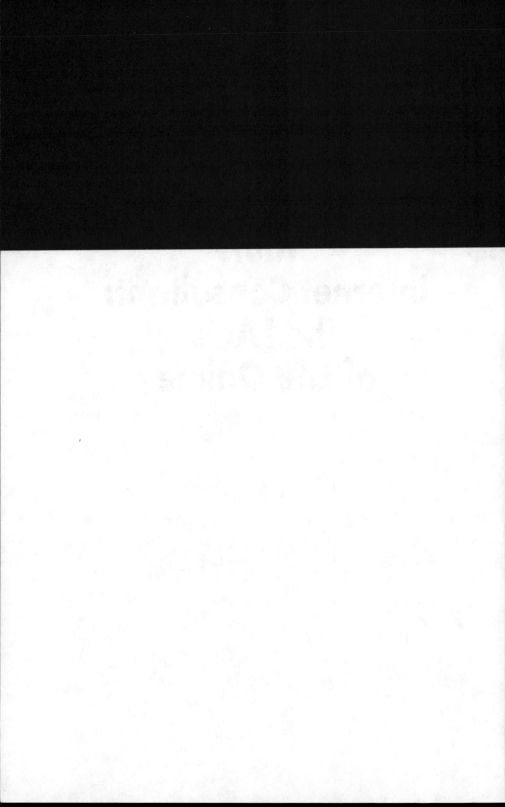

Your Internet Consultant: The FAQs of Life Online

Kevin Savetz

A Division of Macmillan Computer Publishing,
A Prentice Hall Macmillan Company
201 West 103rd Street, Indianapolis, Indiana 46290 USA

For Peace.

International Standard Book Number: 0-672-30520-8

Library of Congress Catalog Card Number: 94-66274

97 96 95 94 4 3 2 1

Interpretation of the printing code: the rightmost double-digit number is the year of the book's printing; the rightmost single digit, the number of the book's printing. For example, a printing code of 94-1 shows that the first printing of the book occurred in 1994.

Trademarks

Composed in AGaramond and MCPdigital by Macmillan Computer Publishing
Printed in the United States of America

Publisher
Richard K. Swadley

Associate Publisher
Jordan Gold

Acquisitions Manager
Stacy Hiquet

Managing Editor
Cindy Morrow

Acquisitions and Development Editor
Mark Taber

Production Editor
Katherine Stuart Ewing

Editor
Susan Christophersen

Editorial and Graphics Coordinator
Bill Whitmer

Editorial Assistants
Sharon Cox
Lynette Quinn

Technical Reviewer
Dave Taylor

Marketing Manager
Gregg Bushyeager

Cover Designer
Tim Amrhein

Director of Production and Manufacturing
Jeff Valler

Imprint Manager
Paul Gilchrist

Manufacturing Coordinator
Barry Pruett

Book Designer
Alyssa Yesh

Production Analysts
Dennis Clay Hager
Mary Beth Wakefield

Proofreading Coordinator
Joelynn Gifford

Indexing Coordinator
Johnna VanHoose

Graphics Image Specialists
Teresa Forrester
Tim Montgomery
Dennis Sheehan
Sue VandeWalle

Proofreaders
Carol Bowers
Ayrika Bryant
Kim Cofer
Kimberly K. Hannel
Greg Kemp
Jamie Milazzo
Ryan Rader
Kris Simmons
SA Springer
Michael Thomas

Production
Elaine Brush
Steph Davis
Angela P. Judy
Ayanna Lacey
Chad Poore
Kim Scott
Scott Tullis
Dennis Wesner

Indexer
Craig Small

Contents

Question Reference

1 Just What Is This Internet? 1

About the Author

Kevin Savetz is a computer journalist and Internet aficionado who lives in Humboldt County, California. He writes for a variety of magazines, including *Internet World, Internet Business Journal, CD-ROM World, Mac Home Journal,* and *Online Access.* He maintains several online Frequently Asked Questions documents, including the Internet Services FAQ and the Unofficial Internet Book List. Kevin graduated from Humboldt State University with a BA in journalism and a minor in computer information systems.

Foreword
by Daniel Dern

Among its other wonders, marvels, and delights, the Internet is home to a mind-boggling sea of questions and answers on what often appears to be every topic under the sun, from "How do I send e-mail from my Internet account to someone on CompuServe?" or "What Firesign Theatre CDs are available?"

Within a given topic, many of these are the basic questions that any newcomer would (or should) ask—that is, *Questions that are Asked Frequently.* Frequently-Asked Questions (FAQ) documents, which collect such questions and answers, are one of the not-at-all-secret Great Resources of the Internet.

Online copies of the Internet's thousands of FAQs are squirreled away in various nooks and crannies across the Internet's global reaches, where the able Internaut can, with a modicum of skill and effort, find and read 'em.

Many of these FAQs contain information invaluable to the Internet newcomer, a.k.a. "newbie"—everything from what TCP/IP software is available for your desktop computer to who offers "Internet accounts" and the Netiquette of participating in a global online society.

The catch-22, of course, is that to find said answers on the Internet, you have to already have access to the Internet, and already know enough about the Internet and its tools to be able to figure out where and how to look.

Even for an experienced Internaut, this can occasionally be a frustrating task. For a newbie only beginning to access and use the Internet—or someone who hasn't yet gotten even that far—being told "it's on the Net" is like telling someone who doesn't have a telephone to call Directory Information.

Enter, among others, Kevin Savetz.

Kevin clearly suffers from a fascination with the Internet and the dreaded Restless Urge to Write. I first encountered Kevin a few years ago—by e-mail, not surprisingly—in the course of an Internet article he was writing. I subsequently had the opportunity to buy several articles from him for *Internet World* magazine, of which I was editor-in-chief for the first six issues.

Through Kevin's articles, I learned a lot more about Internet oddities, such as MUDs and MOOs and MUSHes, the Usenet Oracle, and backgammon in cyberspace. Kevin, in turn, had the dubious pleasure of working with a demanding, nit-picking, curmudgeonly editor who insisted on precision, completeness, and focus as only someone who's already written one Internet book can. (I hope Kevin feels this was a fair trade.)

Kevin also started and took responsibility for maintaining FAQs that are, in my opinion, essential reading for new Internet users, such as the Internet Services FAQ and the Unofficial Internet Booklist.

As Kevin seems to have discovered, the answers to new users' questions about the Internet and how to use it would fill a book—this book, to be specific. And you don't need a computer, modem, or electricity to read a book—unless it's dark out, of course `:-)`.

There's probably some information in here you won't find on the Internet no matter how hard you look—and I guarantee that a lot of what's in here is a lot easier to find by using the book than by pursuing it online. And if you have any other questions about Kevin Savetz or his book, I suggest that the answers are undoubtedly in an FAQ that Kevin has created for just this purpose.

Read, learn, enjoy. And (I predict) within a month or so you'll in turn find yourself answering questions like these that people ask you.

Any questions?

Daniel P. Dern
`<ddern@world.std.com>`
May, 1994

Introduction

Hello, world! Welcome to *Your Internet Consultant—the FAQs of Life Online.* Chances are, if you're new to the Internet or you're just not acronym-adept, you're asking yourself, "What does FAQ mean?" That is a wholly fair and reasonable question. In response to that fair and reasonable question—and future questions, both reasonable and unreasonable—I will try to provide a reasonable answer. So we begin.

I.1. What does FAQ mean?

FAQ is Internet-speak for *frequently asked question.* An FAQ is one of those questions that is so common, so pervasive that, well, it is asked frequently. Every field has its FAQs: ice skating, parenting, the Internet.

Some folks on the Internet who are experts in their fields create lists of FAQs and distribute them. (Actually, they aren't just lists of frequently asked questions; they wouldn't be useful unless they gave the answers, too.) These lists are called FAQ&A lists (FAQ&A means *frequently asked questions and answers*), FAQ lists, or (to confuse the issue) just FAQs. FAQ is pronounced either as *eff aye queue* or simply *fack.* I like the latter pronunciation because it sounds a lot like *facts,* which is, it is hoped, what they are.

I publish one such list, called the Internet Services FAQ. This is a compilation of about 25 frequently asked questions about the Internet and its services. As a long-time Internet user and writer, I read hundreds of the same questions over and over again as each new user explores the Internet and climbs his or her own learning curve. My FAQ list was to be a few pages long and distributed on the Internet to help new users along.

It became clear to me early on that I needed to be very selective as to what questions could be answered in that FAQ list and how in-depth the answers would be, lest the document become a 600-page book. With so many tools and services on the Internet, and so many great questions to be answered, keeping the FAQ list manageable is an inexact science. I have had to pass up some great questions and delightful answers in the quest for brevity.

One major problem is that most users don't know how to find the answers to their all-too-common questions. Although some of this information is available online, a user must know how to navigate the Net in a variety of ways just to find the smattering of documents that are supposed to help. If the user knew how to navigate the Internet, he or she probably wouldn't need help in the first place.

Well, as you can see, my FAQ list has become a 590-page book.

Q I.2. Does the world need another Internet book?

This is an important question, especially to me. About 50 new books about the Internet were published in 1993, certainly with dozens more to follow in 1994. The problem is, most of these books try to be everything to everyone. The world certainly does not need another 1,000-page *All You Need to Know About the Internet* tome. The majority of these books talk about the Internet as if it's a science, but it isn't. The Internet is a living, growing, ever-changing entity. Those books tend to move from start to finish in a methodical fashion: "This is Telnet, here's what you can do with it; this is FTP, here's what you can do with it," and so on.

The world doesn't need any more of those. What people do need, though, is a book that clearly and simply answers the questions they have while exploring the Internet. This book is filled with what people have asked countless times—frequently asked questions.

Admittedly, some of the questions aren't really frequently asked. Some of them are ones that I only wish were asked more often. You can tell those pretty easily: they usually look like "How can I annoy people...?" or something similar. They're my attempt to force-feed the information you need to know, but might not know you need to know.

This book is not geared toward any single type of user. Novices and experienced "Internauts" alike will learn something from this book. If I've done my job, you should be able to come back time and time again for another dose of information, to find the answer to whatever new questions cross your mind.

This book doesn't assume that you have one particular type of Internet access. People connect to the Internet from every conceivable computer system using a variety of access types. You might be using a Sun SparcStation with direct Internet access, or dialing in to a command-line UNIX service from a Macintosh, or sending Internet e-mail from CompuServe with your IBM PC. Readers with (for instance) only electronic mail will still find plenty of useful information herein. When you are ready to venture to new things, you can turn to this book for information on how to get started with the new tools. I hope there is something here for everyone on the Net, using any type of connection.

Q I.3. What won't this book do for me?

This book is just a stepping stone on the path of exploring the Internet. I hope you will find that it makes your learning process easy and fun. There are a hundred ways that you can access the Internet, however, as well as dozens of programs available for sending e-mail, reading Usenet news, and so on, and they each work differently. This book doesn't try to cover them all. Therefore, reading this book will not excuse you from reading lots of online help or perusing online FAQ lists. It also doesn't excuse you from experimenting or making mistakes. Doing all of those things is part of learning about the Internet.

Q I.4. How is this book organized?

From where I sit, musing at the computer files—half-written chapters, cryptic notes to myself, and the like—my reaction is to laugh at the assumption that this book is organized.

From where you sit, however, things should be slightly more

comprehensible. This book is task-oriented, instead of having lumped together all the functions of each Internet tool. The following chapters are arranged by what you want to do; for instance, getting online, using electronic mail, and understanding Internet culture. Here's a brief overview of the chapters:

Just What Is This Internet? Answers questions about the Internet itself: where it came from, what you'll find there, and what makes it tick.

How Do I Get Connected to the Internet? On the way to answering this question, Chapter 2 also explains the types of access, costs involved, and what you should look for when choosing an access method.

How Does the Internet Work? The first get-your-hands-dirty chapter. It shows you the basics of UNIX (the operating system that is a very common diving board into the Internet puddle), how computers on the Internet talk to one another, and why they're called what they're called.

How Can I Communicate with People Around the World? Answers questions about one of the most common and powerful tools, electronic mail. If you want to know how to send e-mail to a user on another network, why your mail keeps bouncing, or how to let others know who you are, check here. Remember that this book is task-oriented, so this chapter meanders off into other cool things like signatures and plan files.

Where Can I Discuss My Favorite Film, Food, or Fetish...and Just About Anything Else? Explores the questions about the Usenet, the Internet's vast, mind-numbingly huge distributed bulletin board. This chapter looks at how to use the Usenet, how it's organized, and why people use it.

How Can I Find and Use Software (and Other Stuff)? Looks at questions about how to find and get software...and stuff. Tools like FTP, FSP, and Archie are covered, as well as tips on finding electronic journals, graphics, and software archives. If you want to know where on the Internet to find software for your particular computer, check here.

How Do I Track Down Information? Answers a variety of questions about finding information online. This chapter tells you specifically where to go if you're looking for headline news or pictures of the weather, and general instructions on finding any other topic online.

Can I Do Business on the Internet? Shows how you can find business information (from stock reports to job listings) online and covers the much-ballyhooed "commercialization of the Internet."

Is There Government Information Online? Answers questions about finding United States and Canadian government resources online.

Where Are All the Fun and Games? Shows how you can play games, chat with newfound friends, and slay dragons.

What Do I Need to Know about Internet Culture and Lore? Looks at "netiquette" (network etiquette) and the language of the Net, such as acronyms and smileys `:-)`. Funky networked appliances like Coke machines and toasters are covered here, too.

How Can I Keep My Privacy and Stay Secure? Answers important questions that affect everyone on the Internet, including how to protect yourself, keep your personal information private, and use anonymous mail servers.

The appendixes. Two appendixes tell you where to look in books, magazines, and (of course) online for more information about the Internet. Another appendix lists commercial Internet service providers.

I.5. What conventions are used in this book?

Commands that you type are in **`bold monospace font`**, and the output from those commands is in `monospace font`.

Within answers, I often need to point to a file on the Internet or tell how to send electronic mail to perform a certain action, like retrieving a file via e-mail. If I'm explaining where to find a file via anonymous FTP (which, by the way, is covered in Chapter 6, "How Can I Find and Use Software?"), you'll see a line like this:

```
rtfm.mit.edu:/pub/usenet/news.answers/internet-services/faq
```

This means to use the FTP command to open a connection to `rtfm.mit.edu`, login as "anonymous," and use your e-mail address as the password. Then, use the `cd` command to change to the directory `/pub/usenet/news.answers/internet-services` and get the file called `faq`.

Note: It's OK if this doesn't make any sense yet. By the way, here's another convention in the book—the note—used for extra-important information, asides, and (sometimes) off-the-topic rambling.

When you need to send electronic mail for a particular reason, this book uses another convention, as follows:

```
To: mail-server@rtfm.mit.edu
Subject: SEND
Body: send usenet/news.answers/internet-services/faq
```

This means to use your electronic mail program to send a message to `mail-server@rtfm.mit.edu`. Give your message the subject line `SEND`. In the body of the message, include the single line `send usenet/news.answers/internet-services/faq`.

Q I.6. How was this book done?

This book was written on a Macintosh IIsi 5/80, using Microsoft Word 5.1a, with the exception of Chapters 6 and 7 (while I was trying out another word processor, which I didn't like very much). Other important software included Zterm, MacPPP, and JetPack, a really spiffy shareware game. Each chapter was e-mailed to my editor using a Supra 14.4KBPS modem through my Internet service provider of choice, A2I Communications. Other gadgetry included a Syquest drive, a cheapo CD-ROM drive (used mostly to play audio CDs, naturally) and a Deskwriter 550C printer.

My brain was powered by large doses of caffeine (in the form scalding hot tea consumed from a BMUG user group mug), darkness and rain (I hardly wrote a thing when the weather was nice—prime napping weather), and many, many hot bubble-baths.

I.7. Can I send e-mail to the author?

I know what happens to authors who publish their e-mail addresses in books, and it isn't pretty: they get deluged with electronic mail. Still, I'm telling you my e-mail address right here because once you read this book, you'll know how to find it anyway `:-)`. It's `savetz@rahul.net`. I do want to hear from you, but please don't be annoyed if I don't reply. The sad truth is that if I sent a personal reply to every e-mail message I received, I wouldn't have time to sleep or do the writing that pays the rent.

I.8. Are we going to make it through the Introduction without a big list of author thank-yous?

No. (Sorry.)

Thanks to Peace Gardiner, who may or may not be my wife by the time this book is published. (Whether she is by then depends on the speed of the gods of publishing and whether she remains as patient with me by the end of this project as she was when I began it.)

Thanks to my mom for always encouraging me in what I do. (Even when she doesn't understand it.) And to my dad, who started my online exploits with an Atari 800 computer and a 300 BPS modem (which, I might add, he still owns).

Thanks to Daniel Dern for his sage advice.

Profuse thanks to Dave Taylor for his ongoing help during this project.

You'll notice that I didn't write every answer in this book. No one can know it all about the Internet, and I certainly don't claim to. Sometimes I've passed a question (or a set of questions) on to other experts. Thanks to the talented folks who assisted by submitting questions and answers for this book.

Thanks to Mark Graham at Pandora Systems for the nifty PPP account that he gave me in exchange for this plug.

Thank you to Laurie Anderson for "Mister Heartbreak" and to the Indigo Girls for *Rites of Passage.*

Thanks to Kinsey, Keyogi, and Arlo for sleeping on my notes, attacking the computer screen at regular intervals, and spreading peace, love, and hair throughout my home. Good kitties.

Finally, thank you to the hundreds of Internet folks who have sent me their feedback, frequently asked questions, and frequently answered answers.

CHAPTER 1

Just What Is This Internet?

This chapter answers questions about the Internet itself: what it is, what you can do with it, and how the "rules" are made. Here also is a look at the Net's past, present, and a few opinions about its future. If you have never used the Internet, start here for insight on how it is put together. (Even if you are already familiar with the Internet, you might find this chapter will tell you more about the Internet's origins. After all, those who do not know history are doomed to repeat it.)

1.1. What is the Internet?

The Internet is the world's largest computer network. It is not a piece of software or hardware. It's a huge collection of computers, cables, and people. When people talk about the Internet, they generally aren't thinking of the physical computers, wires, routers, and other gadgets that compose the network, but of the collection of people, software, and tools that they "see" online.

To the technically minded, the Internet is a network of computer networks that talk to each other using Transmission Control Protocol/Internet Protocol (TCP/IP). TCP/IP is a set of rules that define how messages can be sent between computers. A communications protocol allows different kinds of computers using different operating systems to communicate with each other. That is important because the Internet isn't made up of any single type of computer system. Using TCP/IP, hundreds of different types of computers are able to communicate on the Internet.

This common set of protocols makes it possible for a user plugged into any network on the Internet to communicate with people or software located on any of the other networks connected to the Internet.

The Internet started as a single network, the ARPAnet (the U.S. Department of Defense Advanced Projects Research Agency Network), but it now encompasses about 10,000 other networks of all sizes around the world, including the National Science Foundation Network (NSFnet), the Australian Academic and Research Network (AARnet), the NASA Science Internet (NSI), and the Swiss Academic and Research Network (SWITCH).

To most of the people who use the Internet, the Net isn't about networks, protocols, and operating systems; it's a community of people. A very large community. I might even call it (with a cringe for using such a trite, hackneyed term) a "global village."

The Internet is a locale, a place. It is the closest thing we've got to "Cyberspace" (a term coined by William Gibson in his science fiction classic *Neuromancer)*, an electronic place where people and programs work, learn, and coexist (sometimes peacefully, sometimes not).

NOTE Talking about the Internet is like vocalizing about architecture. You can go on and on about its structure, history, and future, but it doesn't mean anything until you travel around and see it for yourself.

Q1.2. OK, I have Internet access. What can I do?

You can do so much with the Internet that it would be impossible to list everything here. Here's a sampling:

- Send electronic mail to your kid at college.
- View up-to-the-minute satellite weather maps.
- Download the latest and greatest software for your home computer.
- Play chess (or just about any other game you like) with people thousands of miles away or right down the hall.
- Sell your used computer, truck, or Beatles records.
- Subscribe to electronic magazines.
- Order flowers and buy some compact discs.
- Get a complete list of every episode of The Simpsons.
- Have virtual sex.
- Develop an electronic storefront to sell whatever it is that you sell.
- Talk with experts about hypnotherapy, photography, mammography, philosophy, botany, psychology, or Disney.
- Read the complete works of Shakespeare.
- Access a dozen medical databases and directories.
- Find a recipe for tofu enchiladas.
- Search the card catalog at the Library of Congress.
- Send a fax to your mom.

Q1.3. The Internet is free, right?

Wrong. That's a big misconception, probably brought to us by college students and business types who get to play on the Internet at no cost to them thanks to the generosity of their schools, businesses, and/or governments. Most of us actually *pay* to use the Internet. Even if you don't, rest assured that someone else is paying for your connection.

Q 1.4. But access to the Internet's resources is free, right?

That is correct. Those of us who do pay for our Internet access generally pay based on how much time we're online, not by what we do. If your service provider charges $1 an hour, it doesn't matter if you're searching an agriculture database or playing games, because the vast majority of the Internet's resources are free.

The Internet resources are never quite "free" when you consider the amount of time and money invested in making them work. The computers, network equipment, software, and maintenance are paid for by governments, businesses, and personal time and money. However, many resources are accessible without charge, regardless of these expenses. This may come as a surprise to some. There ain't no such thing as a free lunch, right? Why would anyone give away the products of their efforts?

Well, everyone seems to have their own reasons. Academic institutions often make their resources available because it is their purpose to disseminate knowledge. Businesses often offer free services to promote their reputations. "Regular people" donate their time for a variety of reasons—to boost their ego, to give something back to a community they find useful, or simply to do good for the public network.

Q 1.5. I'm a starving student. What can I do online that won't cost me money?

It's pretty easy to tell when you're about to do something that will cost you anything beyond what you pay for Internet access. Here's a big hint: you'll be asked for a credit card number.

Businesses have only recently discovered the power of the Internet, so the number and types of things that can cost you money are increasing. You can find specialized databases and online services that are available for a fee, as well as traditional products and services such as flower delivery and ordering from a catalog. (As a matter of fact, just the other day I bought a Negativland CD from the online Compact Disc Connection.)

Q 1.6. Where did the Internet come from?

The Internet was never truly created as an entity of its own. It is an amalgamation of many earlier networks. The story of how the Internet was born has been told hundreds of times in hundreds of books, magazine articles, and online documents. But I think it's a law that every book about the Internet must tell the story. Without further ado, here it is. (I'll tell it as quickly as I can.)

In 1969, the Advanced Research Projects Agency, a part of the U.S. government's Department of Defense, set up the first parts of the network that would eventually become the Internet. At the time, the network was called the ARPAnet. The ARPAnet would link the military, defense contractors and universities in one seamless computer network.

A major problem with computer networks at the time was that every machine on a network needed to be operating for the network to function at all. Imagine three computers connected in a row; if the machine in the middle went down (for maintenance, for instance) the first and last computers couldn't communicate. If you were the U.S. government in the middle of a cold war, this was bad. Networks of that type could never be very reliable.

The ARPAnet would be the first network of its kind for many reasons—primarily because it was decentralized, with no central computer running the show. Further, if one computer on the network should go down, it was imperative that the others retain the capability of communicating. (You can imagine why this was important to the United States military, which would be more than a little disappointed should their entire network of computers be rendered inoperable by a single, well-placed bomb.) The ARPAnet would need to link any number of computers and automatically reroute information should some of those computers go offline.

The ARPAnet began by linking four locations: Stanford University, UCLA, UC Santa Barbara, and the University of Utah.

The ARPAnet expanded to nonmilitary uses in the 70s when universities and defense-related researchers were permitted to join the network. By the late 70s, the ARPAnet was so large that its original set of standards and communication protocols could not support the growth of the network. After extended bickering and debate, the ARPAnet switched to the TCP/IP communication protocols (still in use today), which would allow further growth in the size of the network. By 1983, all computers on the ARPAnet were using TCP/IP.

By 1983, it became clear that most use of the ARPAnet was for nonmilitary purposes, so it was split into two networks: one part became MILNET, a Department of Defense military-only network, and the rest remained ARPAnet, which would resume its job of connecting research sites and other nonmilitary users. The networks continued to grow.

In 1987, the National Science Foundation created their own network, called NSFnet. The NSFnet would be a high-speed "backbone" network to support the burgeoning number of networked users as well as new bandwidth-intensive applications. The ARPAnet and the NSFnet, similar in structure and purpose, began to cooperate and merge. By the late 80s, the ARPANet was absorbed by the NSFnet. (Today, the NSFnet remains a major "backbone" of Internet connections in the United States.)

In the mid 80s, the National Science Foundation began to provide funding for the establishment of research and academic networks throughout the United States. It began linking those networks to the NSFnet. The same sorts of things were happening all over the world—educators, bureaucrats and hobbyists plugging their computers into networks and those networks into other networks.

The NSFnet's charter's purpose was to support education and research. It was (and is) considered inappropriate to use that network for commercial purposes. Although the guidelines of what you could and couldn't do were vague, the NSFnet's *appropriate use policies* made it clear that for most purposes, commercial activity was forbidden. In many cases, even though it was possible to send business information from two NSFnet-linked networks, it wasn't allowed.

In 1991, a group of small commercial networks created a network of their own—the Commercial Internet Exchange (CIX)—that would allow commercial use and be free of those nasty appropriate use policies. Now, commercial users were able to connect with each other quickly and legally by networking with CIX rather than the NSFnet. What this meant was commercial collaboration, technical support by e-mail, pay-for-use databases, you name it. The formation of the CIX gave yet another boost to the growth of the Internet.

Now it's today and here we are. Commercial activity on the Net is continuing its unprecedented growth, but that certainly hasn't hurt the scientific, educational, and research networks (which are also growing by leaps and bounds). The Internet—a combination of the NSFnet, ARPAnet, the CIX, and about 10,000 other networks—will continue to grow and change, meeting the needs of the people who want it, no matter what they use it for.

NOTE For a more complete history of the Internet, use the anonymous FTP program to get the following files. (If you're a new Internet user, please pardon this lapse into techspeak. I want you to know where to find this information, even if you don't yet know how to get it!) Anonymous FTP is thoroughly covered in Chapter 6, "How Can I Find and Use Software (and Other Stuff)?"

```
ftp.isoc.org:/internet/history/_A Brief
History of the Internet and Related
Networks_ by V. Cerf
ftp.isoc.org:/internet/history/
how.internet.came.to.be
ftp.isoc.org:/internet/history/
short.history.of.internet
```

Q 1.7. What are acceptable use policies?

Acceptable use policies (AUPs for the acronym-inclined) are written statements of what may and may not be done with a particular computer network. AUPs for networks became the norm in the 70s. Most networks were created with specific goals in mind (for instance, for linking research and educational institutions). Their purpose was to promote communication, education, and research. Therefore, many of those networks placed restrictions on what they could be used for: they couldn't be used for financial gain, for instance. These rules came to be known as AUPs.

> **NOTE** The Acceptable Use Policy for the NSFnet is one of the strictest AUPs on the Internet. For better or for worse, the National Science Foundation is removing itself from the duty of maintaining the NSFnet backbone. It's possible that as commercial service providers vie for the role, the rules will change considerably.

Q 1.8. What parts of the world are wired for the Internet?

Most of the world has some sort of access to the Internet. However, if your closest family lives in the Gobi desert, you're out of luck.

At last count, 146 countries had some sort of connection to the Internet and 91 did not. Full Internet access is enjoyed by the United States, Canada, most of South America, all of Australia, Asia, and Europe. Africa is the least-wired part of the world: more than half of Africa has no Internet; most of the rest of that continent has e-mail access only. Most of the rest of the world has access to limited Internet services like BITNET, UUCP, and FidoNet.

Q 1.9. What is BITNET?

BITNET is a major wide area network. It is not based on the TCP/IP protocols that Internet networks must use. Therefore, BITNET isn't truly a part of the Internet. BITNET (BIT stands for Because It's Time) users can send and receive electronic mail to and from the Internet, thanks to gateways that act as "translators" between the different network protocols. Electronic mail is the only tool available—or necessary—for BITNET sites.

Other non-TCP/IP networks are also linked to the Internet using a hodgepodge of gateways, but more commonly, the sites on BITNET and other networks that don't do TCP/IP are switching to networks with the capability of talking in the TCP/IP language so that they can fully utilize the resources of the Internet. BITNET seems to have peaked in terms of its popularity and use; its numbers of sites and users are declining as sites manage to connect directly to the Internet.

1.10. Who uses the Internet?

Today, anyone can get an account on the Internet uses it. As you might imagine, people from every conceivable walk of life use it regularly. It's possible to make assumptions about the types of people using the Internet by looking at the distribution of host computers online. As of January, 1994,

- **605,402 hosts belonged to educational institutions.**
- **567,686 hosts belonged to commercial organizations.**
- **129,134 hosts belonged to governments.**
- **103,507 hosts belonged to the U.S. military.**
- **50,544 hosts belonged to nonprofit organizations and other undefined organizations.**
- **12,608 hosts belonged to other networks.**

NOTE The preceding information primarily counts networked hosts in the United States.

It's interesting to note that of the hosts listed here, the second largest group (about 60 percent) is commercial sites. Remember, until very recently, the Internet was almost entirely comprised of government and educational institutions.

1.11. How many people use the Internet?

No one knows exactly how many people use the Internet because it is impossible to take a census of its users. According to estimates, more than 10 million people currently use the Internet in some fashion. (That number is expected to increase to 100 million by the end of the century.)

The number of people with access to only Internet e-mail is undoubtedly higher, because that's the most common (and least expensive to implement) form of Net access.

Q 1.12. How fast is the Internet growing?

The original ARPAnet connected users at only four locations with perhaps a few hundred users. By 1972, there were 40 sites connected to the ARPAnet. Today, the Internet encompasses more than 10,000 networks. By March of 1993, there were an estimated 2.1 million host computers on the Internet.

It is estimated that the Internet is currently growing at a rate of 65 percent every year! If the Internet continues to grow at its present rate—an impossibility for technical and sociological reasons—the population of the Internet would equal the population of the planet by the year 2003.

A good indication of the Internet's speed of growth is the Internet Index, an interesting little document compiled by Win Treese (`treese@crl.dec.com`). It is reproduced in part here for your edification and enlightenment.

```
                         The Internet Index
                     [Inspired by "Harper's Index"]
            Compiled by Win Treese (treese@crl.dec.com)

Annual rate of growth for Gopher traffic: 997%

Annual rate of growth for WWW traffic: 341,634%

Average time between new networks connecting to the Internet: 10 minutes

Number of newspaper and magazine articles about the Internet during the
        first nine months of 1993: over 2300
Advertised network numbers in October, 1993: 16,533
Advertised network numbers in October, 1992:  7,505

Date after which more than half the registered networks were commercial:
August, 1991

Number of Internet hosts in Norway, per 1000 population: 5
Number of Internet hosts in United States, per 1000 population: 4
Number of Internet hosts in October, 1993: 2,056,000

Number of USENET articles posted in two weeks during December, 1993: 605,000
Number of megabytes posted: 1450
Number of users posting: 130,000
Number of sites represented: 42,000
```

Q 1.13. I sometimes see the word *internet* with a lowercase *i*. Is that different than *Internet* with an uppercase *I*?

Sometimes you'll see the word *internet* with a lowercase *i* rather than an uppercase one. The lowercase *internet* refers to any network based on the TCP/IP communications protocols. The word *internet* originally referred to any *meta-network*, or network of networks. You'll occasionally see it referring to any computer network composed of smaller networks. That's not to be confused with capitalized *Internet*, which refers to a specific network of networks, the largest one of them all. *Internet* with a capital *I* refers to the ultimate in meta-networks, the world's largest network of people and computers.

Q 1.14. So if the Internet is so great, why do I need CompuServe, Prodigy, or another online service?

The Internet is large and vast and wonderful, but when comparing it to traditional online services, there is quite a bit to consider. Some of the information you can find on the Internet is unique; you won't find it on the online services. Similarly, each online service contains a selection of information that you won't find on the Internet. Apple's eWorld service offers articles from back issues of *MacWorld* magazine. America Online has an online encyclopedia. CompuServe offers the Knowledge Index, a database of articles in the areas of computer science, engineering, business, and science. (Those are just three examples of hundreds of cool resources available on those systems.) Sad to say, you can't find any of those things on the Internet.

Also, online services have a major advantage over the Internet: the information there is *organized*. Despite advances in indexing and search technology (such as Archie and Veronica, covered later), the Internet is notoriously unorganized, with a smattering of information here and another dollop there. That is hardly an ideal situation if you're rushing to gather information for a project that was due yesterday.

Online services can't do it all, and neither can the Internet. Don't dismiss one just because you already use the other. (I use the Internet as well as America Online. I try to limit my daily use to those two systems lest I never, ever find time to sleep.)

1.15. What kinds of materials are available for free on the Internet?

The amount of information that is on the Internet is staggering. The quantity and types of information that are being added to the Internet daily are dumbfounding. So while I can't tell you exactly what you can and can't find on the Internet, it is possible to talk in vague generalities about the kinds of information you'll typically find there.

Generally, free materials on the Internet include government documents, works with expired copyrights, works that are in the public domain, and works that authors are making available on an experimental basis to the community.

Conversely, the types of information you are not likely to find available free on the Internet include commercial works that are protected by copyright law. Which leads us right to the next question…

1.16. Why isn't there an encyclopedia available on the Internet?

Although the information on the Internet is certainly encyclopedic in scope, there is no encyclopedia available free to the public on the Internet. (There are indeed encyclopedias on the Net, but they are on closed systems available only to students at a specific university or employees at a certain company.)

The reason for this is about what you'd expect: the companies that make encyclopedias are in business to stay in business, and you don't stay in business by giving away your product. For now, Internet users will have to stick with trekking to the library.

> **NOTE** If you use CompuServe, America Online, or just about any other online service, you have access to an online encyclopedia. Why can those services offer the public access to traditional encyclopedias? They pay stiff fees to encyclopedia creators to do so and then pass the cost on to their customers.

Q 1.17. What's wrong with the Internet?

The Internet isn't perfect. Far from it. Here are four important things that are wrong with the Internet today:

1. **The Internet is hard to learn to use.** (If it weren't, you wouldn't need to read this book.) There are too many programs and tools for doing different things—FTP for file transfers, Telnet for remote login, Gopher, Archie, and so on. If that weren't bad enough, many functions can be done with a variety of "competing" programs that do more or less the same thing.
2. **The Internet is almost completely disorganized.** It's filled with stuff, some of which you'll find useful and some of which is worthless. The Internet is like a junk yard. If you look in the right places (and given a little luck) it is possible to unearth the electronic equivalent of a pristine 1955 Porsche Spyder. If you are without direction, however, you can search for days for something and come away discouraged and dirty. (The Internet is slowly becoming more organized with the help of indexing tools such as Veronica and Archie, but it has a long way to go.)
3. **There is too much information on the Internet.** This is really a throwback to #2, because with better cataloging and retrieval systems, the amount of information on the Internet would be manageable. (With reliable cataloging and retrieval systems, no one complains about "too much information." Have you ever complained about this in your public library? Probably not.) Combine today's software with the fact that everyone on the Internet is a potential publisher of information, and you have a problem of too much content.

4. **The Internet is growing too fast for its own good.** As new networks and hosts are added to the Internet (at a rate of about one every 10 minutes!) the InterNIC, the group that assigns Internet *addresses*, is running out of them. (We'll talk more about addresses in Chapter 3, "How Does the Internet Work?")

Q 1.18. What's allowed on the Internet?

As I said earlier, the Internet is mostly an anarchistic place: what you are allowed to do on the Internet may include quite a bit more than you think. But the Internet's rules and social mores are much affected by the real world, so the Internet is not a free-for-all where anything goes. What you can do is affected by the laws, politics, and ethics of the outside world.

Confusing all the issues is the fact that the Internet is extremely big. It isn't one body with one set of rules; it encompasses other networks, many of which have their own rules (appropriate use policies). It encompasses hundreds of countries, each of which have different laws regarding computer use, copyrights, obscenity, and so on. Sticky export laws come into effect if you're sending data across national boundaries or even from one U.S. state to another.

There aren't too many restrictions regarding what you may do on the Internet, and frankly, those restrictions aren't very clearly defined. When in doubt, ask your service provider if a particular use is acceptable. For instance, commercial activity is not condoned if your service provider is connected via the NSFnet backbone, but if you're connected through CIX, BARRnet, or any of hundreds of other network backbones, commercial activity is okay.

Copyright and intellectual property laws are especially important on the Internet. In the online society, your words are frequently the only way you are known to others. Those words all happen to be in bits and bytes, so it's extremely easy to store, re-transmit, or steal someone else's work (be it an electronic mail message or a book). It helps to know some things about copyright law and intellectual property law. I think no one really understands intellectual property law, including (especially?) the intellectual property lawyers.

1

> **NOTE** Here's a quick story that may or may not have anything to do with what I'm discussing here. In early 1994, I wrote a magazine article about how to send a fax from the Internet. A couple of weeks after it was published, I found that someone (who, although misguided about U.S. copyright law, seemed to find my article useful) had typed in the entire article and posted the whole thing to the Usenet. Accompanying the article was the note: "Please don't distribute this too widely: I am posting this without permission of the author." Although he was concerned about distributing the article too widely, he had just distributed my article on the largest public forum in history! Moral: know who owns something before you zap it across the Internet. If it's not yours, get permission before you use it.

What you can do on the Net boils down to this: if the network you use, or the network it is connected to, is subsidized by the federal government, your activities must be "in support of research or education." If you are on a private commercial network, your activities aren't restricted in that manner. Luckily, even for those on subsidized networks, the phrase "in support of research or education" is fairly broad.

Q 1.19. Who runs the Internet?

No one "runs" the Internet. There is no governing entity or business calling the shots. Remember, the Internet is a decentralized mass of thousands of smaller networks, each running with its own purpose, its own sources of income, and its own rulemakers. The Internet is more or less an anarchy. Every organization that is plugged into the Internet is responsible for its own computers.

The fact that no one runs the Internet has its advantages and disadvantages. On the up side, there are no membership fees, no censorship, and no government control. Unfortunately, when something goes wrong (if an important computer goes down or another user begins annoying you), there's no central authority to ask for help. In the absence of "net cops" policing the Internet, users need to rely on their own judgments and the assistance of the system administrators at their site to solve problems or resolve disputes. Most of the time, you're on your own.

The Internet is guided in its growth, however, by several organizations (loosely called the *Internet technical groups)* that manage it. These organizations attempt to structure the Internet while creating a minimum of restrictions.

Q 1.20. So no one runs the Internet. Then who coordinates the Internet?

A variety of so-called Internet Technical Groups coordinate the Internet's basic workings—how the protocols should talk to one another, how to plan for the Net's future, and other important (but, if you ask me, dull) details of keeping the network alive.

The Internet Engineering Task Force (IETF) coordinates the operation, management, and evolution of the Internet. The IETF develops and maintains the Internet's communications protocols. The IETF is a large, open community of network designers, operators, vendors, and researchers concerned with the Internet and the Internet protocols. This group identifies the Internet's technical and operational problems and proposes solutions, specifies the development of protocols to solve those problems, and provides a forum for the exchange of technical information within the Internet community.

For more information, anonymous FTP to

```
ietf.cnri.reston.va.us:/ietf/*
```

The Internet Research Task Force (IRTF) examines long-term research problems and technical issues currently affecting the Internet. The task force looks at issues that will become important in 5 to 10 years. Current issues include how the Internet will handle a billion users (a rapidly approaching landmark) and how current users will be affected when 100 million U.S. homes are wired for Internet via cable television by the end of this century.

The Internet Architecture Board (IAB) is the master body for technical changes to the Internet. The IAB is concerned with technical and policy issues involving the evolution of the Internet's architecture. IAB members are committed to making the Internet function effectively and to making sure the Net evolves to meet a large-scale, high-speed future. Formed in 1983, the IAB oversees the IETF and IRTF and ratifies major changes that come from them.

The IAB performs the following functions:

- **Reviews Internet standards.**
- **Manages the publication process of Request for Comment (RFC) documents.**
- **Performs strategic planning for the Internet, identifying long-range problems and opportunities.**
- **Acts as an international technical policy liaison and representative for the Internet community.**
- **Resolves technical issues that cannot be treated within the IETF or IRTF frameworks.**

Q 1.21. What is the Internet Society?

Other organizations, not strictly technical groups, exist that facilitate the growth of the Internet and keep the public informed. The Internet Society, the "parent" of the IAB, is an international body made of volunteers providing support to organizations involved in the use, operation, well-being, and evolution of the Internet. The Internet Society doesn't run the Internet either, but its members do work to keep it running smoothly. For more information, send e-mail to `isoc@isoc.org`.

The following goals of the Internet Society are taken from its charter:

> *A. To facilitate and support the technical evolution of the Internet as a research and education infrastructure, and to stimulate the involvement of the scientific community, industry, government and others in the evolution of the Internet;*
>
> *B. To educate the scientific community, industry and the public at large concerning the technology, use and application of the Internet;*

> *C. To promote educational applications of Internet technology for the benefit of government, colleges and universities, industry, and the public at large;*
>
> *D. To provide a forum for exploration of new Internet applications, and to stimulate collaboration among organizations in their operational use of the global Internet.*

More information about the Internet Society is available by anonymous FTP.

```
isoc.org:/isoc/*
```

Information is also available via Gopher, from `gopher isoc.org`.

Q 1.22. Who keeps track of all these Internet addresses?

The InterNIC does (and quite a bit more). The InterNIC is a project supported by the National Science Foundation to provide network information services to the networking community. A Network Information Center (NIC) provides information and help to network users. The InterNIC is a five-year project that began in April of 1993. It is a collaborative project of three organizations, each of which provides a part of the InterNIC's services. General Atomics provides Information Services, AT&T provides Directory and Database Services, and Network Solutions, Inc. provides Registration Services. All the services are provided via the Internet by telephone and (if you can believe it!) on paper.

General Atomics offers a variety of information services for Internet users. It acts as the "NIC of first and last resort" by providing a reference desk for new and experienced users and service providers. The reference desk provides listings of Internet service providers in the United States and internationally, as well as books and documents to assist organizations and individuals in getting connected and pointers to network tools and resources.

AT&T lets your fingers do the walking by maintaining InterNIC's directory services, including the Directory of Directories, Directory Services, and Database Services to store data available to all Internet users.

Network Solutions, Inc. provides Internet registration services including IP address allocation, domain registration, and Autonomous System Number assignment. NSI also tracks points of contact for networks and provides online and telephone support for questions related to IP-address and domain-name registration.

NOTE The InterNIC can be reached by calling 1-800-444-4345 or 1-619-445-4600 or by sending electronic mail to `info@internic.net`. Extensive online information is available at host `is.internic.net`, accessible via FTP, Gopher, and Telnet.

Q 1.23. Hey, wow! I'm sitting in Eureka and talking to a computer in Finland. Who's paying for the phone call when I connect to some far-off host?

Answered by Mitch Patenaude (`mrp@rahul.net`), the guy who scored my first Net connection for me.

The answer to this question is a mixture of "nobody" and "a lot of people." To understand why this is so, you need to know a little about the way the Internet is organized.

First, you have to understand that the Internet transmits the information you send by breaking it up into small pieces called *packets* and sending those packets to the remote machine. The difference between most networks and the Internet is that for most packet-based networks, the machine you are sending information to must be connected to the same network as the computer you are sending it from. Small networks like this are called *local area networks (LAN)*. Internet is a type of *wide area network (WAN)*. WANs typically consist of several LANs hooked together.

When you connect to a host far away, you are not connected by a single phone or data line. The Internet works by connecting lots of little networks with a few big ones. When you communicate with a computer on the other side of the globe, or even just the other end of your state, the information passes through many networks owned and maintained by a variety of organizations.

When you want to communicate with a machine that is not plugged in to your own local network, your computer needs to find a way to get the information to the distant machine. This is like trying to get from an airport in Eureka, California, to one in Helsinki, Finland. There are no direct-connecting flights (that is, no direct network connection from Eureka to Finland). Not surprising.

So your local network asks its Internet travel agent (called a *router,* the machine that connects your local network to the Internet) whether it knows the way to the remote host and how many "hops" it would require to get the information there. (A "hop" is like a stopover at an airport.) One router might find a path from here to there in five hops (Eureka to San Francisco, San Francisco to New York, and so on). Your network then asks for directions from any other routers that are available.

The router that responds with the fewest number of "hops" is given the message to pass along. The network serving as the router does the same thing as your local network, shopping for the shortest route to get your message to its destination. (Your message spends only a few milliseconds at each stopover, a far cry from the endless hours people spend waiting in airports.)

So the information is passed from one network and computer to another until it gets where it's going. Back to the question: the only phone call you're paying for is the one to connect you to your service provider, and your service provider is paying for a connection to some other part of the Internet. Past that, your message uses space on several other networks owned and paid for by many other organizations. You pay a tiny bit, therefore, as does everyone else in the path of your message. Everyone pays, and no one does. Very Zen, don't you think?

NOTE And now, the moral of the everybody-pays-nobody-pays technique: the Internet is an incredible communications network that costs billions of dollars and uncounted millions of man hours to maintain each year. One of the great strengths and great weaknesses of the Internet is that it

depends on mutual cooperation: the trust that people and organizations have in allowing others all over the world to use their resources. If that trust is abused, the Internet will stop being such an open place and everybody loses.

Using a program called *traceroute*, I traced the path of a message from San Jose, California, to Finland. It made the journey in 21 hops (this doesn't have to make sense, but it's interesting to look at).

```
traceroute to tolsun.oulu.fi (130.231.96.16), 30 hops max, 40 byte packets
 1  sj (192.160.13.201)  3 ms  4 ms  4 ms
 2  barrnet-remote (131.119.73.13)  368 ms  409 ms  453 ms
X (131.119.249.1)  404 ms  515 ms  236 ms
 4  SU-SP.BARRNET.NET (131.119.49.1)  424 ms  357 ms  565 ms
 5  fd-0.enss128.t3.ans.net (192.31.48.244)  797 ms  1415 ms  907 ms
 6  * t3-0.San-Francisco-cnss9.t3.ans.net (140.222.9.1)  2776 ms  1420 ms
 7  mf-0.San-Francisco-cnss8.t3.ans.net (140.222.8.222)  933 ms  142 ms  442 ms
 8  t3-0.Chicago-cnss24.t3.ans.net (140.222.24.1)  281 ms  582 ms  840 ms
 9  * t3-0.Cleveland-cnss40.t3.ans.net (140.222.40.1)  705 ms  922 ms
10  t3-1.New-York-cnss32.t3.ans.net (140.222.32.2)  910 ms  654 ms  578 ms
11  t3-1.Washington-DC-cnss56.t3.ans.net (140.222.56.2)  528 ms  464 ms  599 ms
12  mf-0.Washington-DC-cnss58.t3.ans.net (140.222.56.194)  315 ms  1054 ms  910
    ms
13  t3-0.enss145.t3.ans.net (140.222.145.1)  774 ms  1256 ms  1072 ms
14  192.203.229.245 (192.203.229.245)  515 ms  134 ms  113 ms
15  icm-dc-1-H1/0.icp.net (192.157.65.121)  109 ms  241 ms  266 ms
16  192.121.154.233 (192.121.154.233)  925 ms  788 ms  881 ms
17  nord-gw.nordu.net (192.121.154.19)  1031 ms *  813 ms
18  fi-gw.nordu.net (192.36.148.162)  469 ms  532 ms  258 ms
19  ananas-gw.funet.fi (128.214.6.207)  475 ms  748 ms  541 ms
20  oliivi-gw.funet.fi (128.214.254.5)  358 ms  671 ms  656 ms
21  tolsun.oulu.fi (130.231.96.16)  730 ms  424 ms  612 ms
```

> **NOTE** Nets and taxes—If the information is traveling any significant distance in the United States, it will probably travel over a very large and fast network known as the NSFNET. The NSFNET is maintained by the National Science Foundation, which means that it's paid for with your tax dollars, so everybody pays a little. The NSF is slowly backing off from that responsibility. Soon commercial service providers, not the NSF, will maintain that backbone.

Q 1.24. What is an RFC?

Requests for comments (RFCs) are documents that are the working notes of the Internet research-and-development community. An RFC document may be on essentially any topic related to computer communication, and may be anything from a meeting report to the specification of a protocol standard.

According to RFC 1549 (entitled FYI Q/A—for New Internet Users), "most RFCs are the descriptions of network protocols or services, often giving detailed procedures and formats for their implementation. Other RFCs report on the results of policy studies or summarize the work of technical committees or workshops." RFCs can range from only a couple of pages to book-length documents.

RFCs are useful, although not always particularly exciting (unless you are a network engineer). But they are an important part of what goes on "behind the scenes" to make the Internet grow and flourish.

RFCs are numbered sequentially as they are published. Once a document is assigned an RFC number and published, that number is never reused, even if the RFC is revised. That way, there is never a question of having the most recent version of a particular RFC. (By the way, as of the day I'm writing this, RFCs are numbered up to 1609.)

1

NOTE The term *RFC* is a misnomer. Although most RFC authors surely won't mind if you give your opinions about the document, RFCs usually aren't really requesting your comments at all: they're statements or definitions. There are three types of RFCs: *Standards Track,* which specify an Internet standards track protocol for the Internet community; *Experimental,* which define an experimental protocol; and *Informational,* which provide useful information.

Here's a sample list of a few of the most recent RFCs available. Most of it is dry, technical stuff, but some RFCs can be useful, even to beginners.

```
1609 E    G. Mansfield, T. Johannsen, M. Knopper, "Charting Networks in the
          X.500 Directory", 03/25/1994. (Pages=15) (Format=.txt)

1608 E    T. Johannsen, G. Mansfield, M. Kosters, S. Sataluri, "Representing
          IP Information in the X.500 Directory", 03/25/1994. (Pages=20)
          (Format=.txt)

1607 I    V. Cerf, "A VIEW FROM THE 21ST CENTURY", 03/31/1994. (Pages=13)
          (Format=.txt)

1606 I    J. Onions, "A Historical Perspective On The Usage Of IP Version 9",
          03/31/1994. (Pages=4) (Format=.txt)

1605 I    W. Shakespeare, "SONET to Sonnet Translation", 03/31/1994.
          (Pages=3) (Format=.txt)

1604 PS   T. Brown, "Definitions of Managed Objects for Frame Relay Service",
          03/25/1994. (Pages=46) (Format=.txt) (Obsoletes RFC1596)

1603 I    E. Huizer, D. Crocker, "IETF Working Group Guidelines and
          Procedures", 03/24/1994. (Pages=29) (Format=.txt)

1602 I    I. Architecture Board, I. Engineering Steer, C. Huitema, P. Gross,
           , "The Internet Standards Process — Revision 2", 03/24/1994.
          (Pages=37) (Format=.txt) (Obsoletes RFC1310)

1601 I    C. Huitema, I. Architecture Board (IAB), 03/22/1994. (Pages=6)
          (Format=.txt) (Obsoletes RFC1358)
```

```
1600  S   J. Postel, "INTERNET OFFICIAL PROTOCOL STANDARDS", 03/14/1994.
          (Pages=36) (Format=.txt) (Obsoletes RFC1540) (STD 1)

1598  PS  W. Simpson, "PPP in X.25", 03/17/1994. (Pages=8) (Format=.txt)

1597  I   Y. Rekhter, R. Moskowitz, D. Karrenberg, G. de Groot, "Address
          Allocation for Private Internets", 03/17/1994. (Pages=8)
          (Format=.txt)

1596  PS  T. Brown, "Definitions of Managed Objects for Frame Relay Service",
          03/17/1994. (Pages=46) (Format=.txt) (Obsoleted by RFC1604)

1595  PS  T. Brown, K. Tesink, "Definitions of Managed Objects for the
          SONET/SDH Interface Type", 03/11/1994. (Pages=59) (Format=.txt)

1594  I   A. Marine, J. Reynolds, G. Malkin, "FYI on Questions and Answer
          Answers to Commonly asked "New Internet User" Questions",
          03/11/1994. (Pages=44) (Format=.txt) (FYI 4) (Obsoletes RFC1325)

1593  I   W. McKenzie, J. Cheng, "SNA APPN Node MIB", 03/10/1994.
          (Pages=120) (Format=.txt)

1592  E   B. Wijnen, G. Carpenter, K. Curran, A. Sehgal, G. Waters, "Simple
          Network Management Protocol Distributed Protocol Interface Version
          2.0", 03/03/1994. (Pages=54) (Format=.txt) (Obsoletes RFC1228)

1591  I   J. Postel, "Domain Name System Structure and Delegation",
          03/03/1994. (Pages=7) (Format=.txt)

1590  I   J. Postel, "Media Type Registration Procedure", 03/02/1994.
          (Pages=7) (Format=.txt) (Updates RFC1521)

1589  I   D. Mills, "A Kernel Model for Precision Timekeeping", 03/03/1994.
          (Pages=37) (Format=.txt)

1588  I   J. Postel, C. Anderson, "WHITE PAGES MEETING REPORT", 02/25/1994.
          (Pages=35) (Format=.txt)

1587  PS  R. Coltun, V. Fuller, "The OSPF NSSA Option", 03/24/1994.
          (Pages=17) (Format=.txt)

1586  I   O. deSouza, M. Rodrigues, "Guidelines for Running OSPF Over Frame
          Relay Networks", 03/24/1994. (Pages=6) (Format=.txt)

1585  I   J. Moy, "MOSPF: Analysis and Experience", 03/24/1994. (Pages=13)
          (Format=.txt)

1584  PS  J. Moy, "Multicast Extensions to OSPF", 03/24/1994. (Pages=102)
```

Q1.25. What is an FYI document?

FYIs, or *for your information documents*, are a subset of the RFC series of online documents. FYIs are designed to provide Internet users with a central repository of information about any topics that relate to the Internet. FYI documents tend to be more information oriented, whereas RFCs are usually more technically oriented.

FYI topics range from historical memos—why it was done this way—to answers to commonly asked operational questions. FYIs are typically intended for a much wider (read *non-technical*) audience than many of the other RFCs (especially the STDs, which are discussed next).

FYI documents are also numbered: they are assigned both an FYI number and an RFC number. If an FYI document is ever updated, it is issued again with a new RFC number (because RFC numbers are never reused); however, its FYI number remains unchanged. The aim is to help users identify which FYIs are about which topics. For example, FYI 4 will always be FYI 4, even though it may be updated several times and during that process receive four different RFC numbers. You need only to remember the FYI number to find the proper document.

Q1.26. What is an STD?

(No, it doesn't stand for what your high school health teacher told you it stands for!) *STDs*, or *standards documents,* are yet another form of RFC. The intent of STDs is to identify those RFCs that document Internet standards. An STD number will be assigned only to those specifications that have completed the full process of standardization in the Internet.

Like FYIs, once a standard has been assigned an STD number, that number does not change, even if the standard changes over time.

1.27. How can I get copies of RFCs, FYIs, and STDs on the Net?

Use the anonymous FTP program to connect to `ds.internic.net` and look in the `/rfc` directory. See Chapter 6, "How Can I Find and Use Software (and Other Stuff)?" to learn to how use anonymous FTP.

You can also get RFCs by e-mail. To find out how, send a message

```
To: mailserv@ds.internic.net
Subject: <subject line is ignored>
Body: help
```

1.28. So is this the information superhighway?

Oh, how I hate that phrase. The so-called *information superhighway* (also known as the *infobahn* in those sleek cybermedia magazines) is a phrase used by newspapers and television news reporters who don't know how better to describe new technology that they don't quite understand. Not that the term is overused, but I've heard *the information superhighway* used to refer to the Internet, to television-top boxes that will deliver movies on demand, and to personal digital assistants like Apple's Newton. (One of the local TV news shows in Northern California even used the term to describe a program in which college students repair computers from circa 1980 to give to grammar schools. That's the information superhighway?)

At any rate, call it what you will: the Internet is one part of a future where more people will have easier, less-expensive access to technology. That technology could reshape our lives, or we might only be able to order pizza delivery from an on-screen menu. We can only wait and see.

No one can quite define it, but we will know it when we see it.

Q 1.29. What does the future hold?

> **NOTE** Obviously, no one can predict the future, but we're trying to nonetheless. Ask three people what is in store for the future of the Internet and you'll get three different answers. In the humble opinions of myself and two colleagues, the following are three possible answers to that question.

The future of the Internet is going to be a whole lot more exciting than its past. I don't know if people are becoming more creative, smarter, or have been holding back their wonderful ideas until now. Whatever the reasons, the Internet is more exciting today than it has ever been, and its usefulness and the excitement about it will continue to grow.

The past three or four years have seen the most thrilling advances, making the Internet worthwhile and usable to real people, not just computer science and research types. Gopher and WAIS, two applications that have changed the way we navigate the Internet, were released in 1991. The World Wide Web saw the light of day in 1992, and Internet Talk Radio in 1993, as did Mosaic, the application that literally changed the face of the Internet. (All of this sure beats the history of dull old military and government networks forming and merging, doesn't it?)

The Internet is gaining speed and has no intention of slowing down. Gopher, World Wide Web, and Mosaic are just the first steps toward changing the way we communicate, work, and entertain ourselves. In the next two to three years, we will see great strides in what those tools can do. The Internet applications that we'll take for granted in five years haven't been born yet. Now is a great time to be on the Net, because you'll see firsthand how it will change and grow. If you're outspoken, you can even have a voice in its fate.

Although it is gaining speed, the Internet's own popularity will be its biggest obstacle. The network as it is today simply can't handle continued growth at its present rate. Right now, a major limiting factor to getting on the Net is that you need access to a computer. What will happen to the Net when it comes to your TV set via your cable company? How will the network handle 10 million new users converging at once? How will the Internet's current society handle it?

All we can do is wait and see.

Answered by Dave Taylor (dave@netcom.com)

The most obvious changes we'll see on the Internet in the next few years are more users, more sites, and more services. Simultaneously, as everything expands, the challenge of finding information when you want it will become a further burden, certainly exceeding the capabilities of the two most important search databases: Archie and Veronica.

More sophisticated information interfaces will expand (such as Mosaic, a multimedia interface to the Internet), and we will see simpler systems that allow deeper and broader searches of the data on the Net. Computer networks that are not on the Internet (such as CompuServe, GEnie, and America Online) will either add themselves to the network or will begin to automatically clone the most valuable reference information from the Internet.

More business will be done through e-mail and the network, and more companies will offer technical support, sales support, and even product information and ordering through the Internet. This commercialization is just beginning, and if the Internet ends up being the foundation of the so-called National Information Infrastructure, you can expect considerably more commercial use of the network: probably an explosion of companies, each competing for valuable information space.

At the same time, intelligent multienvironment search programs, such as Netfind (a program for finding peoples' e-mail addresses) and Knowbots (intelligent programs that will search out information for users), will become more common, and commercial services that screen vast bodies of information for specific topics will also arise.

One thing that is inevitably going to show up is electronic junk mail. Here's how I envision it beginning: companies will join the Internet and offer product literature through e-mail–based databases. Without users realizing it, their requests will be logged and their electronic mail addresses archived. A few weeks or months later, the company will send an informational mailing to potential customers, including all addresses culled from the e-mail–based data server. Take it one more step, and you have companies that will offer to track who uses commercial information delivery systems and also identify what demographic specialists love to call *opinion leaders*: people who are considered experts in a specific topic by the rest of the user community. These tracking companies will be the equivalent of mailing-list vendors, selling lists of thousands of e-mail addresses and other lists of dozens of the most important and influential members of a particular target community.

Once that happens, programs that intelligently sort incoming electronic mail will become that much more valuable, as users will learn how to program their e-mail–screening robot to politely (or rudely!) reject mail from services of this nature without the human even seeing that it happened. At least five different programs are available today that can perform just such a service, but so far few people need to use them.

The demographics of the Internet are changing, too, and with this change is a change in the culture and society of the network community. Until fairly recently, there have been two primary users of the Internet: researchers and other computer-savvy professionals and students, primarily at universities. As commercial services come online, and as large autonomous networks like America Online and eWorld join the Internet, the Internet will become a more heterogeneous and, I hope, more egalitarian community. Look for groups where it will be frowned on to have computer knowledge and where countercultures will promote a pre-networking era (while on the largest network in the world).

Unfortunately, also expect more obscenity, less reasoned discussion, more personal attacks, and more wandering from the topic, particularly in public forums like Usenet groups. There are currently almost no truly egalitarian communication environments (even the local newspaper has editors who carefully screen the letters they publish) and the Internet will prove to be a fascinating sociological experiment in this regard, though it will also doubtless be frustrating and annoying.

An example of this can be seen when adolescents connect to existing professional conferencing systems, violate the existing behavioral mores, and then turn nasty when their errors are pointed out to them. A case in point: the Indiana Department of Education runs a popular conferencing system called IDEAnet, which is a central place for teachers in the state of Indiana to discuss school-related topics; interact with researchers at various Indiana universities; explore the Internet; and for select K-12 students, learn about computer systems. Recently a few young folk connected and immediately began to post crude and inappropriate messages about each other. When the system administrator chided them for their behavior, they immediately became quite abusive and had their accounts canceled. This is just the beginning, because when the Internet is really spread throughout the world, it will become impossible to enforce any sort of behavioral constraints through means other than peer pressure.

Instead (and perhaps this is the best solution), it will be up to the information consumer to filter intelligently information that is not of interest. This shift from Internet user as passive recipient of information to active participant, teaching sophisticated navigational systems the type of information that is of interest, how to prioritize information found, and which authors are of particular interest (or should be avoided). Primitive versions of these ideas are implemented in some Netnews readers with what are called *kill files.* Expect this to become quite a successful commercial business, too: people will willingly spend a few dollars a month to have a sophisticated software system help them find the information they want and skip the information they don't.

In sum, I think there's going to be a gradual shift on the Internet in the next decade: from a small homogeneous community composed primarily of passive information recipients to an enormous heterogeneous mass of people, producing more information (and misinformation) than any of us are prepared to deal with. It will become imperative to work with software-assisted intelligent, active, information- and network-navigation tools in order to find anything in the information flood.

Answered by Dave Van Buren (`dave@ipac.caltech.edu`)

As this technology matures over the next decade, we will begin to see new patterns of work evolve. Geographically dispersed groups of people will come together online to solve particular problems in the sciences, medicine, engineering, arts, education, business, and politics. Some things we might see in these fields are "critical mass" research groups suddenly able to tackle problems that were too hard or complex; online medical diagnostic services; methods for archiving, organizing, and navigating documents; software and experience for engineering projects; online classes on topics too narrow to support a course at a "physical" university; and emerging artforms based on distributed "hypertext" and other formats. Eventually the services available will move beyond access to archival information and on to providing new information through instruments and sensors hooked directly to computers on the network.

CHAPTER 2

How Do I Get Connected to the Internet?

This chapter covers some of the most frequently asked of the frequently asked questions about the Internet—the ones about how to get connected. There are so many choices to make and ways to connect, newcomers can be overwhelmed. Don't worry. Splay out, laden with your beverage of choice, and consider the possibilities.

Q 2.1. What is an "Internet dial tone?"

Before you can explore the Internet, you need to have access to a computer that is part of the network. When you buy a telephone, it doesn't work right out of the box. Before you make that first call, you need to pay to have the line connected by the phone company, so you can hear a dial tone. Similarly, you can't dial the Internet's services until your modem can connect with a computer that is part of the Internet. Once you have an "Internet dial tone" you will be able to access the Internet's resources.

Getting connected isn't as easy as you might think. One day in our middle future, you may be able to plug your computer into your cable-TV box and have instant access to the information (oh, how I hate this term!) superhighway. Depending on who you ask, this will either be a worldwide free exchange of information available to every American citizen—or a global commercialized nightmare featuring 500 channels of "I Love Lucy" reruns. What will really happen? Your guess is as good as mine. In the meantime, I'll get off my soapbox, and you can think about finding Internet access in today's more mundane world.

The Internet dial tone can take many forms, serving you with any of a variety of tools, toys, and services, so you have many choices and features to consider. Because the Internet is a cooperative effort, there is no Internet, Inc. to sign up with and send a check to. Instead, you must find an online service that is plugged in to the Internet. Not every online service is part of the Internet, and as you will see, the tools available at various services differ considerably.

NOTE The computer to which your computer connects to access the Internet is called your *host*. The company or institution that operates a host is called your *service provider*. Because of the vast array of computers and people that compose the Internet, service providers range from billion-dollar commercial online services to tiny bulletin board systems running out of someone's basement. No matter where you'll be connecting to, when you read about your *service provider*, understand that term to mean the person or company on the other side of your Internet link; when you see *host*, it means the computer you connect to.

Getting telephone service is simple and decision-free: you ask the local phone company for a line and you get it. Getting an Internet dial tone isn't so straightforward. You'll need to choose your access method, think about what services you'll use, compare prices, and finally sign up with a service provider. At the risk of dragging this analogy too far (or is it too late?), imagine having to choose your phone company from a cast of hundreds before you could even make a phone call. It wouldn't be pretty, but you would have the benefit of choosing exactly what services you could use and the price you would pay. That's the way it is with Internet access.

Q 2.2. What kinds of connections are available?

Individuals and small businesses can best access the Internet using a *dial-up connection.* A dial-up connection simply means that when you want to access the Internet, your modem dials a host computer and you can go about your business; when you're done, just hang up the modem to free the phone line. *Dial-up access* means your phone line is only tied up while you're actually using the Internet, and you won't need expensive and complex hardware like a high-speed leased phone line, terminal servers, routers, or a UNIX computer system.

If you're trying to connect a large group of people who require simultaneous, extremely fast connections to the Internet, dial-up access is not the best choice. If you're connecting more than 20 people who require simultaneous and permanent Internet connections, you may very well need that leased line, terminal server, router, and other equipment. This is called a *dedicated connection,* and I won't talk much about these, partly because they frighten me. Luckily, those of us who need simple dial-up access will only need a computer and modem, a phone line, an account with a service provider, and the appropriate software.

NOTE New technologies will add options for accessing the Internet. For instance, Integrated Services Digital Network (ISDN) is offered in some areas and is slowly becoming more readily available. ISDN will bridge the gap between personal dial-up service and a dedicated connection by allowing fast access (at about 57 Kbps, four times faster than today's 14.4 Kbps modems) over inexpensive phone lines. Most phone companies will charge slightly more for ISDN service than for

regular phone service (my phone company, Pacific Bell, charges a monthly fee plus a few cents per minute for connect time), and you'll require special hardware to make your computer talk over ISDN. (Sorry, your regular modem just won't do.) However, if it's available to you, Internet service over ISDN might be the right choice for small businesses and those of us who want access to the Net as fast as we can get it.

There are several types of services you can use to access the Internet.

- **A public-access service provider**
- **A Commercial online service**
- **A Dial-up IP link access**
- **A Community bulletin board system**

Some connections give you access to a wide variety of Internet services and tools; others limit you to only a few tools such as electronic mail and the Usenet. Each type of connection has important features and drawbacks to consider before you make your choice.

2.3. What is command-line access?

Command-line access through a local Internet service provider is one of the most common ways to access the Internet. It is cost-effective, simple to learn, and similar across different computing platforms. The term *command-line access* can be a misnomer, because access through a local Internet service provider might be either via a command line (á la the UNIX operating system) or through a custom menu-driven interface.

Navigating the Net using a command-line or menu-driven interface isn't particularly elegant. A multimedia experience it ain't: you get screens full of text but no online graphics or sound. You can transfer files and access databases, send electronic mail, participate in interactive chat sessions, and lots of other good stuff—but it's not particularly pretty and you don't get to fiddle with a mouse. (The keyboard is usually the only means of input. If you're really lucky, you'll get to learn to use the h, j, k, and l keys like arrows to move the cursor around. Yuk!) Depending on your service, you may see unhelpful prompts and be obligated to type obtuse commands like `trn -xDD alt.internet.services`. Not that I'm complaining (all right, I admit I'm complaining), but I've been using primarily command-line access for years. It works, it's reliable, and it's cheap. Here is an example of reading Usenet news with this type of access:

```
bolero[5] rn
Unread news in alt.fan.laurie.anderson                        1 article
Unread news in alt.internet.services                        453 articles
Unread news in comp.infosystems.wais                         37 articles
Unread news in alt.internet.talk-radio                       11 articles
Unread news in comp.sys.mac.hypercard                       188 articles
etc.

******   1 unread article in alt.fan.laurie.anderson — read now? [ynq]n
****** 453 unread articles in alt.internet.services — read now? [ynq]n
******  37 unread articles in comp.infosystems.wais — read now? [ynq]n
******  11 unread articles in alt.internet.talk-radio — read now? [ynq]n
****** 188 unread articles in comp.sys.mac.hypercard — read now? [ynq]n
******  12 unread articles in alt.etext — read now? [ynq]n
****** 329 unread articles in news.newusers.questions — read now? [ynq]y
Reading overview file....
14245 Re: Fido Net
14246 Using NEWS as a teaching tool
14247 Re: PICO query: including .sigs
14248 Welcome to news.newusers.questions! (weekly posting)
14249 Re: Yes, another .sig question
14250 Re: NEW YORK CITY TRAVEL TIPS
14251 Re: Q: how to create a kill-file
14252 Re: Internet World
14253 Pine mail question
14254 Re: kibo?
14255 Re: Help!
14256 Need contact in US Local Govt. Comp Ops.
14257 Sports scores listservers
14258 Re: vi idiot wants to know: how edit .login?
14259 Re: vi idiot wants to know: how edit .login?
14260 Re: HTTP? WWW Questions
14261 Re: FINDING A NEWSGROUP
14262 This is a test. Do not adjust your set...
14263 Interface TLI
14264 Re: Internet 'Navigator' Software ?
14265 Re: ELM aliases from TIN?
14266 Re: How to choose editor in elm
14267 Assorted questions: where to ask?
What next? [npq] 14248

news.newusers.questions #14248 (328 more)
```

```
From: phillips@syrinx.umd.edu (Leanne Phillips)
Newsgroups: news.newusers.questions,news.answers
Subject: Welcome to news.newusers.questions! (weekly posting)
Supersedes: <news-newusers-intro"760050930@syrinx.umd.edu>
Followup-To: news.newusers.questions
Date: Fri Feb 11 19:30:13 PST 1994
Organization: University of Maryland, College Park
Lines: 314
Distribution: world
Summary: READ THIS BEFORE POSTING TO THIS NEWSGROUP
X-Version: $Id: news-newusers-intro,v 1.24 1994/2/3 02:33:24 phillips Exp $
Originator: phillips@syrinx.umd.edu

Archive-name: news-newusers-intro
Version: $Id: news-newusers-intro,v 1.24 1994/2/3 02:33:24 phillips Exp $

Changes: This is now being maintained by Leanne Phillips
  (phillips@syrinx.umd.edu), rather than by Jonathan Kamens.

  Welcome to the news.newusers.questions newsgroup!  According to the
"List of Active Newsgroups" posting in news.announce.newusers, the
purpose of this newsgroup is "Q & A for users new to the Usenet."  So
if you've got questions about the USENET, this is the place to post
them!

                 Get to know news.announce.newusers.

  However, before you do that, there is another newsgroup with which
you should become acquainted. The news.announce.newusers newsgroup
contains (once again according to the "List of Active Newsgroups"
posting) "Explanatory postings for new users."  Its purpose is to
provide a base set of information with which all participants in the
USENET should be familiar in order to make the USENET a better place
for all of us.
```

Command-line access is easy to set up and is generally less expensive than an IP connection (which is discussed in the answer to Question 2.4) and is usually comparable in price to access to commercial online services. This type of access works reliably from any kind of personal computer because specialized software isn't needed. This can be a benefit if you use, for instance, a Macintosh at home and a 486 PC running Windows at the office. Although the computers are very different, Internet access using a command line would be similar from either machine.

Finding a public access site for a command-line account is usually more difficult than joining a commercial online service. Although there are only a few commercial online services that offer full

Internet access, there are hundreds of public-access UNIX hosts, each offering different features, pricing structures, and local access from different locales. (I find it ironic that finding an access site is difficult because there are so many. Wouldn't it make sense if it were difficult because there were so few?)

With command-line access, your computer is not "on the Internet"; that is, it doesn't have its own Internet name or address. Instead, your host is connected to the Internet, and you access the Net via that remote computer. Although this is an important distinction, know that a command-line account isn't a bad way to use the network: this kind of access is simple to use and (unlike an IP link) doesn't require a complicated software configuration on your own computer.

Because your computer isn't directly on the Internet when you use a command-line account, certain functions require extra steps. A good example is file transfers: imagine there's a new shareware program, a llama racing tracker, for your personal computer available at a popular anonymous FTP site. You decide you must have this program, so you use FTP to get the software. The remote FTP site dutifully sends the file to your service provider's computer, because that is the computer actually on the Internet. When you end the FTP session, you'll notice that a copy of the program is at your host. It doesn't do much good there because you want to run it on your own computer. You need to take the second step: copying the llama tracker from your host to your computer, this time using a file transfer protocol like XMODEM, ZMODEM, or Kermit. This extra step is not much of a hassle, but it is worth noting.

Q 2.4. What is IP access?

Dial-up Internet protocol (IP) links such as serial line Internet protocol (SLIP) and point-to-point protocol (PPP) make your computer a direct part of the Internet while you're online. You can run networking applications for electronic mail, FTP, Gopher, Telnet, and other tools locally from your own computer. Unlike command-line access, with IP links you can connect to multiple sites simultaneously. For instance, you can have an FTP session in one window, Telnet in another, and Gopher in yet another. With the right software, you can even set up your system so that electronic mail comes directly to your computer.

IP access is simply more elegant than command-line access. On most computer systems, you can navigate Internet services (such as Gopher and FTP sites) by pointing and clicking with a mouse. Tools such as Mosaic will bring color graphics and sound to your online world. Using them, you can see the Internet the way it was meant to be seen: as if you're cruising cyberspace in a classic Mustang. Stop off at an online museum and check out photos of the latest exhibits. Make a pit stop in an electronic coffeehouse and see pictures of your comrades. Then use live, two-way video conferencing to get some work done.

Figure 2.1 shows a screen shot of Mosaic, an "Internet browser" application, in action. Mosaic integrates text, graphics, and sound to turn the Internet into a multimedia experience. Cool, huh?

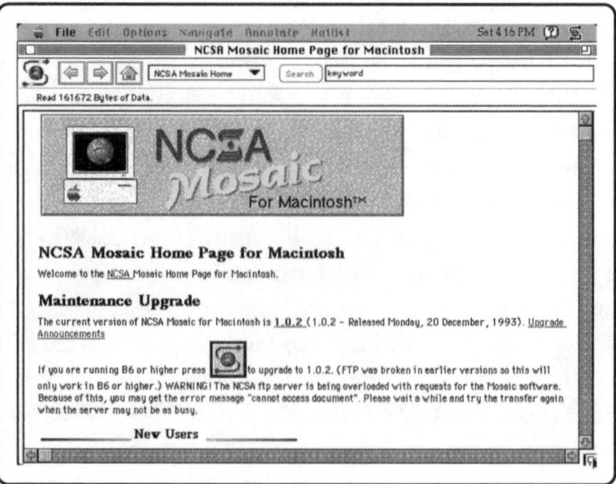

Figure 2.1. *Mosaic in action.*

In the case of the fictional (but highly desirable) llama-race tracking program, using an IP link, you can connect directly to the anonymous FTP site and transfer the program right to your own computer, which eliminates the intermediate stopover at a service provider. Remember that to access the Internet via IP, you do need a service provider, but the host is invisible to you while you go about your business.

Dial-up IP links are usually more expensive than command-line accounts. Also, although you can use a slow (2400 bps) modem for account access, a slow modem just won't do for IP access; you should use a 9600 bps or faster modem. Why? All that whizbang technology—the graphics, moving pictures, and sounds—use an immense amount of bandwidth. It takes a long time to transfer that information to your computer, so a fast connection—or a patient soul—is necessary.

NOTE Bandwidth is a bit of jargon stolen from broadcasting techies. In radio, *bandwidth* refers to the amount of "space" on the airwaves that a given message uses. Faster transmissions with more information require greater bandwidth. When we talk of modems and the Internet, the term is used similarly. A large graphics or sound file takes much more bandwidth than a simple ASCII text message.

Because the software for a dial-up IP link resides on your own computer, you will need to find and install it yourself. You'll need to deal with configuring many pieces of software on your computer, complex steps that command-line users need not worry about. The software you'll need is really several programs: one each for e-mail, FTP, Telnet, Gopher, and so on. In my experience, IP access requires patient tweaking before it works perfectly. If you're new to the Internet, you may want to squash your learning curve by starting with simple command-line access and then moving on to IP access after you know your way around the network.

NOTE It took me, a hardened professional and long-time hacker, a good three or four hours to get my IP access working. I hope it is faster (and less frustrating) for you.

If you are using IP access, you will have to choose between SLIP or PPP access. What you'll use depends on which software is available for your computer and what your service provider offers. Ask your provider whether they support SLIP or PPP and how you can access them using your computer system.

NOTE If you have the choice, choose PPP over SLIP. PPP is better implemented and a little faster than SLIP. (Why? I read somewhere that SLIP was literally designed on a napkin and implemented in one late-night programming session; PPP was better thought out and not rushed through development.) SLIP also has more security problems, a reason that many sites prefer PPP.

Q 2.5. How can my organization get dedicated Internet access?

Any organization can get dedicated Internet access—businesses, nonprofit organizations, computer clubs, schools and colleges, whoever and whatever. You don't even need to be an organization to set yourself up with dedicated Internet access.

A dedicated Internet line provides fast, round-the-clock access for a large group of people. Organizations that want to plug in to the Internet need to consider a variety of issues, problems, and technologies that don't affect those who need individual access. Connecting a large group of people to the Internet takes time, thought, and money. With research, planning, and experimentation, you can find the right kind of access—at the right price—for your organization.

NOTE A dedicated Internet connection links your organization's local area network (LAN), mainframe, or minicomputer to the Internet. Once this connection is made, the connected computer or

computers have a fast, full-time Internet connection. The LAN at your site can include IBM-PC compatibles, Macintoshes, UNIX boxes—in fact, any computers with the hardware to be part of a network.

Dedicated access is expensive. The costs include a high-speed leased telephone line, a CSU/DSU (a kind of high-speed digital modem), a router to connect your LAN to the CSU/DSU, and installation charges. In addition to these, if the computers at your site aren't already networked, they'll need to be before they can access the Internet. A dedicated connection is also expensive in terms of time to set up and maintain. In addition to equipment costs, you will need a person with the expertise to set up and maintain the Internet connection, hardware, LAN, and so on. Of course, you know these things don't appear on their own, but don't underestimate the effort it can take to set them up. Consultation and system set-up can be a full-time job. After things are running smoothly, maintenance may take a part-time or a full-time person, depending on your equipment and the scope of your network link. You will also need technical support personnel to answer questions about and to solve problems with the network.

Q 2.6. What about commercial online services?

Commercial online services are large computer systems that are available around the nation (and around the world). Unlike most public-access UNIX services and IP service providers, commercial online services offer a variety of services other than Internet access, such as databases of information, online games, file libraries, and the like. Commercial online services are slowly venturing onto the Internet as a means of providing an additional service to their customers. You've heard of them: CompuServe, America Online, Prodigy, Delphi, and the Whole Earth 'Lectronic Link are just a few of these services. Some of them offer great Internet access; others barely get by and only offer electronic mail.

An important advantage of commercial online services is that they, unlike most public-access providers, are available via packet-switching networks (covered in the section that follows Question 2.16).

Commercial services do have their disadvantages. Most notably, many commercial services offer very limited access to the Internet. As of this writing, only three major commercial services offer access to the Internet's full range of tools. The rest offer more limited access, usually only electronic mail. Most commercial services also bill by the hour, a rare occurrence with Internet providers.

2.7. What commercial online services offer Internet access?

CompuServe, MCI Mail, and GEnie users can send and receive e-mail via the Internet, but lack other tools. If you'll only use the Internet for electronic mail, you can choose any commercial service, and you'll be able to send and receive mail to your heart's content. But the Internet is much more than e-mail. If you use a service whose only offering is electronic mail, you are missing out on the wealth of good stuff on the Internet. (One commercial service launched a huge advertising campaign promising Internet access, but new users were disappointed to discover that e-mail was the only Internet service actually offered.)

America Online (at the time of writing) offers e-mail and Usenet newsgroups, with plans to add Gopher access. The standouts that offer complete Internet access are Delphi and BIX (which are actually owned by the same company) and the Whole Earth 'Lectronic Link.

Delphi

Delphi was the first nationwide service to provide full Internet access, including electronic mail, Usenet newsgroups, FTP, and Telnet. Delphi uses a decent, text-based, menu-driven system. It's a little funky, but it works well enough with the basic Internet tools. The prices are fair, and after an extensive marketing blitz promoting its Internet access, Delphi seems to have made a real niche for itself.

Here are the costs, but keep in mind that they may have changed by the time you read this. (Indeed, they may change by the time I'm finished typing this paragraph.) Delphi has two membership plans:

the "10/4" plan costs $10 per month and includes four hours of use; additional use is $4 per hour. The "20/20 Advantage" plan is $20 per month, includes 20 hours of use and costs $1.80 per hour for additional time. The Internet service option costs an extra $3 per month. There may be a one-time startup fee, depending on the service plan you choose.

Delphi access during business hours via Sprintnet or Tymnet carries an additional surcharge. Through a trial membership offer, anyone interested in trying Delphi and the Internet can receive five hours of access for free. To join, dial (800) 365-4636 by modem. After connecting, press Return. At the "Username:" prompt, enter `JOINDELPHI` and at the password prompt, type `INTERNET`. If you have questions, call Delphi's voice information line at (800) 695-4005.

BIX

Byte Information Exchange (BIX) offers full access to the Internet, and users can use FTP, Telnet, electronic mail, and other Internet tools. I haven't tried this service, but I get the feeling that for some reason, BIX has always been an underdog among online services. This doesn't seem to have changed much since BIX started offering full Net access. BIX helps the Internet novice along by enlisting the aid of "tour guides" standing by to answer questions about navigating the Net. The service is also home to local conferences, news, and entertainment. BIX is a primarily text-based, menu-driven system, but you can overlay that with custom "navigation" software that lets BIX put on a more graphical face.

Current charges for BIX are $13 each month, plus connect charges of $3/hr for non-primetime use. BIX also offers a "20/20" plan—20 hours of evening and weekend service for $20 a month. For more information, call the voice information line at (800) 695-4775.

WELL

The Whole Earth 'Lectronic Link, or WELL, is one of the best-known California computing services. I hesitate to lump the WELL, a homey electronic community, in the commercial-service category with huge megalopolis services like CompuServe, but the WELL meets the criteria of a nationally available, full-featured commercial service. Besides being a world-famous coffee house built o' electrons, the WELL offers the full selection of Internet services, plus its famous local conferences. However, its text-based command-line interface is among the funkiest to learn to use. Luckily, there's an hour-long interactive tour to help you get familiar with the system.

The WELL costs $15 a month plus $2 an hour. Long-distance usage through the CompuServe Packet Network (a packet-switching service)costs an additional $4 per hour. To sign up online, dial (415) 332-6106 and log in as `newuser`. Callers from out of the area may wish to use the packet network: call (800) 848-8980 to find the nearest CPN number, call that number, and enter WELL at the prompt. The WELL's voice information line is (415) 332-4335.

Here is a sampling of the world of the WELL:

```
This is the WELL

Type   newuser   to sign up.
Type   trouble   if you are having trouble logging in.
Type   guest     to learn about the WELL.



If you already have a WELL account, type your username.

login: savetz
Password:
Last login: Sat Feb  5 18:32:34 from bolero.rahul.net
Sun Microsystems Inc. SunOS 5.3       Generic September 1993

You own your own words. This means that you are responsible for the words
that you post on the WELL and that reproduction of those words without
your permission in any medium outside of the WELL's conferencing system
may be challenged by you, the author.

You have new mail.
PicoSpan T3.3k; designed by Marcus Watts
 copyright 1984 NETI; licensed by Unicon Inc.

OK (type a command or type  opt  for Options): mail
Mail version 5.2d (word-wrap) 9/22/91. Type ? for help.
"/home/s/a/savetz/.inbox": 5 messages 5 new
>N  1 support  Fri Feb  4 14:55  72/2648 "WELLcome to The WELL!"
 N  2 sdf      Sat Feb  5 12:52  14/423 "Welcome"
 N  3 support  Fri Feb 11 02:25  43/1781 "You're invited"
 N  4 rus@bga.com Wed Feb 16 03:59  86/2911 "Spring CyberSpace Community, "
 N  5 support  Fri Feb 18 02:05  43/1786 "You're invited....."
```

```
OK (type a command or type  opt  for Options): confs

                              CONFERENCES

       1 - Conferences on Social Responsibility and Politics (1K)
       2 - Media and Communications (1K)
       3 - Magazines, Publications and Zines (1K)
       4 - Business and Livelihood (1K)
       5 - Body, Mind, Health (1K)
       6 - Cultures and Languages (1K)
       7 - Of Place and Places (1K)
       8 - Interactions (1K)
       9 - Arts and Letters (1K)
      10 - Recreation (1K)
      11 - Entertainment (1K)
      12 - Education, Science and Planning (1K)
      13 - Grateful Dead (1K)
      14 - Computers (1K)
      15 - Conferences About The WELL, Itself (1K)
      16 - Private Conferences (2K)
      17 - Print Out All 200+ Conferences (11K)
```


America Online

Commercial online services are changing what it means to use the Internet. For instance, America Online (AOL) threatens to bring easy-to-use, graphical Internet access to the masses, as shown in Figure 2.2. I say *threatens to* because from where I sit, they haven't done it yet. America Online offers electronic mail to the Internet as well as Usenet newsgroups, Gopher, FTP, and other goodies that may or may not be available by the time you read this. They've been very slow to deliver so far, so I can't tell you if most of these services will work well. America Online runs on Macintosh and IBM-compatible computers and is easy to learn and navigate. The point-and-click interface is certainly easier to learn than the command-line interface on Delphi, BIX, and public-access UNIX providers.

AOL costs $9.95 a month for 5 hours of use, any time of day. Additional time is billed at $3.50 per hour. There is no surcharge for connection through Tymnet and Sprintnet—happy happy, joy joy. For more information, call AOL's voice information line at (800) 827-6364.

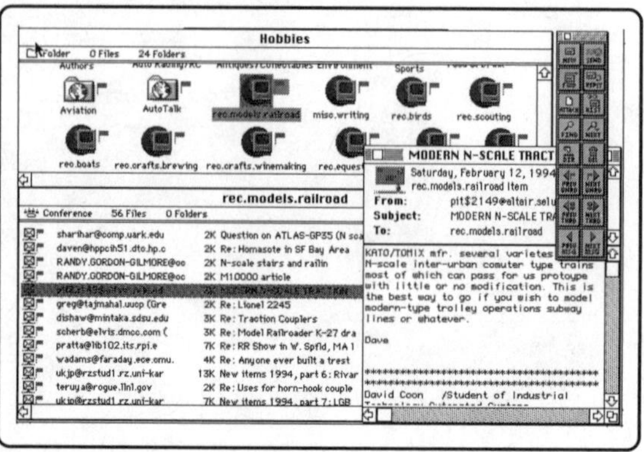

Figure 2.2. *America Online offers Internet e-mail and Usenet newsgroups through a benevolent graphical interface.*

2.8. Can I use the Internet through a bulletin board system?

You may also be able to access the Internet using a local bulletin board system (BBS). This is a dubious proposition at best for many reasons. Although there are tens of thousands of fine bulletin board systems around the world, only about 20 percent of them offer some degree of Internet access. Of those, fewer still offer complete and reliable Internet access.

Finding a reliable BBS for accessing the Internet is truly a crap shoot. Anyone can run a bulletin board: the system operator behind the BBS may be a seasoned professional or a 12-year-old hacking away in his bedroom. Some BBSes are professional, stable operations, others are more fleeting. Some charge for access, some are free. Some have dozens of telephone lines; many have only one or two. Most BBSes are not dedicated to providing Internet access; most of the time, BBSes have their own conferences for chatting and files for downloading. Internet access, if available, usually comes second to the board's own community.

NOTE Of course, in this day and age the 12-year-old could also *be* a seasoned professional!

Some BBSes are part of networks other than the Internet (such as FidoNet or OneNet). Don't be fooled by imitations! Demand Internet by name. : -) Not all types of bulletin boards can offer Internet access, and those that do usually can't offer the full gamut of Internet services. (Several types of bulletin board software can provide Internet e-mail and Usenet newsgroups, but lack programs such as Telnet and FTP with which you can access other systems in real time.) See Figure 2.3.

2

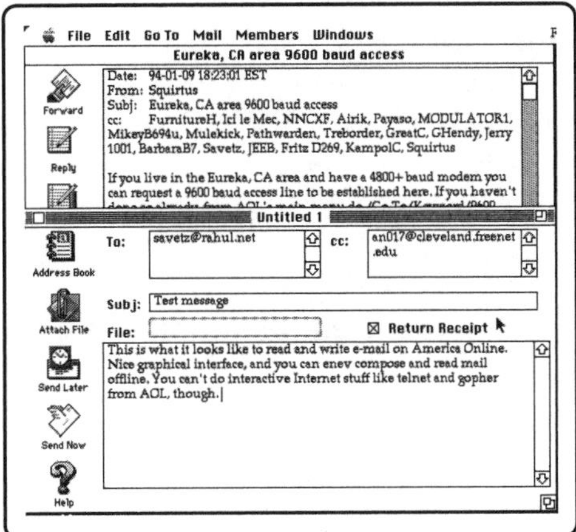

Figure 2.3. *Reading Usenet postings using a FirstClass BBS. (FirstClass is a brand of graphical bulletin board system that can offer e-mail and Usenet.)*

For these and other reasons, accessing the Internet via a bulletin board system is not a reliable choice for any but the most casual user. Stable and reliable BBSes are out there. If you can find one, great, but this can take some real digging.

2.9. Wait a minute! What about free access?

It's a common misconception that access to the Internet is free. The costs of the Internet are shared by those who use it. Many folks get

Internet access at no cost to them through their school or employer (or through the occasional BBS or free-net), which seems to help spread the rumor that the Internet is free for all of us. Sure, it's free to those lucky ones, but you can be sure that someone—such as their school or employer—is paying dearly to provide Internet access.

If you are a college (or even high-school) student or faculty member, check with your campus computer center to learn about the online facilities available to you. Many schools offer free accounts to students and staff. Similarly, your business may offer Internet access to employees—if you know the right person to ask. Finding access at your institution is a great way to get a free Internet account.

Beware of special restrictions on Internet use imposed by your institution. For instance, most schools frown on the use of their accounts for business or other nonacademic activities. Such policies may be as simple as posted rules or as elaborate as firewalls preventing you from using multi-user dungeons, Internet Relay Chat (IRC), and other interesting stuff.

2.10. Where can I get Internet access in my area?

One of the most challenging aspects of using the Internet might surprise you. It's not learning to use a dozen new programs to navigate the network, or even finding out about all of the interesting places to explore. The biggest challenge for most of us—finding Internet access—comes before these other tasks.

Finding the right access may mean one quick phone call to a nearby friend who's "in the know," or it could mean hours of phone calls and research. Is it worth it? Absolutely. Getting on the Internet is like buying a house or planning a vacation: there are options to consider, choices to make, and in the end, a worthwhile prize.

No matter which method of access you want, you need to know specific things about service providers before making the decision as to which one to use. Arm yourself with the information in this section and then begin contacting promising service providers and ask questions—lots of questions.

If you know people who have Internet access, ask them how they got it. If those people live near you and are happy with their service, chances are that service will be right for you, too.

NOTE I hope you will be able to stick with one service for a long time. Staying with one service means you won't have to keep learning new interfaces and commands, because no two services are exactly alike, and you'll have a stable electronic mail address so that your correspondents can find you. Internet service providers vary widely in services and prices. Be sure to check all your options before you sign on the dotted line.

Then again, don't worry too much about finding the perfect Internet service provider the first time around. Getting online the first time is usually the most difficult; once you're online, you'll find a wealth of information about other—possibly better—ways to connect to the Internet. You can change your service provider at any time. Although it's cumbersome to set up a new account, tell your associates your new e-mail address. You shouldn't feel locked in to a particular service provider or type of service.

Q 2.11. What is the PDIAL list?

If you've decided on an IP connection or a UNIX host, you'll need to begin with a recent listing of service providers. One excellent list, PDIAL, is a list of public-access service providers offering dial-up access to Internet connections. Service providers come and go daily, so the PDIAL list is updated on a regular basis.

If you already have an Internet e-mail account (or you know someone who does), you can get the most recent version of PDIAL by sending electronic mail as follows:

```
To: info-deli-server@netcom.com
Subject: Send PDIAL
Message Body: (ignored)
```

To get PDIAL via anonymous FTP, FTP to

```
rtfm.mit.edu:/pub/usenet/alt.internet.access.wanted/P"D"I"A"L"(P)
```

PDIAL is also posted regularly to Usenet newsgroups.

```
alt.internet.access.wanted, alt.bbs.lists, and news.answers.
```

Q 2.12. What is NIXPUB?

NIXPUB is another large listing of public-access and free UNIX providers. Not all the providers in the NIXPUB list offer full Internet service; some only offer e-mail or Usenet newsgroups.

You can get this list via e-mail by sending a request

```
To: nixpub@access.digex.com
Subject: (ignored)
Message Body: (ignored)
```

NIXPUB is available via anonymous FTP at

```
vfl.paramax.com:/pub/pubnet/nixpub.long
```

You can't get the most recent versions of PDIAL or NIXPUB unless you already have an account, right? Isn't that a catch-22? Yes. If you're itching to get on the Net pronto without all this tomfoolery, call Delphi or BIX and you can be online tonight. Once you're exploring the Net, you will be able to find the perfect service provider for your needs. (Or you may decide that Delphi/BIX's menu-driven command-line interface is perfect for you.)

2.13. What's a free-net?

In 1985, Case Western Reserve University began experimenting with offering free, open-access, community computer systems as a new communications and information medium. Called the *Cleveland Free-Net,* the service was to provide free online information access to the community. A cornerstone of the system was (and still is) "community computing," the idea that in cyberspace (as in any new city or town) everything is built by the citizens who inhabit it. The document "The Concept of Community Computing" (available on the Cleveland Free-Net) best describes the motivation behind the free-nets.

```
Anyone in the community with access to a home, office, or school
computer and a modem can contact the system any time, 24 hours a day.
They simply dial a central phone number, make connection, and a series of
menus appears on the screen which allows them to select the information
or communication services they would like. All of it is free and all of it
can easily be accomplished by a first-time user.

     The key to the economics of operating a community computer system is
the fact that the system is literally run by the community itself.
Everything that appears on one of these machines is there because there
are individuals or organizations in the community who are prepared to
contribute their time, effort, and expertise to place it there and operate it
over time. This, of course, is in contrast to the commercial services
which have very high personnel and information-acquisition costs and
must pass those costs on to the consumer.

     Couple this volunteerism with the rapidly-dropping costs of computing
power, the use of inexpensive transmission technology, and the fact that
the necessary software to operate these systems is available for low
cost—and public access computing becomes an economically-viable entity.
```

Free-nets are notoriously easy to use, and most seem to provide adequate Internet access. Although I haven't tried all of them, I know that the Cleveland Free-Net offers Internet e-mail, a small selection of Usenet newsgroups, and the ability to Telnet to selected Internet systems and databases.

Here's what a session on the Cleveland Free-Net looks like:

```
BSDI BSD/386 1.0 (kanga) (ttys8)


                         /\
 WELCOME TO THE... _|  |_
                    _|__  __|_
       __          |          |
     _|  |_        |  |    |  |
    |      |   /\  |  |    |  |
    |      |  |  | |  |    |  |____
    |      | |   | |  |    |  |    |
    |      | |_|_| |  |    |  |    |
    |      |    || |  |    |  |    |
   _|      |    |_|_|         |    |_
  |        |        |_|       |      |
 |                                    |
 |          CLEVELAND FREE-NET        |
 |       COMMUNITY COMPUTER SYSTEM    |
 |____________________________________|

          brought to you by

    Case Western Reserve University
   Community Telecomputing Laboratory


Are you:
        1. A registered user
        2. A visitor

Please enter 1 or 2: 2

Would you like to:
        1. Apply for an account
        2. Explore the system
        3. Exit the system

Please enter 1, 2 or 3: 2
Copyright 1992, Berkeley Software Design, Inc.
Copyright (c) 1980,1983,1986,1988,1990,1991 The Regents of the University
of California. All rights reserved.

BSDI BSD/386 1.0 Kernel #14: Mon Feb  7 11:26:10 EST 1994

Local time is: Fri Feb 18 13:46:50 EST 1994

<<< CLEVELAND FREE-NET DIRECTORY >>>

  1 The Administration Building
  2 The Post Office
```

```
  3 Public Square
  4 The Courthouse & Government Center
  5 The Arts Building
  6 Science and Technology Center
  7 The Medical Arts Building
  8 The Schoolhouse (Academy One)
  9 The Community Center & Recreation Area
 10 The Business and Industrial Park
 11 The Library
 12 University Circle
 13 The Teleport
 14 The Communications Center
 15 NPTN/USA TODAY HEADLINE NEWS
-------------------------------------------------
h=Help, x=Exit Free-Net, "go help"=extended help

Your Choice ==> 15

   <<< NPTN & USA TODAY HEADLINE NEWS >>>

  1 The National Public Telecomputing Network
  2 USA TODAY HEADLINE NEWS
-------------------------------------------------
h=Help, x=Exit Free-Net, "go help"=extended help

Your Choice ==> 2

<<< NPTN/USA TODAY HEADLINE NEWS >>>

  1 About the Electronic News Center

  2 Headline News Summary
  3 Weather
  4 Snapshots

  5 NEWS
  6 MONEY
  7 SPORTS
  8 LIFE
-------------------------------------------------
h=Help, x=Exit Free-Net, "go help"=extended help

Your Choice ==> 2

First message is #515, last message is #525

 **    515. news Fri, Feb 4 1994
       516. news Mon, Feb 7 1994
       517. news Tue, Feb 8 1994
       518. news Wed, Feb 9 1994
       519. news Thu, Feb 10 1994
       520. news Fri, Feb 11 1994
       521. news Mon, Feb 14 1994
```

2

```
     522. news Tue, Feb 15 1994
     523. news Wed, Feb 16 1994
     524. news Thu, Feb 17 1994
     525. news Fri, Feb 18 1994

Enter Command: 525

Article #525 (525 is last):
Newsgroups: usa-today.news,americast.usa-today.news
From: usa-post@AmeriCast.Com
Subject: news Fri, Feb 18 1994
Date: Fri Feb 18 05:16:08 1994

DECISIONLINE: News
USA TODAY Update
Feb. 18-20, 1994
Source: USA TODAY:Gannett National Information Network

TRADE DEFICIT HITS 5-YEAR HIGH:
   The U.S. merchandise trade deficit fell unexpectedly in
December but soared to $115.8 billion for all of 1993. A surge in
aircraft exports helped drive down the December deficit to $7.4
billion, from $9.7 billion in November, the Commerce Department
said Thursday. But 1993's trade gap was the largest since 1988, as
healthy U.S. economic growth boosted imports.
```

Q 2.14. Cool! Is there a free-net near me?

Here's a list of free-nets, along with their dial-in phone numbers. Once you're connected, most of these systems allow you to log in as a "guest" to explore the system and apply for your own account.

Cleveland Free-Net. (216) 368-3888. If you want to talk to a human being at the Cleveland Free-Net, dial (216) 368-USER.

Heartland Free-Net (Peoria). (309) 674-1100

Medina County Free-Net. (216) 723-6732

Tri-State Online (Cincinnati). (513) 579-1990

Youngstown Free-Net. (216) 742-3072

National Capital Free-Net (Ottawa, Canada). (613) 80-3733

Buffalo Free-Net. (716) 645-6128

Columbia Online Information Network. (314) 884-7000

Denver Free-Net. (303) 270-4865

Tallahassee Free-Net. (904) 488-5056

Victoria Free-Net. (604) 595-2300

Big Sky Telegraph. (406) 683-7600

Each of these systems have a feel of their own and its own community of users. Of course, the users on these free-nets aren't limited to those in the physical area in which they're located. Although the systems may focus on their own geographical area, users call in (or Telnet in) from all over the world.

2.15. What Internet tools should I look for?

The tools available to you online will determine what you can do on the Internet. As mentioned, some services offer many tools, others just a few. E-mail, the bare-minimum offering for any service with so-called Internet access, is surprisingly robust alone (see Chapter 4, "How Can I Communicate with People Around the World?" for ideas.) Of course, with more tools in your toolbox you'll be able to do more work.

The most basic level of Internet access is electronic mail, with which you can exchange messages with users on the Internet and other networks.

The next level is a combination of Usenet newsgroups and electronic mail.

The best collection of Internet access includes newsgroups and e-mail as well as the Internet's *interactive* tools—Telnet, FTP, Gopher, and so on. (These tools are called *interactive* because you use them to connect with other people and computers in "real time." E-mail and Usenet groups don't work in real time. When you send an e-mail message, for example, it isn't sent the moment you type it. It may sit in a mailbox for minutes or days before it's read by the intended recipient.)

From the hosts you are considering, find out what Internet tools are available. Some services that claim to offer Internet access offer only a limited selection of tools.

Be sure to plan ahead. For instance, although you may think you only need Internet electronic mail now, you will be gravely disappointed if you later want to try out FTP or Gopher and discover you can't access those services from your host. Tools to ask for are

- **Electronic mail.** Is it "batched" (delivered only a few times a day) or is it delivered the instant you send it? Batching e-mail probably saves your service provider money, but it considerably slows down the delivery of your electronic mail. Also, does the service charge you to send and receive e-mail? A small number of services—especially commercial ones that shall remain unnamed to protect the guilty—charge based on the number of messages delivered or the size of your e-mail. Try to avoid using services that charge this way. Charges based on e-mail usage limit the range of nifty things you will do with electronic mail and can bring unwelcome surprises when the bill comes.
- **Telnet.** The Telnet program, which you use to run programs and access databases on remote computers, is an important interactive tool. Get it if you can.
- **File Transfer Protocol (FTP).** With FTP you can search and retrieve files from various archives throughout the world. If you're interested in shareware, free software, or other information that you might be able to find on a public server, you'll definitely need FTP access! Find out if your service provider offers it. If so, is there a limit to the amount of information you can transfer using it?
- **Usenet News.** Does your host offer a full Usenet feed? How about value-added news like ClariNet (which features UPI newsfeeds, syndicated features, and the like)?
- **Gopher, Archie, and World Wide Web client.** If the service provider runs a special client for accessing these Internet tools, you'll have faster access and (one would hope) more reliability than using public clients run by other organizations.
- **Online help.** Are "manual pages" or other online help systems installed on the host?

Q 2.16. Woe is me! There isn't a service provider in my area. What should I do?

So you've checked PDIAL and NIXPUB and asked your nerdy friends, all of whom admit that you live in a backwater that doesn't have local Internet access. Don't panic. If you've got $20,000 or so sitting around, you might just want to start your own Internet service. Or you could move. Or you could bide your time and pray that your cable company or phone company or Higher Power brings you Internet service. More likely, though, you'll want to go with one of the following options.

Call Out of the Area

If there isn't a service provider in your area (which is likely unless you live in a large, technologically well-developed city), you may choose to use one that's farther away. For instance, if you live in a rural area with no local access, you can connect with a service located in another part of the state or country. Of course, this will raise the cost of getting connected to the Internet because you will need to pay long distance or toll telephone charges. This can be a blessing in disguise; when you use long distance, you have the luxury of choosing any service provider in the nation. This certainly beats being stuck with a mediocre service provider, even one that is a local phone call away.

Depending on your phone company's charges, you may actually save money by using an out-of-state service provider with a long-distance phone call rather than a closer one within your state. Thoroughly investigate the costs of calling various parts of the nation.

If a service provider with the tools you want isn't a local phone call away, a host that is accessible via a packet-switching network or an 800 line can save you from nasty surprises on your phone bill.

Use a Packet-Switching Network

Some Internet service providers and all commercial online services allow connections through a "packet-switching network." These are nationwide systems that users can use to connect to various online services using any of hundreds of local phone numbers. A packet-switching network (like SprintNet and Tymnet) may provide you with a local phone number for access, even though your service provider's computers are actually in Virginia, Cleveland, or wherever. One packet-switching network can provide access to dozens of service providers.

Packet-switching networks are nice, but they can drive up the price of using a service, and they aren't always available in rural areas. They're typically only available for use with larger commercial services. Some services that offer packet-switching access do charge extra for that service.

An important advantage of commercial online services is that they, unlike most public-access providers, are available as a local phone call from hundreds of cities.

Use an 800 Number

Several service providers offer service via a toll-free 800 number. Although access through an 800 number saves surprises on your phone bill, it drastically raises your hourly cost of access. When you use an 800 number, you don't pay for the phone call, but the recipient of the call does. Internet service providers who offer 800 access must pass the cost on to you in the form of inflated hourly charges. Depending on your long-distance telephone charges, using an 800 number may or may not save you money. Surcharges for using an 800 number are generally much steeper than packet-switching surcharges.

WARNING Rates for 800 access to the Internet hover around $10 an hour. That's quite a price to pay for a "free" call.

800 numbers are great if you travel a lot but need to access the Internet wherever you are. It's good to know you can always get online with a nationwide 800 number rather than trying to find your area's local packet-switching network number or paying outrageous hotel long-distance charges.

Q 2.17. What should I look for in a service provider?

Dual air bags, a large trunk, and anti-lock brakes. Whoops, that's something else. Here's what you should look for in an Internet service provider:

Speed

Your fancy 14.4 kilobits per second (kbps) modem won't impress anyone if it can't connect to a system that's as fast as it is. Find out the fastest speed your host can support. Transferring a large file at 2,400 bits per second (bps) can feel like agony, so get the fastest connection you can.

If you'll be connecting via a packet-switching network, find out what modem speed the local network hub will support. Big cities typically have 9,600 bps or faster access. Rural communities typically have to make do with 2,400 bps.

Some services charge extra for connecting with faster modems, so know what you'll be expected to pay based on your modem speed. This practice has decreased in recent years. If you use a quick modem, skip service providers that discriminate against you. Tell them that you're unwilling to connect with them because you're using a fast modem. That should help them phase out that silly bias.

Interface

What does it look like once you're online? What you'll find varies from service to service. There are hundreds of types of computers on the Internet—from tiny personal computers to medium-sized workstations to huge behemoth mainframes—and each one looks different online. The service you choose may feature an elegant graphical interface or, more commonly, a semi-elegant menu-driven interface or a decidedly inelegant UNIX prompt.

Although I've already set myself up to receive tons of hate mail from lovers of UNIX, I will say this. The interface you choose (and ultimately the service provider you use) depends on your expertise and patience. It's a trade-off. Although a command-line UNIX interface is harder at first to use, with practice and patience it is definitely more powerful than any menu-driven program could be.

Storage Space

If you'll be doing business with a command-line service, you'll sometimes need to store some information on your local host computer. Find out how much information you may store there. Some service providers have a strict limit, (say, two megabytes); others may allow you to purchase extra disk space when you need it.

Why should the service provider impose a limit? The hard disk of your host computer can hold only a limited amount of information and the system administrators want to be sure there will be enough to go around.

Software

Don't forget you'll need communications software that lets your computer talk to the modem. Most modems come with software, and there are dozens of software packages available for every computer system. Some are free, some are shareware, and others are commercial software. The software you'll need depends on your computer system and to what service you will connect. Users of public-access UNIX services and text-based commercial services can use freeware or shareware terminal programs. Commonly used communication programs include

Macintosh: Zterm, VersaTerm, Microphone II, Kermit

PC with DOS: Qmodem, Procomm, Telemate, Kermit

PC running Microsoft Windows: Procomm Plus

You need special software to access some commercial online services and BBSes that use graphics instead of text, like Prodigy and America Online. You'll have to get this software from the online service before signing on the first time. You'll also need special software on your computer if you'll be connecting via an IP link.

Access Restrictions

Find out the service's appropriate use policies before you sign up. Each system is run by different folks with varying ideas, ethics, and motivations, so some actions that are acceptable or tolerated on one system can be off-limits on others. Hence, certain systems may be inappropriate for certain activities.

For example, some networks that are part of the Internet are dedicated to education and research; hence they don't allow commercial activity. If you have an account on one of these systems, you shouldn't send junk e-mail advertising your new kitchen gizmo or post your company's press releases to the Usenet. So if you're thinking of putting your business online, find out what the network's appropriate use policies are.

Educational and business institutions can be sticklers about what their students or employees do online. For instance, some schools ban use of online games or multi-user dungeons. Also, it is safe to say that more-conservative sites might become annoyed if you begin posting pictures from your homemade porn movies to the Usenet's `alt.sex.pictures` conference.

If you will be reading news on the Usenet, find out if a site you are considering has a full Usenet feed. A full Usenet feed approaches 100 megabytes of information a day, so many sites cut back less-popular newsgroups to save disk space. (It's likely that you won't miss them unless you want to know about watersports in Finland or the goings-on in a particular literature class at an obscure East-coast university.) Other sites don't feed newsgroups with explicit sexual content.

Reliability and Performance

Nothing in the world is more frustrating than trying to log in to check your electronic mail only to find that your host is down, the phone lines are busy, or network connectivity has been lost. The problem is twice as horrible when you need to send an important piece of e-mail immediately, but alas, your host is in the land of Oz.

Although loss of connectivity right when you need the Internet most can happen with any service provider, make an effort to learn how reliable a host is. Pick up the telephone and call the service's modem number at peak usage times (during the business day and at about 8 p.m.). If you frequently hear a busy signal, the service provider doesn't have enough phone lines to handle its current customers. (It's not unreasonable to get an occasional busy signal, however.) If there is no answer at all, you should wonder aloud why the system is unavailable.

NOTE Many systems have scheduled downtime (usually in the wee hours of the night) for system maintenance and backups.

Even when the system is running, performance is an issue. An overworked computer runs much slower than an underworked one.

Some systems can theoretically handle hundreds of users simultaneously, but get bogged down with more than a few dozen. (Performance also depends on what the users are doing online. Sending e-mail, for instance, uses far less computing power than database searches or compiling programs.) There isn't much you can do to test performance before you try the service for yourself, but you should ask the administrators how many users the system can handle reliably at once, how many typically are online at peak usage times, and if they plan to put a cap on new accounts when they reach a performance limit.

Find out whether there is a service guarantee. If so, what is it?

Security

Find out what measures the system administrators take to ensure that your information remains private. Security isn't an enormous issue for casual Internet users, although most of us want to have some assurance that our files, electronic mail, and other information will be free from prying eyes.

Find out the system's policy on system administrators reading "private" e-mail. This should be of special concern to you if you access the Internet using a BBS. System administrators can peruse anything and everything on their computers, so you must rely on their honesty and integrity to keep their noses out of your files. Some systems try to promise privacy, but others clearly state that nothing is private.

Technical Support

Computers aren't the only component of a successful network; the people who use them make all the difference. While you are asking questions about a host's service, think about their support. Are the people on the other end of conversations helpful and knowledgeable? Are they responsive to your questions and concerns? Are they willing to explain the simple stuff to you or are you treated like a bother? Once you sign on the service, you probably will be asking many more questions. Be sure the technical support team is willing and able to assist.

What methods are provided for you to reach the technical support team? Every online service has tech support via electronic mail, but e-mail won't do you any good if you can't sign on the system or you need immediate assistance. Find out whether there is a tech support hotline, or at least a voice-mail system where you can leave a message.

Finally, don't just take the service provider's word for anything—check references. Get a list of three to five references and call or e-mail those folks. Ask about the service, technical support, system problems (such as unexplained downtime), and so on.

With a little preparation, your first Internet interaction can be a wonderful experience instead of a frustrating, expensive disaster.

C H A P T E R 3

How Does the Internet Work?

This chapter covers questions about what makes the Internet itself tick. Internet gurus like to bandy about lots of terms: domain name, system, host, TCP/IP, URL, WWW, UNIX, and so on. Here we'll decode the catch phrases and the alphabet soup. We'll also look at the basics of getting around on the Internet, such as using the UNIX operating system and getting familiar with important tools.

Making Connections

This section looks at some frequently asked questions about the actual connections that make up the Internet.

Q 3.1. I keep hearing about Internet *hosts*. What is a host?

If you've ever gone to an enjoyable cocktail party, birthday party, luau, or other social event, you already know what a host is—the person who lets you into his or her home and allows you to eat his food, sit on his couch, and generally mess up the place. This type of host is only vaguely similar to the kind of host on the Internet. On the Internet, a *host* is any computer system that is connected to the physical network. More specifically, it's any computer with a distinct identity—a name and a network address. (Your cocktail party host, I hope, also has a name and an address.)

> **NOTE** The words *host, site,* and *computer* can be used interchangeably.

Each Internet host has a name in the form of `system.domain`, where `system` is that computer's own moniker and the `domain` contains information about the organization to which the computer belongs. Examples are as follows:

```
hal.gnu.ai.mit.edu
rs.internic.net
bolero.rahul.net
acadvm1.uottawa.ca
mudhoney.micro.umn.edu
quake.think.com
uunorth.north.net
wirth.ifa.dawaii.edu
```

There are millions more. In any case, the word before the first period is the computer's name. The word after the first period is the domain name. More on domain names in a minute.

3.2. How do computers on the Internet talk to one another, or what is TCP/IP?

TCP/IP (which stands for Transmission Control Protocol/Internet Protocol) is the name of a family of more than 100 data communications protocols used to organize computers into networks. The computers that make up the Internet talk to each other in the language of TCP/IP protocols. Any computer that can talk the language of TCP/IP can be a direct part of the Internet. (That's part of the reason why there is such a wide variety of computers on the Net.)

TCP/IP specifies an addressing scheme for computers on the Internet. TCP/IP sets the rules for how data should move between computers and programs on the network. Its protocols are rules that computers must follow in order to move different types of information from place to place. You have heard—or will hear—of some of the protocols that make up TCP/IP, like the File Transfer Protocol (FTP), the Telnet protocol, and the Simple Mail Transfer Protocol (SMTP).

TCP/IP was developed to interconnect systems on ARPAnet, PRnet (a packet radio network), and SATnet (a packet-based satellite network). Although all these networks are now defunct, TCP/IP lives.

Messages sent over TCP/IP are called *packets.* Each packet of information sent over the Internet can be thought of as a letter. TCP/IP puts each letter in an envelope, addresses the envelope with To and From information, and sends the letter on its way. These packets are designed to be small—usually 1500 bytes or so. Most things you send and receive on the Internet (e-mail messages, Usenet postings, files, and whatnot) are longer than the maximum packet size, so TCP/IP breaks the message up into packet-sized chunks, addresses each packet, and sends them on their merry way. Once at their destination (actually getting them there is another story), TCP/IP reassembles the packets into one coherent message.

NOTE Actually, TCP and IP are two separate protocols that can work in unison. IP moves packets to their destination, whereas TCP checks their integrity and puts them back in their proper order.

Actually getting your message from its source to its destination is fairly painless to understand. The Internet is a *store and forward network*, meaning that those packets can be sent to (and stored on) any number of computers on their way to their destination. If there is a direct network link between two sites—that is, a physical cable linking the two computers—the packets can zip right over, a nonstop flight with beverage service and an in-flight movie. Most of the time, though, there isn't a direct link. So, the sending computer sends the packets to one that's a little closer to the destination. That machine moves the packets farther down the line, and so on, until the packets reach their goal. It's not uncommon for a cross-country message to make 20 or 30 hops. Most of the time, this all happens very, very quickly. Open a Telnet connection from California to New York or Finland and (on a good day) you'll hardly notice any delay at all.

Q 3.3. What is a domain name?

Computers are computers and people are people, and the two species work in very different ways. Computers like to work with lots of numbers, but people generally prefer words and names to numbers. (That's why I'm more likely to walk up to a friend on the street and say, "Hi, Jim!" than call him by, say, his Social Security number.)

Every host on the Internet has an address: a series of four numbers, each less than 256, separated by periods. Although the computers are perfectly happy with this arrangement ("Hello, 137.50.188.22, I have some mail for you from a user at 137.150.10.10."), humans are less than content blurting those numeric addresses. So, for the convenience of humans, computers on the Net also have names.

Each computer's address—formally called its *internet protocol* (IP) address—is made of four numbers separated by dots, like these:

```
137.150.188.22
192.160.13.1
139.130.4.6
140.174.1.1
```

You can generally refer to a computer by its name or its address. For instance, you can type `ftp archie.au` or you can type `ftp 139.130.4.6`. You should connect to the same machine either way. Electronic mail is an exception, using only system names, not addresses. E-mail addresses look like `savetz@rahul.net`, never like `savetz@192.160.13.1`.

Here's an example: one computer at Humboldt State University (my alma matter) is called

```
turing.cnrs.humboldt.edu
```

In this example, there are four words separated by periods. The computer's name (or *hostname*) is `turing. cnrs.humboldt.edu` is the domain of this machine. (And each word of the domain is called a *subdomain.*)

The domains provide information about the computer, from most specific information (on the left) to least specific information (on the right). `turing.cnrs.humboldt.edu` is the fully qualified domain name of the host, a computer with its own IP address. That computer—and its name—is maintained by the College of Natural Resources and Sciences (a.k.a. *cnrs)* department at Humboldt State University. Humboldt is part of a national group (edu) that lumps together all educational institutions. So, by carefully reading the computer's name (and decoding some acronyms), we can learn quite a lot about an Internet site.

Q 3.4. What is a fully qualified domain name?

Fully qualified domain name is the term for a domain name that includes a system name as well as all its relevant higher-level domains. The host name `turing` is not a fully qualified domain name, but `turing.cnrs.humboldt.edu` is the fully qualified domain name for the host at 137.150.188.22.

3.5. Can a computer have multiple domain names?

Yes. It is common for a site to have multiple names that are assigned to the same IP address. For instance, the following names

```
beetle.big-bug.com
ftp.big-bug.com
big.bug.com
stink.bug.com
volkswagen.bug-lovers-association.org
```

could all point to a single computer with one IP address.

It would be very unusual for different top-level domains to point to a single host, however. I think it is more likely that `big-bug.com_` could point to the same address as `ftp.big-bug.com`, `stink.big-bug.com`, and such. It's incredibly unlikely that a host would show up in both .com and .org, that's for sure! —DT

3.6. What is the domain name system?

The computers on the Internet need a way to translate site names to their corresponding numerical addresses. The Internet has a sort of phone book for Internet hosts: a computer can look up another system's name and find out its address. This isn't as simple as it sounds. Millions of hosts on the Internet make for a really thick phone book, even an electronic one. Also, what would happen if two computers on the Internet had the same name? Which address is the right one? Computers don't like ambiguity like that.

When the Internet was much smaller than it is today, the task of maintaining the Internet's address book was simple. The Network Information Center (or NIC) maintained a registry of Internet sites. The document, called a *hosts file*, was distributed periodically to every site on the Internet. As you can imagine, those blissful days have gone the way of the Dodo bird. As the Internet grew, maintenance and distribution of a huge hosts file became unmanageable.

The Domain Name Service (also known as the *Domain Name System*, or *DNS*) replaces the obsolete hosts file. It is a method to administer Internet system names by giving each organization responsibility for maintaining the names at that site. This scheme eliminates the dependence on a centrally maintained file that translates host names to addresses.

There is no longer a centralized list of sites. Instead, each organization keeps track of its own computers on the Internet. Humboldt State University keeps track of only its machines; Fred's Internet and Venetian Blind Company keeps track of its own. If a user at HSU needs to know something about one of Fred's computers, it sends out a query across the Internet that Fred's computer answers. That, in a nutshell, is the domain name system.

NOTE If you've never heard of *MX Records,* they're the little guys with the baseball mitts that catch the queries about a specific domain and field them.

If the system administrator at HSU's College of Natural Resources and Sciences computer lab wants to plug another computer into the Internet, he doesn't need approval from anyone at the Network Information Center, and he doesn't have to wait for someone to add the new machine to a hosts file. With the Domain Name System, he can do all of this himself.

NOTE The IP addresses cannot be assigned randomly, although the NIC still doles out IP address blocks. Before putting any computer on the Internet, an organization must get a block of addresses from the Network Information Center. How many addresses you get depends on how many your organization needs. The smallest is a "class C" address (for instance, 137.150.188.*), which gives the organization room to put 254 computers on the Net. A "class B" address (137.150.*.*) for larger organizations explodes the limit to 64,516 hosts. Finally, those with "class A"

addresses (137.*.*.*) have access to a whopping 16 million number combinations.

Similarly, if someone at that school decided to start a new group (like journalism) and put three computers in that group (we'll call them murrow, rather, and hearst), they could do that without anyone's permission. So, full names of the computers at that school would be

```
turing.cnrs.humboldt.edu
murrow.journalism.humboldt.edu
rather.journalism.humboldt.edu
hearst.journalism.humboldt.edu
```

As long as there are never two computers in one domain with the same name, or two domains with the same name, everything goes swimmingly. If every system administrator makes sure that the names he assigns are unique at his site, there can be no conflicting names to confuse the situation. Given the preceding example, the following host names could be valid additions to the Internet:

```
murrow.cnrs.humboldt.edu
turing.journalism.humboldt.edu
rather.sonoma.edu
```

3.7. What's the *.com, .net,* or *.edu* part of the domain name mean?

You'll always find suffixes like `.com`, `.net`, `.edu`, and `.mil` at the end of Internet domain names. These "top-level" domains were created when the domain system was created. Here's a list of the traditional domain name suffixes:

.arpa	Old style ARPAnet addresses (no longer used)
.com	Commercial site
.edu	Educational institution
.gov	Government site
.mil	U.S. military
.nato	NATO organization (no longer used)

`.net`	Network
`.org`	Other organizations (usually non-profit organizations)

This naming scheme was a less-than-perfect attempt to divide Net addresses into broad categories to help users know something about the organization to which they were connecting or sending mail. This made a lot of sense when the Internet was primarily used in the United States, but the scheme began to show its flaws when an influx of new types of organizations and hundreds of additional countries joined the Internet. For instance, the `.gov` extension means *government site*, but this doesn't mean much if you don't know what country's government owns that computer.

NOTE A newer style of domain name addressing is now in use, in which the final letters indicate the computer's geographical location, rather than organizational domain. For example, the site `well.sf.ca.us` is in San Francisco, which is in California, which is in the United States.

Unfortunately, this scheme is largely ignored in the United States. (I suppose Americans are creatures of habit who don't want to become accustomed to things like country codes in domain names, or the metric system.) Anyway, for now, there is no definitive scheme for reading domain names.

3.8. What country does the country code ___ correspond to?

Following is a list of many of the countries connected in some fashion to the Internet. It is a safe guess that by the time you read this, additional countries will join the Internet, and some of those in this list may have ceased to exist. Still, this list can give you an idea of the vastness of the Net. I use this list all the time to figure out what country I've just received e-mail from.

> **NOTE** This demonstrates another of the limitations of the Internet: things should be readable by humans and translated into machine codes invisibly, but they're usually not. If I get mail from someone at the University of Pisa, Italy, shouldn't I see something that indicates just that, rather than have to decipher a cryptic country code?

AD	Andorra
AE	United Arab Emirates
AF	Afghanistan
AG	Antigua and Barbuda
AI	Anguilla
AL	Albania
AM	Armenia
AN	Netherland Antilles
AO	Angola (Republic of)
AQ	Antarctica
AR	Argentina
AS	American Samoa
AT	Austria
AU	Australia
AW	Aruba
AZ	Azerbaijan
BA	Bosnia-Herzegovina
BB	Barbados
BD	Bangladesh
BE	Belgium
BF	Burkina Faso
BG	Bulgaria
BH	Bahrain
BI	Burundi
BJ	Benin
BM	Bermuda
BN	Brunei Darussalam
BO	Bolivia
BR	Brazil
BS	Bahamas
BT	Bhutan
BV	Bouvet Island
BW	Botswana
BY	Belarus
BZ	Belize
CA	Canada
CC	Cocos (Keeling) Isl.
CF	Central African Rep.
CG	Congo
CH	Switzerland
CI	Ivory Coast
CK	Cook Islands
CL	Chile
CM	Cameroon
CN	China
CO	Colombia
CR	Costa Rica
CS	Czechoslovakia
CU	Cuba
CV	Cape Verde

CX	Christmas Island
CY	Cyprus
CZ	Czech Republic
DE	Germany
DJ	Djibouti
DK	Denmark
DM	Dominica
DO	Dominican Republic
DZ	Algeria
EC	Ecuador
EE	Estonia
EG	Egypt
EH	Western Sahara
ER	Eritrea
ES	Spain
ET	Ethiopia
FI	Finland
FJ	Fiji
FK	Falkland Isl. (Malvinas)
FM	Micronesia
FO	Faroe Islands
FR	France
FX	France (European Ter.)
GA	Gabon
GB	Great Britain (UK)
GD	Grenada
GE	Georgia
GF	Guyana (Fr.)
GH	Ghana
GI	Gibraltar
GL	Greenland
GM	Gambia
GN	Guinea
GP	Guadeloupe (Fr.)
GQ	Equatorial Guinea
GR	Greece
GS	South Georgia and South Sandwich Islands
GT	Guatemala
GU	Guam
GW	Guinea Bissau
GY	Guyana
HK	Hong Kong
HM	Heard & McDonald Isl.
HN	Honduras
HR	Croatia
HT	Haiti
HU	Hungary
ID	Indonesia
IE	Ireland
IL	Israel
IN	India
IO	British Indian O. Terr.
IQ	Iraq
IR	Iran
IS	Iceland
IT	Italy
JM	Jamaica
JO	Jordan
JP	Japan
KE	Kenya

KG	Kyrgyz Republic
KH	Cambodia
KI	Kiribati
KM	Comoros
KN	St.Kitts Nevis Anguilla
KP	Korea (North)
KR	Korea (South)
KW	Kuwait
KY	Cayman Islands
KZ	Kazachstan
LB	Lebanon
LC	Saint Lucia
LI	Liechtenstein
LK	Sri Lanka
LR	Liberia
LS	Lesotho
LT	Lithuania
LU	Luxembourg
LV	Latvia
LY	Libya
MA	Morocco
MC	Monaco
MD	Moldavia
MG	Madagascar (Republic of)
MH	Marshall Islands
MK	Macedonia (former Yugo.)
ML	Mali
MM	Myanmar
MN	Mongolia
MO	Macau
MP	Northern Mariana Isl.
MQ	Martinique (Fr.)
MR	Mauritania
MS	Montserrat
MT	Malta
MU	Mauritius
MV	Maldives
MW	Malawi
MX	Mexico
MY	Malaysia
MZ	Mozambique
NA	Namibia
NC	New Caledonia (Fr.)
NE	Niger
NF	Norfolk Island
NG	Nigeria
NI	Nicaragua
NL	Netherlands
NO	Norway
NP	Nepal
NR	Nauru
NU	Niue
NZ	New Zealand
OM	Oman
PA	Panama
PE	Peru
PF	Polynesia (Fr.)
PG	Papua New Guinea
PH	Philippines
PK	Pakistan
PL	Poland
PM	St. Pierre & Miquelon

PN	Pitcairn
PR	Puerto Rico
PT	Portugal
PW	Palau
PY	Paraguay
QA	Qatar
RE	Reunion (Fr.)
RO	Romania
RU	Russian Federation
RW	Rwanda
SA	Saudi Arabia
SB	Solomon Islands
SC	Seychelles
SD	Sudan
SE	Sweden
SG	Singapore
SH	St. Helena
SI	Slovenia
SJ	Svalbard & Jan Mayen Islands
SK	Slovakia (Slovak Rep)
SL	Sierra Leone
SM	San Marino
SN	Senegal
SO	Somalia
SR	Suriname
ST	St. Tome and Principe
SU	Soviet Union
SV	El Salvador
SY	Syria
SZ	Swaziland
TC	Turks & Caicos Islands
TD	Chad
TF	French Southern Terr.
TG	Togo
TH	Thailand
TJ	Tadjikistan
TK	Tokelau
TM	Turkmenistan
TN	Tunisia
TO	Tonga
TP	East Timor
TR	Turkey
TT	Trinidad & Tobago
TV	Tuvalu
TW	Taiwan
TZ	Tanzania
UA	Ukraine
UG	Uganda
UK	United Kingdom
UM	US Minor outlying Isl.
US	United States
UY	Uruguay
UZ	Uzbekistan
VA	Vatican City State
VC	St. Vincent & Grenadines
VE	Venezuela
VG	Virgin Islands (British)
VI	Virgin Islands (US)
VN	Vietnam

VU	Vanuatu	YU	Yugoslavia
WF	Wallis & Futuna Islands	ZA	South Africa
WS	Samoa	ZM	Zambia
YE	Yemen	ZR	Zaire
YT	Mayotte	ZW	Zimbabwe

For a current list of Internet country codes, read the FAQ "International E-mail Accessibility," which is posted to the Usenet newsgroups `comp.mail.misc`, `news.newusers.questions`, and `alt.internet.services`.

Some of these countries don't have full Internet access; in fact, some have only electronic mail through unstable UUCP or FidoNet gateways. Read the FAQ to find out which countries have what kind of access. It's also important not to send lengthy or useless mail to such countries. The International E-mail Accessibility FAQ says it well:

> *The link to some countries marked as being connected to Internet via UUCP or FIDO is often an expensive telephone dialup link. The people in those countries pay dearly for every byte of information sent to them. It is therefore not advised to send an electronic mail to a remote node in such a country asking, "How's the weather there?" When it comes to money, people take things very seriously, especially since funds are scarce. It is a matter of net etiquette to keep this in mind. Junk mail sent to any node that has to pay a lot for its telephone connection will clearly be dealt with HARSHLY and evasive action may well be taken against those not respecting this notice.*

Q 3.9. I have both a host name and its IP address. Which should I use?

Well, both should work, but you should get in the habit of using a host's name instead of its IP address. IP addresses can change if a host computer is physically moved, but the name should always stay the same. By using the name, you aren't depending on that specific computer remaining at a specific location for any amount of time. Things change. Using names instead of addresses can make those changes less noticeable to you.

3.10. My system doesn't understand site names, but it does understand IP addresses. How do I get a site name resolved into an IP address?

Resolving a site name means finding out its corresponding IP address. Most systems, thanks to the domain name service, automatically translate a site name on the fly when you enter one (for instance, when you type `telnet archie.au`, the system knows you mean the computer at 139.130.4.6). You should never need to look up a name yourself, although you can if you really want.

There should be a name resolver on your system. On UNIX systems, look for a program called nslookup. Type `nslookup` followed by a site name and it will show you that site's IP address. Here's an example of an nslookup session:

```
$ nslookup hal.gnu.ai.mit.edu
Server:   hustle.rahul.net
Address:  192.160.13.2

Name:     hal.gnu.ai.mit.edu
Address:  128.52.46.11
```


Some systems don't know how to translate site names to their corresponding IP addresses. In this case, you can use an e-mail resolving service. Send it a site name and you'll receive a message with the IP address for the site. Send an electronic mail message.

```
To: resolve@cs.widener.edu
Subject: <subject line is ignored>
Body: site hal.gnu.ai.mit.edu


Another e-mail site resolver is available:
To: dns@grasp.insa-lyon.fr
Subject: <subject line is ignored>
Body: ip hal.gnu.ai.mit.edu
```

3.11. How do I get a list of all the hosts on the Internet?

Let me answer that question with another question: why on Earth would you want a list of all the Internet's hosts? You don't. At last count, there were about 800,000 hosts on the Net. Of that number, the vast majority of them are private systems that you can't access, anyway.

3.12. How do I find out whether a certain organization has a computer on the Internet?

There isn't a simple or reliable way to find out whether a specific organization is on the Internet. Your best bet is usually to phone someone at that institution and ask.

You can get some information about Internet sites using the Whois database maintained at the DDN NIC at Network Solutions, Inc. To use the DDN NIC (Defense Data Network, Network Information Center), Telnet to `nic.ddn.mil` and type `Whois` at the `login:` prompt. The Whois database lists many Internet sites, but does not include every site and organization on the Internet. Type `host` followed by the company name to search. Type `help` at the `whois` prompt for information on using Whois.

Here's an example. Is Apple computer on the Internet? Whois says so:

```
Whois:  apple
Apple Computer (APPLE)            [No rolemailbox]

   Hostname: APPLE.COM
   Address: 130.43.2.2
   System: VAX-8650 running UNIX


   Coordinator:
      Fair, Erik E.  (EF16)  FAIR@APPLE.COM

   domain server

   Record last updated on 12-Apr-89.
```

You can also try asking on the Usenet newsgroup `news.config`, or reading the newsgroup `comp.mail.maps`, where maps of the Usenet and the UUCP network are posted.

You may also want to check one of the following references: *!%@:: A Directory of Electronic Mail Addressing and Networks* by Donnalyn Frey and Rick Adams; *The User's Directory of Computer Networks*, by Tracy LaQuey; and *The Matrix: Computer Networks and Conferencing Systems Worldwide*, by John Quarterman.

Q 3.13. How can I tell whether a computer on the Internet is up and running?

If you're trying to connect to another computer on the Internet, but you aren't sure whether it's even running, you can *ping* that computer to find out. The ping command, available on many systems, sends out an "Are you there?" message (called a *ping packet*) to the computer in which you're interested. If the computer is awake, it admits it is there (by sending back what is called, in sillier circles, a *pong packet*) and you'll be told that everything is right with the world. If the remote computer isn't up, you'll know why you haven't been able to Telnet or FTP there, or why e-mail to that site isn't getting through.

3

The ping command can take many forms. On some systems, its output looks like this:

```
$ ping hal.gnu.ai.mit.edu
hal.gnu.ai.mit.edu is alive.
```

On some systems, the ping by default offers quite a bit of useful information. Your host may or may not have an extra-useful ping command. If your system doesn't, don't blame me. It's default of de computer. (I stole that joke from the book *Inside Atari Basic*, written by Bill Carris in 1983. It was stupid then and it's still stupid.)

On my system, when I type `ping -s`, it sends ping packets over and over again until I hit Ctrl-C; then it shows me a status report. In this case, the connection between California and Massachusetts is nice and stable, and it takes about 114 milliseconds for my ping packets to get there and back. This means that my query crossed the United States, was received, acted on, and replied to. That response makes it back to me faster than you can read a single word in this sentence. That's fast!

```
$ ping -s hal.gnu.ai.mit.edu
PING hal.gnu.ai.mit.edu: 56 data bytes
64 bytes from hal.gnu.ai.mit.edu (128.52.46.11): icmp_seq=0. time=116. ms
64 bytes from hal.gnu.ai.mit.edu (128.52.46.11): icmp_seq=1. time=112. ms
64 bytes from hal.gnu.ai.mit.edu (128.52.46.11): icmp_seq=2. time=116. ms
64 bytes from hal.gnu.ai.mit.edu (128.52.46.11): icmp_seq=3. time=117. ms
64 bytes from hal.gnu.ai.mit.edu (128.52.46.11): icmp_seq=3. time=115. ms
64 bytes from hal.gnu.ai.mit.edu (128.52.46.11): icmp_seq=5. time=114. ms
64 bytes from hal.gnu.ai.mit.edu (128.52.46.11): icmp_seq=6. time=111. ms
^C
——hal.gnu.ai.mit.edu PING Statistics——
7 packets transmitted, 7 packets received, 0% packet loss
round-trip (ms)  min/avg/max = 111/114/117
```

NOTE Ping lives in the here-and-now. If the computer in question isn't "alive," you know only that it isn't available on the Internet right now. There's no telling whether it's gone forever, or it crashed, or it's down for system maintenance, or the network link between it and your host has temporarily died.

Q 3.14. What is that strange notation used to indicate file location, or what's a URL?

Uniform resource locators (URLs) are notations for giving the location of *objects* on the Internet—files, Usenet newsgroups, Telnet sites, and other tools and resources. URL's provide simple, easy-to-read one-liners showing how you can access services on the Net.

URLs, besides being easy for us humans to read, are also simple for computers to understand. If you use *World Wide Web* (*WWW*) or other online hypertext tools, you'll often find buttons that do something when pressed—run a program, download a file, Telnet to a certain site, or whatever. Those buttons are linked to URLs: press the button, and the URL associated with it is involved. Use of URLs grew primarily out of the WWW project.

For instance, an online file can be indicated with a URL in the following ways:

```
file://rtfm.mit.edu/usenet/internet-services/FAQ
```

or

```
ftp://rtfm.mit.edu/usenet/internet-services/FAQ
```

Other resources may be indicated by URLs like this:

```
http://info.cern.ch:80/default.html
http://rs560.cl.msu.edu/weather
telnet://well.sf.ca.us
gopher://ux3.cso.uiuc.edu:70/00/Welcome
news:alt.internet.services
```

3

The part of the URL before the colon specifies the access method (such as via Telnet, FTP, or Gopher). The part of the URL after the colon tells what that access method should do, connect to, or display. In general, two slashes after the colon indicate a site name.

3.15. What does HTTP mean?

The URLs that may look the least familiar are those starting with *http*. These indicate files that need to be accessed through the Hypertext Transfer Protocol, and typically they reference files written in Hypertext Markup Language. Hypertext files can contain pointers to text files, graphics, and sounds. A variety of browsers are available (such as WWW and Mosaic) that present a nice interface for exploring the hypertext files.

Tools of the Internet

This section answers FAQs about the Internet's most important tools, such as Telnet, Gopher, Veronica, and WWW. Other tools (like FTP and Archie) are covered later in the book with respect to their particular purpose (such as transferring files). These tools are covered here because they don't easily fit into a single-purpose category; they're useful for thousands of different purposes.

3.16. What is Telnet?

Telnet is a program that allows you to connect to another computer to run software there. Typically, you login either to access a shell (like the UNIX operating system on the remote computer) or some utility, like a weather server or game.

> **NOTE** Most of the time, this book talks about Internet tools when it's most appropriate—for instance, the information about File Transfer Protocol is in Chapter 6, "How Can I Find and Use Software (and Other Stuff)?" But some tools, such as Telnet and Gopher, are used in so many situations that I'm going to talk briefly about them here. Specific examples of using them for particular purposes are covered in later chapters, as appropriate.

To Telnet to a computer, you need to know its name or IP address:

```
telnet bolero.rahul.net
telnet 139.130.4.6
```

Some services require you to Telnet to a specific port on the remote computer. In these cases, that port is usually dedicated to a particular service, so once you've connected, you are whisked directly into that program or tool. Type the port number, if there is one, after the Internet address. For example:

```
telnet nri.reston.va.us 185
telnet lambda.parc.xerox.com 8888
```

Q 3.17. I can't Telnet to a site. What's wrong?

Telnet is nearly idiot-proof. Unlike some of the Internet's tools that require infinite patience, a degree in cryptography for decoding error messages, and manual pages as thick as your skull, Telnet is simple. It either works or it doesn't.

If you try to connect to a site that doesn't exist or can't be Telnetted to (for instance, a UUCP feed) you'll see an `unknown host` message. There isn't much you can do but check your spelling and try again.

```
$ telnet nonexistent.com
nonexistent.com: unknown host
```

Once you've successfully Telnetted to a host, there's no telling what you're expected to do. In the best case, you'll instantly see a message telling you what to do. In the worst case (if you're expecting something more), you'll only be greeted with:

```
login:
```

or

```
Username:
```

If you don't know what you are expected to enter at one of these prompts, perhaps you shouldn't be Telnetting to that host.

3

> **NOTE** I asked Daniel P. Dern to answer a couple of questions about the Internet's tools. Well, Daniel can be a little verbose. His idea of a "a couple of questions" spans the rest of the "Tools of the Internet" section. Daniel Dern (`ddern@world.std.com`) is an Internet author/analyst and independent technology writer based in Newton Centre, MA. He is author of *The Internet Guide for New Users* (McGraw-Hill, 1993) and creator of the Internet Learner's Permit and Driving Test.

3.18. What is Gopher?

Gopher is a menu-oriented way to "cruise and browse" the Internet. Gopher presents you with lists of the Internet's files, programs, resources, services, and other menus, in the form of easy-to-read point-and-click menus. By simply positioning the cursor or entering the appropriate item number, you make selections and thereby cruise much of the Internet using nothing more than a few keystrokes.

More than 4,500 businesses, government agencies, individuals, and others around the world are making their information and services available to Internet users via Gopher, making it one of the most popular user tools on the Internet today.

Gopher was originally created by people in charge of microcomputer support at the University of Minnesota as a better way to let users access several thousand files of online answer information. The name *Gopher* reflects its capability of "going fer" things. (The gopher is also the University of Minnesota's mascot.)

Gopher lets the support staff structure these thousands of files into a hierarchy of menus that users navigate by using some combination of arrow keys, the Enter key, mouse clicks, or selecting by number.

Each menu contains selections with one-line text descriptions. A Gopher menu selection can be a file containing text or any other type of documents (such as a weather map, file of mail messages, or an image); access to another program, such as Telnet, FTP, WAIS, finger, a searching tool, and so on; or another menu. When a file is selected, it is retrieved and presented to the user at his or her screen. Gopher also lets you save the selection as a file in your local account, or you can e-mail it to someone, or print it.

A Gopher menu can contain any mix of these items as well as an almost unlimited number of them—hundreds, to be sure. With Gopher, users can define *bookmarks* to save and quickly relocate specific items without having to search and navigate to them step by step.

The Gopher *server* program handles management and "serving" of files. Each user runs a Gopher *client* program, which handles things like displaying the received menus and files.

Users at other Internet locations began using Gopher as an easier way to make information available to other Internet users. *Gopherspace*—the Gopher servers available to Internet users—rapidly climbed to 1,000, then 2,000, then 3,000 Gopher servers (and still growing), holding over 2,000,000 menu items!

Gopher clients are available for every popular type of PC and computing environment—DOS, Windows, Mac, Amiga, and UNIX (using ASCII and X Windows). Gopher servers are available for almost as many types of computers.

Here's an example that shows you how Gopher allows you to seamlessly zip among Internet hosts, services, and tools just by picking from a menu:

```
Internet Gopher Information Client v1.11

                    Gopher headquarters (gopher.tc.umn.edu)

      1.  Information About Gopher/
      2.  Computer Information/
      3.  Discussion Groups/
      4.  Fun & Games/
      5.  Internet file server (ftp) sites/
      6.  Libraries/
 -->  7.  News/
      8.  Other Gopher and Information Servers/
      9.  Phone Books/
      10. Search Gopher Titles at the University of Minnesota <?>
      11. Search lots of places at the University of Minnesota  <?>
      12. University of Minnesota Campus Information/


Internet Gopher Information Client v1.11

                                News

 -->  1.  Cornell Chronicle (Weekly)/
      2.  French Language Press Review/
      3.  Minnesota Daily/
      4.  NASA News.
      5.  National Weather Service Forecasts/
      6.  Other Newspapers, Magazines, and Newsletters /
      7.  Purdue University News/
      8.  Technolog (Institute of Technology, University of Minnesota)/
      9.  The Bucknellian Student Newspaper at Bucknell University/
      10. The Daily Illini (University of Illinois)/
      11. The Gazette (University of Waterloo)/
      12. The University of Chicago Chronicle (biweekly)/
```

3

```
13. USENET News (from Michigan State)/
14. University of Minnesota News (U Relations)/
15. Wire Service News (Reuters/AP/UPI) U of Minnesota Only/
```

Q 3.19. What's Veronica?

Very easy rodent-oriented net-wide index to computerized archives (Veronica) is a system that indexes the entire set of Gopher menu items and with which users can search quickly for specific information.

Unfortunately, Veronica has proven to suffer from numerous problems, some inherent to Gopherspace. The nature of Gopherspace—in which entries can easily point to items at distant servers, and a given server hierarchy can have a complex and even recursive structure—makes proper indexing difficult.

Further, Gopher menu items are often terse to the point of obscurity when viewed out of the context of their menu. Thus, it is not obvious whether the results of a Veronica search are different items or multiple listings. (Further, there are currently only three or four publicly accessible Veronica servers.)

Searches using Veronica can be hit-and-miss. The search in the following example for macrobiotic milk turned up 10 hits. Searches for `supersonic aircraft` turned up zero. `Iran contra` hit one. `Fleas and ticks`, zero. `Gopher` hit `too many items` to list. Can you believe it?

```
+------Search Gopher Directory Titles via U.Texas, Dallas------+
|                                                               |
| Words to search for  macrobiotic milk                         |
|                                                               |
|                          [Cancel ^G] [Accept - Enter]         |
|                                                               |
+---------------------------------------------------------------+
```

```
        Search Gopher Directory Titles via U.Texas, Dallas: macrobiotic milk

   -->  1.  The Milk Round/
        2.  Division of Milk Control/
        3.  58 FR 50511: Milk in the New York-New Jersey and Black Hills, Sout../
        4.  58 FR 50526: Milk in the Louisville-Lexington-Evansville Marketing../
        5.  58 FR 50511: Milk in the New York-New Jersey and Black Hills, Sout../
        6.  58 FR 50526: Milk in the Louisville-Lexington-Evansville Marketing../
        7.  Subpart I — Condensed Milk Subcategory/
        8.  Subpart J — Dry Milk Subcategory/
        9.  Healthy Milk/
        10. 637.1  Milk production/


  Press ? for Help, q to Quit, u to go up a menu                    Page: 1/1
```

Q 3.20. What is WAIS?

Wide-area information system (WAIS, which is pronounced *ways* or *wase*) is a search engine designed to help Internet users find the online equivalent of needles in haystacks. That is, WAIS is a program for searching large databases, lists, documents, directories of files, and so on.

Hundreds of WAISed information collections are available via the Internet, including everything from lists of Usenet newsgroups to scientific and government databases, as well as numerous books and lists. WAIS can be used to provide search access to collections of audio, video, image, and multimedia information.

WAIS has demonstrated that it's possible to do fairly powerful searches with remarkably less computer power than was once thought; and equally, that it's possible to do a full-text search of vast data holdings (for example, several years' worth of the Wall Street Journal) if you've got the right software and a big enough computer.

These files may be local to your own hard disk, such as five years' worth of accumulated e-mail messages, or nearby files (stored on your host) such as your company's memos and policy handbooks.

Or these files may be across the Internet, such as the Internet's Jargon File, technical abstracts, or any of hundreds of other free-for-access, pay-for-access, or private datasets.

For example, suppose that you're looking for an Internet FAQ that talks about TCP/IP for PCs. If there's a WAIS database available containing the FAQs, you could do a WAIS search looking for FAQs containing `TCP/IP` and `PC` (or perhaps you'd try `Windows` and `DOS`). You'd get back a list of results, *weighted* (sorted) by how well they match. You would then select one or more of these to be displayed, saved to your account, e-mailed, or whatever.

Some versions of WAIS support a feature called *relevance feedback,* which basically means *find me more like this one.* If a search gives one result that you particularly like, you can use that result as the *search criteria* for the next search, against the other results or against new datasets.

There are ASCII and other clients available for WAIS. Most popular Internet navigators and front-ends, such as Gopher, Mosaic, and most other WWW clients, initiate WAIS searches.

In this example, the database of WAIS databases at `wais.com` harbors 476 troves of information.

```
SWAIS                          Source Selection                    Sources: 476
  #            Server                              Source                   Cost
001:   [            archie.au]  aarnet-resource-guide                       Free
002:   [ndadsb.gsfc.nasa.gov]  AAS_jobs                                    Free
003:   [ndadsb.gsfc.nasa.gov]  AAS_meeting                                 Free
004:   [      munin.ub2.lu.se]  academic_email_conf                         Free
005: * [     archive.orst.edu]  aeronautics                                 Free
006:   [bruno.cs.colorado.ed]  aftp-cs-colorado-edu                        Free
007:   [nostromo.oes.orst.ed]  agricultural-market-news                    Free
008:   [     wais.oit.unc.edu]  alt.gopher                                  Free
009:   [     wais.oit.unc.edu]  alt.wais                                    Free
010:   [      munin.ub2.lu.se]  amiga_fish_contents                         Free
011:   [    coombs.anu.edu.au]  ANU-Aboriginal-EconPolicies          $0.00/minute
012:   [    coombs.anu.edu.au]  ANU-Aboriginal-Studies               $0.00/minute
013:   [         150.203.76.2]  ANU-ACT-Stat-L                       $0.00/minute
014:   [    coombs.anu.edu.au]  ANU-Ancient-DNA-L                    $0.00/minute
015:   [    coombs.anu.edu.au]  ANU-Ancient-DNA-Studies              $0.00/minute
016:   [    coombs.anu.edu.au]  ANU-Asian-Computing                  $0.00/minute
017:   [    coombs.anu.edu.au]  ANU-Asian-Religions                  $0.00/minute
018:   [    coombs.anu.edu.au]  ANU-AustPhilosophyForum-L            $0.00/minute

Keywords:

<space> selects, w for keywords, arrows move, <return> searches, q quits, or ?
```

Q 3.21. What's the World Wide Web?

The *World Wide Web* (a.k.a. *WWW*) is like Gopher: a system for organizing, linking, and providing point-and-click access among related Internet files, resources, and services.

WWW employs the hypertext, or "hypermedia," approach, in which cross-references are embedded within documents and other entries. Each cross-reference is a pointer to another document or to other actions, lists, or menus. Think of it as being able to click a footnote and being instantly taken to the corresponding place in another book or to hearing the sound of someone explaining something or to being automatically logged in to a corresponding service, such as the Library of Congress.

During 1993 and 1994, the use of WWW rapidly caught up with Gopher as a way to make information available to the Internet community, further spurred by Mosaic and Lynx, two World Wide Web "browsers."

NOTE A WWW browser, or *front-end*, is the program that you run to access the information stored in the Web. Two popular browsers are Lynx, an ASCII-based browser, and Mosaic, a multimedia browser for the Macintosh and Microsoft Windows. You'll see the word *Mosaic* many more times online and in this book: it's a program that has changed the way people use the Internet, by letting them easily access text, sounds, and graphics, and use "hypertext links" to navigate through information.

The text-based WWW browser in the following example is a bit of an eyesore, but it harbors a vast amount of information. Graphical browsers like Mosaic make WWW easier—and more fun—to use.

```
NJIT Information Technology Entry Point (20/20)
   (WWW) software developed at CERN[3] with  modifications[4] by NJIT.  With
   the NJIT Screen Mode browser use either the cursor keys or the item number,
   followed by the return key to select the topic of interest.    Goals[5] of
   the NJIT-IT.            HELP[6]

        Test[7] menu                                              EMERGENCY[8]
  University[9]   Directory[10]   Information Systems  NJIT Police        3111
    Calendar[11]    Faculty[12]       NJIT Library[13] Rutgers Police 648-5111
      Events[14]      Staff[15]    Other Libraries[16] Newark Police  733-6080
Publications[17] Phone Book[18] Other Info Systems[19] UMDNJ Hospital 456-4300
        News[20]      Hours[21]  Computing Systems[22] Health Services    3621
   Information Topic:
     Student[23]   Academic[24]     Administration[25]        Facilities[26]
        What is new on njIT[27]            Weather[28]        Known Bugs[29]




                                                                   http://it/


Next  Back  Up  Find  List  Recall  Top  End  Go  saVe  eXit  Query  Preceding
 Succeeding  Home  Instructions
go Home to initial start-up document         ( ? help, - escape, ++ homebase )
HYPERTEXT ACTION CHOICE>
```

Notice that in these Web menus, various words are followed by numbers in brackets. Using this browser, I typed the number of the item that I wished to jump to. In a more elegant browser, like Mosaic, I could simply point-and-click on a keyword.

NOTE See Figure 2.1 for an illustration of Mosaic in action.

```
                                                        News Available Online
                              NEWS AVAILABLE ONLINE

      News sources include:

      A full list of the news groups available via the Internet and Bitnet News
      Groups[1].

      News Group Frequently Asked Questions Archive are maintained at
      ohio-state[2] and rtfm.mit.edu[3] and also available for searching via
      WAIS at wais@rtfm.mit.edu[4]  Note:  These hosts limit the maximum number
      of users.  If you experience a problem please try again later.

      USA Today[5] News via Nova



                                              http://it/njIT/News/General.html

Next  Back  Up  Find  List  Recall  Top  End  Go  saVe  eXit  Query  Preceding
 Succeeding  Home  Instructions
Query hypertext links                           ( ? help, - escape, ++ homebase )
HYPERTEXT ACTION CHOICE> Q
```


3.22. Why are there so many different (competing) Internet tools?

First, sheer numbers. There are many different Internet tools for a variety of reasons. One, Internet users need a lot of different services because there are lots of things they want to do. Originally, each service was aimed at a specific niche: FTP was for file transfer; Archie was a database of FTP files; Gopher was a distributed menu-based document server. For example, they need Telnet to do remote login, FTP to do file transfers, and so on. Each tool has its own purpose. For this reason alone, users end up with a lot of tools.

Second, the Internet community is vast, wide, and dispersed. It's not uncommon for many individuals or communities (sometimes unknown to each other) to be working on similar problems and to come up with their own solutions to those problems.

For example, Gopher, Hytelnet, TechInfo, and WWW all, to some extent, represent solutions to several problems. Similarly, in the "how do I find someone's e-mail address" arena, there's Michael Schwartz' NetFind, Daniel Kegel's uwho, whois++, and so on. Many problems can have more than one solution.

Each tool was created to meet its own organization's needs, so each works differently and usually offers slightly different features. We don't all work the same way—you'll like some tools more than others, or pick one based on price, availability, or the computer environment with which it works.

> **NOTE** So, often a number of tools exist that let you do basically the same thing. As if that weren't enough, often many ways exist to access any given tool. Consider three of the ASCII-oriented clients for WWW—there's a *line browser* (generally named *www*), screen-oriented browser (called *web*), and (most popularly) one called *Lynx* (*lynx*), which seems to do ASCII access to the Web best. Differences include the commands to move the cursor, get help, and so on (the "look and feel" of the programs); what types of computers they're available for; and how well they perform. Users with the proper type of connections probably prefer to use Mosaic, yet another Web browser, which handles text documents as well as still images, sounds, and movies.

Q 3.23. What's all this talk of *indexers* and *navigators*?

An *indexer* involves a component to gather the data, build the index, and handle user queries. An example is Archie, a tool that catalogs the holdings of thousands of anonymous FTP sites. Indexes are efforts to do virtual look-ups across thousands of Internet servers, like the holdings of anonymous FTP sites, or the menus in

Gopher servers. The idea is to collect a list from each participating server, and then collect these lists into one database that can be searched, so that a single query seems to search the entire Internet.

A *navigator* provides the user with a view of this information, and a way to search, browse, and select things. It provides an Internet-wide view rather than a connection to only one site. For example, a single screen of a Gopher menu may point to resources at a dozen locations around the world!

Q 3.24. Why do we need navigators and front ends for the Internet?

The Internet is a continually growing and changing universe of resources: files that can be read and retrieved, computer programs that can be run, databases that can be queried, and so on.

Back when the Net was smaller and a given user could easily know everyone in his or her field, as well as every relevant site and resource, navigation wasn't as much of an issue. Also, users were more likely to be computer-savvy (able to use UNIX, VMS, and other non-user-friendly interfaces). Plus, the percentage of new users was small enough that their learning curve and questions weren't a significant burden to the rest of the community. Today, almost none of this is true.

One last thought: As of early 1994, these Internet navigators and front ends helped ameliorate many of the immediate, obvious, and relatively easy aspects of navigating and using the Internet, but the real problems—the ones that make the Internet "the librarian's Full Employment Act for the 1990s"—have yet to be solved.

Q 3.25. Can I get more information online about tools for navigating the Internet?

Yes. There are many, many guides online to help you learn to use Gopher, Veronica, World Wide Web, Telnet, and a dozen other programs. Check Appendix B, "Information About the Internet, on the Internet," for a big list of them, but before you do, I'll tell you a few of my favorites for beginners:

Big Dummy's Guide to the Internet. A book in itself, the Big Dummy's Guide will show the ins and outs of navigating the Net. Available by FTP: `ftp.eff.org:/pub/Net_info/Big_Dummy/*`

There's Gold in Them Networks! A classic guide to exploring the Internet. Available by FTP: `nic.merit.edu :/documents/fyi/fyi_10.txt`

John December's Internet Tools List. (Part of which is reproduced in Appendix B.) A wonderful list of informational documents and services. If you want to know more about something online, check here for the place to find it. It is also available via FTP: `ftp.rpi.edu :/pub/communications/internet-tools`.

Fun with UNIX

This section covers the basics of UNIX, a *de facto* standard interface for many Internet users. Even if you don't access the Internet through a UNIX host, chances are you'll run across it sooner or later.

Q 3.26. What is UNIX?

UNIX is one of the most popular operating systems used on the Internet. UNIX is available for a wide variety of computer platforms. It's a multiuser, multitasking environment. This means that several people can use a UNIX computer simultaneously, and each person can run several programs at once. This makes UNIX a very powerful system.

UNIX was developed in the 1960s at AT&T Bell Labs. Since its creation, UNIX has seen countless updates, revisions, and spinoffs. Today, there are flavors of UNIX with names like SCO UNIX, BSD, and System V.

Q 3.27. Why is UNIX so prevalent on the Internet?

Answered by Dave Taylor (`taylor@netcom.com`)

If you're connected to the Internet, it's entirely possible that you are using a Macintosh, PC, or other machine, but odds are that you're actually using a UNIX system. Indeed, UNIX computers are the backbone of the Internet, and the heart of much of its design. If you've been on the Net for any length of time, this isn't news to you, but do you know why?

The Internet grew out of various projects in the 1960s and 1970s, many associated with the U.S. Department of Defense Advanced Research Projects Agency (DARPA). One place you'll be familiar with the name of this organization is ARPAnet, the precursor to the Internet.

There were many goals of the federally funded ARPAnet, but the most important was that it would be a vehicle for universities and research facilities to share information about government-related projects. Through targeted funding of various organizations, utilities and tools were born that gradually evolved into services we know as e-mail (based on the simple mail transport protocol, SMTP), remote logins (Telnet), and remote user interaction (talk, finger).

Almost all these development machines were running the UNIX operating system, a system particularly suited for software development and much favored at research institutions and universities where the programmers could actually work with the source code to the operating system itself (which was quite a difference from such stalwarts as IBM and DEC, who wouldn't even talk about the operating system internals, let alone open the system up to university students!). Further, most of these machines were Digital machines, mostly VAX and PDP series minicomputers, with UNIX replacing the then-aging VMS operating system, mostly due to its greater flexibility.

The TCP/IP protocol was also developed significantly with Department of Defense ARPA funds. The story goes that there were two groups developing competing TCP/IP protocols, one at UC Berkeley and one at AT&T, and to everyone's surprise, the Berkeley version was chosen by ARPA as the standard. The machines that were used at UC Berkeley were UNIX machines, and AT&T's Bell Laboratories was the birthplace of that operating system.

Without doubt, one of the changes that has occurred on the Internet in the last few years is that the number of non-UNIX machines has dramatically increased, as programmers and users on other platforms require the many networking services available on UNIX-based TCP/IP networks.

Much of the continued evolution of the Internet and its tools and interfaces are still UNIX-based, with the UNIX systems offering the combination of price and performance that allows them to work with the volumes of information flying through the wire without stopping the user from working on his or her own tasks. On an inexpensive UNIX workstation, for example, a user can work on a word processing document without any delays, never realizing that an electronic-mail based server, Gopher server, and FTP archive are all actively being utilized simultaneously.

3.28. Ugh! Do I really have to learn UNIX?

As you explore the Internet, chances are that you will use a computer system that works with the UNIX operating system. If you're familiar only with DOS or Macintosh computers, trying to use UNIX can make you feel like a stranger in a strange land. Read on and you will have a better understanding of the basics of UNIX. Also, you'll learn how to find more information about UNIX when you need it.

To access a UNIX system, you'll need the system administrators to set up your very own *account*. Every person who is authorized to use a particular UNIX system has an account; when you want to use the computer, you tell it your account name and a secret password. The computer uses this information to verify who you are, give you access to the information that belongs to you, and keep others out of your files. If you're legit, you'll see the UNIX prompt, the sign that the computer is ready to take a command.

If you use DOS, you're familiar with a prompt like C:\ >. UNIX prompts vary from system to system, but yours is most likely to be a dollar sign ($) or a percent sign (%).

When you log on, you may also see the *system message of the day* (or *MOTD*, pronounced *mot-dee*) announcing anything the system administrator thinks you need to know. You may also see a message if you have any unread electronic mail.

To log off the system, simply type `logout`. It is important to do this to tell the computer that you don't plan to use it for a while. This prevents others from walking up to your terminal and looking through your files.

The following is an example of logging onto a UNIX system.

```
login: savetz
Password:
Unix System V Release 3.1 AT&T 3B2
ziggy
Copyright (c) 1984 AT&T
All Rights Reserved

Last login: Sat Dec 26 20:49:52 on ttyp1

              *Welcome to BigCorp's Big Powerful Unix computer*
             This machine is provided solely for authorized use.
         * System will be down from 2AM - 3AM Tuesday for maintenance *

There are 2 messages in your mailbox.
$
```


3.29. What should I know about files and directories in UNIX?

If you've used any other computer operating system, you are familiar with the concepts of files and directories. Files are individual collections of information stored on a computer (for instance, a letter to Aunt Zelda, a picture of the moon, or a game program). Directories allow you to place files in a logical manner so that you can find them later. UNIX files and directories are very similar to those on DOS computers.

Your account has a *home* directory, the directory you use by default when you log on to the system. You can change your current directory, list a directory's contents, and create and remove directories that are part of your home directory. Like DOS, UNIX uses a hierarchical directory structure. This means that there is one *root* directory and many subdirectories in which to store files. Figure 3.1 shows what a simple directory tree might look like.

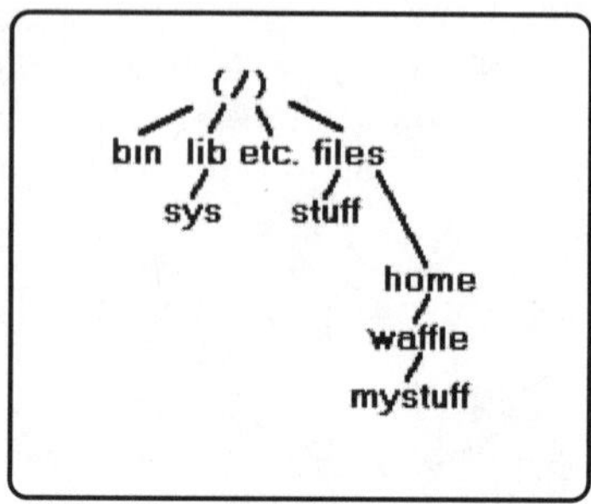

Figure 3.1. *A simple directory tree.*

A file in the `mystuff` directory can be referred to as follows:

```
/files/home/waffle/mystuff/filename
```

This is referred to as the filename's *full path.* The first / must be there for it to be a full path. If you leave it off, UNIX will look for the file starting in your present directory. This is useful because having to constantly refer to files by their full pathnames would get tedious. If you were in `waffle` and wanted to refer to `filename` in `mystuff`, you could call it `mystuff/filename`. Or if you are already in `mystuff`, just use `filename`.

If you use DOS on your home computer, note that UNIX uses a forward slash between directory names rather than a backslash.

NOTE If you use DOS, you're also used to restrictive filenames with eight letters, a period, and an extender of three more letters (for example, `grandmas.ltr`). If you use a Macintosh, you have the luxury of filenames of up to 31 characters. Depending on what flavor of UNIX you're using, you may be allowed filenames from 14 to 255 characters. And, unlike DOS, which likes only A-Z, 0-9, and the underline in filenames, UNIX filenames can contain just about any character you can type on the keyboard. (Some characters are possible as part of a filename, like the space character, brackets, and the asterisk, but can get you in sticky situations later. It's best to avoid using them.)

3.30. How do I manipulate files with UNIX?

Following are some important commands for manipulating files and directories. I've put them more or less in the order of most common use. First things first, though: use and love the `man` (manual) command. Typing `man cp`, for instance, will tell you everything you could want to know about the `cp` command. Type `man man` and `man intro` for general system help. Most of the following commands take special options, called *arguments*, for tweaking how they work. There isn't room here to list each command's options and arguments, so make judicious use of the `man` command.

pwd. Stands for Present Working Directory. It will tell you what directory you're currently in. Log on to your system and type `pwd` to find out what your home directory is called. Mine is `/files/home/waffle`.

ls. Lists all the files and directories under your present working directory. There's a problem, though: the `ls` command doesn't tell you whether you're looking at the names of files or directories. Not to worry: if you type `ls -CF`, you'll get a nicely formatted list, with executable files (programs) indicated by an asterisk and directories indicated by a slash.

NOTE Some files in UNIX are normally invisible (or *hidden files*). Any filename that begins with a period, such as `.newsrc` and `.login`, isn't normally shown with the `ls` command. You can see them, however, if you explicitly ask to see all

files by adding the a argument to the `ls` command: type `ls -a` or `ls -aCF` (yes, capitalization matters!) to see your invisible files. Invisible files usually specify your system configuration and preferences information—or, perhaps you simply have something to hide.

`cd`. Stands for *change directory*. You can move to a directory that is under your present directory by typing something like `cd mystuff`. To move to the directory above your current one, type `cd ..` (that's two dots. Why two dots? It's a mystery to me). If you know exactly what directory you want to go to, you can type a command like `cd /lib/sys`.

`cp`. An abbreviation for *copy*. Not surprisingly, the `cp` command lets you copy a file. Typing `cp file1 file2` will create an exact copy of `file1` in your present directory. Typing `cp file1 /files/home/wombat` will create a copy of `file1` in another directory.

`mv`. An abbreviation for *move*. Lets you move files around directories. Moving a file copies a file to your specified directory, then deletes the original.

`rm`. Stands for *remove*. This command will let you erase files that you no longer need. Be careful! There is no "undelete" command in UNIX; once your file is gone, it's gone forever. `rm file2` will erase one file in your present directory. Typing `rm *` will delete every file in the directory. In UNIX, like in DOS, the asterisk means *all files*.

`cat`. Stands for *catenate*, an obscure word meaning *to form a chain or series*. In its most basic use, `cat` works just like DOS' `TYPE` command: it displays the contents of a text file. Actually, you can use it to display the contents of any file, but binary files (like programs and digitized pictures) will only appear as garbled data. To display a file, just type `cat letter_to_grandma` and the computer will dump the letter to your screen. If the text in the file is too long, the beginning will scroll off the top of the screen faster than you can read it. This brings us to the next command.

`more`. Shows you the contents of a text file one page at a time. To use it, type `more letter_to_grandma`. After each screenfull of text, you'll see the word `more`. Strike the space bar to see the next page of text. Your system may also have a program called `less`, which does the same as `more`, only better. Just as they say, less is more. : -) As always, type `man less` or `man more` for complete information.

`chmod`. Can be used to change the permissions of files. UNIX permissions can be tricky. Remember that UNIX is a timesharing system that can be used by many people simultaneously. You might want to keep some of your files—for instance, your electronic mail—private, but let other users read or modify certain files. So `chmod`, which stands for *change mode*, makes it possible to allow or deny yourself, all system users, or certain users to read, write, or execute your files. For more information (you saw this coming, right?) type `man chmod`.

3.31. What other important UNIX commands should I know about?

The following are some commands that are important.

`man`. OK, I already mentioned this one, but I'm mentioning it again to make sure that you know how to RTFM (read the manual). The `man` command shows you the manual page for a particular command. For instance, `man grep` will give you lots of information about the `grep` command.

The following is an example of a manual page.

```
$ man grep
Reformatting page.  Wait... done
GREP(1V)                 USER COMMANDS                 GREP(1V)

NAME
     grep, egrep, fgrep - search a file for a string  or  regular
     expression

SYNOPSIS
     grep [ -bchilnsvw ] [ -e expression ] [ filename... ]
```

```
DESCRIPTION
     Commands of the grep family search the input filenames  (the
     standard  input default) for lines matching a pattern.  Nor-
     mally, each line found is copied  to  the  standard  output.
     grep  patterns  are limited regular expressions in the style
     of ed(1).   egrep  patterns  are  full  regular  expressions
     including  alternation.   fgrep patterns are fixed strings -
     no regular expression metacharacters are supported.

OPTIONS
     -b    Precede each line by the block number on which  it  was
           found.  This is sometimes useful in locating disk block
           numbers by context.
```

vi or emacs or others. Text editors, or programs that allow you to create text files (such as e-mail messages, programs, or letters to Aunt Zelda). Ask your local guru what editor you should use. The `vi` editor is simple but not exceptionally easy to learn. In contrast, `emacs` is a software behemoth that will edit files, tell your fortune, and teach you to make cookies. (Really.)

lpr or print. May let you print a text file on a printer connected to the UNIX computer. Two caveats: first, never try to print a nontext file. Anything that looks like gibberish when viewed onscreen with the `cat` command will look worse on paper. Second, if you're hacking from a college computer lab or your office and you know there's a printer down the hall, feel free to use the `print` command. If you're using a dial-up UNIX system hundreds of miles away, however, don't use the printer unless you intend to drive there to pick up your printout!

grep. Stands for Global Regular Expression Print, which is a verbose way of saying that this program will search through files and output any lines that contain text that you specify. If you've ever read Usenet news, your home directory contains a hidden file called `.newsrc`, which lists all the newsgroups available to you. Typing `grep amiga .newsrc` will list all the lines in the file that contain the word *amiga*.

passwd. Allows you to change your password. Typing **passwd** will prompt you for your old password, then ask you to type your new password twice. Passwords you type should never be visible on your screen.

Q 3.32. Where can I get more help with UNIX online?

Congratulations! You now have enough information about UNIX to be dangerous. UNIX is a complex operating system made up of hundreds of commands, oddball nomenclature, and countless little quirks. Don't worry. The Internet is rife with beginner's information about UNIX. To explore more of the basics, read the following.

- **The UNIX Frequently Asked Questions list.** This huge, seven-part list of questions and answers explores the ins and outs of UNIX. Users of all knowledge levels will learn something from this file. It is available via FTP:

  ```
  rtfm.mit.edu:/pub/usenet/news.answers/unix-faq/
  faq/*
  ```

  It is also available via e-mail:

  ```
  To: mail-server@rtfm.mit.edu
  Subject: <subject line is ignored>
  Body: send usenet/news.answers/unix-faq/faq/*
  ```

- **The `comp.unix.user-friendly` Frequently Asked Questions (FAQ) list is another great source of helpful information.** It is available via anonymous FTP `ftp.wfu.edu:/pub/usenet/cuuf-FAQ`

- **Also, peruse the Usenet newsgroups `comp.unix.user-friendly`, `comp.unix.questions`, `comp.unix.shell`, and `news.answers`.**

3

Q 3.33. What's a good book to help learn more about UNIX?

Dozens of fine UNIX books exist. Be sure that the book you pick out is tuned to the version of UNIX you use (for instance, System V, Solaris, or BSD). If you're not sure which book to read, start with one of these:

- ***Teach Yourself UNIX in a Week* by Dave Taylor.** Published by Sams Publishing, ISBN 0-672-30464-3. This book, written by the technical editor of the book you're reading now, is a grassroots, seven-day guide to learning UNIX. This is a great hands-on, learn-by-doing book. It covers dozens of facets of UNIX, from file handling and text editing to job control and UNIX's Internet tools. If you're willing and able to digest nearly 90 pages a day, you really can teach yourself UNIX in a week.

- ***Learning the UNIX Operating System, 3rd edition,* by Grace Todino, *et al.*** Published by O'Reilly & Associates, ISBN 1-56592-060-0. An introduction to UNIX, including information on electronic mail, networking, and X-Windows. Geared toward users who need to better understand UNIX to make the most of the Internet.
- ***UNIX for Dummies* by John Levine and Margaret Levine Young.** Published by IDG, ISBN: 0-878058-58-4. An informal and nontechnical introduction to UNIX.
- ***Exploring the UNIX system, Third Edition,* by Stephen Kochan and Patrick Wood.** Published by Hayden Books. ISBN: 0-672-48447-1. A basic overview of UNIX structure and commands from the ground up. (This was my first UNIX book.)
- ***A Student's Guide to UNIX* by Harley Hahn.** Published by McGraw Hill. ISBN: 0-07-025511-3. A superb introduction to UNIX. In a clear and lively language, the author tells novice users everything they need to know about UNIX and the Internet. The book covers commands, utilities, shells, vi, X-Windows, e-mail, and other topics.
- ***UNIX in a Nutshell* by Daniel Gilly.** Published by O'Reilly & Associates. ISBN: 1-56592-001-5. A complete reference guide containing all UNIX commands and options, along with lots of examples and descriptions of the commands. Versions for System V releases 3 and 4 and Solaris 2.0, SCO UNIX, and BSD systems are available.

NOTE For a more complete list of books covering all levels of UNIX, read the UNIX Books FAQ, listing selections of the best books and documentation on UNIX and related subjects (such as UNIX editors and shells). This list is obtainable via anonymous FTP from `rtfm.mit.edu:/pub/usenet/news.answers/books/unix`

You can also get it by e-mail.

```
To: mail-server@rftm.mit.edu
Subject: <subject line is ignored>
Body: send usenet/news.answers/books/
unix
```

CHAPTER 4

How Can I Communicate with People Around the World?

Electronic mail, known to its friends as *e-mail*, is the lowest common denominator of Internet service. Even if you have an account that can't access Gopher and the Usenet; even though it can't slice, dice, and mix drinks; any service that is part of the Internet can—at a minimum—send and receive electronic mail. If you can't use fancier Internet tools with your service, don't feel left out, because electronic mail offers a wealth of information and fun—and access to the single greatest resource on the Internet: people. Scattered throughout this book, you'll find tidbits on using e-mail for searching databases, transferring files, and other good stuff, but this chapter focuses on using e-mail for communicating with people.

4.1. What's so great about electronic mail?

What makes electronic mail nifty? A combination of things make e-mail the useful tool that it is. It allows you to send information: advertisements, spreadsheets, game programs, and love letters more or less privately across the Net.

E-mail is surprisingly fast. Depending on the type of your connection, the condition of computers on the Net and the phase of the moon, your e-mail message can arrive at its destination in as little as a few seconds. (OK, the phase of the moon probably won't affect your e-mail at all. The point is that conditions far beyond your control will indeed affect it.) Most messages make it to their destinations in just a few hours, but sending mail to and from some subnetworks (like FidoNet) can take several days.

E-mail is also inexpensive. It doesn't matter if you pay a flat monthly fee or several dollars an hour for your Internet access; firing off an e-mail message is almost certainly cheaper than making a telephone call, or even using the post office (affectionately called "snail mail" by Netters). Electronic mail messages can be large or small, and contents aren't measured by weight or by volume. It's also distance-independent: you can send mail across the city for the same cost as across the Atlantic.

Of course, electronic mail does have its faults. You can't tell whether your electronic mail message has been read, for instance. Also, text messages lack tone and body language, which can lead to confusing situations and mixed meanings. And although we hope for the best, e-mail isn't necessarily private. (See Chapter 12, "How Can I Keep My Privacy and Stay Secure?" for more on this.)

4.2. What should I know about proper e-mail etiquette?

Truth be told, no one really asks this question, but I wish they would. Allow me to climb on this soapbox briefly and share some uncommon sense about the etiquette of electronic mail.

Get your point across. Any message, electronic or otherwise, is useless if it doesn't convey the right information. Think back to grammar school and remember to include the five Ws: who, what, where, when, and why. Make sure each element is present in your message.

Put a meaningful subject line on your message. The subject line will help remind the reader what the topic of discussion is. A bad subject line doesn't give a clue as to the content of the message. Some bad subject lines are, `Send info.`, `Stuff`, and `What Joe said at lunch`. Better subject lines are more descriptive, such as, `Requesting info re: WombatNet`, `Wanna hear a dirty joke?` and `Joe's comments on the proposal`.

Type complete sentences. Brief, choppy sentences are often nothing more than incomplete thoughts and are vague and confusing.

Be brief. No one wants to read a novel-length message. Correspondents who read their mail on-line and are paying for the privilege will resent having to read a long diatribe when just a few lines will do. In less than thirty seconds, a reader will choose to delete the message, save it for later, or continue reading. (This is actually a journalistic rule of thumb: you have thirty seconds to hook the reader. If the first paragraph doesn't excite them to read more, you've lost them and the rest of the article is irrelevant.) Make those thirty seconds count.

DON'T TYPE IN ALL CAPITAL LETTERS. It's not considered friendly. Your corespondents are likely to think you're shouting at them.

Proofread your mail before you send it. I couldn't count the number of messages I've seen—and probably sent—that had meanings which were totally obscured by a missing word or an errant typo. (Legend has it that one poor soul used electronic mail to send a resume to a potential employer. The cover letter said, "If you have any questions, please hesitate to call me." This is *bad.*) Spelling is equally important. Many online services have some sort of spell-checking facility. Find out if it does and if so, use it!

Think before you send your message. Sending electronic mail is like driving: you shouldn't do either while intoxicated or emotionally charged. Consider the tone of your message and think about the content. If you're angry at a correspondent, relax a bit before you decide to send a flaming missive his way. You would be wise to follow the "Read it Twice" rule of e-mail: Read through your entire message two times before you send it.

Beware of the infamous smiley :-). I won't tell you not to use smileys for fear of retribution by pro-smiley groups. I'll just say that some of us are annoyed by smileys, believing that if something is truly funny or ironic, happy faces aren't necessary. On the other hand, smileys serve as important visual cues that would otherwise be missing in the writing, and it takes a fairly good writer to be able to convey irony or satire to a wide and diverse audience. (For more on smileys, see Chapter 11, "What Do I Need to Know About Internet Culture and Lore?")

Sign your name. Although every mail system attaches the sender's name to the message, it's nice to see a proper sign-off to a message.

If you compose your e-mail off-line using a word processor, don't forget to save it in ASCII format before sending it. Many word processors include information that on-line systems won't understand. By saving your message in ASCII format, you can be sure that when you upload it, it will be free from funky control codes. (For instance, my version of Microsoft Word can use these cool "smart quotes," but when uploaded to e-mail, smart quotes look `Qlike thisR`. Pretty irritating.) The length of your lines is equally important. The vast majority of Internet users have 80-character screens. On such a screen, it is hard to read a message where each line is 95 characters long.

Don't participate in chain letters or get-rich-quick schemes. Not only are these an enormous waste of time and computer resources, you're likely to lose mail privileges if the system administrator catches you sending them. 'Nuff said.

Keep in mind that your recipient might not check his or her e-mail regularly, or at all. Mail sent is not necessarily mail received.

Q 4.3. What goes in an e-mail header?

Every e-mail message has two parts: the header and the body. The message header is a lot like the front of an envelope. It contains the information needed to deliver the message, such as whom it is to and whom it is from. The header also contains a subject line. The message body, as you might expect, contains the actual text of your message. You don't need to worry much about your e-mail's headers, but they do prove useful. When you send e-mail, your mail program will prompt you for the recipient's name, a message subject, and other vital information and will automatically format the headers for you. In some circumstances, (a couple of them are mentioned in the following questions) you may want to manually edit your message headers.

Here is a list of the basic Internet mail headers and what they do:

`From: Arlo T. Kitty <arlo@meow.kitty.com>`
The From: line shows who a message is from. It always includes an e-mail address and sometimes includes the sender's "real" name, too. Luckily, my cats don't really send me e-mail.

Note: There are two basic formats for the From: line. One is in the form `From: Arlo T. Kitty <arlo@meow.kittty.com>` as shown above. The other is `From: arlo@meow.kittty.com (Arlo T. Kitty)`.

`To: savetz@rahul.net`
The To: line contains the address of the primary recipient (or recipients) of the message. I say *primary* because other folks can get copies, too, as specified in the Cc: and Bcc: header lines. A To: line can contain as many addresses as you care to include. The addresses can be those of individuals, mailing lists, or programs that accept e-mail.

`Message-Id: <00174.7464859954.7645@bolero.rahul.net>`
Message-Id is a unique numeric identifier for the message. I have never found it useful, but it's always there.

`Subject: We're low on cat chow!`
The subject line is basic enough; it contains the sender's idea of the message's topic.

`Date: Sun, 20 Feb 1994 11:11:36 PST`
The Date: line tells you when the message was actually sent. Date lines can be mildly confusing—some of them tell you the send time at the originating computer site, and others convert the time to Greenwich Mean Time (GMT)—the time in Greenwich, England. I can never remember if California is seven or eight hours behind GMT because the time difference changes when daylight savings starts in late April.

Note: GMT is "ground zero" from the International Date Line, which is exactly 12 time zones away in either direction from Greenwich. Modern conventions have renamed GMT as Universal Time Coordinated (UTC) so you may see that notation, too.

`Organization: Fuzzy Kitties R Us`
The Organization: line is optional and may tell you who the senders work for or where they go to school, or it may contain a tiny advertisement for their service providers. Lots of people who choose to deny affiliation with any organizations use the field for silly messages and bogus firm names.

`Cc: president@whitehouse.gov`
`Bcc: admin@northcoast.net`
Cc stands for Carbon Copy and Bcc stands for Blind Carbon Copy. These fields help electronic mail mimic what you can do with traditional mail. Specifically, fire off copies to multiple people, either while announcing it or surreptitiously. Remember, the recipient never sees the Bcc: line. See the following questions for more on carbon copying.

Q 4.4. How do I send an e-mail message to multiple recipients?

Specify a list of recipients (rather than just one) and your mail program will build To: or Cc: lists for you. Your message will be sent to everyone listed on the To: and Cc: lines. Your mail program may automatically prompt you for names to carbon copy to or it may not.

There is no functional difference between listing addresses in the To: or Cc: header lines. But from the user's point of view, it is implied that any Cc: recipients are receiving the message for informational purposes only, and no reply is desired. If anyone on the To: or Cc: list should reply to your message, the reply can (at the sender's option) go to all the recipients of your message.

The ability to send e-mail to multiple recipients is a useful tool: you can all at once (if you desire) send one message to several Internet users, an America Online account, a few fax machines, and a mailing list.

Q 4.5. What's a "blind carbon copy"?

If you wish to send a copy of an electronic mail message to someone without the knowledge of the folks listed in the To: and Cc: header lines), you can use the blind carbon copy (Bcc:) header item. Addresses listed in the Bcc: line will receive a stealth copy of your outgoing message. They will not, however, receive copies of any replies to your message. If you send your message to multiple blind carbon copy recipients, these are also hidden from each other.

NOTE I've found the Bcc: function to be very reliable, but you should test your system's Bcc: function to make sure your system really strips the Bcc: line out of your message's header.

You'll never see the Bcc: line in mail that you receive: it's only there for the actual submission of the first mail item, then it is removed.

Q 4.6. My e-mail keeps bouncing. What's wrong?

When your e-mail can't get to its intended destination for any reason, it "bounces" back to you. A bounce message is usually a lengthy, cryptic message from a program called MAILER-DAEMON. Hidden in the message, you'll find a line telling you what went wrong. Assuming your site's e-mail facilities are working properly, e-mail typically bounces for one of two reasons.

First, the host you're mailing to may not exist. The host (or site, the part of the e-mail address after the @ sign) must be listed in appropriate *name servers.* If the host you specify can't be found, your e-mail message has no destination and must be bounced back to you. When this happens, double-check your intended e-mail address and try to resend your message to the right place. Here's an example of a message bounced because there was no such site:

```
Date: Sun, 30 Jan 1994 20:40:38 -0800
To: waffle
Subject: Returned mail: Host unknown

   ---- Transcript of session follows ----
554 smith@nonexistent.com... 550 Host unknown (Authoritative answer from name
server)

   ---- Recipients of this delivery ----
Bounced, cannot deliver:
   smith@nonexistent.com

   ---- Unsent message follows ----
```

The other likely reason your e-mail may bounce is this: although the destination host has been verified, there is no user that answers to the name you specified. (The name is the part of the e-mail address that comes before the @ sign.) When this happens, double-check the name or username of your intended recipient and resend your message. Here's an example of a message that bounced because my cat doesn't have an account at apple.com:

```
From daemon Sun Jan 30 20:42:03 1994
Received: by bolero.rahul.net id AA25984
  (5.67a8/IDA-1.5 for waffle); Sun, 30 Jan 1994 20:41:50 -0800
Date: Sun, 30 Jan 1994 20:41:50 -0800
From: Mail Delivery Subsystem <MAILER-DAEMON>
Message-Id: <199401310441.AA25984@bolero.rahul.net>
To: waffle
Subject: Returned mail: User unknown
```

```
    ---- Transcript of session follows ----
While talking to apple.com:
>>> RCPT To:<Kinsey_Michelle_Kitty@apple.com>
<<< 550 <Kinsey_Michelle_Kitty@apple.com>... User unknown
550 Kinsey_Michelle_Kitty@apple.com... User unknown

    ---- Recipients of this delivery ----
Bounced, cannot deliver:
   Kinsey_Michelle_Kitty@apple.com

    ---- Unsent message follows ----
```

Q4.7. How do I know if my e-mail got there?

You don't, really. A problem with Internet e-mail is that you are usually told only if your message *doesn't* get through—for instance, if the destination host name is invalid. By default, if your mail does get to its destination intact, you won't be informed.

This can be annoying. Even more annoying is the fact that your mail's intended recipients might not check their mailboxes for weeks at a stretch—if ever. There's nothing you can do about that, but most UNIX-esque systems understand a special header item called `Return-Receipt-To:` that will cause the recipient's host to send you mail verifying delivery of your message. `Return-Receipt-To:` can't tell you when the recipient reads your message; it can only tell you that your message was received by the destination computer and placed in the recipient's mailbox. It's actually a confirmation of delivery rather than a confirmation that mail has been received by the recipient.

`Return-Receipt-To:` is a mail header item, just like the `To:` and `Cc:` fields. The `Return-Receipt-To:` command won't do anything if it is in the body of the message. To verify receipt of your mail, you need to know how to edit the mail *headers* before sending your message (see the next question to find out how). In the headers, add a line like

```
Return-Receipt-To: keyogi@kitty.com
```

but use your own e-mail address instead of Keyogi's.

The receiving host must understand the Return-Receipt-To: command to act on it. If you're mailing to a user on another network (like FidoNet or America Online), you're not likely to receive confirmation when your mail is delivered.

As soon as your mail is delivered, you will receive a message with a subject line of

```
Subject: Returned mail: Return receipt
```

and you will rest content in the knowledge that your mail is safe and sound in somebody's e-mailbox.

4.8. How do I edit a message's headers?

Sometimes you'll want to edit a message's headers before you send it—for instance, to add your own `Return-Receipt-To:` or `Bcc:` lines. There is no standard means of doing this; you'll need to read the documentation for your mail program. There are dozens of programs for sending mail and each one works differently.

In Elm, a wholly nifty mail program for UNIX systems, compose your message as usual. Before you send it, however, press the `h` key to edit the headers:

And now: `Headers`

```
e)dit message, h)eaders, c)opy, i)spell, !)shell,
s)end, or f)orget
```

Press `u` for user defined header:

```
Choose header, u)ser defined header, d)omainize, !)shell, or <return>.
Choice: u
```

Then type your special header.

```
Enter in the format "HeaderName: HeaderValue".
Return-Receipt-To: savetz@rahul.net
```

Now send your message as usual. Voilà!

And now Send

```
     e)dit message, h)eaders, c)opy, i)spell, !)shell, s)end, or f)orget
Sending mail...
```

Q 4.9. I got a message saying my message can't be delivered for three days. What should I do?

Lots of strange things happen in the great lottery of Internet mail. En route from your host to its destination, your mail might pass through several other computers, over gateways, and around roadblocks. Once in a rare while you'll receive an automated message saying your mail can't be delivered for a certain amount of time. There's nothing you can do but wait. Your mail will go through eventually. Don't fret: it will still probably get there faster than "snail mail" would.

Q 4.10. Can I send programs, pictures, and sounds through e-mail?

Although it isn't obvious, you can send binary files—such as executable programs, sound files, and GIF images—though electronic mail.

The Internet's e-mail system usually handles basic text files nicely, but doesn't reliably handle binary ones. Text messages are called 7-bit files because characters in the *low ASCII* character set—which contains the letters A through Z, the numbers, some punctuation, and some special symbols—only use seven of the eight bits that make up each byte. Binary files such as graphics images, sampled sounds, Microsoft Word documents, and many others use all eight bits of each byte. The problem is that many of the hodgepodge of computers on the Internet can't handle 8-bit messages, only 7-bit ones. If you send electronic mail that contains a binary (8-bit) file, chances are that by the time it reaches its destination, it will be stripped of all those eighth bits, something that will completely upset your graphics program, sound player, or word processor.

The solution is to convert those 8-bit files to 7-bit ones before the e-mail trip. The recipient of the message must then convert the file back to eight bits before using the data. There are three common schemes for translating between eight- and seven-bit files: binary to ASCII/ASCII to binary (BtoA/AtoB), uuencode, and binhex. You also may stumble upon xxencoded files, a rare conversion scheme that was supposed to be better than uuencode but never seemed to gain wide acceptance.

BtoA conversion is most popular among UNIX folks. uuencoded translations are popular in the UNIX and IBM PC worlds. Binhex files seem to be preferred by the Macintosh crowd. All of these conversion schemes cause the resulting ASCII file to be larger than the original binaries due to the overhead of all that bit shuffling.

To send a binary file in e-mail, both you and the message's recipient must have a utility to translate between one of these formats.

Q4.11. How can I tell whether a file has been converted with BtoA?

Files encoded with any of the conversion programs look like gibberish, but it isn't hard to tell what format they're in, and hence, how to decode them.

If you can see the filename (that is, if the mystery file is sitting in your hard disk or included in the subject of a message), BtoA-encoded filenames usually end in the extension `.btoa` or the more verbose `.MBin.ascii`. If you can't see the filename, look at the first line of the message. The first line of a BtoA file starts with something similar to `xbtoa Begin`.

Q4.12. How can I tell if a file is uuencoded?

uuencoded files usually end with the extension `.uu` or `.uue`. The first line of a uuencoded document starts with something similar to `begin 644myfile.txt`.

4.13. How can I tell if a file is in binhex format?

Binhexed files typically end with the extension `.hqx`. You can easily eyeball the file to tell if it's binhexed. The first line is a complete giveaway: (This file must be converted with BinHex 4.0).

4.14. How long can my e-mail be?

This is a sticky question with no definite answer. The maximum length of electronic mail files depends on the computer you send mail from, the recipient's computer, and all the machines along the route from here to there. Some situations allow for enormous, megabyte-long messages and other situations limit e-mail to relatively itty-bitty 30-kilobyte chunks.

Even the most verbose of writers' messages easily fit under the limitations of the most restrictive networks. E-mail messages are usually one to three kilobytes long. In comparison, this chapter (just the text, sans formatting) is about 75 kilobytes long. (If you're reading this, you'll know that it successfully made the trip from the Internet to my editor's CompuServe account.)

I have sent e-mail messages that included large binhexed programs that were 3 or 4 megabytes in length. I sent these messages between sites in the continental United States over connections that I knew could handle the obtuse files.

You shouldn't send huge e-mail messages over transcontinental links. Many of these Internet connections are excruciatingly expensive, and the folks who use them often pay for each byte that passes their way. Similarly, networks such as FidoNet are passed between computer systems by long-distance phone calls. Their owners pay the bills out of the goodness of their hearts, but they become annoyed when forced to pay for wasteful use of the network bandwidth. Gratuitous use of electronic mail in both these situations annoys people and is likely to get you yelled at.

Q 4.15. How do I send mail from the Internet to another network or online service?

In the best of worlds, our "global village" of electronic mail would be linked by one main street. Alas, it is actually composed of hundreds of small networks linked using *gateways.* One main street is the Internet, but jutting off of it are dozens of side roads leading to other networks. It's always simplest to send mail to a recipient on the same online service as yourself—say, from your America Online account to another—but sometimes you may need to send mail to someone who doesn't have an account on the system you use. Although it's usually possible to mail from one network to another, you need to know the right route. To send any mail, you need to know the online service your recipients use and their names (or usernames) on that service.

For a complete and up-to-date listing of how to send mail from just about any network to any other, read the "Inter-Network Mail Guide" edited by Scott Yanoff. You can fetch this guide by anonymous FTP in `csd4.csd.uwm.edu:/pub/internetwork-mail-guide`.

It's also available on the Usenet newsgroups `comp.mail.misc`, `alt.internet.services`, and `news.answers`.

America Online. *`user`*`@aol.com`
Use all lowercase and remove any spaces in the AOL username. For example, `savetz@aol.com`. AOL splits long Internet e-mail messages into chunks under 27K. Users of the DOS-based PC/AOL software are limited to a maximum mail size of 8Kb. For all AOL users, funky characters (hearts, moons, clovers, diamonds and any other non-alphanumeric characters your terminal can conjure up) are replaced with spaces.

Applelink. *`user`*`@applelink.apple.com`
AT&T Mail. *`user`*`@attmail.com`
Bitnet. *`user`*`@`*`host`*`.bitnet`

(The Bitnet hostname isn't necessarily the same as the Internet host name.) If this fails, your machine's SMTP server may not be up to date, so try directing your mail through a gateway such as `cunyvm.cuny.edu, pucc.princeton.edu,` or wuvmd.wustl.edu. The address would be as follows: user%domain.bitnet@pucc.princeton.edu (or cunyvm or wuvmd).

BIX. *user*@bix.com

Compuserve. *userid*@compuserve.com

Use the recipient's numeric CompuServe identification number, but use a period instead of a comma to separate the number sets. For example, to send mail to CompuServe user 17770,101, mail to 17770.101@compuserve.com.

Connect. *user*@dcjcon.das.net

Delphi. *user*@delphi.com

eWorld. *user*@eworld.com

Fidonet. *firstname.lastname*@p#.f#.n#.z#.fidonet.org

To send mail to FidoNet users, you not only need the names, but the exact FidoNet addresses they use. FidoNet addresses are broken down into zones, net, nodes, and (optionally) points. For example, the address of one Fido BBS is 1:102/834. The zone is 1, the net is 102, the node is 834. A user's address could include a point as well: 1:102/834.1; the final 1 is the point. So to send mail to John Smith at Fido address 1:102/834, e-mail to John.Smith@f834.n102.z1.fidonet.org. To send mail to that user at Fido address 1:102/834.1, e-mail to John.Smith@p1.f834.n102.z1.fidonet.org.

GEnie. *user*@genie.geis.com

Where user is their mail address. If a user tells you their mail address is xyz12345 or something similar, it isn't. It usually looks like A.BEEBER42 where A is their first initial, BEEBER is their last name, and 42 is a number distinguishing them from all other A.BEEBER's.

Internet. *user*@host.domain

Where user is the recipient's login name, and domain is the full name and location of the computer where he or she receives e-mail. Examples are savetz@rahul.net and an017@cleveland.freenet.edu.

MCI Mail. *user*@mcimail.com

User can be a numeric identification (which is always 7 digits long or 3 zeroes followed by 7 digits), their account name (which is one word) or first and last names separated with an underline. (for example, `0001234567@mcimail.com`, `123-4567@mcimail.com` or `John_Edward_Doe@mcimail.com`.)

National Videotext Network. *user*@nvn.com
NVN is another national online service, a la Delphi, but less well known. I think it should stay.

NVN and eWorld and the WELL conform to the basic `user@host.domain` format, agreed. However that doesn't mean that the reader-user knows what the host.domain is for a particular service. That's why they are included, and why I think they should stay.

PC Link. *user*@aol.com
Incoming mail is limited to 27K. (There is no `pclink.com` domain. PC Link is owned by America Online, hence the `aol.com` domain.)

Prodigy. *userid*@prodigy.com
A user ID looks like `BVXF64A`.

Whole Earth 'lectronic Link (WELL).
user@well.sf.ca.us

4.16. How do I send mail from another network or online service to the Internet?

Suppose you're using an online service and want to send mail to someone on the Internet. Can you do it? Probably. Sometimes it's easy, but other times the steps are more convoluted. Have patience and if you can't seem to get your mail out, ask someone using that network or service.

America Online. *user*@host.domain
AppleLink. *user*@host.domain@internet#
This is one of the only cases that I know of where you'll send e-mail with two @s in the To: line. I don't know why they do it that way; it's bad form. To send mail from AppleLink, the destination address must be fewer than 35 characters.

AT&T Mail. internet!*domain*!*user*
For example: `internet!rahul.net!waffle`.

BITNet.
Methods for sending mail from BITNet to the Internet vary depending on what mail software is running at your BITNet host. In the best case, users should be able to send mail to `user@host.domain`. If this doesn't work, try *`user%domain@gateway`* where `gateway` is a BITNet-Internet gateway site (such as `cunyvm.cuny.edu`, `pucc.princeton.edu`, or `wuvmd.wustl.edu`.)

CompuServe. `>INTERNET:`*`user`*`@host.domain`
Connect. `DASN`
Make the first line of the message
`"`*`user`*`@host.domain"@DASN`

Fidonet. *`user@machine.site.domain`* `ON 1:1/31`
Use the normal Internet address followed by `ON 1:1/31`.

GEnie. *`user`*`@host.domain@INET#`

MCI Mail.
At the `To:` prompt, type your recipient's name followed by `(EMS)` For instance, `John Smith (EMS)`. At the `EMS:` prompt type `INTERNET`. Finally, at the `Mbx:` prompt type *`user`*`@host.domain`.

WWIVnet. *`user#machine.site.domain`*`@506`.
If the destination username begins with digits, begin the address with a quote mark This is a low-traffic site, so use it sparingly and only for short, infrequent messages.

4

4.17. Is there a way to search the user directory at CompuServe (or another online service) to find out the e-mail address of one of its users?

You can't use the Internet to look up users on most commercial online services. If you know that associates have accounts on CompuServe, for example, the only way to find out their CompuServe e-mail address is to call them and ask.

The only exception that I know of is MCI Mail. Its users are listed in the Knowbot Information Service (see the answer to Question 4.20.)

If you have a CompuServe account, you can log in and check the user directory, but even that directory doesn't list all CompuServe users. Subscribers can elect to have their names and addresses taken out of the directory. Most other online services have similar directories that are only available to their own users.

> **NOTE** Some services will identify a subset of their users if you try to send mail and it's not a unique descriptor. For example, there are probably a half-dozen Dave Taylor's on CompuServe, so sending mail to `Dave.Taylor@compuserve.com` might result in a message back from the system indicating that there is more than one, and listing them. This doesn't always work, but it's worth trying!

4.18. How do I find out someone's Internet e-mail address?

Because there are so many computer systems and users in the world, it is impossible to keep a complete "white pages" of the Internet. The problem is compounded because people—especially students—constantly come and go from the Net. Trying to store and update a complete directory of e-mail addresses would be an impossible task.

However, it's not impossible to find people on the net. Several tools are available that can help you search for a person's e-mail address, given some amount of information about your victim—er, associate. Each tool works in a different way. Some tools keep a huge database of names and addresses, and others search the Net for you "on the fly" without a prestored database. Quite often one of the following tools will succeed although the others fail, so it pays to try them all.

The more information you know about your associates—names, places of business or schools, and so on—the greater your chances are of finding them. If you want to get in touch with a pal from your past but you don't know where he or she works, or what city he or she lives in, you're less likely to locate him or her—even if he or she is on the Net.

Of course, to be listed in any of these services, you need to have an account on the Internet, and to some extent, you need to want to be found. Don't forget about other ways to find someone: write a letter or pick up the phone and call.

For more information on finding someone's e-mail address, read: "FAQ: How to find people's E-mail addresses," available via e-mail from `mail-server@rtfm.mit.edu` by sending `send usenet/news.answers/finding-addresses` in the body of the message. This document is also posted regularly to the Usenet group `news.answers` and is available via FTP as

```
rtfm.mit.edu:/pub/usenet/news.answers/finding-
addresses
```

Another document, specifically with help on finding college student's e-mail addresses, is available. It is also posted on a regular basis to `news.answers`. You can also get the file by anonymous FTP as

```
rtfm.mit.edu:/pub/usenet/soc.college/
Student_Email_Addresses
```

or by sending a mail message to `mail-server@rtfm.mit.edu` with a message body of `send usenet/soc.college/Student_Email_Addresses`.

When all other methods of searching for an e-mail address have failed; after you've tried using the following user-lookup services and calling your associate's old roommates, you can consider posting a message to the newsgroup `soc.net-people` asking for help locating your target. Before doing this, read the document "Tips on using soc.net-people" which is posted to that group regularly. This file is also available via FTP (the filename will be slightly different):

```
rtfm.mit.edu:/pub/usenet/soc.net-people/
Tips_on_using_soc.net-people_[l.m._13_09_92]
```

Remember, posting to the Usenet costs many people real money, and your chances of finding someone on `soc.net-people`—especially if other search methods have failed—are slim.

Many Internet systems support a command called `finger`, which can give basic information about a user on a given computer. `finger` usually allows searches by first, last, or login names. To list users named *Ron* on your local system, typing `finger ron` should list everyone with *Ron* as part of their name or login. `finger` may return information including the user's real name, login, a phone number, and other personal information if these are supplied.

On many systems, `finger` allows you to peruse the users of other computers as well. Entering the command `finger ron@hal.gnu.ai.mit.edu` will tell you about the *Rons* with accounts on a certain computer at Massachusetts Institute of Technology. This in itself is not too powerful, however, because it requires that you know the exact name of the computer system you are searching. When you are searching for an associate's e-mail address, this isn't the case. Once you know the computer system and login name of a person, you know enough to send electronic mail.

`finger`'s power, however, grows when used in conjunction with services such as Netfind, which scour the network for the names you give without any other information except an idea of where to look.

4.19. What is whois?

Whois is a program that can give you contact information for users on the Internet. In addition, you can use whois to find information on Internet sites also (more on this later.)

Be warned that there are almost 100 different whois servers, and your results might vary based on which server you use. I looked up Ed Krol (author of the *Whole Internet User's Guide and Catalog*, a fine book about the Internet) with the InterNIC system by using `Telnet rs.internic.net`, and here's how it looked. (Notice that you can perform a variety of different databases searches, not just whois. and queries from this site.)

```
$ telnet rs.internic.net
Trying...
Connected to rs.internic.net.
Escape character is '^]'.
```

```
SunOS UNIX (rs) (ttyp3)

**************************************************************************
* -- InterNIC Registration Services Center  --
*
* For gopher, type:                    GOPHER <return>
* For wais, type:                      WAIS <search string> <return>
* For the *original* whois type:       WHOIS [search string] <return>
* For registration status:             STATUS <ticket number> <return>
*
* For user assistance call (800) 444-4345 ¦ (619) 455-4600 or (703) 742-4777
* Please report system problems to ACTION@internic.net
**************************************************************************
Please be advised that the InterNIC Registration host contains INTERNET
Domains, IP Network Numbers, ASNs, and Points of Contacts ONLY. Please
refer to rfc1400.txt for details (available via anonymous ftp at either
nic.ddn.mil [/rfc/rfc1400.txt]  or ftp.rs.internic.net [/policy/
rfc1400.txt]).

Cmdinter Ver 1.3 Mon Apr 11 01:00:12 1994 EST
[vt100] InterNIC > whois krol,ed
Connecting to the rs Database . . . . . .
Connected to the rs Database
Krol, Ed (EK10)          Krol@UXC.CSO.UIUC.EDU
   University of Illinois
   Computing and Communications Service Office
   195 DCL
   1304 West Springfield Avenue
   Urbana, IL 61801-4399
   (217) 333-7886

   Record last updated on 27-Nov-91.
```

4

4.20. How can I access the "whois" program?

Your system might have whois installed. Try typing `whois` to find out. If your site doesn't have its own copy of whois, Telnet to `rs.internic.net` and login as `whois`.

4.21. I received e-mail from someone on a host called *panix.com*. Can I use whois to learn more about that site?

Yes. Whois can tell you about Internet hosts, not just users. On my computer, I simply type `whois panix.com` and `learn`.

```
Panix Public Access Unix of New York (PANIX-DOM)
   c/o Alexis Rosen
   110 Riverside Drive
   New York, NY 10024

   Domain Name: PANIX.COM
Administrative Contact, Technical Contact, Zone Contact:
      Rosen, Alexis  (AMR8)  hostmaster@ACCESS.NET
      (212) 877-4854

   Record last updated on 12-Apr-93.

   Domain servers in listed order:

   NS1.ACCESS.NET              198.7.0.1
   NS2.ACCESS.NET              198.7.0.2
   NYU.EDU                     128.122.128.2, 192.76.177.18
   EGRESS.NYU.EDU              128.122.128.24, 192.76.177.17
```

Q 4.22. How do I use Netfind?

Netfind is a "white pages" service that uses a number of sources to find electronic mail addresses. Netfind can locate users at over 5,000 sites worldwide. The majority of the domains it can access are educational institutions, so this service is good for locating students. However, Netfind can also access a vast number of commercial, military, government, and other organizational computers. Its operators estimate that it can locate about 5.5 million people.

It works best for sites that do not insulate themselves from the outside world. Some sites, for privacy or security reasons, do not allow offsite users to `finger` their computers or access other information. Although this may be best for the company, it hinders Netfind, which uses this information, when it can, during its search.

Netfind can be used either as a client program running on your local computer or by Telneting to one of several public servers. The public servers don't require the Netfind software to be on your local host, so we'll look at that venue for searching.

To use Netfind, Telnet to `bruno.cs.colorado.edu` (or another Netfind server, listed in following text), armed with the names to search for and their places of business or schools. At the `login` prompt, type `netfind`. Most servers are limited to a certain number of searches at any given time, so you may be denied access. If so, try again later or choose a different server.

Netfind displays a menu of selections. For searching for a specific person, enter `2` (search). You'll then be asked to `enter person and keys`. Enter one word for the name followed by one or more words defining where to look. For instance, entering `simon san diego state university` will check for San Diego State in Netfind's "seed database." If it has something to go on, it will begin checking domain names for the keys. If not, try a less restrictive key (in this case, just `san diego`). Next is a search for hosts. Netfind uses several remote services, including the `finger` command and the Simple Mail Transfer Protocol (SMTP) to query each computer that might have an account name, in this case `Simon`. (A more complete explanation of this process is available in Netfind's online help.)

If Netfind finds too many machines that match your keys, it will list them and ask you to choose up to three.

If a match is made, Netfind gives you as much information as it can about the match. If there is no match, or it can't get access to information from a secure site, you are told why.

Example:

```
$ telnet bruno.cs.colorado.edu
Trying 128.138.243.150...
Connected to bruno.cs.colorado.edu.
Escape character is '^]'.

SunOS UNIX (bruno)

Login as 'netfind' to access netfind server

login: netfind

=====================================================
Welcome to the University of Colorado Netfind server.
=====================================================
Top level choices:
        1. Help
        2. Search
        3. Seed database lookup
        4. Options
        5. Quit (exit server)
```

```
--> 2
Enter person and keys (blank to exit) --> savetz a2i
Searching rahul.net
( 1) SMTP_Finger_Search: checking domain rahul.net
SYSTEM: rahul.net
        Login: waffle                           Name: Kevin Savetz
        Directory: /files/home/waffle           Shell: /local/bin/tcsh
        Mail last read Fri May 13 20:27:22 1994
        On since Fri May 13 19:43 (PDT) on ttyp8

        Freelance computer journalist.

        Publisher of the Internet Services Frequently Asked Questions List.
        Publisher of the Unofficial Internet Book List.
        Publisher of the Internet Fax FAQ.
           All of these documents are available via e-mail. For info, send
mail
           To: savetz@rahul.net            Subject: send help

        Author, "Your Internet Consultant - the FAQs of Life Online" (Sams
        Publishing to be released June 1994.)
```

NOTE Telnet to the nearest address, login as `netfind`

`archie.au.` AARNet, Melbourne, Australia

`bruno.cs.colorado.edu.` University of Colorado, Boulder

`dino.conicit.ve.` National Council for Technical and Scientific Research, Venezuela

`ds.internic.net.` InterNIC Directory and DB Services, S. Plainfield, NJ

`eis.calstate.edu.` California State University, Fullerton, CA

`hto-e.usc.edu.` University of Southern California, Los Angeles

`krnic.net.` Korea Network Information Center, Taejon, Korea

`lincoln.technet.sg.` Technet Unit, Singapore

malloco.ing.puc.cl. Catholic University of Chile, Santiago

monolith.cc.ic.ac.uk. Imperial College, London, England

mudhoney.micro.umn.edu. University of Minnesota, Minneapolis

netfind.anu.edu.au. Australian National University, Canberra

netfind.ee.mcgill.ca. McGill University, Montreal, Quebec, Canada

netfind.icm.edu.pl. Warsaw University, Warsaw, Poland

netfind.if.usp.br. University of Sao Paulo, Sao Paulo, Brazil

netfind.oc.com. OpenConnect Systems, Dallas, Texas

netfind.sjsu.edu. San Jose State University, San Jose, California

netfind.vslib.cz. Liberec University of Technology, Czech Republic

nic.uakom.sk. Academy of Sciences, Banska Bystrica, Slovakia

redmont.cis.uab.edu. University of Alabama at Birmingham

4.23. What is the Knowbot Information Service?

The Knowbot Information Service (KIS) is another "white pages" service that performs a broad name search, checking MCI Mail, the X.500 White Pages Pilot Project, various Whois servers at various organizations (Whois is yet another directory service), and the

UNIX `finger` command. It can be used either as a client program resident on your local machine, through e-mail, or by Telneting to a public server.

KIS uses subprograms called *Knowbots* to search for information. Each Knowbot looks for specific information from a site and reports back to the main program with the results.

Two hosts running KIS servers are `info.cnri.reston.va.us` and `regulus.cs.bucknell.edu`. You can access either one by electronic mail (send mail to `netaddress@nri.reston.va.us`, for instance) or using Telnet. (If you Telnet to a KIS server, you need to request port 185: instead of typing `telnet regulus.cs.buckness.edu`, you'd actually type `telnet regulus.cs.buckness.edu 185`.)

Because searching can take several minutes, I prefer to use the e-mail method; once KIS knows the results of the search, it mails them back to you.

In the body of your mail message to netaddress, put names of your associates, one per line. You may use first and last names or a login if you know them. Sending `johnson` will search the default list of directory servers for user `johnson`. Because KIS checks a predefined set of services, you do not need to supply an organization name to check for.

KIS also includes commands for narrowing your search and searching for an organization. For more help, include the word *man* in your e-mail to KIS or your interactive session.

4.24. How do I use the Usenet addresses search?

The Usenet search is a unique variation in methods of looking for people on the Net. This tool checks your search request against a list of people who have recently posted to the Usenet. If you think your associate is a regular poster to the Usenet, you might want to try this. This search is beneficial because you do not need to know where your associate works or goes to school; a name can be enough.

You use the Usenet search by sending electronic mail to a server that processes your query and replies by e-mail. To look up a name, send a message to mail-server@pit-manager.mit.edu. The server will ignore the subject line. In the body of your message, send send usenet-addresses/keys. keys can be one or more search words separated by spaces. It can be the first and last name, a login name, or the name of an organization. (If you send only the name of an organization, you will receive a list of all the posters from that place.)

You can guess about the words that may appear in the address of the person you are searching for; it's okay if some of the keys don't appear in the address. The search program uses "fuzzy" matching and tries to find the addresses that are closest to your keywords. Forty or fewer matches will be returned, ranked from best to worst.

For more information, send a message to mail-server@pit-manager.mit.edu with a message body of send usenet-addresses/help. If you need to talk to a real person, send mail to postmaster@pit-manager.mit.edu. The online help should be all you need, though.

The Usenet addresses database is also accessible via WAIS on two hosts: rtfm.mit.edu and cedar.cic.net. In both cases, the database is called usenet-addresses and is on port 210. The version on rtfm is slightly more up-to-date with respect to the master address list than the version on cedar.

Here's an example of a Usenet addresses search. No Paul Simon, but lots of near misses:

```
Date: Sun, 23 Jan 1994 03:51:14 -0500
To: Kevin Savetz <savetz@rahul.net>
Subject: mail-server: "send usenet-addresses/paul simon"

simon@fehen.demon.co.uk (Simon Bisson)@fehen.demon.co.uk (Simon Bisson) (Dec
5 93)
paul@mtnmath.UUCP (Paul Budnik paul@MTNMATH.COM)       (Jan 20 94)
paul@mtnmath.UUCP (Paul Budnik uunet!mtnmath!paul)     (Jan 2 94)
paul-hertz@nwu.edu (Paul Hertz) (Paul Hertz)    (Jun 14 93)
uunet!mtnmath!paul@ncar.UCAR.EDU (Paul Budnik uunet!mtnmath!paul)    (Jun
3093)
simon@brome.iro.umontreal.ca (Daniel Simon)     (Apr 1 93)
Paul_Roberts@p100.f2003.n241.z2.fidonet.org (Paul Roberts)      (Apr 1 93)
simon@moscow.uidaho.edu (Mike Simon)    (Apr 21 93)
```

```
paul.britton@f54.n54.fido.zeta.org.au (Paul Britton)    (Apr 21 93)
paul@hpwrce.mayfield.hp.com (Paul Beatrice)     (Apr 21 93)
Paul.E..King@f716.n109.z1.his.com (Paul E. King)        (Apr 21 93)
paul@castle.ed.ac.uk (Paul Haldane)     (Apr 1 93)
paul@gaitlab1.uwaterloo.ca (paul j guy) (Apr 21 93)
Paul_Fishwick@p100.f2003.n241.z2.fidonet.org (Paul Fishwick)     (Apr 1 93)
Simon Aitken <simon@brolga.cc.uq.oz.au> (Apr 11 93)
```

4.25. What is a mailing list?

A mailing list is simply an electronic mail address that redistributes its mail to other addresses. It is a way to reach a few, a few dozen, or a few thousand people who are interested in a specific topic. People who are interested in a particular discussion or topic can "subscribe" to a list. When someone sends mail to the mail list, the message is redistributed via e-mail to the list's subscribers.

Most mailing lists are available to the Internet public, so anyone interested in that topic may join that list. Some mailing lists have membership restrictions, others have message content restrictions, and still others are moderated; that is, only messages that have been approved by a moderator pass through the gates to your e-mailbox.

4.26. How do I subscribe to or unsubscribe from a mailing list?

Answered by Arno Wouters (`Arno.Wouters@phil.ruu.nl`*) in his FAQ, "How to (un)subscribe to a mailing list."*

There are two types of mailing lists: manually maintained lists and automated lists.

In its manual form, the list of subscribers is maintained by a person: the list's administrator. To subscribe to such a list, one should ask the list administrator to add your name to the list. Typically the administrator can be reached at `listname-request@host.domain`.

An automated list is maintained by a program (called a *mailserver*) that handles subscriptions and mail redistribution. To subscribe to an automated list, one should send a message to the mailserver.

To subscribe, send the command `SUB listname Yourfirstname Yourlastname` to the designated mailserver. Obviously you should use your own name in the subscription request. To stop receiving information from a mailing list, send `SIGNOFF listname` to the mailserver.

A mailserver is a program that interprets the lines in a message as a series of commands to act on; for example to mail a file or to add a person to a mailing list. To learn how to handle a mailserver, you should send a one-line message containing the command `help` to the mailserver's address. (In some rare cases, the mailserver needs an empty message with `help` in the subject header).

4.27. What's a Listserv?

Listserv is the name of a very common mailserver. Listservs are the *de facto* standard on Bitnet, and there are versions that work on the Internet as well. Listservs provide three kinds of services: mailing list management, file archives, and address registration.

You can receive a manual on using Listservs by sending the command `INFO GENERAL` to any Listserv (for instance to `LISTSERV@BITNIC.BITNET`). The command `HELP` will get you a short list of commands, `INFO REFCARD` a longer list.

Be aware that not all lists are run on Listservs. If you want to subscribe to a mailing list but you aren't sure if there's a person or a program behind the scenes, assume the list is maintained by a human. Don't send listserv commands unless the contact address starts with `majordomo` or `*listserv` or the instructions explicitly say to send listserv commands. Some list owners will get annoyed if you send them listserv commands rather than polite messages complete with "please" and "thank you."

If you're not sure if a human or a machine is on the receiving end, send a message like this:

```
SUB listname My Name
Hi! If a human is reading this, please sign me up! Thanks!
```

4

Q 4.28. How do I contact the administrator of a mailing list rather than sending my message to everyone on the list?

Few things are more annoying (or more common) for mailing lists subscribers than to see a message saying "Please add me to this list" or "Remove me from this list." This kind of message should be sent to the list administrator, not the mailing list itself.

Never send requests or commands for subscribing or unsubscribing to the list itself. Such messages bother all the participants and aren't likely to get you removed from the list, either. Instead, send requests of an administrative nature to the moderator of the list. Typically, the administrator can be reached at `listname-request@host.domain` or `listname-owner@host.domain`.

Q 4.29. How can I find mailing lists that interest me?

There are zillions and zillions of mailing lists available. How do you find the ones that you are interested in? Grab one of the following lists of mailing lists and peruse it for the topics that most interest you.

The SRI NISC "Interest Groups" List of Lists

This is a list that describes most of the special-interest group mailing lists, explains their primary topics, and tells how to subscribe to them. Unfortunately, it has not been updated since June, 1993, and no updates are in sight. Although the list is still handy for finding interesting mailing lists, keep in mind that some of the mailing lists have died, changed location or moderator, or have been otherwise affected by the winds of change.

A hardcopy, indexed version is available from Prentice Hall under the title "Internet: Mailing Lists" (ISBN 0-13-327941-3). It is also available online for free, but watch out: it's more than a megabyte long.

```
via anonymous FTP: sri.com:/netinfo/interest-groups
via e-mail To: mail-server@sri.com
           Body: send interest-groups
```

A typical entry in the lists of lists looks like this one:

```
4DOS on ListServ@IndyCMS       ListServ@IndyCMS.IUPUI.Edu
     4DOS (4DOS command interpreter) is dedicated to discussion of the 4DOS
command interpreter, or "DOS Shell," produced by JP Software Inc. 4DOS (the
list) is completely independent of 4DOS (the command interpreter) and JP
Software Inc (the manufacturer).

     To subscribe to 4DOS send the following command
SUB 4DOS yourfirstname yourlastname in the BODY or mail (or an interactive
command on BITNET) to Listserv@INDYCMS.BITNET or Listserv@INDYCMS.IUPUI.EDU.
4DOS is owned and coordinated by an interested user (John B Harlan).
```

4.30. Publicly Accessible Mailing Lists

Stephanie da Silva maintains the list of "Publicly Accessible Mailing Lists." The list includes the list names, contact information, and short descriptions of the purpose of the lists. It is available via

Usenet. updated monthly on `news.lists` and `news.answers`
anonymous FTP. `rtfm.mit.edu:/pub/usenet/news.answers/mail/mailing-lists`
e-mail. `mail-server@rtfm.mit.edu` with `send usenet/news.answers/mail/mailing-lists/*` in the body
World Wide Web. `http://www.ii.uib.no/~magnus/paml.html`

4

```
Glass Arts
    Contact: glass-request@dixie.com

    Purpose: For stained/hot glass artists.

glbpoc
    Contact: glbpoc-request@ferkel.ucsb.edu
```

```
    Purpose: glbpoc is a mailing list for lesbian, gay, and bisexual
    people of color.  To be added to the list you must provide your full
    name and a complete internet address.

glove-list
    Contact:  (machine) listserv@boxer.nas.nasa.gov
              (human)   jet@nas.nasa.gov (J. Eric Townsend)

    Purpose: Discussion of the Nintendo PowerGlove, a < $100 dataglove
    available on the remaindered racks of Toys 'R Us and other big
    toy stores.
    To subscribe, send email to listserv@boxer.nas.nasa.gov with a
    *body* of "subscribe glove-list  your_full_name".

gnu-manual
    Contact: internet: gnu-manual-request@a.cs.uiuc.edu

    Purpose: "gnu-manual" members are volunteers who write, proofread,
    and comment on documents for a GNU Emacs Lisp programmers' manual.
```

The Dartmouth SIGLIST

David Avery from Dartmouth maintains an edited list of mailing lists on both Bitnet and Internet. The list includes short descriptions of the purpose of the lists and is sorted by category (such as computing, science, humanities, and so on).

SIGLIST is available via

> **anonymous FTP.** dartcms1.dartmouth.edu:/SIGLISTS/*
> **e-mail.** listserv@dartcms1.bitnet with INDEX SIGLISTS in the body

```
AFA-HEAL@WSUVM1.BITNET   LISTSERV@WSUVM1.BITNET  AFA-HEAL Health Finance
AFA-INT@WSUVM1.BITNET    LISTSERV@WSUVM1.BITNET  AFA-INT International Finance
AFA-INV@WSUVM1.BITNET    LISTSERV@WSUVM1.BITNET  AFA-INV Investments
AFA-LE@WSUVM1.BITNET     LISTSERV@WSUVM1.BITNET  AFA-LE Law & Economics
AFA-MATH@WSUVM1.BITNET   LISTSERV@WSUVM1.BITNET  AFA-MATH Mathematical Finance
AFA-PUB@WSUVM1.BITNET    LISTSERV@WSUVM1.BITNET  AFA-PUB Public Finance
AFA-REAL@WSUVM1.BITNET   LISTSERV@WSUVM1.BITNET  AFA-REAL Real Estate
AFA-S-IV@WSUVM1.BITNET   LISTSERV@WSUVM1.BITNET  AFA-S-IV Small Investors
AFA-SBUS@WSUVM1.BITNET   LISTSERV@WSUVM1.BITNET  AFA-SBUS Small Business
Finance
AFAM-L@UMCVMB.BITNET     LISTSERV@UMCVMB.BITNET  African-American Research
AFRICA-L@BRUFMG.BITNET   LISTSERV@BRUFMG.BITNET  FORUM PAN-AFRICA
AIAA@ARIZVM1.BITNET      LISTSERV@ARIZVM1.BITNET AIAA Listserv
AIL-L@austin.onu.edu     listserv@austin.onu.edu Artificial Intelligence and
Law
```

```
ALIENS-L@UTKVM1.BITNET  LISTSERV@UTKVM1.BITNET  Taxation/Witholding/Reporting
Re
quirements f
all-of-elsa@jus.uio.no  akj@jus.uio.no  European Law Students Assocication
ALLMUSIC@AUVM.BITNET    LISTSERV@AUVM.BITNET    Discussions on all forms of
Musi
c
ALSBNEWS@MIAMIU.BITNET  LISTSERV@MIAMIU.BITNET  Academy of Legal Studies in
Busi
ness (ALSB)
ALSBTALK@MIAMIU.BITNET  LISTSERV@MIAMIU.BITNET  Academy of Legal Studies in
Busi
ness (ALSB)
AltInst@cs.cmu.edu      AltInst-request@cs.cmu.edu      Alternate
Institutions
ALTLEARN@SJUVM.BITNET   LISTSERV@SJUVM.BITNET   Alternative Approaches to
Learni
ng Discussion
AMERCATH@UKCC.BITNET    LISTSERV@UKCC.BITNET    History of American
Catholicism
America@xamiga.linet.org        subscribe@xamiga.linet.org      American
Governm
ent
AMFCH-L@UCHCECVM.BITNET LISTSERV@UCHCECVM.BITNET        Noticias Acerca de la
Co
operacion Franco-Chile
AMIGA-TR@TREARN.BITNET  LISTSERV@TREARN.BITNET  Turk Amigacilar listesi...
AMINT-L@PSUVM.BITNET    LISTSERV@PSUVM.BITNET   Academy of Management
Internatio
nal
AMLIT-L@UMCVMB.BITNET   LISTSERV@UMCVMB.BITNET  American Literature
Discussion L
ist
AMWEST-H@USCVM.BITNET   LISTSERV@USCVM.BITNET   American West History Forum
ANCIEN-L@ULKYVM.BITNET  LISTSERV@ULKYVM.BITNET  History of the Ancient
Mediterra
nean
```


The NEW-LIST New Mailing List List

The NEW-LIST mailing list provides announcements of new mailing lists. To subscribe via

> **e-mail.** LISTSERV@NDSUVM1.BITNET with SUB NEW-LIST Yourfirstname Yourlastname in the body
> **Usenet.** bit.listserv.new-list

You can also search a database of information in "interest-groups," "list of lists," and the "new-list" interest group. Letting a computer search for mailing lists that interest you certainly beats perusing megabyte-long lists yourself. For information on accessing the database, send e-mail to LISTSERV@NDSUVM1.BITNET with INFO DATABASE in the body.

Here's an example of a list announced on the Usenet's bit.listserv.new-list:

```
ABooks-L on ListProc@scu.edu.au

   ANet is a networked electronic forum in the broad accounting and
   auditing discipline.  It has been established by Southern Cross
   University in conjunction with the School of Business at Bond
   University.

   ANet announces ABooks-L.  A mailing list which allows authors and
   publishers to advertise the arrival of new books in the broad
   accounting and auditing discipline.  Be warned - unashamed
   advertising allowed.

   To subscribe to the ABooks-L mailing list, send a message to the
   mailing list management software:
      ListProc@scu.edu.au
   with the following text in the body of the e-mail:

      subscribe ABooks-L firstname surname

   Archives of this ANet mailing list are held and can be accessed by
   sending a message to:
      ListProc@scu.edu.au
   with the following text in the body of the e-mail:

      index ABooks-L

   The archives are also available from the ANet Gopher (see signature
   below) or by anonymous FTP from "anet.scu.edu.au".

   Roger Debreceny, ANet,            |E-mail: ANetAdm@ANet.scu.edu.au
   The Intl. Accounting Network      |Fax:    +61 66 22 1724
   Faculty of Business and Computing |Phone:  +61 66 20 3837
   Southern Cross University         |ANet is a co-operative venture
   PO Box 157                        |between Southern Cross Uni
   Lismore, NSW, 2480, Australia     |& Bond University.
   +-----------------------------------------------------------------+
   |For background on ANet, email "ANet@scu.edu.au". No text needed. |
   |ANet Gopher URL -> gopher://ANet.scu.edu.au/11/anet/             |
   |ANet Home Page  -> http://ANet.scu.edu.au/ANetHomePage.html       |
   |Can you help by becoming an Associate of ANet? Contact ANetAdm   |
   +-----------------------------------------------------------------+
```

For More Information

If you want to know still more ways to find mailing lists of interest, read the FAQ "How to find an interesting mailing list," edited by Arno Wouters (`Arno.Wouters@phil.ruu.nl`). Available are:

> **e-mail.** `listserv@vm1.nodak.edu` with `GET NEW-LIST WOUTERS` in the body
>
> **anonymous FTP.** `vm1.nodak.edu:/new-list/new-list.wouters`

Q 4.31. What is MIME?

MIME stands for *Multipurpose Internet Mail Extensions.* MIME beefs up the capability of electronic mail so that it can handle more than boring, low ASCII text (letters, numbers, and punctuation). If dull 80-column, single-font text is beginning to bore you, consider that with MIME, you can send and receive multimedia e-mail messages with a variety of beautiful fonts and color pictures.

MIME makes e-mail more powerful by adding the capability to exchange messages in languages with different character sets and with character sets other than ASCII. MIME mail can also include pictures, sounds, PostScript images, file pointers to FTP sites, and other good stuff.

MIME isn't a program; it's a specification. Many of today's e-mail programs understand the MIME specification, but remember that not everyone has access to programs that understand MIME. If you aren't sure whether your message's recipients can read MIME messages, stick with plain old text, the lowest common denominator of electronic mail.

Discussions about MIME take place on the Usenet's `comp.mail.mime` newsgroup. There is also a mailing list gatewayed with `comp.mail.mime`. If you are unable to read Usenet news, send a subscription request to `info-mime-request@thumper.bellcore.com`.

If you're in the United Kingdom, you can receive info-mime by sending a request to `info-mime-uk-request@mailbase.ac.uk`.

An overview of the MIME specification is available by FTP from ftp.netcom.com:pub/mdg/mime.txt for the text version or ftp.netcom.com:pub/mdg/mime.ps for the PostScript version.

For more information, read the comp.mail.mime frequently asked questions list on Usenet at comp.mail.mime or available by FTP from rtfm.mit.edu:/pub/usenet/comp.mail.mime/c.m.m_f_a_q_l_(F)_(1_3).

Q 4.32. Can I send a fax from the Internet?

Indeed. Electronic mail is not limited to sending information between Internet hosts. Creative folks have plugged a variety of appliances into the Internet, including toasters, cola machines, and fax machines. In fact, there are several services for sending a fax via Internet mail; some are free but others are pay services. (With at least one service, users can receive a fax via Internet mail.) Four mail-to-fax services that I know about are discussed in the following text. Others will likely be available by the time you read this.

Free "Remote Printing"

One fax-from-the-Internet service is the brainchild of Carl Malamud (the creator of Internet Talk Radio) and Marshall Rose. They're doing research on how to integrate special-purpose devices, like facsimile printers, into the fabric of the Internet. The experiment is a good hack. It works simply enough: send electronic mail to a special address and soon after (if your recipient's fax machine is in the covered area) out comes a freshly-minted fax.

How does it work? A variety of companies, institutions, and citizens linked to the Internet have joined the experiment by linking a computer and fax modem to the Net. When an organization joins the remote-fax service, it specifies what areas it is willing to send faxes to. In most cases, an organization will allow faxes to be sent to any machine that is a local call from its location.

This service itself is free; rather, it costs no more than sending a standard e-mail message. Malamud wrote in an e-mail message, "First, it costs you money to send e-mail... so faxing is not free, it is cost-effective and distance-insensitive." The recipient is only out the cost of a sheet or two of fax paper. However, the creators are investigating ways of recouping a nominal fee for sending faxes to help reimburse institutions for the cost of sending faxes.

"The point of this experiment is not 'here is a way we can freeload on altruistic people,' but 'here is a way we can all pitch in and work together to provide telephone service,'" Malamud says.

When you send an e-mail fax message, you (naturally) must include the phone number of the recipient's fax machine. A computer looks at the phone number and determines whether any participating fax machines cover the area you want to fax to. If so, your message is routed to the appropriate machine for faxing. Otherwise, you will receive electronic mail with the disappointing news that your fax couldn't be delivered.

Can you send a fax anywhere? Well, no. This is an experiment, so only a smattering of participants have enlisted their fax machines in the quest to send outgoing messages from total strangers to other total strangers. As this is written, the set of locales to which you can send faxes is bizarre, including all of Australia, New Zealand, Washington DC, big chunks of Central California, some of Southern California, and parts of Michigan, Massachusetts, and New York. More locales undoubtedly will be added to the list soon, including Denmark, Finland, Ireland, Japan, Sweden, and more parts of the United States.

To send a fax over the Internet, compose an e-mail message. The body of the message should contain the contents of your fax message. The `To:` line is the most important part of your fax-mail, because it must contain the phone number of the recipient's fax machine as well as the recipient's name.

The `To:` line should look something like this:

```
To: remote-printer.Arlo_Cats/
Room_123@12025551212.iddd.tpc.int
```

To the left of the `@` symbol, you must include the identity of the recipient. The words `remote-printer` tell the fax server the type of access. (In this case, faxing or remote printing.) Because some mailers have difficulty dealing with addresses that contain spaces, you should be careful as to what characters you use to identify the recipient. It is safest to use upper- and lowercase letters, digits, the _ and the / character. When the fax cover sheet is generated, the _ will turn into a space and the / will become a line break. So the preceding address would generate a cover sheet such as

Please deliver this facsimile to

```
Arlo Cats
Room 123
```

The mess of numbers to the right of the preceding example identifies the telephone number of the remote fax machine. Exchanges must be specified by country code and phone number. This means you must specify the country code and then the phone number of your intended recipient. If you're sending to a machine in the U.S., you need only send a 1, the area code, and the phone number. Next, add the Internet domain `.iddd.tpc.int.`

You can send a fax to multiple fax machines or even a combination of faxes and traditional e-mail recipients. After the deed is done, you will receive electronic mail telling you whether your fax was successfully sent.

For more information or for a copy of the Frequently Asked Questions list on faxing from the Net, send mail to `tpc-faq@town.hall.or`, and you will automatically receive the FAQ via e-mail. The FAQ also covers advanced topics such as using MIME to send fancy formatted text or graphics and how to operate your own fax server for the good of the world.

Fax sites are being added to the network on a regular basis. For a current list of faxable areas, send e-mail to `tpc-coverage@town.hall.org`. There is also a mailing list for discussion of the fax service and its implementation. To join, send a request to `tpc-rp-request@aarnet.edu.au`.

InterFax

You can use InterFax to send faxes via e-mail within the U.S. or internationally. InterFax costs money to use (billed to your credit card) but, unlike the remote printing experiment described previously, with InterFax you can send faxes anywhere, not just to select locations. As of this writing, InterFax costs $5 per month, which includes the first five fax pages. Additional pages cost 50 cents each.

There is a one-time sign-up charge of $25. For further information, send e-mail to `faxmaster@pan.com` or contact InterFax at PO Box 162, Skippack, PA 19474 USA. (215) 584-0300; FAX: (215)584-1038.

FAXiNET

Another fax-by-mail service is FAXiNET, with which you can send any text (ASCII) or PostScript documents to fax machines worldwide. FAXiNET can send faxes to more than 50 countries and plans to add more. The company also says it can receive faxes for you, which will be delivered to you via electronic mail. I haven't used their service, but if it works, the ability to receive faxes in e-mail is a unique one.

Accounts for individuals cost 75 cents per page, plus a one-time $20 activation fee. Additional services, including adding your custom logo and signature to your faxes, are available at extra cost. Corporate accounts are also available.

More information is available from AnyWare Associates, FAXiNET, 32 Woodland Road, Boston, MA 02130. (617) 522-8102. E-mail: `sales@awa.com`

Unigate—for Faxing to Russia

Unigate is another pay-for-use service that you can use to send faxes to and from Russia and the Commonwealth of Independent States. Unigate is a commercial service that also handles "snail mail." Most of us probably don't need to fax Russia, but if you should need to, Unigate is probably much less expensive than whatever method you're using now. Fax service from USA to Russia (or back) is $1.59 per page. I've never needed to fax Russia, so for more information, e-mail `yuri@atmos.washington.edu`.

Q 4.33. How can I find out about users on an Internet system?

By `finger`ing them. `finger` is a program that returns information about a registered user on a computer. Typing `finger` alone will show the users who are logged into the system you are using. `finger @host.domain.foo` may show you who's currently using some other computer on the Internet. Certain computers have variations on `finger` support, where `finger ron` will show information on `ron` at your site, and `finger ron@hal.gnu.ai.mit.edu` will show you all the `rons` with accounts on a certain computer at MIT.

Note that some finger programs don't take arguments, some will accept only a userid (the exact login name of a user,), and still others will search using a first or last name. If your system has manual pages installed, type `man finger` for more information. If your system has Internet access but not `finger`, there are several freely distributable versions, including GNU finger and BSD finger.

Here's an example:

```
bolero[3] finger ron@hal.gnu.ai.mit.edu
[hal.gnu.ai.mit.edu]
Users who have 'ron' in their names:

Aaron Putnam (putnam)
Home: /home/fsg/putnam
Shell: /usr/local/bin/cracked
No mail.
Aaron Putnam (putnam) is not presently logged in.
Last seen at hal.gnu.ai.mit.edu on Sun Apr  5 14:03:27 1992


No plan.

Carol Botteron (botteron)
Home: /home/gp/botteron
Shell: /bin/csh
New mail since Tue Feb 22 00:30:55 1994
Has not read mail for 13:52:00.
Carol Botteron (botteron) is not presently logged in.
Last seen at geech.gnu.ai.mit.edu on Mon Feb 21 13:15:05 1994


No plan.

Ronnie Gay Strong (strongr)
Home: /home/fsg/strongr
Shell: /usr/local/gnubin/bash
No mail.
Ronnie Gay Strong (strongr) is not presently logged in.
Last seen at hal.gnu.ai.mit.edu on Tue Feb 23 10:22:49 1993
```

4.34. How can I let others know more about myself?

People will learn about you and form opinions about you based on the words and actions you use on the Net. The newsgroups you frequent, your sense of humor (if any), and your opinions will be duly noted by the masses. There are more overt ways of making information available about yourself. Among them are the `finger` command and your `electronic mail and Usenet posting` "signature."

finger and Your Plan

Systems that support the `finger` command can typically show basic information about you and your account, such as your name, when you last read your electronic mail, and whether you are currently logged on. Your mileage may vary; there are nearly as many implementations of `finger` as there are computers on the Internet.

On many systems, you can add to the information provided by `finger`. UNIX computers (and others) allow you to create a file in your home directory called `.plan`. Your plan file will be appended to your vital statistics whenever anyone `finger`s your account. At last, you can share your life's plan with the world. If you were to `finger` me on the day I wrote this, you would see what's below. Everything after "On since..." is my plan file, but it's there because it's information I think anyone `finger`ing me might want to know.

4

```
Login: waffle                                Name: Kevin Savetz
Directory: /files/home/waffle                Shell: /local/bin/tcsh
Mail last read Wed Jan 19 17:06:52 1994
On since Wed Jan 19 21:45 (PST) on ttyp9

Freelance computer journalist.
Publisher of the Internet Services Frequently Asked Questions List.
  This file is posted weekly to the newsgroup "alt.internet.services"
  and posted twice monthly to "news.answers" and "alt.answers" It is also
  available via anonymous FTP:
  rtfm.mit.edu:/pub/usenet/news.answers/internet-services/faq

Author, "Your Internet Consultant - the FAQs of Life Online" (Sams
Publishing.)
```

Your Signature

Your “signature” may be automatically appended to your postings to the Usenet and electronic mail, depending on what news and mail software you use. Check with the manual for your favorite software to learn how to make it do this.

Your signature can be a few lines that briefly tell others who you are or how to contact you. Some signatures contain cute quotes, disclaimers that the writer’s opinions aren’t necessarily the opinions of his employer, and a myriad of other information. Here are a few examples:

```
[ Kevin M. Savetz -- savetz@rahul.net              ]
[                 -- faq-book-info@northcoast.net ]
```

And one that’s a little more elaborate.

```
Grady Ward       ¦ compiler of Moby lexicons:       ¦ finger grady@netcom.com
+1 707 826 7715  ¦ Words, Hyphenator, Part-of-Speech ¦    for more information
(voice/24hr FAX) ¦ Pronunciator, Thesaurus          ¦ 15 E2 AD D3 D1 C6 F3 FC
grady@netcom.com ¦ and Language, all royalty-free   ¦ 58 AC F7 3D 4F 01 1E 2F

E. Jay O'Connell___________________________________ejo@world.std.com
"God does not play dice with the Universe"--A Einstein
"No, she plays SuperScratch-Card Wingo (TM)"--Me.
___________________________________________________________________
```

Be careful about what information you share with the world in your signature and plan files. Think twice—or three or four times—before publishing your home phone number, credit card number, shoe size, or other information that will make you miserable when 14 million of your closest neighbors have it.

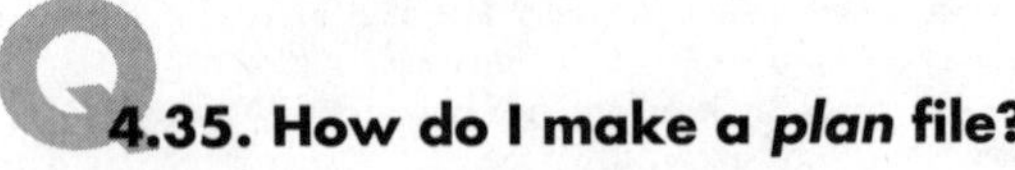

4.35. How do I make a *plan* file?

This will work on UNIX systems and its variants. You can also create a file called *.project* in a similar manner, but this can only be one line. The project line will also be displayed when you’re `fingered`.

1. Go to your home directory by typing `cd`.
2. Create and edit a file called `.plan` and fill it with good stuff by typing `vi .plan` (you can use your favorite text editor in place of vi).
3. Make `.plan` readable by everyone by typing `chmod a+r .plan`.
4. Make your home directory searchable by everyone by typing `chmod +x .` (don't forget the period on the end).

4.36. How do I create a "signature file"?

1. Go to your home directory by typing `cd`.
2. Create and edit a file called `.signature` and give your name, rank, and serial number by typing `vi .signature` (use your favorite text editor in place of vi).
3. Make .plan readable by everyone by typing `chmod a+r .signature`.
4. Make your home directory searchable by everyone by typing `chmod +x .` (don't forget the period on the end).

Check with the instructions for your Usenet news and e-mail software to learn what (if anything) you'll need to do to tell it to append your signature to messages.

4.37. How can I best annoy people with my signature?

This question isn't actually frequently asked, but perhaps it should be. Allow me to climb (once again) on my soapbox…

1. Make a very long signature file. Make sure that it exceeds the length of any Usenet post or e-mail message you send. (Many systems, run by fascist system administrators intent on stifling your creativity, truncate signature files after four lines.)
2. Draw a picture out of ASCII characters and put that in your signature. Use tabs instead of spaces so that your picture doesn't even look right.

3. Somehow goof so that every message you send has two or three signatures.

There are other ways to annoy people with your signature, which are left as an exercise for you to do. Use discretion.

If you want to be annoyed by other people's signatures, read the newsgroup `alt.fan.warlords`, which is devoted to critiquing signatures that go too far. Here's an example of what you'll find there:

```
>           /\
>          / /
>         /\ \/\
>         \ \  /  __
>       __ \ \/  / .\__
>....../ .\_\/../\  __/
.........................................................
>     /\  __/  / /\ \       __________
>    / /\ \   /\  /\/    .- __   / -- -\          Eric Uner
>   / /\/\/   \ \  /    / <___> ___ ¦ ¦\-         ericu@comm.mot.com
>   \  / /  ___\ \/  .^¦ _--_ /   \ =   / \
>    \  /o / ____/   ¦o ¦  =  / o ¦ ¦   ¦¦  ¦     Motorola, Schaumburg, IL
>     \/  /\ \       =0=======0==¦  ¦----¦  ¦=
>      o  \ \ \       \_\_/    \_\_/   \_\_/
>        /\ \ \/
>        \ \/ /  It's an Oval Window, It's a Sunroof, It's a 3.0L!
>........\  /
.....................................................................
>          \/
```

This one was also posted to `alt.fan.warlords`. Although I'm pretty fond of this one, most users would ask that you keep this carp off the Usenet. : -)

```
>                                                    .             ,
>                                                                .:/
>     Rosemary Dean Mackintosh                        .       ,,///;,   ,;/
>     rosemary@clam.rutgers.edu                         .    o:::::::;;///
>"Set the gearshift to the high gear of your soul!"        >::::::::;;\\\
>                                                           ''\\\\\'" ';\
>                                                              ';\
```

4.38 How can I change how my name appears?

On some UNIX systems you can change some of the information about you, such as your name and office location by typing `chfn`, which stands for "change finger name."

If `chfn` is not available, try typing `passwd -f`.

For more information see the `chfn`, `passwd`, and `finger` manual pages or online help.

4.39. How do I send e-mail to the White House?

You can send e-mail to the President at `president@whitehouse.gov`. Mail for the Vice-President should be sent to `vice.president@whitehouse.gov`. Although you may receive a confirmation that your e-mail was received, be sure to include your name and address; the White House sends form letter responses only by snail mail.

According to an article by Michael Strangelove in the January, 1994, issue of *Online Access* magazine, messages sent to the White House are actually processed 30 miles away by the computers of Trusted Information Systems in Glenwood, Maryland. TIS processes between 1,000 and 6,000 e-mail messages for the White House daily. Strangelove writes, "You have a better chance of receiving a personal reply from Elvis than you do from Bill."

4.40. Wow! I just got e-mail from Elvis! (Is it possible to forge e-mail?)

A few years back, I started receiving electronic mail from `Easter.Bunny@never.never.land`. Mr. Bunny, ever a kind-hearted soul, wanted to know what color eggs I wanted come Easter. It didn't take an expert Internaut to discover there was no `never.never.land` on the Internet, and there is certainly no Easter Bunny. Sad but true on both counts.

Although silly and harmless, I had received forged electronic messages. It is indeed possible to forge electronic mail, making it appear to the untrained eye that it came from a user that didn't really send it. If you should receive mail from the Easter Bunny or Brooke Shields, or if you get mail that doesn't sound like it came from someone you know, although it seems to be signed by that person, try to confirm that the message is legitimate before proceeding. Forged e-mail is not common, but it's something to keep in mind.

4.41. How can I forge electronic mail?

I'm not answering that here, no way, no how. Maybe I'll write an article for *2600* magazine about it one day, but until then, I'll tell you this: Forging electronic mail is easy… once you know how to do it.

4.42. Wow! Did I really get e-mail from Santa Claus?

Quite possibly, if you sent mail to him first. Lately, around December, electronic mail Santa servers have been popping up on the Net. You can send Santa your wish list, and when he has time he'll send an e-mail reply. Here's what my letter from Santa looked like. (By the way, Santa granted only one of my wishes!)

```
From daemon Thu Dec 23 07:54:05 1993
Date: Thu, 23 Dec 93 10:19:58 -0500
To: Kevin Savetz <savetz@rahul.net>
From: "Santa Claus" <Santa@north.pole.org>
Organization: The North Pole (A Public Benefit Corporation)
Subject: Re: Dear Santa

> Dear Santa,
>
> All I want for Christmas is a decent SLIP or PPP connection locally.
> Oh, and I'd like my book contract to go through.

Greetings from the North Pole! What a week, what a week! Its really busy
getting ready for the big day. We've been feeding the reindeer extra carrots
and the elves are all looking forward to a week on the beach.
```

```
Do you realize that we have to visit 2 billion children in one night? That's
822.6 visits per second, barely enough time to snarf down those cookies!

I've checked my database (twice) and its clear that you've been very good
this year. I'm going to do the very best I can to get you all the neat
stuff that you are hoping for. Still, when all is said done, I hope you get
peace and happiness in 1994, the best presents of all.

Merry Christmas and a Happy New Year!

Santa Claus
(and the Elves! *<:-))
The North Pole

P.S. Rudolph sends his regards. He's drooling all over the rug just thinking
about all those carrots and stuff kids are leaving out for him. What a mess,
what a mess!
```

CHAPTER 5

Where Can I Discuss My Favorite Film, Food, or Fetish...and Just About Anything Else?

Usenet is world's largest distributed bulletin board system, shared by millions of people using hundreds of thousands of computers scattered along the Internet highway. Folks on the Usenet talk about everything—everything!—you can think of, from square dancing to motorcycle maintenance...from the Swedish Chef to Ronald Reagan.

5.1. What is the Usenet?

Answered by Dave Taylor (`taylor@netcom.com`*)*

If you've spent any time near the so-called information highway that is today's Internet, you can't help but hear about all these fantastic netnews groups that are part of something called the *Usenet.* Not a network in the common sense of the word (that is, a bunch of wires connecting machines together), the Usenet acts like more of an intellectual connection system, where you can become involved in any of thousands of specialized groups discussing topics ranging from suicide and Pakistani culture to modem protocols, C++ programming, hang-gliding, or upcoming Grateful Dead concerts.

The Usenet is simply the largest, most active, and most varied discussion forum in the world. Imagine a bulletin board on the wall. Imagine that as people pass it, they glance at what's there, and if they have something to add, they stick their note up, too. Now (here's the big leap), imagine that there are thousands of bulletin boards in this building, and that there are actually tens of thousands of buildings throughout the world, each with its own identical copy of the bulletin boards. Got it? That's Usenet.

Usenet was created in 1979 when two graduate students at Duke University, Tom Truscott and Jim Ellis, hooked their computer to another at the University of North Carolina. In 1980, there were *two* sites with Usenet. At the end of 1993, there were an estimated 120,000 sites on Usenet, representing over 4.2 million participants.

A true experiment in free speech and barely controlled anarchy, the Usenet's range of discussions, called *newsgroups,* is astonishing, all the way from computer modem protocols (on `comp.dcom.modem`) to Macintosh programming (on `comp.sys.mac.programmer`) to topics of relevance to single men and women (on `soc.singles`) abortion (on `talk.abortion`) and even the wonderful TV show Mystery Science Theater 3000 (on `alt.tv.mst3k`).

5.2. How does the Usenet work?

Answered by Dave Taylor (`taylor@netcom.com`)

To understand what Usenet is, you need some idea of how it works. First, there is no central Usenet authority, unlike online services such as CompuServe or AppleLink. All systems participating in the Usenet act like super copying machines, in that an article that you send to the Usenet (this is commonly known as a *posting*) is saved on your local machine and an exact duplicate is sent to a group of other machines that your system "talks" to directly. Each of these machines keeps its copy and forwards duplicates to the machines that it talks with, and so on, until your words might well have been duplicated tens of thousands of times!

The great thing about this strategy for distributing postings is that at any given time your local system will have all the relevant postings in the groups that you're interested in reading, with more coming in hourly (if not more frequently!). Because they're all on your local computer, you can usually read the group or groups that interest you quickly, certainly without any lag as a central system doles out individual items. Indeed, many people actually set up their home computer systems to have the Usenet articles sent to them automatically. Then they can use Mac or Windows newsreading software to peruse the new information at their leisure.

Q 5.3. How is the Usenet organized?

Because I cringe at the assumption that the Usenet is actually organized, this one is also answered by Dave Taylor (`taylor@netcom.com`).

In the beginnings of the Usenet, back in the early 80s, all newsgroups were organized under a single umbrella prefix of `net`, so a group discussing editors was called `net.editors` (you should always pronounce the . as *dot*, so this group would be called *net dot editors*) and a group that focused on social issues important to single people was called `net.singles`.

Around the middle of the 80s, it became clear that this organization wasn't going to work too well and was causing confusion. Instead, a seven-part hierarchy was suggested, where sets of groups were organized by major topic: all computer-related discussion fell into the `comp.` hierarchy, recreational activities were put in the `rec.` hierarchy, and so on. In the last few years, the Usenet has dramatically increased in size and now has considerably more than just the original seven. On my main news machine, Netcom, I can find an astounding 284 different top-level newsgroup domains (*domain* is a fancy, but common, way of talking about the top level names for each group. For example, `comp.` is the domain of the computer-related discussion groups).

Q 5.4. What are the Usenet's top-level domains?

Usenet newsgroups are divided into broad categories. Groups that are distributed worldwide are split into seven classifications: `comp`, `misc`, `news`, `rec`, `soc`, `sci`, and `talk`. Each of these classifications is organized into groups and subgroups according to topic.

> **`comp` groups are topics in computer science and information on hardware and software systems.** Groups are9 of interest to hobbyists as well as computer professionals. Examples are `comp.apps.spreadsheets`, `comp.binaries.atari.st`, `comp.databases.object`, and `comp.lang.scheme`.
>
> **`misc` groups address themes that are not easily classified under any of the other headings or which incorporate themes from multiple categories.** Examples are `misc.jobs.offered`, `misc.misc`, `misc.invest`, and `misc.books.technical`.
>
> **`news` groups are concerned with the Usenet news network and associated software.** Examples are `news.announce.newusers`, `news.software.readers`, and `news.groups`.
>
> **`rec.` groups are oriented towards the arts, hobbies, and recreational activities.** Examples are `rec.arts.comics.strips`, `rec.arts.sf.starwars`, `rec.autos.antique`, `rec.radio.amateur.policy`, and `rec.sport.baseball.college`.
>
> **`sci` groups are discussions marked by special, and usually practical knowledge, relating to research in or application of the established sciences.** Examples are `sci.bio.technology`, `sci.physics.research`, and `sci.skeptic`.
>
> **`soc` groups address social issues and socializing.** Examples are: `soc.culture.african.american`, `soc.religion.quaker`, and `soc.rights.human`.
>
> **`talk` groups are largely debate-oriented and tend to feature long discussions without resolution and without appreciable amounts of generally useful information.** For example: `talk.politics.guns`, `talk.rape`, and `talk.rumors`.

Some hierarchies exist that are not formally a part of Usenet because they have different conventions than mainstream newsgroups. For example,

`alt.` groups are an anarchic alternative to mainstream Usenet groups. These groups are not carried on all systems. Although *alt.* stands for *alternative*, note that some of the best stuff on Usenet is part of the `alt.` hierarchy. (`alt.` groups are an alternative to the "big seven" news domains and not necessarily discussions of an alternative nature.) Because the creation of `alt.` groups is less formal than standard groups, you are likely to find some funky topics here. Examples are `alt.alien.visitors`, `alt.internet.services`, `alt.architecture.alternative`, `alt.banjo`, and `alt.barney.dinosaur.die.die.die`

`bit` groups are a collection of newsgroups distributed only by sites that choose to carry them. The bit newsgroups are redistributions of the more popular Bitnet Listserv mailing lists. Examples are `bit.org.peace-corps`, `bit.listserv.aidsnews`, `bit.listserv.wx-talk`, and `bit.listserv.hindu-d`.

`biz` groups are for business-related postings. Here you'll find company press releases, product information and other commercial traffic. Examples are `biz.comp.telebit.netblazer` and `biz.zeos.announce`.

`k12` groups are carried at some sites. Their content is aimed at kindergarten, elementary and secondary teachers, and students. Examples are `k12.chat.elementary`, `k12.ed.art`, and `k12.ed.life-skills`.

`clari` groups come from ClariNet Communications and are only available on systems that pay for them. These groups feature wire service news and syndicated columnists such as Miss Manners and Dave Barry. For more information, read the answer to "Where on the Internet can I find national and world news?" in Chapter 7, "How Do I Track Down Information?" Examples of ClariNet groups are `clari.feature.dave-barry`, `clari.world.europe.eastern`, and `clari.news.books`.

> Even if you don't get the full ClariNet feed, you can probably see a sample of what they do on `biz.clarinet.sample`. (For more information on ClariNet, call 1-800/USE-NETS.)

One other hierarchy worth further discussion is the `alt.` organizational domain. The `alt.` groups are the most anarchic arm of the Usenet. Although some controls have been placed on the creation of new newsgroups in the "big seven" Usenet hierarchies, there are no such restrictions for `alt.` groups. In the interest of letting the Usenet sprawl and evolve without too many constraints, the alt. domain is the one space where newsgroups can be created without a consensus from the masses (this is covered later in the chapter); if you want a group, create it!

The results of this are, predictably, some weird groups that sometimes have no discussion within and are attempts at humor, sarcasm, or something similar. If you've ever seen the Muppet Show you might remember Jim Henson's Swedish Chef who was often caught chopping madly and saying, "bork bork bork." Someone created a newsgroup called `alt.swedish.chef.bork.bork.bork`—and somehow that hit a popular note on the Net. Now there are a variety of newsgroups in the `alt.` domain that have similar names. Examples:

> alt.adjective.noun.verb.verb.verb
>
> alt.american.automobile.breakdown.breakdown.breakdown
>
> alt.american.olympians.choke.choke.choke
>
> alt.christnet.bible-thumpers.convert.convert.convert

Notice that no topics are off-limits here and people often create groups that are of interest for a few weeks, or days, and then vanish.

Various sex-related groups have popped up within the `alt.` domain too, including `alt.sex.movies`, `alt.sex.bondage`, `alt.sex.motss`, `alt.binaries.pictures.erotica`, and `alt.sex.fetish.foot`. The Usenet is chockablock with acronyms; MOTSS stands for "members of the same sex," the topic covering gay, lesbian and bisexual issues and interests.

Another interesting space within the `alt.` domain is a set of groups that are for fans of specific individuals. The list of people is extensive (over 100) and range from people such as Dan Quayle, Rush Limbaugh, Gene Scott, and Clarence Thomas; to authors such as

Tom Robbins, Dave Barry, Douglas Adams, and Piers Anthony; to musicians and music groups such as Madonna, Run DMC, Spinal Tap, Wang Chung, Devo, and Laurie Anderson. If you like a person or group, chances are someone else does too!

Q 5.5. What is a local newsgroup?

Thousands of newsgroups are *local* where discussions are in and about specific geographic areas. These newsgroups are a great way to communicate with folks in your city, state, college, or country, but they're usually wholly uninteresting to everyone outside that area. There is at least one local newsgroup for every state and province in the U.S. and Canada plus thousands more for people in every country that's plugged into the Internet. Local groups allow New Yorkers to discuss the best restaurants in New York City, for example, but not waste disk space on a machine in Sao Paulo or Hong Kong.

The names of local newsgroups look just like global Usenet groups, except the first part is an initial for the location name. For example, `atl` groups are for Atlanta, Georgia, and `ab` groups are for Alberta, Canada. Here are some examples:

`ab.general`	Items of general interest in Alberta, Canada
`ab.jobs`	Jobs in Alberta, Canada
`ab.politics`	Discussion of politics in Alberta, Canada.
`atl.general`	Items of general interest in Atlanta, GA.
`atl.jobs`	Jobs in Atlanta, GA
`atl.olympics`	The Olympics in Atlanta, GA
`atl.resumes`	Resumes in Atlanta, GA

5

Other local newsgroups have different prefixes. For example:

`aus`	Australia
`ba`	San Francisco Bay Area
`bc`	British Columbia
`bln`	Berlin
`boulder`	Boulder, Colorado
`brasil`	Brazil
`br`	Britain

`ca`	California
`cam`	Cambridge, Massachusetts
`dk`	Denmark
`hsv`	Huntsville, Alabama
`pnw`	Pacific Northwest
`ri`	Rhode Island
`tamu`	Texas A&M University

To find local newsgroups in your area, try using your newsreader to search for groups with your location's initials or name. (Use the initials of your state, province, or country.) Of course. you can also ask someone in the know (such as your system administrator) what your local newsgroups are called.

Dave Taylor says, "There are also organizational domains within companies on the Internet and network access firms like Netcom, Software Tool and Die, and the Whole Earth 'Lectronic Link. These can be recognized by the similarity between the domain name and the organizational name. Some examples: `hp.` are groups within Hewlett-Packard, `apple.` for Apple Computer, `purdue.` for Purdue University, `ucb.` for the University of California at Berkeley, `netcom.` for Netcom local newsgroups, `world.` for The World, and `well.` for the Whole Earth 'Lectronic Link. You probably won't be able to access most of these—particularly the corporate ones that often are a hotbed for discussion of company internal information and projects.

5.6. How many Usenet newsgroups are there?

In January, 1994, there were about 7,000 newsgroups, with 20 to 30 being added every week. Reading the entire list reveals an incredible breadth of human experience, and insight into the teeming melting pot of cultures and languages on the Net. It's also a good way to waste an afternoon.

5.7. Where can I find a list of all the Usenet newsgroups?

If your system carries Usenet, you might have a file called `/usr/lib/news/newsgroups`, which contains just the information you seek. Try typing `more /usr/lib/news/newsgroups` to view it.

If you don't have that file, you should know that a list of active newsgroups, many including descriptions, is available via FTP from `ftp.uu.net:/networking/news/config/newsgroups.Z`. (You'll need to uncompress this file with the UNIX `uncompress` command before reading it.) It is also posted occasionally to the Usenet newsgroup `news.lists`.

The list looks something like this, only much longer:

```
alt.1d                  One-dimensional imaging, & the thinking behind it.
alt.2600                The magazine or the game system.  You decide.
alt.3d                  Three-dimensional imaging.
alt.abortion.inequity   Paternal obligations of failing to abort unwanted
child.
alt.abuse.recovery      Helping victims of abuse to recover.
alt.activism            Activities for activists.
alt.activism.d          A place to discuss issues in alt.activism.
alt.activism.death-penalty      For people opposed to capital punishment.
alt.adoption            For those involved with or contemplating adoption.
alt.aeffle.und.pferdle  German cartoon characters das Aeffle und das Pferdle.
alt.agriculture.misc    All about cultivating the soil and raising animals.
alt.aldus.pagemaker     Don't use expensive user support, come here instead.
alt.alien.visitors      Space Aliens on Earth!  Abduction!  Gov't Coverup!
alt.amateur-comp        Discussion and input for Amateur Computerist
Newsletter.
alt.amazon-women.admirers       Worshiping women you have to look up to.
alt.amiga.demos         Amiga demonstration programs.
alt.amiga.slip          ???
alt.angst               Anxiety in the modern world.
alt.animals.lampreys    They're eel-like, and they suck.
```

Q 5.8. How much stuff passes through the Usenet?

A lot! In the two-week period before I wrote these words, Usenet traffic approached 90 megabytes per day. You can find out how busy the Usenet is by reading the messages `Total traffic through uunet for the last 2 weeks`, which are posted periodically to the newsgroup `news.lists`. These messages detail the number and size of all the messages that pass through UUNET Communications, a major Internet hub and service provider. They also show what newsgroup hierarchies see the most use. Here's an example:

```
news.lists (moderated) #1013 (7 more)
From: newsstats@uunet.UU.NET
Subject: Total traffic through uunet for the last 2 weeks
Date: Mon Jan 24 09:08:44 PST 1994
Organization: UUNET Communications


673328 articles, totaling 1251.764104 Mbytes (1607.763435
including headers), were submitted from 43439 different
Usenet sites by 141421 different users to 8910 different newsgroups
for an average of 89.411722 Mbytes (114.840245 including headers)
per day.

Only categories receiving an average of 1 or more article per day
are listed.
                                  Article                 Total
        Category          Count   Mbytes        Percent  Mbytes
        alt              173977 558.572659       44.6%  655.361424
        rec              138678 210.941356       16.9%  282.061621
        comp             116142 181.985099       14.5%  243.368251
        soc               52397 110.112458        8.8%  140.527408
        misc              26957  39.500316        3.2%   53.869506
        talk              18405  39.457156        3.2%   51.367199
        de                10700  37.951659        3.0%   44.142952
        sci               19820  34.986043        2.8%   45.692273
        bit               22798  33.823799        2.7%   50.226438
        news               4450  28.623819        2.3%   31.309438
        relcom            34356  28.225976        2.3%   51.535220
        zer               18443  26.276050        2.1%   39.191961
        clari             34149  25.542684        2.0%   44.816616
        fj                10013  19.357237        1.5%   25.526185
        cbd                7119   9.626486        0.8%   12.965948
        americast          2857   8.750183        0.7%    9.900073
        maus              12481   7.078011        0.6%   14.258556
        ba                 5214   6.660749        0.5%    9.211163
        ncar               4229   5.991553        0.5%    7.817455
        sfnet              4466   5.332375        0.4%    7.700691
        gnu                2119   4.938273        0.4%    6.053602
        ca                 1607   4.605775        0.4%    5.455496
```

Q 5.9. What are the most heavily used newsgroups?

You can find out which Usenet newsgroups have the highest volume of messages by checking the newsgroup `news.lists`. This newsgroup features fascinating up-to-date statistics about Usenet use. In particular, the periodic posting called `Top 25 News Groups for the last 2 weeks` will tell you what newsgroups that passed through UUNET had the highest volume of messages.

The following list ranks newsgroups by number of kilobytes posted, not the number of articles. Digitized pictures and sounds use much more bandwidth than basic text messages, so it's not surprising that numerous newsgroups featuring `pictures` top the list. During this two week sample, erotica, politics, and sound effects were prominent.

Rank	Kbytes	No. of Articles	$ Cost per Site	% of Total	Cumulative % of Total	Group
1	82465.2	2369	217.62	6.6%	6.6%	alt.binaries.pictures.erotica
2	43757.3	1402	115.47	3.5%	10.1%	alt.binaries.pictures.misc
3	26838.1	552	70.82	2.1%	12.2%	alt.binaries.sounds.misc
4	19887.1	541	52.48	1.6%	13.8%	news.answers
5	18882.2	478	49.83	1.5%	15.3%	alt.binaries.pictures.erotica.male
6	16203.2	403	42.76	1.3%	16.6%	de.alt.binaries.pictures.relay-party
7	15739.7	765	41.54	1.3%	17.9%	alt.binaries.pictures.supermodels
8	11900.2	236	31.40	1.0%	18.8%	alt.binaries.sounds.movies
9	10786.6	429	28.46	0.9%	19.7%	alt.binaries.pictures.erotica.orientals
10	9357.1	369	24.69	0.7%	20.4%	alt.binaries.pictures.erotica.female
11	9160.6	199	24.17	0.7%	21.2%	alt.binaries.pictures.fractals
12	8597.6	3722	22.69	0.7%	21.9%	talk.politics.misc
13	7784.2	4383	20.54	0.6%	22.5%	cbd.procurements
14	7680.7	732	20.27	0.6%	23.1%	alt.binaries.pictures.utilities
15	7652.5	248	20.19	0.6%	23.7%	alt.binaries.pictures.tasteless
16	7624.3	190	20.12	0.6%	24.3%	comp.answers
17	7398.5	285	19.52	0.6%	24.9%	alt.binaries.pictures
18	7155.4	189	18.88	0.6%	25.5%	rec.answers
19	7098.0	3078	18.73	0.6%	26.0%	alt.fan.rush-limbaugh
20	6684.4	3592	17.64	0.5%	26.6%	talk.politics.guns
21	6056.4	165	15.98	0.5%	27.1%	alt.sex.pictures
22	5991.6	4229	15.81	0.5%	27.5%	ncar.weather
23	5931.0	518	15.65	0.5%	28.0%	alt.sex.stories
24	5824.5	133	15.37	0.5%	28.5%	de.alt.binaries.pictures.female
25	5138.0	1975	13.56	0.4%	28.9%	soc.culture.indian

Q 5.10. What program should I use to read news?

Dozens of programs exist with which you can read Usenet news. These pieces of software—appropriately called *newsreaders*—may be complex or simplistic, but they all show you the Usenet news. The programs available to you depend on what system you're reading news on. If you are accessing the Internet by running SLIP on a Macintosh, your choices are completely different than if you're dialing into a VAX to read news. Because the majority of Internet folks use UNIX, this answer focuses on popular newsreaders available for UNIX. A full overview of all newsreaders for every system could take a chapter of its own and bore us all to death.

If you do use a UNIX system, remember that not every site will have all of the following newsreaders, so your choices may be more limited. If you don't use UNIX, check with your system administrator to see what newsreaders are available to you.

> **NOTE** The following part of the answer was provided by Rahul Dhesi (`dhesi@rahul.net`)

You can read news by using any of a number of news reading programs. To help you decide which you should use, a brief description of each is given in the following text. Most Usenet users prefer to use `nn`, `trn`, or `tin`.

`readnews`. This is one of the simplest news readers available. It is line-oriented, so it does not make much use of cursor movements. It will show you each newsgroup one by one. Within each newsgroup, it will show you each article one by one. For each newsgroup or article, answer with `y` to see it or `n` to skip it. Due to the high volume of postings on Usenet, it will take you a long time to go through them with readnews; it is not very good at letting you select a small subset of articles to read except by answering yes or no to each. You should use readnews only if you want to get started reading news right away without spending much time learning to read news. As soon as you are comfortable with readnews, you should switch to one of the more powerful news readers.

vnews. This is screen-oriented, so it will position article headers and other information at the top and bottom of the screen. This makes it a little friendlier to the eyes than readnews. Vnews also gives you more options than readnews. It is approximately as easy to use as readnews. Like readnews, vnews is not very good at letting you select a small subset of articles to read, except by answering yes or no to each. You should use vnews if you want a screen-oriented display and if you want to get started reading news right away without spending much time learning to read news. As soon as you are comfortable with vnews, you should switch to a more powerful news reader.

rn. This is more powerful than readnews and vnews and has much more online help. It is also a little harder to learn. You can easily skip all articles on any topic that does not interest you. You should use rn only if you are already familiar with it. If you are not already familiar with rn, try trn instead; it does everything that rn does and quite a bit more.

trn, nn, and tin. These three news readers are quite powerful and flexible, and it is not easy to decide which is the best. Each one has some interesting features. nn is oriented toward selecting articles to read on the basis of their subject heading; it recognizes all articles with the same subject and can present them as a single menu item. Both trn and tin are oriented towards tracking "threads" of discussion, based on who responded to which article, independent of what the subject headings might be. And nn and tin are also very good at letting you decode software posted to the newsgroups in various encoded formats. The nn program is excellent when you are searching for articles with specific subjects. You should probably try all three news readers or ask other people what they think.

gnus. This is a mode within the emacs editor. If you are not a regular user of emacs, you should probably not use gnus; many of its subcommands assume familiarity with emacs. If you do use emacs, you might find it interesting to try gnus. It has many of the good features of the other news readers, but its drawback is its slow speed. To invoke gnus, first invoke emacs, type ESC, ^X (Ctrl-X), and then `gnus`. To get online help from within gnus, type ^C ^I.

Others. There is a news reader called *tass* which is old; it was adapted to create tin, which replaced it. There might be sites that have tass and not tin. There is also software called *notes* that is not much used any more. It was independently created to do the same thing as Usenet news software, but later it got gatewayed to Usenet and just became an alternative interface for the same thing. I have never used it, but some sites might still have it.

Help! Too many choices? Don't let all these choices confuse you. If you want to keep it simple and can't decide which news reader to use, begin with vnews. After one or two weeks of using vnews, you can explore the other news readers. If in doubt, try trn, because it is slightly easier to use than nn and is faster than tin.

NOTE By the way, Rahul prefers nn, Kevin prefers trn, and Dave Taylor likes tin best, proving that no program is perfect for everyone.

Here's an example of what the trn newsreader looks like. (You should try it. It's my favorite newsreader, but it's not particularly easy to learn.)

```
======  6 unread articles in alt.fan.laurie.anderson — read now? [+ynq] n
====== 24 unread articles in comp.infosystems.wais — read now? [+ynq] n
======  4 unread articles in alt.internet.services — read now? [+ynq] y
Reading overview file...
alt.internet.services          4 articles

a+Thomas Dowling    1  >Stock quotes from the Internet
b Dave Taylor       1  >The internet mall
d DaveHatunen       1  >Anonymous mail
e Rick Duffy        1  >How many people are on the Internet? (Flame!!)

— Select threads (date order) — All [Z>] —
```

Here's what the tin newsreader looks like. tin uses a friendly screen-oriented display.

```
    1     6  alt.fan.laurie.anderson               Will it be a music conce
    2     4  alt.internet.services                 Not available in the uuc
    3    24  comp.infosystems.wais                 The Z39.50-based WAIS fu
    4    15  alt.internet.talk-radio               Carl Malamud's Internet
    5   151  comp.sys.mac.hypercard                The Macintosh Hypercard:
    6        alt.radio.internet
    7     5  alt.etext
    8        a2i.announce
    9        a2i.general
   10        a2i.modems
   11        news.announce.important               General announcements of
   12        news.announce.newusers                Explanatory postings for
   13   233  alt.config                            Alternative subnet discu
   14   804  news.answers                          Repository for periodic
   15     7  news.lists                            News-related statistics
   16    42  news.misc                             Discussions of USENET it

      <n>=set current to n, TAB=next unread, /=search pattern, c)atchup,
  g)oto, j=line down, k=line up, h)elp, m)ove, q)uit, r=toggle all/unread,
    s)ubscribe, S)ub pattern, u)nsubscribe, U)nsub pattern, y)ank in/out

Threading articles...
                          Group Selection (77)                       h=help


                    alt.fan.laurie.anderson (3T 6A 0K 0H R)          h=help

   1  +    Laurie Anderson's _Nerve Bible_ book          woody
   2  + 3  Lovely Laurie                                 Godes Shimon
   3  + 2  William S. Burroughs                          Rob Hilton
```

Yuck! Everyone (except perhaps beginners) should avoid readnews at all costs. It's so simple that it's impossible to use for any length of time.

```
--------------------------------
Newsgroup alt.fan.laurie.anderson
--------------------------------

Article 394 of 398, Fri 06:31.
Subject: Re: William S. Burroughs
From: steve@dusty.unet.umn.edu (Steve Fletty @ University of Minnesota, Networki
ng Services.)
(34 lines) More? [ynq] n

Article 395 of 398, Wed 04:35.
Subject: Re: Lovely Laurie
From: godes@decscc.tau.ac.il (Godes Shimon @ Tel-Aviv University Computation Cen
ter)
```

5

```
(14 lines) More? [ynq] n

Article 398 of 398, Mon 16:16.
Subject: Laurie Anderson's _Nerve Bible_ book
From: C562611@mizzou1.missouri.edu (woody @ University of Missouri, Columbia)
(17 lines) More? [ynq] n

-----------------------------
Newsgroup alt.internet.services
-----------------------------

Article 17557 of 17560, Wed 10:20.
Subject: Re: Stock quotes from the Internet
From: tdowling@lib.washington.edu (Thomas Dowling @ University of Washington)

(18 lines) More? [ynq] y
```

5.11. What newsgroups should be required reading for newcomers?

With so much to choose from, everybody has their own Usenet reading list. But there are a few newsgroups that are particularly of interest to newcomers. Among them are

news.announce.newusers. This group consists of a series of articles that explain various facets of Usenet.

news.newusers.questions. This is where you can ask questions about how the Usenet works.

news.announce.newsgroups. This is where you'll find information about new newsgroups and proposed additions to the Usenet.

news.answers. This newsgroup is the central trove of frequently asked questions postings. Most FAQs for other newsgroups show up periodically in news.answers. Just sifting through a week's worth of postings can take hours, but you're guaranteed to come across so much good information (about the Internet, religion, entertainment, and hundreds of other topics) to make it worth your while.

alt.internet.services. This is the place to ask questions about any and all Internet services. Here you'll also find announcements of new Internet tools and toys and more useful FAQ lists.

alt.infosystems.announce. Announcements about new Internet information services appear here.

I checked out news.answers to see what FAQs were posted in the past few days. Here are some examples:

```
====== 796 unread articles in news.answers — read now? [+ynq]
Reading overview file..........
REC.NUDE FAQ—The Questions, Part I of III
FAQ: rec.games.pbm Frequently Asked Questions
soc.religion.quaker Answers to Freque...Asked Questions
Info-VAX: Introduction to Info-VAX
Info-VAX: "Basic" Common Questions
Info-VAX: "Advanced" Common Questions
Info-VAX: How to find VAX/VMS software.
[rec.scuba] FAQ: Frequently Asked Que...Monthly Posting
[alt.fan.howard-stern] FAQ: Frequentl...Monthly Posting
[rec.sport.pro-wrestling] FAQ: Wrestling Relations
FAQ: rec.audio (part 1 of 4)
comp.lang.c Answers to Frequently Asked Qu...(FAQ List)
comp.protocols.ppp part1 of 8 of f...wanted information
Project Management Programs - Frequen...Questions (FAQ)
comp.compilers monthly message and Fr...Asked Questions
Catalog of compilers, interpreters, and...tools [p1of3]
Amateur Radio: Elmers List Quick-Search Index
Amateur Radio: Elmers Resource Directory
A Guide to Buying and Selling on Usenet
Midi files/software archives on the Internet
Computer Music bibliography
Bisexual Resource List (monthly posting)
monthly rec.games.pinball FAQ, one of two
Music Notation Programs - a list to answer a FAQ
Welcome to Misc.kids/FAQ File Index (Updated 1/17/94)
Alt.beer faq 940117 revision
comp.periphs.scsi FAQ part 1 of 2
Sci.physics Frequently Asked Questions - Feb...Part 1/2
Cryonics FAQ 1: Index
Welcome to rec.radio.shortwave
Welcome to soc.religion.bahai
alt.fan.dave_barry Frequently Asked Questions
Space FAQ 01/13 - Introduction
Economists' Resources on the Internet
```

Q 5.12. Some of these posts in *rec.humor* (and elsewhere) are gibberish. What's with that?

In an effort to keep clean minds clean (while allowing those of us with our minds in the gutter to wallow there), you'll find some postings that appear as gibberish at first glance. They're encoded with *rot13*, a popular Net cipher. Rot13 is sometimes used to "hide" dirty jokes and "spoilers" (posts that can ruin your fun by, for example, giving video game hints or telling you what happens in each episode of the Prisoner).

It's entirely up to the person who posts the message whether it will be encoded with rot13 or not. It's pretty easy to read rot13-encoded text. In fact, it's supposed to be easy. With rot13, each letter is replaced by the letter 13 farther along in the alphabet (cycling around at the end). Most newsreaders have a built-in command to decrypt rot13 articles. By pressing the special keys, you acknowledge that you're about to see something that may annoy or offend you.

Program	*Command*
readnews	`D`
nn	`D`
emacs/gnus	control-C control-R
rn/trn	`X` or control-X
notes	`%` or `R`
VMS news	`read/rot13` command

Here's a message with rot-13 encoding:

```
                    Gur Frk Yvsr bs na Ryrpgeba

                        ol n Qvfgbegrq Jnir

Bar avtug jura uvf punetr jnf cyragl uvtu, zvpeb snenq qrpvqrq gb
trg  n  phgr yvggyr pbvy gb yrg uvz qvfpunetr. Ur cvpxrq hc zvyyv
nzcf naq gbbx ure sbe n evqr ba uvf zrtnplpyr. Gurl ebqr npebff n
jurng-fgbar oevqtr naq fgbccrq va n  zntargvp svryq  arne n fznyy
fgernz bs rqql pheeragf.
```

And without

```
                The Sex Life of an Electron

                     by a Distorted Wave

One night when his charge was plenty high, micro farad decided to
get  a  cute little coil to let him discharge. He picked up milli
amps and took her for a ride on his megacycle. They rode across a
wheat-stone bridge and stopped in a  magnetic field  near a small
stream of eddy currents.
```

5.13. Some people seem to post inane drivel: is there some way that I can avoid seeing their articles?

Some newsreaders, such as tin and trn, include a useful feature called the *kill file*, which you can use to skip articles you don't want to see. Kill files can be local (hiding from your weary eyes certain posts in a particular newsgroup) or global (hiding certain posts in all newsgroups). With kill files, you can skip articles with a particular subject line, from a particular poster, from a certain site, and articles cross-posted from any other group (as well as other criteria).

I use a kill file to hide all posts with the subject line of `MAKE.MONEY.FAST`, thus avoiding a pyramid scheme that won't die and messages from the people it annoys. You might use a kill file to hide the weekly-posted FAQ in a favorite newsgroup or to kill messages from a particularly annoying Usenet poster.

Read the documentation for your newsreader to find out how to use kill files. If you use rn or trn on a UNIX system, read the `rn KILL file FAQ` that's available on Usenet at `news.newusers.questions`, by anonymous FTP at `rtfm.mit.edu:/pub/usenet/news.newusers.questions/rn_KILL_file_FAQ` or by e-mail to `rtfm.mit.edu` (put `send usenet/news.newusers.questions/rn_KILL_file_FAQ` in the body of the message).

5.14. How can I search all newsgroups for stuff that interests me?

Until recently, you couldn't search all the newsgroups at once for information that interests you—for example, selecting only articles with certain keywords. However, this changed in February, 1994, with the introduction of the Stanford Netnews Filtering Service. This tool is free (even though the word "service" might suggest it's fee-based) and has changed the way I read Usenet news.

The Stanford Netnews Filtering Service is a tool for personalized netnews delivery. You subscribe to the service by establishing "profiles" describing your interests. Netnews articles that match your profiles are sent to you periodically via e-mail. The best part is that this automated program searches all newsgroups (well, all those available at `stanford.edu`) for interesting articles. For instance, if you're interested in UFOs and a conversation about them should pop up in `alt.fan.laurie-anderson` (an altogether unlikely place for such a conversation, admittedly), the filtering service will be sure you won't miss out, even if you don't normally read about Laurie Anderson.

The profiles are plain English text, with no boolean `and`s, `or`s, or `not`s—for instance, `object oriented programming` or `nba golden state warriors basketball`. Based on the statistical distributions of the words in the articles, scores are given to evaluate how relevant they are to your profile. You can specify the minimum score for an article to be delivered. After you receive useful articles, you can feed them back to the service to improve its search strategy. You can also adjust the frequency of delivery, the volume of articles, and the length of your subscription.

You can access the service from any World Wide Web reader, such as Mosaic:

```
http://woodstock.stanford.edu:2000
```

The service also supports e-mail access. To get the instructions on the e-mail interface, send a message with the word `help` in the message body to `netnews@db.stanford.edu`

Here is an example to give you some idea of how the service works. Suppose that you subscribe to the service with a profile `online information services`. Then periodically you will receive e-mail messages like this:

```
Subscription 1: online information services

 Article: misc.activism.progressive.11965
 From: hn0003@handsnet.org
 Subject: HandsNet WEEKLY DIGEST 1/15-21
 Score:  84
 First 15 lines:
  HANDSNET WEEKLY DIGEST  January 15 - 21, 1994
  News from HandsNet's Information Forums
  HandsNet is a national, nonprofit network connecting organizations working
 on social and economic justice issues.  Members use HandsNet to make new
contacts, work collaboratively and to find and publish information, news
....

 Article: ca.politics.38420
 From: rlm@helen.surfcty.com (Robert L. McMillin)
 Subject: GOV-ACCESS #5:Cal.Emergency Svcs.online + Net-fax + MINN Pub Info Net
 Score:  82
 First 15 lines:
  Jan. 22, 1994
  CALIFORNIA OFFICE OF EMERGENCY SERVICES INFO AVAILABLE ONLINE
    <a recent exchange of messages>
  The state Emergency Digitial Information Service is working fine
    Telnet to telnet oes1.oes.ca.gov 5501
```

Q 5.15. What should I know about Usenet "netiquette" before posting?

Each message posted to the Usenet can reach millions of people scattered around the globe, so your words and actions (however insignificant they may seem) can affect lots of real people. All of the etiquette guidelines for sending electronic mail count doubly for Usenet postings. Use the following guidelines coupled with your own common sense (now there's an oxymoron) when you post to the Usenet.

Think about where your article is going. If you are posting to one of the top-level hierarchies, your message will find its way to an audience of more than three million potential readers.

Keep your message at or under 72 characters per line. Not everyone uses the 80-column by 25-row text that you may be accustomed to, so shorter lines mean your message will look cleaner to more people. Also, remember that if anyone follows up to your message and "quotes" it, your lines will become longer. Further follow-ups mean longer lines. Here's some visual aid:

```
I like Oreos!

>I like Oreos!
Me too!

>>I like Oreos!
>Me too!
I like Tim Tams better.
```

Speaking of quoting previous articles—make careful use of quoted material. If you reply to a posting without including some of the text you're referring to, it's very likely many of your readers won't know what you're talking about. But too many quoted lines preceding your own message will annoy people. So use quoting when you have to, but don't quote the entire text of a novel-length article. Especially if your only addition is `Me too!`

While we're on the subject, don't post messages of which the entire content is `Me too!` You probably have seen some of these: someone posts a message asking for a recipe for malted milk balls, then four or five people post `Me too!` Imagine what would happen if 1,000 or 10,000 people did the same thing. The Usenet would be both overloaded and a bore to read. If you really must have the information also, send an e-mail message to the original posters and ask them to pass along the information when they find it.

Refer to articles by their Message-ID and never by the article number. The article's number varies from computer to computer: #1502 on `news.answers` on your computer is almost certainly not the same message as #1502 on mine.

Use a good subject line, just as with e-mail. Often, your subject line is the only thing that potential readers have as a gauge to decide whether they'll read your message. Postings with no subject or uninformative subject lines—such as `READ THIS NOW!`, `Question`, and `Help needed`—are likely to be ignored.

The Internet is laden with a variety of FAQs and other documents to help you avoid being a social misfit on the Usenet. Start with `Rules for posting to Usenet`, which is posted to `news.announce.newusers` and `news.answers`. This message describes some of the basic rules of conduct on the Usenet.

> **NOTE** If you're still thirsty for information, read `Hints on writing style for Usenet` and `A Primer on How to Work With the Usenet Community`, which are posted regularly to `news.newusers.questions`.

5.16. Hey, I'd like to post a test message. Where should I send it?

Sometimes you might want to post a test message to the Usenet to make sure your news software is working or to see what the headers of your posts look like. By sending your message to one of several special test-ground newsgroups, you can try your posting software, see what your message looks like, and verify that your site actually propagates Usenet messages. Special newsgroups exist for test messages. You can send your test message to one of them with impunity. Don't post your message to `alt.internet.services` or `alt.personals` or `talk.poitics.guns` or anywhere else that isn't just for test messages. Doing so will annoy thousands of folks who were minding their own business until your message came along and told them to ignore it because it's only a test.

Just so there are no excuses, here's a list of several places to which you may post test messages. Send as many as you want!

```
alt.test
atl.test
austin.test
ba.test
bit.test
biz.test
ca.test
```

```
can.test
de.alt.test
de.test
de.test.egon
eunet.test
fj.test
fr.test
k12.test
misc.test
mit.test
news.test
nj.test
ny.test
psu.test
relcom.test
sbay.test
scruz.test
seattle.test
sfnet.test
su.test
tx.test
ucb.test
uiuc.test
uk.test
vmsnet.test
```

Q 5.17. How do I know my messages are really propagating on the Usenet?

When you post a message to any newsgroup, it should—depending on your type of Internet access—start showing up on other sites within a few minutes or hours.

If you are not sure whether your postings are leaving your site, post a test message to one of the major Usenet testing grounds such as `alt.test` or `news.test`. Out in the vast reaches of the Usenet, some sites have set up programs, called *autoresponders*, that automatically send e-mail replies to messages posted to the biggie test newsgroups. The autoresponders are cool because: 1) you get to see that your message is reaching other sites, and 2) you get lots of e-mail from all over the world. Here's a typical automatic reply to a message I sent to the newsgroup `ca.test`:

```
To: waffle@rahul.net
From: testrep@xyzoom.info.com
Subject: Re: My Funky Test
Precedence: junk


Your test message posted to ca.test was received at xyzoom.info.com on
Wed Feb 23 07:45:23 PST 1994.

xyzoom.info.com is located in the Hollywood Hills, California, USA.
(specifically, just below the Hollywood sign)

Your email address was derived from the From: line of your test posting.
Your entire message is enclosed below shifted by '>'.

No response is required from this message. It's just to let you know that
your test was received. If you feel that you must respond, please do so to
"rob@xyzoom.info.com" as replies to the sender of this message are
automatically discarded.


If you would rather not see these automatic responses, please include the
text 'ignore' in the body of future messages.
        -Rob
—
Rob Lingelbach KB6CUN ¦ 2660 Hollyridge Dr LA CA 90068 213 464 6266 (voice)
rob@xyzoom.info.com   ¦ "I care not much for a man's religion whose dog or
robl@netcom.com       ¦  cat are not the better for it."  —Abraham Lincoln

>Newsgroups: ca.test
>From: waffle@rahul.net (Kevin Savetz)
>Subject: My Funky Test
>Message-ID: <CLo8Et.CyM@rahul.net>
>Summary: Won't you take me to Funky Town?
>Sender: news@rahul.net (Usenet News)
>Date: Wed, 23 Feb 1994 09:44:53 GMT
>Lines: 9
>
>Some day I hope post test messages FOR A LIVING.
>
>-Kevin Savetz
>
>--
> "Anybody who uses email probably has three times more opinions per head
> than people who don't." -Scott Adams, "Dilbert"
>[ Kevin M. Savetz -- savetz@rahul.net             ]
>[                 -- faq-book-info@northcoast.net ]
```

5

If you don't want automatic replies to your test messages, put the words `no reply` or `ignore` in your test post's subject line.

> **NOTE** Probably useless trivia: some test reflectors will also ignore your posts if your subject line includes any of these words and phrases: `no replies`, `keine antwort`, `fresse`, `maul`, `schnauze`, `klappe` and `sei still`.

5.18. What is a moderated newsgroup?

Answered by Dave Taylor (`taylor@netcom.com`)

I've seen lots of metaphors for the Usenet, and one of the most colorful is that it's an information tsunami—a massive wave of words that floods over your machine—divided into thousands of little waves showing up in each newsgroup. It doesn't take long to realize that a system where anyone can publish (*post* in Usenet parlance) anything results in an unbelievable flood of information. If you're interested in a specific topic like reviews of current movies, the last thing you want to read are fifty articles that start out talking about the type of camera used to film a particular sequence and end up in an esoteric discussion of Japanese export tariffs! Yet not only can this happen, it very commonly does happen in Usenet groups.

There are a variety of solutions, and one that has proven highly successful as the network has grown and expanded is to have a person or group of people act as newspaper editors, moderating the flow of information on the net, acting as moderators.

Groups that are designated as *moderated* have all articles posted by the moderator: postings from other people are sent to the central moderation site (which differs for each moderated newsgroup) and, if the article is approved and meets the guidelines of the group, it is posted by the moderator. I view it as analogous to a magazine editor: lots of articles may be submitted to the magazine, but only a subset of them are appropriate for the readership that is served by the group.

Many moderated newsgroups are reserved for very specific types of postings and consequently have a low volume of high quality information. Examples abound, including `comp.sys.sun.announce` for information of importance to Sun Microsystems users, `news.answers` with answers to common questions about the Internet, Usenet, specific newsgroups, and other topics, and `comp.internet.library` with discussions of Internet access issues that relate to public or institutional libraries.

I would estimate that almost 25 percent of the Usenet groups I personally read are moderated, and they are the source of some of the most valuable information I find on the network. Which groups? Some of the moderated groups I follow are

`comp.binaries.mac.`	Free and shareware Macintosh programs
`comp.internet.library.`	
`comp.sources.unix.`	
`comp.sys.mac.announce.`	Macintosh-related announcements
`comp.sys.sun.announce.`	Sun-related announcements
`rec.arts.movies.reviews.`	Covers just movie reviews, with discussion elsewhere

Q 5.19. How can I tell if a newsgroup is moderated?

Answered by Dave Taylor (`taylor@netcom.com`)

Depending on your software, it may or may not be easy to identify whether a particular newsgroup is moderated. Some news reading programs (like rn and tin) denote whether a group is moderated or not. If you see a notation such as `Approved:` in a Usenet article, you can safely assume that the group is moderated, too.

One way to make sure, of course, is to try to post an article to the group: if it's moderated, you'll see a brief note indicating that your article has actually been e-mailed to the newsgroup's moderator. Usually the mailing address of the moderator is based on the name of the group and is routed through a system called `uunet.uu.net`. For example, the newsgroup `comp.sources.unix` is moderated, and articles posted to that group are mailed electronically to `comp-sources-unix@uunet.uu.net`. The good news is that the news posting programs can e-mail your article to the right person without your having to remember any esoteric e-mail addresses at all.

5.20. How do I choose a "distribution" area when posting to the Usenet?

As you post to the Usenet, your posting software (Pnews or postnews for UNIX users) will ask for a distribution. It wants to know how widely distributed you want your article: who should see it? Just people in your city, your state, or the whole wide world?

You may be shown a list of distribution areas; the list differs depending on your site's location. My site offers the following distribution choices:

```
Your local distribution prefixes are:
local          this site only
ba             Bay Area
ca             California
usa            USA
na             North America
world          the universe
```

If you send your posting everywhere—that is, to "world" distribution—your message will indeed go everywhere the Usenet goes: Finland, Korea, even Cleveland. Consider whether your message really needs to go to these places. A used car ad or request for a bridge partner in your city shouldn't leave your city, let alone the state and country.

It is generally impossible to post an article to a distribution that your own machine does not receive. For instance, if you live in California, you can't post an article for distribution only in Toledo or Botswana unless your site happens to exchange those particular distributions with another site. If you need to post to a local newsgroup that's not local to you, try mailing the article to someone in that area and ask them to post it for you.

Q 5.21. What is crossposting? How do I do it?

Answered by Prof. Timo Salmi of the University of Vaasa, Finland (`tw@uwasa.fi`)

If you want your message to appear in more than one newsgroup (such as `comp.sys.mac.wanted` and `misc.forsale.computers.mac`) you can achieve this by *crossposting*. If you look at the header in the news you will notice the item `Newsgroups:`. Put the names of the newsgroups in this item separated by commas. Scan the headers of almost any newsgroup, and you are bound to see how it is done.

Example:

```
Newsgroups:
comp.sys.mac.wanted,misc.forsale.computers.mac,ca.wanted
```

The number one rule of crossposting is that it should never be done indiscriminately. If you feel that it is necessary to crosspost, consider carefully your selection, and keep crosspostings to a minimum. Avoid crossposting to groups that are branches of the same subhierarchy (such as `comp.sys.mac.wanted` and `comp.sys.mac.misc`).

What goes for newsgroup selection in general also applies to crossposting. Never crosspost to newsgroups that do not coincide with your subject.

There is one very important *don't* in crossposting. Do not send the same message separately to different newsgroups. Always use the crossposting facility of the Usenet (with multiple groups in the `Newsgroups:` header line). If you repeat a message separately in different newsgroups, readers will have to see your posting many times over, and will get annoyed.

5

Be careful, however, if you edit the headers. Learn their exact requirements. If you make mistakes, the posting may fail, or the followups to it by other users may fail because of your editing errors. For example

```
Newsgroups:
comp.lang.pascal,comp.os.msdos.programmer,
```

would result in an error in follow-up because of the trailing comma.

NOTE Timo has a great collection of Internet FAQs of his own, which are available via FTP from `garbo.uwasa.fi` as `/pc/ts/tsfaqn39.zip`

5.22. What's the *Followup-To:* news header?

When you crosspost messages, you might want to direct any replies to your posting to a single newsgroup, to prevent any follow-up discussion from living parallel lives in several places. You can do this by using the `Followup-To:` field in the headers of Usenet news messages. `Followup-To:` forces any replies (or follow-ups) to the place of your choosing. (For example, you might crosspost a dirty joke to `alt.tasteless` and `rec.humor`. Inserting the line `Followup-To: rec.humor.d` will force any replies to go to that newsgroup instead of the others.)

Some users put the word `poster` in the `Followup-To:` field to send any replies directly to them by e-mail. However, this isn't guaranteed to work. Some system configurations and newsreaders do not handle `Followup-To: poster` correctly.

5.23. When I crosspost an article to a moderated group and unmoderated groups, it gets mailed to the moderator but isn't posted to the unmoderated groups. Why?

Because that's the way it works, although some folks don't like it. When you post to a moderated and an unmoderated group, the post is sent to the moderator where it waits for approval. Moderators have the option of crossposting your article so that it appears in the unmoderated newsgroups as well as in the moderated ones. Or they could post it only to the moderated group. Or they could choose not to post it at all.

If you want your article to go out immediately to the unmoderated groups, you could post it twice—once to the unmoderated group and once to the moderated groups. Posting a message in multiple places without crossposting is bad karma, though.

5.24. How can I post messages to the Usenet via electronic mail?

There are a few sites on the Usenet that offer e-mail to Usenet gateways so that you can post to any newsgroup by sending e-mail. This isn't the usual way for most of us with Usenet readers to post, but it works if your site doesn't have Usenet or if your news posting software is broken.

One mail-to-news gateway is at `decwrl.dec.com`. To use it, mail your message to `newsgroup@decwrl.dec.com`. For example, to post to `alt.internet`.services send your message to `alt.internet.services.usenet@decwrl.dec.com`.

5.25. How are mailing lists different from Usenet newsgroups?

Answered by Dave Taylor (`taylor@netcom.com`)

The Internet is full of subtle but important distinctions between different types of data. One of the more subtle distinctions is how newsgroups differ from electronic mailing lists. When you consider that there are two main types of electronic mailing lists (those that forward to all members any mail sent and those that have a moderator who screens messages for appropriateness) and two types of Usenet newsgroups (moderated and unmoderated), the lines definitely blur.

There are two primary considerations for building and maintaining a special interest discussion group: control and dissemination. Why is control important? If you're a member of a discussion group you want to ensure that the information you receive is relevant and appropriate for the audience. That is, if you're involved with discussion of high-level physics string theory (or some other specialized discussion), there is an expectation of a certain amount of knowledge on the part of the participants.

Control is also a means of maintaining the quality of information in a discussion. The more narrowly focused a discussion, the more you might want to consider imposing some sort of controls on the group, either at the point when people join (for example, by sending a note indicating that there are certain expectations of knowledge or interaction inherent in the discussion) or when they submit information (by moderating the discussion). Both work for mailing lists, and moderation works, quite effectively, on the Usenet.

Dissemination is the other half of the coin: although it may appear that the Internet is free and infinitely powerful, that just isn't the case, unfortunately. With the Usenet, only one copy of each article is present on any given computer, whether 100 or 0 people read that discussion. However, with a mailing list, each recipient gets an individual copy of the message. A large mailing list leads to hundreds of messages filling up mailboxes left and right! If you have 70 people on a single machine and they are all subscribed to a mailing list with 20 new messages each day, you're talking about 1,400 messages every day; the resource demands can be quite high. Expand this across thousands of systems and 10,000 readers, and it becomes clear that at a certain point it makes more sense to use a newsgroup rather than a mailing list.

The reverse holds true too: a Usenet group discussing 1967 Chevy Cameros is far too specific to be of interest to a lot of people, but it might make a nice 40-person mailing list, where participants can learn about each other's interests.

NOTE **Rule of Thumb #1:** If there are less than a couple of hundred people interested in the subject, it will probably work better as a mailing list.

NOTE **Rule of Thumb #2:** If it seems as though there are going to be a lot of irrelevant or inappropriate articles in the group (either mailing list or

newsgroup), assign or nominate a moderator who can screen submissions and just let the highest quality articles through to the readership.

There is indeed a blur between mailing lists and Usenet groups, and it's a healthy mix. Many times mailing lists will grow and grow as they become popular and ultimately spawn Usenet groups as the resource demands increase.

As I said, it's a subtle distinction and there are a variety of different factors that affect whether a particular discussion is best as a mailing list or newsgroup, but the most important ones are resource demands and dissemination of the material.

5.26. How do I start a Usenet group?

It's simple to actually create a Usenet newsgroup, but it is a much more complicated matter to have your newsgroup accepted by the Usenet community, allowed onto the millions of Internet hosts, and actually read.

It is simplest to create an `alt.` hierarchy newsgroup and have it accepted. The sprawling `alt.` newsgroups are largely unregulated. Although it is considered polite to post to `alt.config` a message requesting comments on the creation of a newsgroup, it's clear to anyone who watches as new `alt.` newsgroups magically appear (without so much as a hint of discussion on `alt.config`) that this doesn't happen all the time. If the general consensus is that the group should be created, talk to your news administrator about actually creating it.

The ability to create newsgroups on the spur of the moment often leads to newsgroups that are silly, or very topical. For instance, a newsgroup for discussion of the January, 1994, Los Angeles earthquake appeared only moments after the first shake.

The guidelines for creating local newsgroups may differ depending on where you are. Users in some areas may enforce complex rules for group creation or have a more lax attitude. Find out your area's rules (written or unwritten) before you create your own group for discussion of the wanton destruction of lemming habitat in the greater Walla Walla area.

No matter what hierarchy your newsgroup is part of or how it is created, the decision whether to allow a newsgroup on a given computer on the Internet rests with the administrator of that machine. Some systems hand pick which newsgroups are invited in; some let them all in.

Before you create a Usenet group or start a discussion about creating one, make sure that no such group already exists. With upward of 7,000 newsgroups out there, there's a very good chance there's already a place to talk about what you want to talk about.

If you think your newsgroup should exist as part of one of the standard Usenet hierarchies—`comp`, `misc`, `news`, `rec`, `sci`, `soc` or `talk`—your task is more complicated and convoluted:

First, a request for discussion (RFD) on creation of a new newsgroup should be posted to `news.announce.newgroups` and also to any other groups or mailing lists that are related to the proposed topic. Follow-up discussion should take place on `news.groups`. During the discussion period, several things need to be ironed out, including the name and charter of the proposed group and whether it will be moderated or unmoderated. If it's to be moderated, who should the moderator be?

If there is no general agreement on these points among the proponents of a new group at the end of 30 days of discussion, the debate should be taken out of `news.groups` and sent into e-mail for further deliberation. Luckily, you're not defenseless in the world of newsgroup creation: group advocates seeking help in choosing a name to suit the proposed charter or looking for guidance in the creation procedure can send a message to `group-advice@uunet.uu.net`. A few seasoned news administrators there may assist you.

Once all the preceding has been agreed on, and it is determined that the new newsgroup is really desired, a call for votes should be posted to `news.announce.newgroups` and any other places where interested parties are likely to read. There are various procedures for taking votes, but the vote period should be from 21 to 31 days. The exact date that the voting period will end should be stated in the call for votes. Only votes e-mailed to the vote-taker count; votes posted to the Usenet or mailing lists can't be counted.

At the end of the voting period, the vote taker must post the vote tally and the e-mail addresses of the voters to `news.announce.newgroups` and the newsgroups where the original call for votes was posted. After the vote result is posted, there is a five-day waiting period, during which the Net has a chance to correct any major errors or raise serious objections.

After the waiting period, and if at least two-thirds of the total number of valid votes are in favor of creation and there are 100 more "yes" votes than "no" votes, the newsgroup may be created. If the 100-vote margin or two-thirds percentage is not met, the group should not be created and the topic should not be brought up for discussion for at least six months.

Whew! That was the Reader's Digest condensed version. For the full story, read `How to Create a New Usenet Newsgroup`, a document that will tell you everything you wanted to know (and more) about creating a new newsgroup. It is available on Usenet at `news.announce.newusers`, `news.announce.newusers`, `news.groups`, `news.admin.misc`, `news.announce.newgroups`, and `news.answers`; by e-mail to `pit-manager@rtfm.mit.edu` (in the message body `send usenet/news.announce.newusers/How_to_Create_a_New_Usenet_Newsgroup`); and by anonymous FTP to `rtfm.mit.edu:/pub/usenet/news.announce.newusers/How_to_Create_a_New_Usenet_Newsgroup`

To find out more about creating an `alt.` group, read `So You Want to Create an Alt Newsgroup`, a guide for anyone interested in creating a newsgroup within the `alt.*` hierarchy. It is posted every 14 days to `alt.config` and `news.answers`.

For a cynical and humorous list of how not to go about creating a newsgroup, read `Emily Postnews answers your questions on how to create a new alt. group`, which is also posted periodically to `alt.config` and `news.answers`.

Q 5.27. Do I really want to go through the trouble of creating a new newsgroup?

Maybe. Unless you plan on railroading the creation of a new `alt.` newsgroup, creating a newsgroup takes time and patience. It will take from two to three months of your time from the beginning of the initial discussion period to the final tally of the Call for Votes. In that time, you'll have to devise a way to collect and count the votes and endure the endless bickering of highly opinionated people on news.groups.

If you're faint-of-heart or don't think there is enough interest in your idea for a Usenet group, consider creating a mailing list. Mailing lists can be set up quickly and work well with small readerships. Best of all, you don't need anyone's permission to make one.

CHAPTER 6

How Can I Find and Use Software (and Other Stuff)?

The Internet is an enormous warehouse of computer programs, graphics, and electronic magazines. This chapter looks at questions about how to rent a forklift, search the Internet's software warehouses, and make it out alive with what you're looking for.

Q 6.1. What is FTP?

FTP stands for *file transfer protocol.* It is a tool you can use to copy files among computers on the Internet. With the FTP program, you can log into an account on a remote computer in order to send files to it or receive files from it. FTP, in contrast to Telnet, isn't used for running programs; you use it just to move among files and among computers.

Before you can use FTP to transfer files between your host and a remote site, you need to have access on the remote computer. You need an account of your own before you can Telnet into most computers, and, similarly, you need permission to use FTP to access a computer. After all, system administrators usually don't want total strangers going through the files on their system or downloading and uploading files without permission. (This is akin to going into someone's else's office and taking some of his or her stuff.)

If you have full access on two Internet hosts, you can use FTP to copy files from your account on one to your account on the other. This is sometimes known as full-privilege FTP.

Honestly, FTP by itself isn't very exciting, but it's the *de facto* standard for transferring files on the Internet. FTP is kind of like my old Pontiac Sunbird hatchback: ugly and hard to get around in, but it gets the job done. (Actually, my Sunbird became engulfed in flames once and later died on the side of the road somewhere in Nowheresville. FTP seems to do these things sometimes, too.) Despite its drab interface and single-mindedness of purpose, FTP shines when coupled with the Internet's anonymous FTP archives.

6.2. What is anonymous FTP?

The majority of FTP use isn't done by people moving their own files between computers. (That's like moving your stuff between your home and your office: sometimes it's useful, but it's still the same old stuff.) Instead, most FTP use is to access archives of software. Gargantuan libraries of software are available for the taking, using anonymous FTP. Thousands of sites provide anonymous FTP service, so you can download everything from electronic books and magazines to satellite pictures of the weather to public-domain utilities and games for your personal computer.

Some system administrators have chosen to make their computers available for everyone on the Net to stop by and share files. Unlike full-privilege FTP, you don't need your own account to access an anonymous FTP site; all you need is the not-so-secret word *anonymous.* Whereas almost all Internet sites support full-privilege FTP, only a small percentage of them allow anonymous FTP access. (Still, on a network the size of the Internet, that small minority of sites offering anonymous FTP quickly adds up to thousands.)

The term *anonymous FTP* is a misnomer. When you access an anonymous FTP site, you are not necessarily anonymous at all. In fact, many sites insist that you "sign in" using your electronic mail address before you scramble to transfer copies of every program known to mankind. A few FTP sites log all files transferred to and from the computer. So the word *anonymous* means that anyone can access the archive, not merely those people with full-privilege accounts on that computer.

6.3. How do I use FTP?

Using FTP is similar to using UNIX. Some of FTP's commands (such as `cd`, `pwd`, and `ls`) work just as their UNIX counterparts do. This is great news if you're already familiar with UNIX, because there isn't much new to learn. Even if you don't use UNIX, don't cringe; you'll find FTP is trivial to use.

To use FTP, you need the FTP program on your local host, and you need to know where you want to connect. On my system, I start FTP by typing (stay with me, now) `ftp`, and then I open a connection by typing `open` followed by a site name.

> **NOTE** You can also type `ftp sitename`, thereby combining the tasks of starting the FTP program and opening a site. For example, to connect to netcom's FTP server, type `ftp ftp.netcom.com`.

If you're FTPing to your own account (that is, you're using full-privilege FTP instead of anonymous FTP), enter your own username and password at the prompt. On systems that allow anonymous FTP access, use the username `anonymous`. You'll probably be asked to enter a password, too. When prompted for a password, type your e-mail address. This isn't always necessary, but it's a courtesy to site administrators who like to know who is using their facility. Some sites require a valid e-mail address before you'll be allowed in, but most don't. On some systems you must use the generic password "guest" rather than an e-mail address.

NOTE A neat trick: many FTP programs can automatically append your hostname if you just enter your username followed by the `@` without any further information (for instance, `savetz@`). I don't know if that's useful, but it can save a wee bit of strain on those fingers.

Be careful not to enter your own account's password when logging on to an anonymous FTP site. You should enter your e-mail address or, in some cases, the word *guest*.

NOTE In true password style, you won't see the password on the screen when you log in with FTP, even when you're just entering your e-mail address for a password using anonymous FTP.

Here's an example of starting an FTP session.

```
$ ftp is.internic.net
Connected to is.internic.net.
220-
220-    ****************************************************
220-    **                                                **
220-    **  Welcome to the Internic InfoGuide Archive     **
220-    **                                                **
220-    ****************************************************
220-
220-
220-
220 is FTP server (Version wu-2.4(2) Thu Apr 14 13:25:36 PDT 1994) ready.
Name (is.internic.net:waffle): anonymous
331 Guest login ok, send your complete e-mail address as password.
Password:
230-
230-Logged Access from: bolero.rahul.net
230-
230-IMPORTANT NOTE:
230---------------
230-If you have problems accessing this archive:
230-Try using a dash (-) as the first character of your password
230-This will turn off the continuation messages that may
230-be confusing your ftp client.
```

```
230-
230 Guest login ok, access restrictions apply.
ftp>
```

Although FTP's commands look a lot like UNIX commands, there are a few commands needed in FTP that don't exist in UNIX itself. The first command with which to become familiar is `help`, which should list the FTP commands available on your system.

Once you're connected, you will be able to navigate the remote system's directory and transfer files. Here are the commands for moving around directories:

> **`cd`.** With the `cd` command you can change your directory on the remote computer. Typing `cd /pub/games` will change your current directory to `/pub/games`. Typing `cd ..` (that's two dots) will move you up one directory—for instance, from `/pub/games` back to `/pub`. If your FTP host is running on a UNIX system, you can also type `cdup` to move up a directory; on VMS hosts, you can type `cd [-]`.

NOTE Typically, all the interesting stuff on anonymous FTP sites is in a directory called `pub` (which stands for public).

> **`lcd`.** Stands for *local change directory*. You can use this command to change the current directory on your local host. It doesn't affect what directory you're using at the FTP site. If you decide that you want the next file you retrieve to end up in the directory `/usr/potato` on your system, you can type `lcd /usr/potato`.
>
> **`pwd`.** Shows your present working directory on the FTP site.
>
> **`lpwd`.** This cryptic-sounding command means *local present working directory* and will tell you your present directory on your local system.
>
> **`ls` or `dir`.** These commands list the files in the current directory on the remote computer. I like the output from `dir` better than from `ls`, but take your pick. With most systems,

you use UNIX-style wildcards with these commands; for example, `dir inter*` will list all the files with names that start with *inter*.

Use these commands when you're through with FTP:

`close`. Typing `close` disconnects you from the remote FTP host, but leaves you in the FTP program so that you can connect to another site.

`quit`. Type `quit` to disconnect from the remote host and leave the FTP program.

> **NOTE** Is it a noun? Is it a verb? Both, sort of. Although my eighth-grade grammar teacher would cringe at the thought, I (along with everyone else on the Internet) use FTP interchangeably as a noun and a verb. "How do I use FTP?," "Hey! FTP to sunsite," and "Have you FTPed my spreadsheet yet?" are all understood. Don't let this confuse you; just remember that any noun can be verbed.

Q 6.4. How do I receive a file with FTP?

Once you're connected to an FTP site and have found the files you want, you can use the following commands to retrieve the files in which you are interested.

`ascii`. This command tells the system that you plan to transmit text (seven-bit) files. `ascii` mode is the default transfer mode and is the opposite of binary mode.

`binary`. This command switches to binary mode. You must be in binary mode to transfer binary (eight-bit) files such as .ZIP, .SIT, or .GIF files. In fact, I use binary mode all the time, even for transferring text files.

`get` and `mget`. The `get` command copies one file from the remote FTP site to your local host. If you want to grab multiple files using a wildcard, you can use `mget` instead. For example, `get rutabaga.zip` will transfer one file; `mget rut*` will transfer all files that start with the letters *rut*.

Unless your computer is directly connected to the Internet (that is, if you are connected through an intermediary remote host), software for use on your home computer needs to be FTPed to your local host, and then downloaded to your PC, using Xmodem, Zmodem, Kermit, or some other transfer protocol—a two-step process.

Here's a sample FTP session:

```
$ ftp mac.archive.umich.edu
Connected to mac.archive.umich.edu.
220 pogue.admin.lsa.umich.edu FTP server (ULTRIX Version 4.1 Tue Mar 19 00:38:17
EST 1991) ready.
Name (mac.archive.umich.edu:waffle): anonymous
331 Guest login ok, send ident as password.
Password:
230 Guest login ok, access restrictions apply.
ftp> lcd /nobak/waffle
Local directory now /hustle/stuff/nobak/waffle
ftp> cd /mac
250 CWD command successful.
ftp> ls
200 PORT command successful.
150 Opening data connection for /bin/ls (192.160.13.1,1268) (0 bytes).
.AppleDouble
.cache
00help
00introduction
00ls-lRfile
00newfiles
development
game
graphics
hypercard
incoming
misc
powerpc
sound
system.extensions
util
226 Transfer complete.
168 bytes received in 0.05 seconds (3.3 Kbytes/s)
ftp> cd misc/update
250 CWD command successful.
ftp> ls ram*
```

```
200 PORT command successful.
150 Opening data connection for /bin/ls (192.160.13.1,1278) (0 bytes).
ramdoublerup1.01.cpt.hqx
226 Transfer complete.
remote: ram*
26 bytes received in 0.021 seconds (1.2 Kbytes/s)
ftp> get ramdoublerup1.01.cpt.hqx
200 PORT command successful.
150 Opening data connection for ramdoublerup1.01.cpt.hqx (192.160.13.1,1280)
(79182 bytes).
226 Transfer complete.
local: ramdoublerup1.01.cpt.hqx remote: ramdoublerup1.01.cpt.hqx
79182 bytes received in 50 seconds (1.5 Kbytes/s)
ftp> quit
```

6.5. How do I send files with FTP?

Using FTP to send a file to another site is a simple process. Rather than "get" files from the remote host, you "put" them there using (what else?) the `put` command. And, as with getting files, you can send multiple files in one batch with the `mput` command.

For instance, say that the present working directory on your local computer contains five files, as follows:

```
Atari_8bit_FAQ
Internet_Services_FAQ
Internet_Services_List
Internet_Tools
Privacy_Anonymity_FAQ
```

You can send any or all of these to a remote FTP site. Connect to another host via FTP, find the remote directory in which you want to deposit the goods, and then use the `put` or `mput` commands to send the files on their merry way.

```
put Privacy_Anonymity_FAQ -- will send one file
```

> **NOTE** Some anonymous FTP sites don't allow you to send files; you only can receive them. More commonly, there is a specific directory where you're allowed to put file submissions for the FTP site. Check to see whether the FTP site has a directory called `/incoming`. If so, you're expected to deposit any incoming files there. If you're using full-privilege FTP, you can put files anywhere on the system on which you have permission to write files.

Here's an example of using the `put` command. (By the way, here I'm putting a file on a computer in Finland.)

```
$ ftp garbo.uwasa.fi
Connected to garbo.uwasa.fi.
220 garbo.uwasa.fi FTP server (Version 5.77 ...) ready.
Name (garbo.uwasa.fi:ts): anonymous
331 Guest login ok, send ident as password.
Password:
230 Guest login ok, access restrictions apply.
ftp> cd /pc/incoming
250 CWD command successful.
ftp> binary
200 Type set to I.
ftp> put myprog.zip
200 PORT command successful.
150 Opening BINARY mode data connection for myprog.zip
226 Transfer complete.
local: myprog.zip remote: myprog.zip
37775 bytes sent in .13 seconds (2.8e+02 Kbytes/s)
ftp> quit
221 Goodbye.
```

Q 6.6. How can I read a text file while on an FTP site without ending my FTP session?

Often, when you're exploring FTP sites, you'll see text files—such as file indices or `README` files—that you'll want to read immediately, without leaving the FTP session. If you're using UNIX, an easy way to get a file (in this example, it's called README) and view it in one fell swoop is by typing the following:

```
get README /dev/tty
```

Depending on the UNIX shell you use, you may also be able to use

```
get README ¦more
```

which will let you read the file one screenful at a time.

> **NOTE** Because many FTP sites allow only a small number of simultaneous users, if you plan to peruse a lot of long text files, don't read them while you're tying up an FTP connection. Instead, get them all at once and read them offline at your leisure.

Q 6.7. I can't FTP to a certain site. What could be wrong?

There are a few basic problems you might run into when trying to connect to an FTP site. Luckily, most of the error messages you'll see are straightforward; for instance, you might see a message that a particular site is temporarily down for maintenance or unavailable during business hours. In these cases, all you can do is try again later.

Because sites come and go on the Internet daily, the FTP site you read about in last week's *Internet Bliss* magazine (I just made that name up, but it sounds good, doesn't it?) may not exist anymore, or the archive may have moved to a computer with a different name. Trying to connect to a system that isn't there (because it's permanently offline or you mistyped the system name) will yield an "unknown host" message.

```
ftp> open nonexistent.com
nonexistent.com: unknown host
```

When this happens, check your spelling and punctuation (the Internet treats `big-bug.com` as a different name than `bigbug.com`) and try again. If things still don't go right, perhaps the system doesn't really exist or doesn't operate an FTP service.

You may also find that the FTP site is not currently on the network. If this happens, you'll get a `host unavailable` message. There's nothing to do but try again a few hours later or use one of the system's mirrors if there are any (see Question 6.10 later in this chapter). A `connection denied` message means that the computer is known on the network but isn't accepting FTP connections.

```
ftp> open ftp apple.com
ftp.apple.com: host unavailable
```

The most common (for me, anyway) problem when trying to connect to popular anonymous FTP sites is that the host computer has reached its maximum user capacity. If a system has reached its preset limit of FTP users, you'll be turned away when you try to connect. In this case, all you can do is wait a few minutes and try again. Or try using a mirror site.

```
ftp> open mac.archive.umich.edu
Connected to mac.archive.umich.edu.
220-
220-  Welcome to                               wuftpd 2.1c installed
220-  the U of M Software Archives                     -- rjc@umich.edu
220-
220-  Local Time:  Sun Mar 13 14:30:09 1994
220-
Name (mac.archive.umich.edu:savetz): anonymous
530-
530-    All allowed connections are being used at this time.
530-
530-Due to overwhelming usage during business hours, restrictions to ftp access
530-are now being enforced.  PLEASE be considerate and ftp during non-"business
530-hours" as much as possible.  Also, please keep connection times short.
530 User anonymous access denied.
Login failed.
```

Even if the site exists, is up and running, and isn't overloaded, there is one problem you might encounter: fumble fingers while logging on. If you misspell *anonymous* when logging in (something that's surprisingly easy to do), you'll see a message telling you a password is required. Whoops. Next time, type more carefully. Alternately, try using the login `ftp` rather than `anonymous`—this works on many systems and is a whole lot easier to type.

```
ftp> open mac.archive.umich.edu
Connected to mac.archive.umich.edu.
220-
220-  Welcome to                                 wuftpd 2.1c installed
220-  the U of M Software Archives                     -- rjc@umich.edu
220-
220-  carpediem.ccs.itd.umich.edu is brought to you by
220-          U of M's Campus Computing Sites
220-
220-  Local Time:  Sun Mar 27 21:22:46 1994
220-
220 carpediem.ccs.itd.umich.edu FTP server (Version wu-2.1c(1) Thu Feb 3 22:20:5
0 EST 1994) ready.
Name (mac.archive.umich.edu:waffle): anonymouse
331 Password required for anonymouse.
Password:
530 Login incorrect.
Login failed.
```

6.8. I'm trying to FTP a really large file, and it sure is taking a long time. How do I know whether it is still transferring or my connection died?

During your online exploits, you may find yourself FTPing a multimegabyte file from halfway across the globe and wondering whether that file is really on its way or your FTP connection silently and surreptitiously died. (The Internet is a lot of things, but it is usually neither fast nor reliable during very-long-distance file transfers.)

Well, the FTP program includes a command called `hash`, which forces the program to print a hash mark (also known as a pound sign, #) for every few kilobytes transferred by FTP. (How frequently seems to vary. On many systems you'll see a hash after every kilobyte; my system likes to send one every 8K.) This can be useful to reassure you that information is really flowing.

Use the `hash` command before you start a transfer if you suspect that your FTP connection is flaky. You probably won't want to use this command regularly unless you are particularly fond of those little # characters.

> **NOTE** You can also use the `hash` command for any really large transfer (even ones from nearby sites) so that you know the data is flowing and so you can get a visual clue about how fast the information is pouring through the wires.

```
$ ftp rahul.net
Connected to rahul.net.
220 bolero FTP server (Version 6.59 Sat Feb 26 23:52:17 PST 1994) ready.
Name (rahul.net:waffle): waffle
331 Password required for waffle.
Password:
230 User waffle logged in.
ftp> help hash
hash            toggle printing '#' for each buffer transferred
ftp> hash
Hash mark printing on (8192 bytes/hash mark).
ftp> get my-small-file
200 PORT command successful.
150 Opening ASCII mode data connection for my-small-file (49322 bytes).
#######
226 Transfer complete.
local: my-small-file remote: my-small-file
50309 bytes received in 2 seconds (24 Kbytes/s)
```

Q 6.9. How fast do files travel across the Internet?

That depends on the speed of the connection between your site and the remote host. When an FTP file transfer finishes, you'll see a line that says something like

```
37111 bytes received in 14 seconds (2.5 Kbytes/s)
```

which will tell you how fast your files are traveling. In this case, a 37K file was transferred in 14 seconds.

6.10. What is a mirror FTP site?

You'll sometimes log on to an FTP site and see a message announcing other sites that are so-called "mirrors" of that system. A mirror site is a computer system that maintains exact duplicates of all the files on some other system. The copy, or mirror, is updated on a regular basis (usually daily or weekly) to ensure that the mirrored information remains up to date.

Mirror sites are useful for a variety of reasons. They reduce the usage load on popular FTP sites by giving users alternative locations to use. Most computers on the Internet can handle only 50 to 100 FTPing users at once, so rather than have 500 people vying for space on a particularly popular site, some of those users can instead connect to mirrors of that site.

> **NOTE** You can be reasonably sure that files on a mirror site are the same as the files on the host that is being mirrored, but remember that mirror sites are synchronized on a regular basis—usually daily or weekly—so the very freshest, most recent files may take a day or two to make it to a mirror.

You can often use mirror sites to connect to a host that's physically closer to your local host, ensuring faster, more reliable, less expensive connections. Why should users in the United States connect to a host in Finland (using an expensive transatlantic link) when an exact duplicate of the site is available in their own state? Mirror sites can allow this convenience.

> **NOTE** A site may have multiple mirror sites. In fact, the most popular Internet FTP sites have dozens or hundreds of mirrors scattered around the globe.

6.11. How do I know whether a particular FTP site has mirrors?

There's no sure way to find out whether a favorite FTP site is mirrored. (Sometimes the FTP site administrators don't even know who keeps mirrors of their site.) The best thing you can do is look around the site for notices or help files when you log in with FTP. Many sites have files with names like `read-me-before-FTPing` placed in visible locations, as in `/pub`. I know that most of us don't like to read the documentation, but believe it or not, actually reading those files can provide a wealth of useful information.

> **NOTE** Remember that not all sites are mirrored. In some situations, you may have no choice but to grab that file from an FTP site on the other side of the planet.

6.12. I can't seem to send a file to a mirror of my favorite FTP site. Why not?

Although mirror sites are useful for receiving files available on popular anonymous FTP hosts, they can't be used for sending files to the mirrored host. That is, you can't send a file to a site's mirror and expect it to find its way to the original FTP site. The reason is that mirroring is a one-way exchange: A host's mirror checks in periodically to see what's changed and what new files are available at the main host, but the computer that is being mirrored doesn't check to see what's new at the mirror site. If you want to send a file to an FTP site, you'll have to send it directly to that site, not to one of its mirrors.

```
ftp.mirror-2.com
          ^
          |
          |
     ftp.big-bob.com   ----->  ftp.mirror-1.edu
          |
          |
          V
    another-mirror.gov
```

6.13. I constantly hear rumors about "pirate" FTP sites that contain commercial software. Do they exist? Can someone send me a list of them?

Looking for the latest version of PageMaker, SimCity 2000, or Windows but unwilling to pay outrageous prices for software? Welcome to the club. Seriously, the answers to these questions are yes and no. FTP sites specializing in pirated (also known as bootlegged) software do indeed exist. You probably won't find out about any of them, however.

In most civilized countries, wanton duplication of commercial software is illegal and carries a severe criminal penalty. The people who operate and use pirate FTP sites and bulletin board systems realize this, so they give access information only to a select few trusted friends, lest the FBI, SPA (Software Publishers Association), or any other group with an acronym for a name should find out about it. Unless you are known and trusted by someone who uses or runs a pirate software site, no one will tell you about them.

Public knowledge of such a site would cause it to come crashing down in a matter of days, either by sheer mass of users glutting themselves on free software or by the law. Or both.

NOTE The short answer is that software piracy is illegal and the use of the Internet to make illegal copies of commercial software is illegal, too.

Q 6.14. I grabbed a program with FTP, but it won't run on my system. What's wrong?

If you've downloaded a program (or graphics file, sound file, or whatever) to your computer from the Internet, but it won't run (or display or play or do whatever it is supposed to do), take heed: Any of a hundred little things could have gone wrong to mung your copy of the file.

> **NOTE** Thousands of files are copied each day from public archives such as anonymous FTP sites. Most of these sites are moderated; that is, before a file is made available to the public, someone checks it to make sure it works. It's not impossible that a the file you downloaded from a public archive is corrupt, but it is unlikely.

A common mistake is failing to transfer binary files (such as programs, archives, graphics, and such) in binary mode. If you don't explicitly specify binary transfer mode when FTPing a file and downloading it from your host to your PC, most programs assume that you want text mode. Copying a binary file in text mode is a sure way to make it unusable. Don't worry, everyone occasionally forgets to use the right transfer mode.

Inexperienced users often fail to translate or "uncompress" files before trying to use them. Most archive sites on the Net use some form of file compression and/or translation on their files. File compression allows files to use less hard disk space. Naturally, compressed files need to be uncompressed before use. Translated files are those that have been converted from eight-bit (binary) format to seven-bit format. Again, you'll have to turn these files back into binary before you can use them.

You need to know how those files have been tweaked before you can make them usable again. You will find some files that have been tweaked in multiple ways; for instance, compressed and translated.

Chapter 4, "How Can I Communicate with People Around the World?" contains questions and answers concerning how to tell if your file has been translated with `BinHex`, `uuencode`, or `btoa`, three popular translation formats.

Q 6.15. What's with all these filename extensions, file formats, and archiving systems?

How a file has been translated and compressed is usually indicated by the filename's suffix. Normally a file will have a name something like `filename.sit.hqx`. In this example, `sit` indicates how it was compressed and `hqx` indicates how it was translated. Before you can use any programs or view any graphics tweaked with any compression or translation tools, you'll need to turn the file back into its pristine original; for instance, by un`BinHex`ing and then un`Stuff`ing the file. (By the way, `BinHex` is used exclusively on Macintosh files.)

Some anonymous FTP sites make a habit of modifying files twice, first compressing them and then changing binary files to text format (so that they can easily pass through mail gateways and other computer systems that don't handle binary files).

There is a wonderful document that lists zillions of file compression, translation, and archiving formats along with their filename extensions and information on where to find the software to uncompress, translate, and "unarchive" files in these formats. It lists file formats that I never knew (and would rather not know) existed: ones with names like BLU, Disk-Masher, Ish, terse, Whap, and yabba. (May the gods of Internet smile on you and keep those arcane files far away from you.) Anyway, get this document, available by FTP:

```
ftp.cso.uiuc.edu directory:/doc/pcnet/compression
```

There is a FAQ posting that deals exclusively with picture file formats. It is posted regularly to `alt.binaries.pictures.fine-art.d`. It is available via anonymous FTP.

```
rtfm.mit.edu:/pub/usenet/news.answers/pictures-faq/part1
rtfm.mit.edu:/pub/usenet/news.answers/pictures-faq/part2
```

For e-mail access, send a message

```
To: mail-server@rtfm.mit.edu
Subject: <subject line is ignored>
Body: send usenet/news.answers/pictures-faq/*
```

Here's a list of some of the most popular archive systems, translation methods, and file formats. Rest assured that there are hundreds more.

Archive	*Compression Standards*
.ARC	Archive (typically, but not necessarily, for IBM-PC compatible computers)
.BSC	BinScii file for Apple II [TEXT]
.CPT	Compactor pro archive (Macintosh)
.GZ	GNU Compress (a.k.a. GnuZip, becoming popular on UNIX systems)
.HQX	BinHex file, most likely for a Macintosh [TEXT]
.LHA	LHA archive (used on IBM, Amigas, and other systems)
.LZH	LZH archive (used on IBM, Amigas, and other systems)
.SEA	Self-extracting archive (might be Mac, might not)
.SHAR	UNIX shell archive [TEXT]
.SIT	Macintosh stuffit archive
.TAR	UNIX tape archive
.Z	UNIX compressed file
.ZIP	IBM zip archive
.ZOO	IBM zoo archive

continues

Archive	*Compression Standards*
Translation standards	
`.BTOA`	UNIX binary-to-ASCII file [TEXT]
`.HQX`	BinHex file [TEXT]
`.UU`	UNIX uuencode file [TEXT]
`.UUE`	UNIX uuencode file [TEXT]
`.XXE`	UNIX xxencode file [TEXT]
Graphics file formats	
`.BMP`	Windows and OS/2 bitmap picture file
`.EPS`	Encapsulated postscript
`.GIF`	Graphics interchange format
`.IFF`	Amiga Interchangeable file format
`.JPEG`	(sometimes .JPG) joint photographic experts group graphics file
`.PICT`	Macintosh PICTure format
`.TIFF`	Tag image file format graphics file

6.16. How do I tell whether a file is compressed?

There are a variety of programs for compressing files, like the DOS tool PKZIP (which creates files with the extension .ZIP) and the Macintosh shareware program StuffIt Lite (which makes files with the filename extension .SIT). UNIX has a file compression method of its own, simply named `compress`. Files compressed with the UNIX compress program end in the extension `.Z`.

Many of the files available from Internet archives are compressed to save disk space and reduce file transfer time. Similar to .ZIP files on a DOS computer and .SIT files on a Macintosh, UNIX's compressed files take up relatively little space, but aren't useful while in compressed form; you need to uncompress them before use.

6.17. How do I uncompress a UNIX compressed file?

Just type `uncompress filename.Z`. The program will create an uncompressed version of the file (with the same name, *sans* the `.Z` extension) and delete the compressed version.

> **NOTE** You didn't ask, but in case you were wondering, you can compress a file by typing `compress filename`. The program will compress your file, add the .Z extension, and delete the original file.
>
> Further, if you type `compress filename` and it's already compressed, the program is smart enough to figure that out, add the .Z suffix, and uncompress it! Pretty handy, eh?

6.18. Is there a list of all anonymous FTP sites?

There probably isn't a list of all the world's anonymous FTP sites, but there is one—a behemoth seven-part tome—that is certainly close enough to complete. It should keep you busy for a long, long time.

A typical entry in the FTP list looks like this:

```
Site   : explorer.arc.nasa.gov
Country: USA
GMT    : -8
Date   : 06-Jan-94
Source : MODERxx.ZIP; old ftp-list
Alias  :
Admin  : yee@atlas.arc.nasa.gov (Peter Yee)
Organ  : NASA - Ames Research Center, , California
Server :
System : Unix
Comment: A CD-ROM farm with 84 NASA image and data discs on-line, /cdrom
Files  : Images and data mostly of Jet Propulsion Laboratory space probes,
Viking, Voyager, Magellan etc.
```

It is available via FTP.

```
rtfm.mit.edu:/pub/usenet/news.answers/ftp-list/sitelist/*
oak.oakland.edu:/pub/msdos/info/ftp-list.zip
ftp.edu.tw:/documents/networking/guides/ftp-list
garbo.uwasa.fi:/pc/doc-net/ftp-list.zip
```

It's also available via e-mail.

```
To: mail-server@rtfm.mit.edu
Subject: <subject line is ignored>
body:  send usenet/news.answers/ftp-list/sitelist/*
```

Q 6.19. Where can I get updates on new software and stuff on the Internet?

The Usenet group `comp.archives` is home to information about the latest updates to many Internet file archives. This newsgroup is a great place to find out about recent additions to file archives and learn about new ones. Here's some of what was announced on `comp.archives` today: pictures from the movie *Deliverance*, relief maps of United States geography, a movie archive, and lots of other good stuff.

```
[comp.speech] "rsynth" text-to-speech code f...and SGI
[comp.robotics] 'F1 controller software
[comp.sys.ibm.pc.games.action] * * * SPISPOPD V2...* *
[alt.games.doom] ** JUMBLE v3.0 RELEASED **
[comp.os.ms-windows.announce] 26 New...CICA [02/23/94]
[comp.os.ms-windows.announce] 43 New...CICA [02/23/94]
[comp.sys.atari.8bit] 8-Bit Emulator on ftp.wustl.edu
[comp.music] >>>> QSEQ v1.0c acce...mailer <<<<<<<<<<
[comp.infosystems.www] [ANNOUNCE] RosettaMan v2.0 alpha
[rec.games.board.marketplace] [VidBits]...Out Already!
[rec.arts.fine] A Free Digital Gallery
[rec.games.bolo] Amoeba's personal Bolo WWW page
[comp.lang.tcl] ANNOUNCE: xibc-0.3...Backgammon Server
[comp.ai.neural-nets] ANNOUNCEMENT cont...RNS Features
[comp.lang.functional] Announcing MacGofer 0.22
[alt.sources.d] announcing ncurses 1.8.5
[sci.crypt] Announcing pgptalk
```

```
[comp.infosystems.www] ANNOUNCING: the...Movie Archive
[comp.sys.apple2] Apple II emulator ready (well, kinda)
[sci.archaeology] Archaeological...server announcement
[rec.audio] AUDIO-related Mac software by ftp
[rec.music.christian] Deliverance JPEG's
[comp.infosystems.announce] digital USA relief maps on WWW
```

Q 6.20. I don't have access to FTP! Am I cut off from the world of software archives?

No! Anonymous FTP isn't the only way to browse and retrieve software from the Internet's archives. Many sites allow retrieval of their software using Gopher, WWW, and WAIS. These services make searching much easier, but require special client software to be installed on your host machine. You can also get files using electronic mail, which everyone on the Internet can do.

For more information on using Gopher, WWW, and WAIS, read the Usenet newsgroup `comp.infosystems.gopher`, `comp.infosystems.www`, or `comp.infosystems.wais`.

There are plenty of Usenet newsgroups dedicated to postings of software binaries (ready-to-run programs) and source code. These groups are great ways to find the most recent versions of popular programs with a minimum of fuss, but they aren't useful as long-term archives. After the messages expire, the software is gone from the Usenet until the next time it is posted (if there is a next time).

The easiest way to find them is to look for Usenet groups that begin with `comp.sources` or `comp.binaries`. For example, the group `comp.binaries.mac` contains new versions of a variety of shareware programs, in BinHex format.

Q 6.21. I don't have access to the FTP program. How can I get files via e-mail?

A variety of servers are available that will send you files by electronic mail. These are useful for folks (like BITNET and UUCP users) who don't have access to FTP, Gopher, or the other methods of accessing Internet file archives.

If you are looking for FAQ documents, for instance, you can access the mail server at `rtfm.mit.edu`. A mail server is a program that takes requests for information and mails back to you what you want to know. `rtfm.mit.edu` is home to thousands of the Internet's frequently asked questions and answers lists, which you can retrieve via e-mail. (Actually, this is nothing new. In previous chapters, I've showed how to get a variety of files from the MIT document server.) For information, send e-mail

```
To: mail-server@rtfm.mit.edu
Subject: <subject line is ignored>
Body: help
```

You will receive a document explaining how this document server works.

You can also search for and transfer programs, graphic files, and other good stuff from FTP sites using mail servers. A number of FTP-by-mail servers are available. You should use the one that's closest to you.

> **NOTE** Please make sure that your system administrator has approved the use of mail servers. Files can take system resources not only at your site, but also on computers "up the stream." Telephone line charges for some electronic mail services—such as FidoNet and UUCP connections—cost real people real money. Your administrator probably won't like you much if he is forced to pay for a three-hour, long-distance phone call because you decided to grab a million files using an e-mail server.

Remember that binary files can't be sent through e-mail, so any files you request will be translated to a seven-bit format. You may be able to choose how your desired files will be encoded—with uuencode or BinHex, for example. Read the server's documentation thoroughly, and experiment by retrieving small files before trying to download every program ever written for your computer.

> **NOTE** Electronic-mail gateways can be fickle, limiting the size and type of incoming e-mail, so with FTP-by-mail servers you can set the maximum size of messages sent to you. These servers can split huge files into smaller chunks that your e-mail gateway can better handle. When you receive the files, you'll need to put the pieces back together, in the right order.

Here's a partial list of FTP-by-mail servers:

```
ftpmail@ftp.dartmouth.edu (USA)
ftpmail@decwrl.dec.com (USA)
ftpmail@sunsite.unc.edu (USA)
ftpmail@cs.uow.edu.au (Australia)
ftpmail@ftp.uni-stuttgart.de (Germany)
ftpmail@grasp.insa-lyon.fr (France)
ftpmail@src.doc.ic.ac.uk (Great Britain)
ftpmail@ieunet.ie (Ireland)
ftpmail@lth.se (Sweden)
ftpmail@ftp.edu.tw (Taiwan)
bitftp@pucc.princeton.edu (USA)
bitftp@plearn.edu.pl (Poland)
bitftp@vm.gmd.de (Germany)
```

If you are on BITNET, send your mail to one of the following:

```
BITFTP@PUCC
BITFTP@PLEARN
BITFTP@DEARN
```

Commands for using these services are similar to using the FTP program: You put your FTP commands, one per line, for the server to act upon. For information on using one of these services, send e-mail to one of the preceding addresses:

```
Subject: <subject line is ignored>
Body: help
```

6.22. Where can I find the program called ______, or what is Archie?

Answered by Dave Taylor (taylor@netcom.com)

Imagine that you've just walked into a library but aren't familiar with the organizational system it uses. You thought you'd figured out the Dewey Decimal System, and almost have a handle on the Library of Congress organizational scheme, but this appears to just be a semi-random ordering of books, sorted by whether they're intended to be for the public, for special groups, or others. Now multiply that by a few thousand libraries and try to find a copy of *The New Holistic Herbal.* It's impossible.

On the Internet, FTP archives are akin to libraries of information. Imagine it: thousands of repositories of information and no way to know which might have the information you seek.

It's enough to cause a headache, and indeed it did for a creative team at McGill University in Canada. The result, however, wasn't that they went to lie down, but that they created a centralized database of all files available on all anonymous FTP sites throughout the world. All sites. Over 2.5 million different files! Then, because this is the Internet, they designed a server that would allow other systems to connect and find information without having to replicate the massive database on each computer on the network. The result is Archie.

They did a fantastic job, and Archie is a lifesaver if you ever search for specific files or programs, no matter what computer they run on. But that's not all, because FTP archives include all sorts of curious things, so there's also a large recipe database, and Archie can find all the cookie recipes if you're interested!

There are caveats to this service, though. The greatest is that the program doesn't really know anything about any of the millions of files listed in the database other than the name of the file, the name of the computer on which it lives, and the directory within which it resides. If you are looking for a program called Wanda but it's in the archives as "wnd," searching for Wanda will not find it. If you want a specific version of the program, you might find yourself retrieving and examining a half-dozen copies before you find the one you want; Archie doesn't know about version numbers, either.

6.23. How do I access Archie?

If your Internet host has its own Archie client installed, you should be able to simply type the word `archie` to start the program. If your site doesn't have Archie installed, you can Telnet to one of the Internet's public Archie server sites. They're listed in the next question, but be warned that they can be very busy!

Once you connect, login as `archie` (no password is needed) and type `prog filename` to search for a specific file. Specify an exact program name for it to seek and it will list the matches it finds in the database. For instance, you would type `prog Wanda` to search for a convenient FTP site for a program that you know is called Wanda. Archie searches can include options, so you can search for your word within other words (for example, *edit* could match *editor* or *to-edit*) or specifically on all uppercase or lowercase letters only. You can type `help` for detailed instructions from Archie.

In the following example, in just under a minute, Archie found more than a thousand files with the name `nethack` scattered around the Internet.

```
$ telnet archie.unl.edu
Trying 129.93.1.14 ...
Connected to crcnis2.unl.edu.
Escape character is '^]'.

SunOS UNIX (crcnis2)

login: archie
Password:

##############################################################################

        #     # ####### ######  ######     #     #####  #    #     #
        ##    # #       #     # #     #   # #   #     # #   #     # #
        # #   # #       #     # #     #  #   #  #       #  #     #   #
        #  #  # #####   ######  ######  #     #  #####  ###     #     #
        #   # # #       #     # #   #   #######       # #  #    #######
        #    ## #       #     # #    #  #     # #     # #   #   #     #
        #     # ####### ######  #     # #     #  #####  #    #  #     #

     Welcome to the ARCHIE server at the University of Nebraska · Lincoln
```

6

```
    If you need further instructions, type help at the unl-archie> prompt.

################################################################################

# Bunyip Information Systems, 1993

# Terminal type set to 'vt100 24 80'.
# 'erase' character is '^?'.
# 'search' (type string) has the value 'sub'.
unl-archie> prog nethack
# Search type: sub.
# Your queue position: 9
# Estimated time for completion: 00:51
working... -

Host ftp.wustl.edu    (128.252.135.4)
Last updated 10:08 25 Dec 1993

    Location: /mirrors/cabrales.cs.wisc.edu/TOP/USR/GAMES
      FILE    -r--r--r--   50983 bytes  23:00 18 Oct 1989  nh305_NETHACK3DIR.t.Z

    Location: /systems/os9/cabrales/TOP/USR/GAMES
      FILE    -r--r--r--   50983 bytes  23:00 18 Oct 1989  nh305_NETHACK3DIR.t.Z

    Location: /mirrors/cabrales.cs.wisc.edu/TOP/USR/GAMES/CMDS
      FILE    -r--r--r--  228643 bytes  00:00 30 Dec 1988  nethack.Z

    Location: /systems/os9/cabrales/TOP/USR/GAMES/CMDS
      FILE    -r--r--r--  228643 bytes  00:00 30 Dec 1988  nethack.Z

    Location: /mirrors/cabrales.cs.wisc.edu/TOP/USR/GAMES/CMDS
      FILE    -r--r--r--  384212 bytes  23:00 18 Oct 1989  nethack3.Z

    Location: /systems/os9/cabrales/TOP/USR/GAMES/CMDS
      FILE    -r--r--r--  384212 bytes  23:00 18 Oct 1989  nethack3.Z

    Location: /systems/amiga/aminet/fish/ff822
      FILE    -rw-rw-r--  783224 bytes  00:00  8 Mar 1993  NetHack.lha
```

You can also use Archie via an electronic mail interface. You can get details on using Archie by e-mail by sending mail

```
To: archie@archie.mcgill.ca
Subject: <subject line is ignored>
Body: help
```

Many other Archies that you can Telnet to also have e-mail interfaces.

6.24. Where can I get a list of sites that run Archie?

Right here.

`archie.unl.edu` (Nebraska)

`archie.internic.net` (New Jersey)

`archie.rutgers.edu` (New Jersey)

`archie.ans.net` (New York)

`archie.sura.net` (Maryland)

`archie.au` (Australia)

`archie.edvz.uni-linz.ac.at` (Austria)

`archie.univie.ac.at` (Austria)

`archie.uqam.ca` (Canada)

`archie.funet.fi` (Finland)

`archie.th-darmstadt.de` (Germany)

`archie.ac.il` (Israel)

`archie.unipi.it` (Italy)

`archie.wide.ad.jp` (Japan)

`archie.kr` (Korea)

`archie.sogang.ac.kr` (Korea)

`archie.rediris.es` (Spain)

`archie.luth.se` (Sweden)

`archie.switch.ch` (Switzerland)

`archie.ncu.edu.tw` (Taiwan)

`archie.doc.ic.ac.uk` (United Kingdom)

To get a current list of Archie servers, Telnet to any Archie and type `server`.

6.25. Where can I find a program to do ________?

If you don't know the name of a specific program, but you do know that you want a program that does a specific thing, you can let your fingers do the walking with archive sites that maintain file description abstracts. Connect to your favorite archive site, find the directory that sounds like it holds the kind of program you're looking for, and look at a description of the files there. OK, so it's not high tech, but it works.

Most anonymous FTP archives include index files that briefly describe the various programs available at the site. Generally, each subdirectory has its own abstract file that lists the programs available therein. Abstract file names typically begin with `00` and end with either `.txt` or `.abs`. (I keep writing *generally* and *typically* because the folks behind the scenes at each FTP site are free to index the system any way they want—or not index it at all. Your mileage may vary.) For instance, `00index.txt`. Some FTP sites have a complete list of all the files and abstracts. Try looking for a file called something like `/pub/00all-abstracts`.

So if I were looking for a freeware Tetris-like game for the Macintosh, I would FTP to `mac.archive.umich.edu`, go to the directory `/mac/game/arcade`, and get the file `00index.txt`. I would peruse the index offline and reconnect later to grab the files that interest me.

6.26. What should I know before submitting files to a software archive?

The Internet's software archives thrive when its users submit an abundance of new software, art, sound files, and so on. Sharing is a two-way street ('tis better to give than to receive and all that), so if you come across a great program (or wrote one yourself), by all means share it with the Internet community!

Of course, there are some things to bear in mind before you submit your new *Star Trek* trivia quiz, word processing program, or scans of your Cindy Crawford art deco placemat collection.

- **First, is the software appropriate for that archive?** Of course, you shouldn't send Macintosh games to a site dedicated to MS-DOS programs. Some sites specialize in scientific papers, finance information, and other technical information and reject everything outside their specific area.
- **Send only quality files.** A good rule of thumb is to only submit software that you would bother to download yourself.
- **If you created the software (or graphics file or whatever it is) make sure that you clearly indicate its status.** Is it in the public domain or is it copyrighted software? Do you expect a shareware payment, or is your software free to use? For your own protection, make these things clear.
- **If it's not your original work, make sure that the file may be legally distributed.** For example, is it public domain or shareware? If you scan a photo of Cindy Crawford, for example, upload it, and then are caught, you'll face some pretty serious legal charges from the owner of the original work. This is doubly so for anything typed from a magazine or book.

Once you've decided that a file is suitable for a certain software archive, you can help the site administrators and draw positive attention to your submission by following these guidelines:

- **Include a version number with all programs uploaded.**
- **Use unique filenames that stand out and tell something about the program.** GIF2PICT.ZIP is certainly a better filename than UTIL.ZIP.
- **Be sure to send your file using the preferred archive and/or translation format of the archive moderators.** (For instance, they may prefer .ZIP files over .ARC files or Stuffed and BinHexed files over Compact Pro archives.) Most sites discourage use of self-extracting archives, except in rare cases. You probably don't need to make your archive self-extracting.

Q 6.27. What is AFS?

AFS is another way to move files around the Internet. It is a distributed file system that allows hosts to share files across local area networks—and bigger networks, such as the Internet. AFS, also known as *Andrew File System*, was originally developed at the Information Technology Center at Carnegie Mellon University.

The nifty thing about AFS is that, from the user's point of view, there is no difference between perusing directories and downloading files on your local computer's hard disk drives and those linked by AFS. All the commands that you normally use to access local files, move around directories, and so on, can be used to access files in AFS. You don't need to run a special program (as with FTP); you just go to a special directory (usually called `/afs`) and use the commands with which you are already familiar.

So instead of FTPing to `spider.big-bug.com`, you could just type `cd /afs/spider.big-bug.com/pub`.

Unfortunately, not many Internet sites offer AFS access. In order to use AFS, both your local host and the remote site from which you wish to grab files must be part of the AFS network. From what I understand, AFS is a pain to configure, and it runs only on UNIX systems (such as HP, NeXT, DEC, IBM, and Suns). For these reasons, AFS isn't very common despite its niftiness.

NOTE AFS is a commercial product that is supplied and maintained by Transarc Corporation. The company can be reached via e-mail at `information@transarc.com`, by phone at (412) 338-4400, and by fax at (412) 338-4404.

For more information about AFS, read the Usenet newsgroup `alt.filesystems.afs`. There is an anonymous FTP site with information about AFS: `grand.central.org`. The `/pub` directory contains newsletters, release notes, and technical information about AFS.

Also, check out the AFS FAQ.

FTP:

`grand.central.org:/pub/afs-contrib/doc/faq/afs.faq`

E-mail:

```
To: mail-server@rtfm.mit.edu
Subject: <subject line is ignored>
Body: send usenet/news.answers/afs-faq
```

Usenet:

`alt.filesystems.afs`

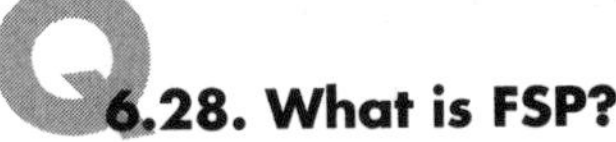

6.28. What is FSP?

FSP is a file transfer protocol, similar to FTP, but it's healthier, better for the environment, and won't lead to tooth decay. The FSP FAQ says, "FSP is what anonymous FTP *should* be." It's designed for anonymous archives, and includes protection against overloading the FSP server and the network itself.

I've never used FSP, so I'll leave it to the FSP FAQ to explain why FSP is so wonderful in comparison to FTP.

```
From the user's point of view, the differences are not that great, except that
some of the more annoying features of FTP are gone.  Here are the main
differences.

a. The protocol can stand things going down: if the server or the network
falls over in the middle of a transfer, you can just wait until it comes back
up. You don't have to reconnect, and even better, if the server went down 90%
through grabbing a file, you can continue from where you left off.

b. The protocol doesn't need a username or password. You just throw packets at
the server.  You don't have to identify yourself (though you're not completely
anonymous).

c. It's harder to kill off a site with an FSP server than with an FTP server.
The FSP daemon is designed to be as lightweight as possible:  it doesn't fork
off any sub-processes, and it takes steps to limit the amount of traffic it
handles.

d. The user interface is completely different.  The interface that comes with
the package consists of eleven commands that you can call from the shell.  In
```

```
effect, your shell is providing all the nice functions like command line
editing. This makes the interface much more versatile than FTP's.

e. FSP is a bit slower than FTP. This is a feature, not a bug. The point is
to keep the communication lightweight, and not to flood the Net.
```

Discussion about the implementation and usage of FSP takes place on the Usenet newsgroup `alt.comp.fsp`. You can get a current list of FSP sites by fingering `charro@bode.ee.ualberta.ca`.

6.29. Where can I get the FSP software?

The official place for FSP distribution is `ftp.germany.eu.net:/pub/network/inet/fsp`. It is available both by FTP and FSP; the FSP server is on port 2001.

Another official site is `taxus.uib.no:/fspdist`, which only runs an FSP server on port 9000. Sorry, you can't FTP there.

6.30. What are electronic journals?

Electronic journals (e-journals) are publications that are distributed online rather than in traditional formats like printed magazines. Publishing a printed magazine is an expensive and laborious process, but e-journals are inexpensive to create and distribute. Global computer networks are giving more people a quick and inexpensive means to be heard. With electronic journals, freedom of the press isn't limited to those with access to a printing press.

Through electronic journals, anyone with access to a computer and a modem can produce and distribute a magazine using computer networks such as the Internet. At last count there were more than 400 electronic journals covering every conceivable topic, including poetry, health issues, mass transit, the environment, and art. When there isn't a magazine that fits a need, starting one requires only a computer and access to a network. These periodicals typically have a more diverse, although smaller, audience than traditional magazines. The editors range from young crackers and "phone phreaks" to scientists and journalists.

Most publishers of electronic journals would have been unable to produce a traditional magazine, due to cost and time constraints. Online publishing offers the ability to create a professional-looking publication using minimal resources.

Most electronic journals are free. "Subscribing" means nothing more than asking to automatically receive new issues in your electronic mailbox. E-journals also generally lack advertising. Until there is a method for profit in electronic distribution, e-journals won't become a mainstream medium.

NOTE What e-journals are available? Try *InterText*, a bimonthly fiction magazine, or the *Health Info-Com Network Newsletter*, focusing on health issues for doctors.

Perhaps you're more in the mood for the *Unplastic News*, an ASCII free-form punk extravaganza. The cover says that *Unplastic* is for those who "like to read short odd pieces arranged in absolutely no order whatsoever." Its purpose, according to publisher Todd Tibbetts, (`tt1@netcom.com`) is to make you giggle or think. The *Unplastic News* is the sort of nutty fun that probably couldn't exist without electronic distribution. "The *Unplastic News* is more of a symbol than anything else," he says. "A symbol of what is yet to come. A symbol of free information. I love to receive mail from readers in Kaliningrad or Kyoto or Zanzibar—places I didn't even think had electricity. And these people are just like us...reaching out to try to touch the planet."

```
**                               *******
    *                               *  *  *
    *                                  *
    * **     * ******* ***** ****      *  ***** **   ** *******
    *  **    * *  *  *  *     *  *     *   *      * *   *  *  *
    *  * *   *    *     *     *   *    *   *      * *      *
    *  *  *  *    *     *     *   *    *   *       *       *
    *  *   * *    *     ***   ****     *   ***     *       *
    *  *    **    *     *     *  *     *   *      * *      *
    *  *     *    *     *     *   *    *   *      * *      *
    *  *     *    *     ****  *    *   *   ****  *   *     *

=======================================
InterText Vol. 4, No. 3 / May-June 1994
=======================================

  The Watcher   by Jason Snell
==============================

  The watcher had just passed middle age when it felt it for the
  first time, a little breath of cold as it passed by just out of
  reach. It was the first cold the watcher had felt in the
  millions of years since its coalescence.

  Time moved along, balls of mud and gas spinning in their orbits,
  the cold touch a long-forgotten memory. The small life-things
  still clung to one of the balls of mud, taking hesitant steps
  toward their brothers. The watcher continued its silent vigil.

  Then, again, the cold breath blew into its heart. Stronger this
  time, and the watcher could feel its claws as it passed. A black
  icy bird, with a sharp beak and razor-sharp talons. Moving
  through the darkness like quicksilver.
```

Q 6.31. Where can I find electronic journals?

On the Usenet, read `alt.etext`, `alt.zines`, and `rec.mag` for information about electronic journals.

The FTP site `ftp.cic.net` is a clearinghouse for hundreds of e-journals. Look in `ftp.cic.net:/pub/e-serials/ej.lst` for an extensive list of e-journals, complete with descriptions and information on finding them online.

You'll also find hundreds of e-journals at the following FTP sites:

```
ftp.eff.org:/pub/journals
etext.archive.umich.edu
```

```
quartz.rutgers.edu
ftp.msen.com
ftp.halcyon.com
netcom.com:/pub/johnl/zines
grind.isca.uiowa.edu:/info/journals
nin.cic.net:/norcomm/gopher/e-serials
```

Various sites also offer e-texts by Gopher, including

```
gopher.eff.org
etext.archive.umich,edu
gopher.cic.net
gopher.well.sf.ca.us
gopher.unt.edu
```

Once you find an electronic journal you would like to subscribe to, you'll find an editor's e-mail address somewhere in each issue. Send an e-mail note to the editor asking to be added to the subscriber list, or follow any specific instructions for subscribing listed in the journal.

NOTE A disclaimer at `etext.archive.umich.edu` nicely sums up the content of the more subversive e-journals.

The files on this archive server are presented as a contribution to scholarly research, documenting cultural phenomena and movements. Some of them may be offensive to you. In fact, it is a near certainty that you will find some of them morally repugnant, politically incorrect, and/or subversive. If this bothers you, you may disconnect now.

6.32. Where can I find computer graphics, pictures, and fine art?

The Usenet is rife with graphics and art. Check out the newsgroups `alt.binaries.pictures.fine-art.graphics` (for those pictures created with computer graphics programs) and alt.binaries.pictures.fine-art.digitized (for reproductions of paintings, drawings, prints, and so on). Discussion of the art on these groups takes place on alt.binaries.pictures.fine-art.d. If you are interested in fractal imagery, look at alt.binaries.pictures.fractals.

The newsgroup alt.binaries.pictures.erotica is where you can find pictures featuring human nudity or pornography. And in case you were wondering, alt.binaries.pictures.tasteless is for tasteless and bizarre pictures. Pictures that don't fit elsewhere can be found on alt.binaries.pictures.misc.

Archives of the Usenet fine-art groups can be perused using anonymous FTP.

```
uxa.ecn.bgu.edu:/pub/fine-art.
```

Another art archive is available via FTP at the following:

```
sunsite.unc.edu:/pub/multimedia/pictures/OTIS
```

There's an online art gallery accessible via Gopher at gopher.mta.ca. A WWW version that wasn't complete when I wrote this is available at the following:

```
hhtp://cs1.mta.ca/FineArts/FineArts.html
```

Another computer graphics mecca is ftp.informatik.-unioldenburg.de (located in Germany). Because cross-pond FTP is slow and wastes bandwidth, it is better to get it at a mirror site such as wuarchive.wustl.edu:/graphics/graphics/mirrors/ftp.informatik.uni-oldenburg.de.

For more information, read the alt.binaries.pictures FAQ. It is posted every other Monday to the newsgroup alt.binaries.pictures. It is also available by anonymous FTP.

```
rtfm.mit.edu :/pub/usenet/news.answers/pictures-
faq/*
```

It is also available via e-mail. Send a message

```
To: mail-server@rtfm.mit.edu
Subject: <Subject line is ignored>
Body: send usenet/news.answers/pictures-faq/*
```

Q 6.33. Where can I get software for my IBM PC computer?

The Usenet is home to several newsgroups for software for DOS machines.

The group comp.binaries.ibm.pc is where you'll find "binaries," or ready-to-run software, for DOS machines such as the IBM PC, AT, and compatible computers. On the day that I looked at comp.binaries.ibm.pc to see what was up, it was filled with new releases of virus-scanning software.

```
======  17 unread articles in comp.binaries.ibm.pc -- read now? [+ynq]=
Reading overview file.
 1351 v25i085: scanv113.zip, VirusScan V113 Virus Scanner (part 01/06)
 1352 v25i086: scanv113.zip, VirusScan V113 Virus Scanner (part 02/06)
 1353 v25i087: scanv113.zip, VirusScan V113 Virus Scanner (part 03/06)
 1354 v25i088: scanv113.zip, VirusScan V113 Virus Scanner (part 04/06)
 1355 v25i089: scanv113.zip, VirusScan V113 Virus Scanner (part 05/06)
 1356 v25i090: scanv113.zip, VirusScan V113 Virus Scanner (part 06/06)
 1357 v25i091: clean113.zip, Clean-Up V113 Virus Remover (part 01/07)
 1358 v25i092: clean113.zip, Clean-Up V113 Virus Remover (part 02/07)
 1359 v25i093: clean113.zip, Clean-Up V113 Virus Remover (part 03/07)
 1360 v25i094: clean113.zip, Clean-Up V113 Virus Remover (part 04/07)
 1361 v25i095: clean113.zip, Clean-Up V113 Virus Remover (part 05/07)
 1362 v25i096: clean113.zip, Clean-Up V113 Virus Remover (part 06/07)
 1363 v25i097: clean113.zip, Clean-Up V113 Virus Remover (part 07/07)
 1364 v25i098: vshld113.zip, VirusShield V113 TSR Virus Protection (part 01/04)
 1365 v25i099: vshld113.zip, VirusShield V113 TSR Virus Protection (part 02/04)
 1366 v25i100: vshld113.zip, VirusShield V113 TSR Virus Protection (part 03/04)
 1367 v25i101: vshld113.zip, VirusShield V113 TSR Virus Protection (part 04/04)
What next? [npq]
```

The group comp.binaries.ibm.pc.d is for discussions and bug reports about the programs posted to comp.binaries.ibm.pc. comp.binaries.ibm.pc.wanted is for file requests and replies concerning where to find programs for IBM PCs. These newsgroups are only for distribution of public domain, freeware, and shareware programs for DOS machines; commercial programs and OS/2 aren't dealt with there.

The newsgroup comp.archives.msdos.announce is a moderated newsgroup for announcements about MS-DOS archives.

Via FTP, check out the following:

```
ftp.cica.indiana.edu:/pc
ftp.uu.net:/systems/msdos
wuarchive.wustl.edu:/systems/ibmpc
sunsite.unc.edu:/pub/micro/pc-stuff
ftp.cso.uiuc.edu:/pc
gatekeeper.dec.com:/micro
oak.oakland.edu:/pub
```

NOTE You'll find more discussions about MS-DOS computers on `comp.os.msdos.apps`, `comp.os.msdos.misc`, `comp.os.msdos.programmer`, `comp.sys.ibm.pc.games`, `comp.sys.ibm.pc.hardware`, and `comp.sys.ibm.pc.digest`.

6.34. What about the site *wsmr-simtel20.army.mil* that I heard about?

One of the most popular FTP sites for programs for the IBM PC was Simtel20, an enormous archive based at the U.S. Army's White Sands Missile Range. Simtel is long gone, however; it was closed at the end of September, 1993. Fear not, because several sites still carry mirrors of Simtel, and although these mirrors are no longer updated, you can still peruse one of the largest software collections on the Internet.

(Michigan) `oak.oakland.edu:/pub/msdos`
(Missouri) `wuarchive.wustl.edu:/systems/ibmpc/msdos`
(Oregon) `archive.orst.edu:/pub/mirrors/oak.oakland.edu/simtel20/msdos`
(Falls Church, VA) `ftp.uu.net:/systems/ibmpc/msdos/simtel20`
(Australia) `archie.au:/micros/pc/oak`
(England) `src.doc.ic.ac.uk:/pub/packages/simtel20`
(Finland) `ftp.funet.fi:/pub/msdos/SimTel-mirror`

(Germany) ftp.uni-paderborn.de:/msdos
(Israel) ftp.technion.ac.il:/pub/unsupported/dos/simtel
(Switzerland) ftp.switch.ch:/mirror/msdos
(Taiwan) NCTUCCCA.edu.tw:/PC/simtel
(Thailand) ftp.nectec.or.th:/pub/mirrors/msdos

Q 6.35. Where can I get software for OS/2?

On the Usenet, look in comp.binaries.os2 for programs that run under OS/2.

There's also an OS/2 home page available with WWW. Its address is as follows:

```
http://www.mit.edu:8001/activities/os2/os2world.html
```

You'll find lots of great information about OS/2 in the OS/2 FAQ list.

You can obtain the OS/2 FAQ via FTP.

```
ftp-os2.cdrom.com:/pub/os2/all/info/faq/faq21d.zip
```

(Actually, the filename changes with each version number and probably will have changed by the time you read this.)

NOTE Other newsgroups are available for discussion of OS/2, including comp.os.os2.multimedia, comp.os.os2.setup, comp.os.os2.bugs, comp.os.os2.advocacy, comp.os.os2.networking, comp.os.os2.apps, and comp.os.os2.announce.

6.36. Where can I find software for Microsoft Windows?

A huge repository of Windows shareware and freeware is `ftp.cica.indiana.edu:/pub/pc/win3`. It has everything, including editors, games, waveform files, programmer utilities, and Windows NT programs. Check it out and download to your heart's content. You can also Gopher to `gopher.cica.indiana.edu` to browse the archives.

On the Usenet, look in `comp.binaries.ms-windows` for current ready-to-run Windows programs.

> **NOTE** You'll find discussions about Windows in a variety of Usenet forums, including `comp.os.ms-windows.advocacy`, `comp.os.ms-windows.apps`, `comp.os.ms-windows.misc`, and `comp.os.ms-windows.programmer.misc`.

6.37. Where can I find software for my Macintosh?

This answer is longer than the ones on finding software for other computer systems. I apologize to all you non-Mac folks; I'm biased heavily in favor of the Macintosh.

My favorite archive site for Macintosh stuff, complete with games, utilities, developer's tools, virus programs, and anything else your heart could desire, is as follows:

`mac.archive.umich.edu:/mac`

The University of Michigan Mac archive can be pretty busy, so you may want to use one of its mirrors.

(Missouri) `wuarchive.wustl.edu:/systems/mac/umich.edu`
(Oregon) `archive.orst.edu:/pub/mirrors/archive.umich.edu`

(Iowa) `grind.isca.uiowa.edu:/mac/umich`
(Australia) `archie.au:/micros/mac/umich`
(Israel) `ftp.technion.ac.il:/pub/unsupported/mac/umich`
(Switzerland) `nic.switch.ch:/mirror/umich-mac`
(United Kingdom) `src.doc.ic.ac.uk:/packages/mac/umich`
(Japan) `ftp.u-tokyo.ac.jp:/pub/mac/umich`
(Sweden) `ftp.sunet.se:/pub/mac/mirror-umich`
(Taiwan) `nctuccca.edu.tw:/Macintosh/umich-mac`
(Taiwan) `ftp.ccu.edu.tw:/pub/mac`
(France) `anl.anl.fr:/pub/mac/umich`
(Germany) `ftp.uni-paderborn.de:/mac`

Files from the University of Michigan Mac archive are also available via electronic mail. For information, send an e-mail message

```
To: mac@mac.archive.umich.edu
Subject: <subject line is ignored>
Body: help
```

One of the finest collections of Macintosh software is `sumex-aim.stanford.edu`, housed at Stanford University. Sumex is home to hundreds of megabytes of Macintosh freeware, shareware, and demonstrations of commercial software. You can get there by FTPing to

`sumex-aim.stanford.edu:/info-mac.`

Sumex is an extremely popular FTP site, and it can be difficult to access it. A slew of mirror sites are also available for your FTPing pleasure, however. So, if you can, use your nearest mirror site rather than `sumex.aim.stanford.edu`.

You can find a complete and current list of Sumex mirrors via FTP.

`sumex-aim.stanford.edu:/info-mac/help/mirror-list.txt`

Here is an abbreviated list of Sumex mirrors:

(Arizona) amug.org:/pub/ftp1/info-mac
(Hawaii) ftp.hawaii.edu:/mirrors/info-mac
(Massachusetts) gopher.lcs.mit.edu:/pub/INFO-MAC
(Virginia) ftp.uu.net:/archive/systems/mac/info-mac
(Iowa) grind.isca.uiowa.edu:/mac/infomac
(Missouri) wuarchive.wustl.edu:/systems/mac/info-mac
(Australia) archie.au:/micros/mac/info-mac
(Austria) ftp.univie.ac.at:/mac/info-mac
(Finland) ftp.funet.fi:/pub/mac/info-mac
(Germany) ftp.cs.tu-berlin.de:/pub/mac/info-mac
(Japan) ftp.center.osaka-u.ac.jp:/info-mac

You may also access Sumex via e-mail. For help, send electronic mail

```
To: LISTSERV@RICEVM1.RICE.EDU
Subject: <subject line is ignored>
Body: $MACARCH HELP
```

Another useful site is ftp.apple.com. This is Apple's semi-official repository for system software, developer tools, source code, technical notes, and other things that come more or less straight from Apple's mouth. Unfortunately, the materials at ftp.apple.com are arranged pretty badly, but you can unearth some of Apple's treasures. Some material at this site may not be distributed outside the U.S. or by other sites that don't have an official license to distribute Apple system software, so read the various README documents online here.

NOTE If those three sites don't fill your desire for Mac software, read the Mac FTP list, an enormous list of sites featuring software for the Macintosh. It is posted periodically to the Usenet newsgroups comp.sys.mac.misc, comp.sys.mac.apps, and comp.sys.mac.games.

On the Usenet, you'll find Mac software on the newsgroups `comp.binaries.mac` and `alt.sources.mac`. Discussion of `alt.sources.mac` takes place on `alt.sources.mac.d`.

NOTE Other conversations about the Macintosh can be found on the Usenet newsgroups `comp.sys.mac.apps`, `comp.sys.mac.digest`, `comp.sys.mac.games`, `comp.sys.mac.hardware`, `comp.sys.mac.programmer`, `comp.sys.mac.system`, `comp.sys.mac.wanted`, `misc.forsale.computers.mac`, `comp.sys.mac.portables`, `comp.sys.mac.databases`, and a variety of others.

Q 6.38. Where can I find software for the Amiga?

Aminet is a group of Internet archive sites holding software for the Amiga. The Aminet archives are available at the following FTP sites:

(Missouri) `ftp.wustl.edu:/pub/aminet`
(Texas) `ftp.etsu.edu:/pub/aminet`
(California) `ftp.cdrom.com:/pub/aminet`
(Iowa) `ftp.isca.uiowa.edu:/amiga/fx`
(Hawaii) `ftp.hawaii.edu:/pub/amiga/fish`
(Scandinavia) `ftp.luth.se:/pub/aminet`
(Germany) `tp.uni-kl.de:/pub/aminet`
(Germany) `ftp.uni-erlangen.de: /pub/aminet`
(Germany) `ftp.cs.tu-berlin.de:/pub/aminet`
(Germany) `ftp.th-darmstadt.de:/pub/aminet`
(Germany) `ftp.uni-paderborn.de:/pub/aminet`
(Germany) `ftp.uni-oldenburg.de:/pub/aminet`
(Switzerland) `ftp.eunet.ch:/pub/aminet`
(Switzerland) `litamiga.epfl.ch:/pub/aminet`
(United Kingdom) `src.doc.ic.ac.uk:/pub/aminet`
(Australia) `splat.aarnet.edu.au:/pub/aminet`

For updates on Amiga software availability, read "Recent-uploads-to-Aminet," which is posted weekly to the Usenet group `comp.archives`.

Also, check out the following Usenet groups: `comp.binaries.amiga` (for ready-to-run Amiga programs), `comp.sources.amiga` (for the source code to compile programs yourself), `alt.sources.amiga` (another repository for program source code), and `alt.sources.amiga.d` (for discussion of Amiga source code posts).

> **NOTE** By the way, the Usenet features dozens of other Amiga-related newsgroups, including `comp.sys.amiga.announce`, `comp.sys.amiga.applications`, `comp.sys.amiga.games`, `comp.sys.amiga.graphics`, `comp.sys.amiga.hardware`, `comp.sys.amiga.introduction`, `comp.sys.amiga.marketplace`, `comp.sys.amiga.programmer`, and many others.

6.39. Where can I find software for the Vax and VMS?

The following FTP sites have significant collections of VAX/VMS software:

```
acfcluster.nyu.edu
Black.Cerritos.EDU
dmc.com
ftp.spc.edu
White.Cerritos.EDU
```

For a current list of VMS FTP-sites, FTP to `info.rz.uni-ulm.de:pub/VMS/ftp-sites`.

These FTP sites and their contents are discussed in the newsgroup `vmsnet.sources.d`.

The following e-mail servers deal primarily with software for VMS:

```
fileserv@shsu.edu
FILESERV@WKUVX1.BITNET
nrl_archive@nrlvax.nrl.navy.mil
MAILSERV@Cerritos.EDU
vmsnet-sources-serv@dmc.com
VMSSERV@NYUACF.BITNET
```

For help, send e-mail to one of these addresses with the word *help* in the body of your message. Full instructions on their use appear regularly in the `vmsnet.sources.d`, `vmsnet.misc`, and `vmsnet.tpu` newsgroups.

6.40. Where can I find software for my Apple II?

The following is a list of FTP sites with Apple II related files:

wuarchive.wustl.edu:/systems/apple2
wuarchive.wustl.edu:/usenet/comp.binaries.apple2
wuarchive.wustl.edu:/usenet/comp.sources.apple2
wuarchive.wustl.edu:/mirrors/archive.umich.edu/apple2
apple2.archive.umich.edu:/archive/apple2
cco.caltech.edu:/pub/apple2 (mostly files for the II GS)
f.ms.uky.edu:/pub/appleII
grind.isca.uiowa.edu:/apple2
plains.nodak.edu:/pub/apple2
calvin.sfasu.edu:/pub/apple2
cs.bu.edu:/PC/APPLE
pindarus.cs.uiuc.edu:/pub/apple2
ftp.apple.com:/dts/aii (system software, technical notes)
slab.slip.uiuc.edu:/apple2
ucrmath.ucr.edu:/PC/apple2
ftp.uni-kl.de:/pub/apple2
ftp.hawaii.edu:/incoming/apple2
iskut.ucs.ubc.ca:/pub/apple

On the Usenet, you'll find public domain and shareware software for the Apple in `comp.binaries.apple2` and `comp.sources.apple2`.

NOTE Apple fans will also want to check out the Usenet discussions `comp.sys.apple2` (with general discussion and questions), `comp.sys.apple2.comm` (for communications and networking issues), `comp.sys.apple2.marketplace` (for buying and selling stuff), `comp.sys.apple2.programmer` (for programmers), and `comp.sys.apple2.usergroups` (for discussion of users groups).

You can get Apple games via e-mail from the mailing list APPLE2-L. For information, send mail to `LISTSERV@utarlvm1.uta.edu`. You can also request Apple files via e-mail from `archive-server@plains.nodak.edu`.

You can get the Apple II FAQ list (talk about finding files and lots of other good stuff!) via FTP from `apple2.archive.umich.edu:/apple2/faq/faq1.txt`.

Q 6.41. Where can I find software for my Atari computer?

No, I'm not going to tell you how to find software for every computer ever invented, but I do want to show you that there's software out there for every computer system you can imagine. Systems you might have thought were long dead, like the Commodore Vic-20, the Vectrex video-game system, and the Atari 800 are still used and loved, and talked about on the Net.

On the Usenet, check out `comp.binaries.atari.st` and `comp.sources.atari.st` for software.

The Atari Archive is a section of the University of Michigan/Merit Software Archives that holds a huge number of files covering all Atari products. It is available via anonymous FTP at the following sites:

```
atari.archive.umich.edu:/atari/8bit
wuarchive.wustl.edu:/mirrors/archive.umich.edu/
atari/8bit
```

The Atari Archive can also be accessed in Gopher. If your system has a Gopher client, try the command `gopher gopher.archive.merit.net 70` to connect directly to the Merit Gopher server, and choose Merit Software Archives.

The Atari Archive is also served by its own mail server. To learn how to access it via e-mail, send a message

```
To: atari@atari.archive.umich.edu
Subject: <subject line is ignored>
Body: help
      send 8bit/0index
```

A separate archive of Atari software is FTPable at

```
cs.bu.edu:/PC/ATARI.
```

> **NOTE** You'll find other talk about Atari computers on the newsgroups `comp.sys.atari.advocacy`, `comp.sys.atari.st`, `comp.sys.atari.st.tech`, `rec.games.video.atari`, and `comp.sys.atari.8bit`.

CHAPTER 7

How Do I Track Down Information?

Without a doubt, the most common question on the Internet is one that takes the form "How do I find" followed by something—anything. It can range from the name of a specific DOS program to a government edict on pesticide storage to a schedule of tour dates for Pink Floyd in the Southwestern United States. Although many aspects of the Internet have had years to evolve and mature to the point of being robust and reliable, the big missing link all these years has been resource identification; that is, finding information.

In this chapter I'll take you by the hand and show you the basic information retrieval tools on the Internet, how to use each one, and, more importantly, *when* to use each one. Once we've looked at Gopher, Veronica, WAIS, FAQ archives, and such, it'll be time to move into exemplary questions about identifying specific resources on the Internet, with an explanation of which tools to use and why. You'll also see the results of a search.

7.1. What are the tools I'll need to find information?

The initial answer to this question is that there are two: Gopher and WAIS. In fact, though, there are a variety of different possibilities. The searching tool within Gopher is Veronica (which stands for *very easy rodent-oriented net-wise index to computerized archives.* Really!). Veronica is almost always a great starting point for any information search. Next on the list is WAIS, the Wide Area Information Server. If you're looking for a specific file, program, or document, you can always try your luck with Archie, the searching tool for the many FTP archives on the Internet. (Archie is covered in Chapter 6, "How Can I Find and Use Software (and Other Stuff)?") Those are the easy ones.

Other possibilities include looking through the plethora of Frequently Asked Questions documents distributed through the Usenet community, and, of course, searching within Usenet itself. As a last resort, you can always identify an appropriate Usenet group or mailing list and post a question to the group regarding the information you seek.

7.2. Wait a second. You mean I have to learn to use a bunch of different tools?

Yup. There is a variety of projects seeking to integrate the many different sources of information on the Internet. For example, you can find the results of an Archie search automatically while in Gopher, but those programs are not reliable, and they're pretty hard to use. Don't worry, though—today's tools are pretty easy to use.

7.3. How much data is in these different archives?

The size of things varies (you already know that) because the Internet is growing on a daily basis. With that in mind, at last count, there were 4,500 Gopher servers with archived information in the Veronica database (each server has, as a guess, at least 200 items of information, meaning that the total Veronica database encompasses roughly 900,000 documents and files). Archie servers typically have archives of over 2,000,000 files and documents, and there are over 500 known WAIS databases. (WAIS is really a database of databases, where each database within is known also as a WAIS database. Is this confusing enough yet?)

There are over 6,000 Usenet newsgroups distributed throughout the world (though probably 60 percent of those are regional or organizational in distribution, such as `seattle.*` for the Seattle-Tacoma area of Washington or `netcom.*` for groups that are for Netcom users only). Within that, there are, I would estimate, about 1,800 FAQ documents that "live" in one specific newsgroup or another. For example, the Internet Services FAQ list lives in the Usenet newsgroup `alt.internet.services`.

7.4. What do I need to know about Gopher and Veronica?

Gopher is one of the most fascinating and valuable information sources on the Internet because, unlike almost all the others, it's designed for both browsing and searching for information. If you think about it for a second, you'll realize that these are two very different strategies for finding information. Many books are designed for both: You can flip through this book, scanning questions until you find one that catches your eye, or you can use the table of contents or index to zero in on specific information without wasting time. Books on computer are becoming even more sophisticated, allowing searches for information that aren't included in the predefined index, combinations of keywords, and so on.

Internet tools are constrained to either one or the other information retrieval paradigms; WAIS is a search-only database system, whereas Usenet is a browse-only environment. The cross-over is Gopher, with the Veronica search application.

The idea behind Gopher is simplicity itself. Every document and file stored on a computer in, say, an FTP archive, has a description of some sort, even if it's just the name of the file. What if you could have a menu of items available on the computer? Add to this the ability to have menu items that are actually arrows pointing to other menus or even to programs themselves. Now you're talking!

That's exactly how Gopher works. It's a huge, interwoven menu of information available on the Internet, organized through thousands of submenus broken down by topic, geographic location of server, service, and just about any other way you can imagine. Think of it as a big tree with a myriad of branches. Any Gopher menu item will either move you to another menu (on the same machine or another), or it will do something like display a document, play a sound file, show a graphic, or invoke a program.

Q 7.5. What is Gopherspace, anyway?

Gopherspace is the term for the collected set of information, documents, and menus available within the Gopher tool. I can only assume the word is derived from the oft-used term *cyberspace.* How do you move around in Gopherspace? You burrow, of course!

Q 7.6. How does Gopher move me to other machines?

The real power of Gopher, and why it—along with the WWW—is one of the most exciting developments on the Internet is that you can switch from one machine to another without knowing you've done it. In the dark, early days of the Internet, each machine existed as a little tiny island in a huge ocean of information; you *never* got to that island without explicitly requesting it by name (for instance, by opening an FTP session or logging in with Telnet). That works if you want to keep an information archipelago, but the Internet is really more of a single land mass than a peppering of small islands, and that's why the ability to transparently move from machine to machine is so important.

Gopher is a fine example of this ability to transparently move from machine to machine. I've been exploring Gopherspace and have spent hours browsing, all the while blissfully unaware that I'm hopping from machine to machine, server to server, even overseas and back.

The secret is that when you're using Gopher, you're never connected to any computer other than your own Internet host. What happens is that your local system sends a request for the list of menu items from the server computer, which it then receives and displays so that you can peruse it to your heart's content. While you're doing that, however, you aren't connected to the remote machine. (This is a very important distinction, and we'll explore it more later in this chapter.) The biggest win from this design is that if the item you choose to browse is actually on a different server than the one that gave you the menu, you simply connect directly to the new machine without any intermediaries.

Once your computer receives the menu of possibilities from the server, the connection is severed and that server can work with other people while you browse the list, looking for your information. If you were to choose the menu item that corresponded to "look on server #2," the request would go directly to server #2, and server #1 would be out of the picture.

7.7. How does Veronica work with Gopher?

When you think about this design, one thing stands out: a program can ask a server what information it has and save it into a file so that you can look at it later. Multiply this by the number of possible menus on a server and multiply the result by the number of servers on the Internet, and you have an idea of how the Veronica system works. Fortunately, the system doesn't actually chat with each of the thousands of servers for each of the searches you make! Instead, there are a small number of Veronica servers that actually collect the tons of information out there in Gopherspace and then make that database available for anyone who is searching for information.

The benefit of this is that with Veronica, you can easily narrow in on only the information you're interested in.

7.8. When I type *gopher* I see *command not found!* How can I access Gopher?

There are two possibilities. If you're on the Internet and have the Telnet program, you can try connecting to any host on the following list of systems, logging in as `gopher` or the account name specified.

Hostname	*Login*
`cat.ohiolink.edu`	
`consultant.micro.umn.edu`	
`ecosys.drdr.virginia.edu`	
`gopher.msu.edu`	
`gopher.virginia.edu`	`gwis`
`grits.valdosta.peachnet.edu`	
`infopath.ucsd.edu`	`infopath`
`inform.umd.edu`	
`infoslug.ucsc.edu`	`INFOSLUG`
`nicol.jvnc.net`	`NICOL`
`panda.uiowa.edu`	
`seymour.md.gov`	
`solar.rtd.utk.edu`	
`sunsite.unc.edu`	
`telnet.wiscinfo.wisc.edu`	`wiscinfo`
`twosocks.ces.ncsu.edu`	
`ux1.cso.uiuc.edu`	
`wsuaix.csc.wsu.edu`	`wsuinfo`

Here are the overseas options:

Hostname	*Login*	*Geographic Location*
`ecnet.ec`		Ecuador
`finfo.tu-graz.ac.at`	`info`	Austria
`gopher.brad.ac.uk`	`info`	England
`gopher.chalmers.se`		Sweden
`gopher.denet.dk`		Denmark
`gopher.isnet.is`		Iceland
`gopher.itu.ch`		Switzerland
`gopher.th-darmstadt.de`		Germany
`gopher.torun.edu.pl`		Poland
`gopher.uv.es`		Spain
`hugin.ub2.lu.se`		Sweden
`info.anu.edu.au`	`info`	Australia
`info.sunet.se`		Sweden

```
siam.mi.cnr.it                         Italy
tolten.puc.cl                          Chile
```

To use any of these, you would type `telnet hostname` and then log in with `gopher` or the appropriate login specified in the table. For example, `UNC` is the University of North Carolina (one of the first two Usenet sites!), and I would like to see how they've set up their Gopher system. I type `telnet sunsite.unc.edu`, and when I'm prompted for an account, I type `gopher`. It immediately shows me the choices at UNC.


```
1.  About Ogphre/
2.  Sun and UNC's Legal Disclaimer
3.  Surf the Net! - Archie, Libraries, Gophers, FTP Sites./
4.  Internet Dog-Eared Pages (Frequently used resources)/
5.  Worlds of SunSITE — by Subject/
6.  SUN Microsystems News Groups and Archives/
7.  NEWS! (News, Entertainment, Weather, and Sports)/
8.  UNC Information Exchange (People and Places)/
9.  The UNC-CH Internet Library/
10. UNC-Gopherspace/
11. Link-Info
12. What's New on SunSITE/
```

7.9. I don't have Telnet or any other direct Internet connection. Can I use Gopher through electronic mail?

A small number of sites on the Internet are experimenting with electronic mail-based query systems for Gopher. This service certainly isn't as elegant as using Gopher the standard, interactive way, but it does provide a wealth of information for the millions of folks without interactive Internet accounts.

There are four GopherMail addresses at the time of this writing.

```
gopher@solaris.ims.ac.jp
gophermail@calvin.edu
gophermail@ncc.go.jp
gopher@earn.net
```

You can start by sending mail to `gophermail@calvin.edu`; subject line and message body are ignored. GopherMail will reply with its home page. You then use your e-mail program to reply to that message, including it in the text of your reply. Mark the menu choices that you are interested in by putting an *X* before the menu numbers of the interesting menu choices. From there you can just keep repeating the process, sending replies back to Gopher while marking your desired items.

Let's let the `calvin.edu` service speak for itself.

```
You can get started by sending mail to gopher@calvin.edu with any
or no subject and any or no message body. GopherMail will reply by
sending you it's main gopher menu. You then use your email program
to reply to that message, including it in the text of your reply.
Mark which menu options you want to follow-up by putting an "X"
(or "x") anywhere near the beginning of the line, before the menu
numbers for those options.

From there you can just keep repeating the process, sending
replies back to gopher with the desired items marked with an X. To
make it more efficient, you could edit your replies so they
contain just the gopher link information for the items that you
want. You'll find all the link information after the menu, at the
bottom of the menu messages that GopherMail sends to you. Some
items on gopher menus are database searches and college phone
books. To search for a particular name or keyword(s), you simply
send them on the "Subject:" line of the message in which you've
Xed the phonebook or WAIS database menu option.
```

Note that these services are all experimental and might well have changed by the time you try to use them. Also, if you have access to Gopher, it's a *much* better choice!

7.10. How do you find a Veronica server?

Within the Gopher system you need merely to find a Veronica service, and then you will be ready to search through the millions of items of information in Gopherspace for the information you seek.

Most Internet systems offer the Gopher service, either through a simple terminal-based interface or through one of the more sophisticated graphical programs such as TurboGopher for the Macintosh or HGOPHER for Windows.

NOTE The menu that you see when you first fire up Gopher depends entirely on the Gopher server you're using. The Gopher server at `netcom.com` has entirely different menu selections than the one at `bolero.rahul.net`. If you don't like your system's main Gopher menu, you can always connect to another site's Gopher server.

Start up and you'll probably have a menu similar to the following:

```
1.  About this GOPHER server.
2.  Information about NETCOM/
3.  Internet information/
4.  Jughead - Search High-Level Gopher Menus (via Washington & Lee) <?>
5.  Search Gopherspace using Veronica/
6.  Other Internet Gopher Servers (via U.C. Santa Cruz)/
7.  Weather (via U. Minnesota)/
8.  Worldwide Directory Services (via Notre Dame)/
9.  Interesting items/
10. ATTENTION NETCOM users.
```

Because I'm using a text-based interface, the program can't display whizzy little graphics to indicate what kind of file each of these items is, so instead it shows this on the very last character of each line. In a nutshell, any line that ends with a period (`.`) is a file or document; any line ending with a forward slash (`/`) leads you to another menu; and anything that has `<?>` (such as item #4) will connect to a program. You can see here that most of the menu items at the top level are pointers to other menu items. Numbers 1 and 10 are text files, and number 4 will run a program called *Jughead.*

By contrast, here's what it looks like when you start up Gopher on the Whole Earth 'Lectronic Link (WELL):

```
1.  Information About Gopher/
2.  Computer Information/
3.  Discussion Groups/
4.  Fun & Games/
5.  Internet file server (ftp) sites/
6.  Libraries/
```

```
7.  News/
8.  Other Gopher and Information Servers/
9.  Phone Books/
10. Search Gopher Titles at the University of Minnesota <?>
11. Search lots of places at the University of Minnesota <?>
12. University of Minnesota Campus Information/
```

Here the folks at the WELL have opted to have people start right out with the University of Minnesota (UMinn) Gopher server, a wise choice because Gopher started at the University of Minnesota. From here, I can choose #8.

```
1.  All the Gopher Servers in the World/
2.  Search titles in Gopherspace using veronica/
3.  Africa/
4.  Asia/
5.  Europe/
6.  International Organizations/
7.  Middle East/
8.  North America/
9.  Pacific/
10. South America/
11. Terminal Based Information/
12. WAIS Based Information/
13. Gopher Server Registration
```

And now I can see the Veronica options.

Q 7.11. There are lots of Veronica servers! Which should I use?

Choosing `Search titles in Gopherspace using veronica` leads to a screen similar to the following on just about any Gopher system:

```
1.  Search gopherspace by veronica at NYSERNet <?>
2.  Search gopherspace by veronica at SCS Nevada  <?>
3.  Search Gopher+ ABSTRACTs (50 sites) via SCS Nevada  <?>
4.  Search gopherspace by veronica at University of Pisa <?>
5.  Search gopherspace by veronica at U. of Manitoba <?>
6.  Search gopherspace by veronica at University of Koeln <?>
7.  Search gopherspace by veronica at UNINETT/U. of Bergen <?>
```

```
8.  Search Gopher Directory Titles using NYSERNet <?>
9.  Search Gopher Directory Titles using SCS Nevada  <?>
10. Search Gopher Directory Titles using University of Pisa <?>
11. Search Gopher Directory Titles using U. of Manitoba <?>
12. Search Gopher Directory Titles using University of Koeln <?>
13. Search Gopher Directory Titles using UNINETT/U. of Bergen <?>
14.                                 .
15. Script to automate your local veronica menu (maltshop-0.2c)..
16.                                                             .
17. FAQ:  Frequently-Asked Questions about veronica  (1993-08-23).
18. How to compose veronica queries .
```

Here you can see that almost all the options are actually programs (the lines end with <?>), but they are at data servers throughout the world. In fact, here's the rundown:

NYSERNET is New York City
SCS Nevada is Nevada
University of Pisa is in Pisa, Italy
University of Manitoba is in Manitoba, Canada
University of Koeln is in Koeln (Cologne), Germany
University of Bergen is in Bergen, Norway

You can, in theory, choose any of them, but you'll find with experience that some are more reliable (and less busy) than others.

Q 7.12. How do you search for something in Gopherspace?

You probably thought it would take a dozen more pages before I actually searched for anything, but let's have a quick look now. The first search will be for documents or files that have something to do with physiology.

To start a search, simply move the cursor on your screen to the item of your choice and press Return or type the number of the item. I'll use the latter and type #4, which results in the following:

```
+---  Search Gopherspace at the University of Pisa  -----+
¦                                                        ¦
¦ Words to search for  physiology                        ¦
¦                                                        ¦
¦                         [Cancel ^G] [Accept - Enter]   ¦
¦                                                        ¦
+--------------------------------------------------------+
```

To my surprise, there are quite a few matches: well over 200 documents match the word "physiology." Here are the first fifteen matches listed:

```
1.  Physiology of feeding-preference patterns of female black blowfli.
2.  The sensory physiology of host-seeking behavior in mosquitoes.
3.  acj6: A gene affecting olfactory physiology and behavior in Droso.
4.  Blood-feeding by vectors: physiology, ecology, behavior, and vert.
5.  Metabolic physiology of alcohol degradation and adaptation in Dro.
6.  Comprehensive insect physiology, biochemistry and pharmacology. V.
7.  Morphology, physiology, and behavioral biology of ticks.
8.  Olfactory physiology in the Drosophila antenna and maxillary palp.
9.  Nitrogen fertilization influences the physiology of apple leaves.
10. Contributions to sensory physiology of the tick Amblyomma testudi.
11. Physiology of an ATP [adenosine triphosphate] receptor in labella.
12. Physiology of an ATP [adenosine triphosphate] receptor in labella.
13. Cellular and Molecular Physiology.
14. Cellular and Molecular Physiology.
15. Cellular & Molecular Physiology.
```

Worth noting here is that the last three documents are probably the same file (as are #11 and #12). A document can show up in more than one Gopher menu (or more than one computer system), but the archival software can't distinguish between them and shows you all of the matches.

To read any of these documents, again either move the cursor to the document and press Return or simply type the number of the document itself. I'll have a quick peek at #8 (not that I can figure out what it's about from the title!).

```
Ayer, R. K., Jr., Carlson, J.. Olfactory physiology in the Drosophila
   antenna and maxillary palp: acj6 Distinguishes two classes of
   odorant pathways. Journal Of Neurobiology, 1992  8. 23. 965-982.
```

```
A-B 89-6,93

Press <RETURN> to continue, <m> to mail, <s> to save, or <p> to print:
```

The document consists of a bibliographic citation to a journal article.

Q7.13. Once I've found a document I like, what can I do with it?

The last line shown on the preceding information holds the secret: When you get to the bottom of a document, you can press Return to return to the Gopher menu, *m* to e-mail the document to yourself, *s* to save it to a file, or *p* to print it on a local printer. (Many sites don't allow the print option, however.)

Q7.14. What does it mean when I see *too many items found*?

This is the bane of all Veronica searches and it means that the word or set of words that you've used are insufficient to narrow the search down to a reasonable number of hits. There are several ways to address this problem: specify that Veronica can show you more than the default 200 matches, specify that it should look only for specific types of menu items, or add further keywords.

NOTE If you get that annoying `too many items found` message, try changing the order of the keywords. Put less common words first, followed by more common ones. In multiword searches, Veronica searches for the first word first, and then moves on to the next keyword. In the interest of performance, if there are too many "hits" on the first word, Veronica gives up with the `too many items` message before scanning the rest of the words. I searched for `David Letterman` and saw `too many items`, but searching for `Letterman David`

worked. The word `David` probably hit thousands of times, causing Veronica to give up early. The word `Letterman` hit relatively few times, so the program could continue.

Veronica can search with more sophisticated patterns than just a word like `physiology`. In fact, there is a variety of file types that it can match, each of which is specified in the Veronica search string by prefixing `-t` to the item type indicated in the table that follows.

Type	*Item Description*
0	File
1	Directory
2	CSO (qi) phonebook server
4	BinHexed Mac file (discouraged)
5	DOS binary archive of some kind (discouraged)
6	UNIX uuencoded file (discouraged)
7	Index-Search server
8	Pointer to a Telnet session
9	Binary file of some sort

For example, if I wanted to search for directories on any Veronica server that had the word `chicken` in them, I could use the search string `chicken -t1` (and find that there are over 2300 matches, incredibly enough!).

7.15. What does it mean when I see *too many connections – try again soon*?

This is the other bane of Veronica searches. It means that the server you chose has too many people using it and cannot process your request. As it suggests, try again in a few minutes or pick another Veronica server.

Q 7.16. Where can I find information about IDEANet, the State of Indiana Department of Education computer system?

This is a great example of where Veronica can help you! I chose a Veronica server and entered `ideanet` as the pattern. Here's the result:

```
1.  How do I access IDEAnet?.
2.  How do I send e-mail to Ideanet?.
3.  IDEAnet: Indiana Department of Education/
4.  IDEAnet: Indiana Department of Education/
5.  New File <OTH099> IDEAnet: Indiana Department of Education (fwd).
6.        New File <OTH099> IDEAnet: Indiana Department of Education.
7.        New File <OTH099> IDEAnet: Indiana Department of Education.
8.  IDEAnet: Indiana Department of Education/
9.  IdeaNet.
10. IDEAnet: Indiana Department of Education <TEL>
11. IDEAnet: Indiana Department of Education <TEL>
12. IDEAnet (Indiana Department of Education) <TEL>
13. IDEAnet: Indiana Department of Education <TEL>
14. Search Community Ideanet <?>
```

Quick and painless, and if I now choose #1, I can even find out how to connect to the system itself.

Q 7.17. I've heard about an electronic mail system called *Elm*. How can I find a copy of it on the Internet?

Again, here's a great chance to work with Veronica, only this time you'll want to do a slightly more sophisticated query. I connected to NYSERNet and used `elm and mail -t0` to find only documents that included *elm* and *mail* as words. It found well over 200 matches. Here are the first few:

```
1.  Elm Mail User Agent FAQ - FAQ
2.  comp.mail.elm.
3.  Re: ELM New Mail Question... Pl. Help.
4.  Re: Elm 2.4 PL 2 & a reply to local mail problem.
```

```
5.  Re: How to "efficiently" send MIME mail with elm?.
6.  Re: ELM 2.4PL6 - Big problem! Changing permissions on /usr/mail.
7.  Re: ELM 2.4PL6 - Big problem! Changing permissions on /usr/mail.
8.  mail status in elm.
9.  Re: elm won't pipe mail via .forward.
```

You can see that there's even a FAQ about the program, as well as a Usenet group (that's what the second document talks about). Either would be a great place to start searching for information on how to obtain a copy, if you were so inclined.

7.18. What about looking for specific programs or documents? Isn't that what Archie is for?

Archie is useful, but it isn't the only way to find files. Gopher and Veronica can help, too. Because there isn't a unified information space on the Internet, resources can appear in one area but be excluded from another simply due to the methods that are used to collate data. In a nutshell, Gopher usually isn't the best choice if the information you seek is likely to be found in an FTP archive. Instead, that's where the Archie program comes in handy. (Archie is covered in Chapter 6, "How Can I Find and Use Software (and Other Stuff)?") If you have it on your system, you'll be able to type `Archie` and work directly with the program. If not, don't despair; there are a number of hosts on the net that support remote Archie queries.

For example, I might have some documents that I make available through anonymous FTP and register with the local Archie server. Because I don't have Gopher available, it doesn't end up cited in Gopherspace, so a search for my document with Veronica will fail, whereas a search for the same document in Archie will succeed. Often the opposite is true, too. That's why there are some new, smarter, information-searching tools popping up, such as Knowbots.

7.19. Knowbots? Cool! What are those?

Well, it sounds much cooler than it is, at least in my opinion. Knowbots are an organized set of autonomous programs that know how to search a specific database of information on the Internet. When they're done, they report all their results to a master program, which can then report back to you the results of the multiresource search. The problem is that this service is just fantastically resource-expensive, so as fast as people are learning about Knowbot sites, those sites are limiting their access or shutting down completely. A quick search with Veronica found lots of descriptive documents, including one that explains that the Knowbot service is available through the Corporation for National Research Initiatives computer in Virginia. Based on that information, you can check out the Knowbot Information Service by using Telnet to connect to `nri.reston.va.us`. You'll need to specify that you want to connect to port 185 (for example, on UNIX, you can type `telnet nri.reston.va.us 185` to do this).

7.20. I've heard that there's an old computer game called Hunt the Wumpus and I'd like to find a copy to try. Where should I look?

This is another job for Archie, I think, although frankly, having to search multiple databases can get old pretty quickly. Why Archie? Because we're looking for a specific file. Let's find out. I search by using `archie -s wumpus` to find no matches! Next, I'll try Veronica, where I use the search string `wumpus`. There are ten matches, one of which is a file called `wumpus.c`. I choose it and there's the source code to an old version of the program!

7.21. I have heard that there's a way to synchronize the time on your computer with a network time server. How do I do that on my Mac?

This is a job for Veronica! Let's search for `network and time -t0` to find documents that have both `network` and `time` in their title.

There are tons of matches, and from a cursory inspection you can see that the standard name for this service is "NTP," the Network Time Protocol. Now let's revisit the search, because we want information on NTP and the Macintosh. This time we search for `NTP and Mac? -t0` (the question mark is so that we can match `Mac` and `Macintosh`) and see one match, `net_machine.h`, which isn't what we want. Hmmm. Let's skip the "NTP" stuff and try a variant of the original query: `network and time and mac? -t0`. Ah ha! This yields the following:

```
1.  Network Time for Mac - Info required.
2.  Network Time for Mac - Info required.
3.  SUMMARY - Network Time for Mac.
4.  SUMMARY - Network Time for Mac.
```

The third entry is what we're looking for. I type `3`, press Return, and see the following:

```
This is from the document '/lists-k-o/mac-supporters/archives/09-1993'.

From: Vlastimil Malinek <v.malinek@mrc-apu.cam.ac.uk>
Date: Wed, 29 Sep 93 14:37:54 BST
To: mac-supporters@mailbase.ac.uk
Subject: SUMMARY - Network Time for Mac

I asked:

> I run NTP (Network Time Protocol) at this site. ........
> Does anyone know of an application (or anything else) that will allow
> the mac's clock to be set at boot time from a datehost?

A host of helpful replies arrived. Unfortunately I wasn't able to try them
out immediately as the hard disks on my mac decided to go down.... However,
here is summary of the replies:

1) 'VersaTerm Time Client' which is shipped by Synergy Software with
   VersaTerm PRO and VersaTerm.

I have VersaTerm Pro in-house but only a couple of copies which are used by
other people so I didn't test this one. However, it is being used by some of
the respondees.

2) 'Tardis' This is part of the CAP package. It sits in the 'Chooser' and
will connect to a CAP 'Timelord' server. Or, it will connect to another mac
acting as 'Timelord' (better than nothing I suppose).

3) Network Time. sumex: /info-mac/Communication/Network/network-time-20.hqx
Excellent! This is the business. Allows you to make an Extension once you've
configured which you can punt out to your machines. Will run at boot time or
```

```
when a TCP/IP connection is made or both. Very configurable. You can also make
your own timezones (you'll need one for the UK because of Daylight Savings).

Takes IP addresses as well as names and has a list of timeservers.
Only drawback. Manual comes in MacWrite Pro format and the postscript comes set
for US letter. As the whole thing is done as odd/even pages it's very difficult
to get at if you don't have MacWrite Pro. However, one of my colleagues wrote me
a nice unix script that will convert the postscript to A4 if anyone wants it.

Thanks again to everyone for the very helpful replies.

Vlastimil Malinek
MRC Applied Psychology Unit
15 Chaucer Road
Cambridge CB2 2EF

%%%%%%%%%%%%%%%%%%%%%%%%%%%%%%%%%%%%

Press <RETURN> to continue,
   <m> to mail, <D> to download, <s> to save, or <p> to print:
```

7.22. Where can I find education-related information on the Internet?

This is definitely a job for Veronica, so I'll search for `education -t1` to find just directories. Thousands of matches! Here are the top twenty:

```
1.  COCAMED  - Computers in Canadian Medical Education/
2.     Education-TC/
3.  Academic and Education-related Gophers/
4.  ADULT AND TEACHER EDUCATION (AdEd)/
5.  AGRICULTURAL EDUCATION (AgEd)/
6.  ART EDUCATION (ArEd)/
7.  BUSINESS AND MARKETING EDUCATION (BME)/
8.  EDUCATION (Educ)/
9.  ELEMENTARY EDUCATION (Elem)/
10. HOME ECONOMICS EDUCATION (HEEd)/
11. INDUSTRIAL EDUCATION (Ind)/
12. MATHEMATICS EDUCATION (MthE)/
13. MUSIC EDUCATION (MuEd)/
14. PHYSICAL EDUCATION (PE)/
15. SECONDARY EDUCATION (SeEd)/
16. VOCATIONAL EDUCATION (VoEd)/
17. Education/
```

```
18. HIGHER EDUCATION/
19. MUSIC  EDUCATION/
20. 14:Professional Activities, Education, Employment/
```

Note that if I specify `-t0` for documents instead, the top twenty are as follows:

```
1.  New Horizons in Adult Education: The First Five Years (1987-1991)..
2.  The Canadian Network for the Advancement of Research, Industry, an...
3.  94-06-25World Conf on Education.
4.  Assessment of Multimedia in Education - bibliography.
5.  Assessment of Multimedia in Education - bibliography.
6.  the Internet - a Higher Education Communications Revolution.
7.  Science Education
8.     Ag Education Club.
9.     Stds for Pro-Life Education and Aid.
10.    U of MN Coalition for Higher Education.
11. Education-TC, Students, Twin Cities Campus, U of MN, US.
12. Treen, Chip (Continuing Education and Extension).
13. DIRECTOR OF SPECIAL EDUCATION AND PUPIL SERVICES—Manitowoc, WI.
14. AdEd 5103    Adult Education Workshop.
15. AdEd 5205    Field Experience in Adult Education.
16. AdEd 5301    Designing the Adult Education Program.
17. AdEd 5501    Continuing Education and the Professions.
18. AdEd 8302    Problems: Adult Education.
19. AgEd 3029    Directed Experience in Agricultural Education.
20. AgEd 3041    Practicum: Agricultural Education Technology.
```

Q 7.23. Where on the Internet can I find national and world news?

There is a wide variety of sources. Three examples follow.

Voice of America News

The Voice of America's international News and English Broadcasts radio newswire is available via anonymous FTP and the Internet Gopher, along with a variety of other information from VOA and Worldnet Television.

The News and English Broadcasts wire service includes the texts, in English, of radio reports prepared by VOA staff correspondents, contract news reporters, and feature and documentary writers. The wire provides a comprehensive daily report of news events worldwide. It is one of the core news products of the Voice of America, and is used as the basis for much of VOA's programming in all languages. The public Internet server is updated within a few minutes after each report is issued by the VOA central news department; a seven-day archive of the wire is available on the public server.

Selected VOA and Worldnet program schedules, shortwave radio frequency and satellite downlink information, public announcements from the Voice of America and Worldnet, and technical documents on international radio and television broadcasting are also available on the public Internet server.

All the materials on the server are available by anonymous FTP and the Internet Gopher. Schedules and other general information materials may also be requested via electronic mail; the News and English Broadcasts newswire is not available via e-mail because its contents change so rapidly.

The Voice of America and Worldnet are, respectively, the international radio and television networks of the United States Information Agency. They operate out of headquarters in Washington, D.C. VOA has news bureaus in many major world cities.

You can access the VOA archives via anonymous FTP to `ftp.voa.gov` or by Gophering to `gopher.voa.gov, port 70`. For more information, send e-mail to `info@voa.gov`. To request instructions on how to use the e-mail server, send a message with the contents "send help" to the preceding address.

To request an index of available files, send a message with the contents "send index" to the preceding address.

ClariNet

ClariNet offers what its designers call an electronic newspaper, broken down into categories by specific topics. If your Usenet provider subscribes to the service, you'll be able to read news from the Associated Press and Reuters newswires as well as a variety of syndicated news and analysis columns. (You can even see the Dilbert comic strip. Nifty!)

You'll definitely want to subscribe to the "top" news groups in any categories you're interested in tracking. `clari.news.top` covers top

U.S.-related news, whereas the popular `clari.news.top.world` group focuses on international stories. Sports fans also read the group `clari.sports.top`, whereas business readers want `clari.biz.top`. Too much information? Try `clari.news.briefs`, offering short summaries of the current top news.

You can get subscription information on ClariNet by sending e-mail to `info@clarinet.com`, browsing `ftp.clarinet.com`, or phoning (800) USE-NETS or (408) 296–0366.

PeaceNet World News Service

The PeaceNet World News Service (PWN) is a daily newspaper of world news delivered to you through electronic mail. Each day a digest of news stories is sent, and subscribers can choose among a variety of different issue- and regional-oriented digests, too.

PWN features important international news about government, politics, the environment, human rights, development, the United Nations, and the work of nongovernment organizations.

To learn more about PWN, you can send an e-mail message to `pwn-info@igc.apc.org`, and for more general information about PeaceNet itself, send a message to `peacenet-info@igc.apc.org`.

7.24. What libraries are available on the Internet?

You can't even begin to believe how many different libraries are accessible through the Internet. The majority of large universities have their entire catalog system available online. One great resource is MELVYL, the University of California online library system (holding over 7 million volumes). A list of online libraries is available through the FTP service.

```
ariel.unm.edu:/library/internet.library
```

It's a huge file—more than 8,800 lines of text, so make sure that you have room on your computer disk before you attempt to grab your own copy.

Here's the introduction to this document:

```
Internet-Accessible Library Catalogs and Databases is coauthored by Dr. Art St.
George of the University of New Mexico and Dr. Ron Larsen of the University of
Maryland. Dr. St. George says this document, "began as an effort to provide
additional service to the network community locally. However, it became
apparent that the library resources were of broader appeal than that."

It contains a listing of over 100 online library catalogs and databases
available within the United States and beyond. It contains listings of U.S.
and international library catalogs and databases, dial-up libraries, Campus-
Wide Online Information Systems, and bulletin board systems. Each listing
gives a brief description of the resource and instructions on how to access
it, as well as places to contact for more information. Listings include such
material as Columbia University's online library catalog (CLIO), Pennsylvania
State University's online card catalog system (PENpages), and the Colorado
Alliance of Research Libraries (CARL) and its 25 individual resource listings
of libraries and information databases, such as the Metro Denver Facts
database. This catalog is an ongoing project. If you have any suggestions,
comments, or additions, please send them to Dr. Art St. George by electronic
mail to stgeorge@unmb.bitnet or stgeorge@bootes.unm.edu.
```

If you're at all interested in libraries on the network, this is a great place to start. If you just want to try one or two, here are a couple I use:

> **MELVYL.** The University of California Library System; Telnet to `melvyl.ucop.edu`
>
> **CARL.** The Colorado Alliance of Research Libraries; Telnet to `pac.carl.org`
>
> **Massachusetts Institute of Technology.** Telnet to `library.mit.edu`
>
> **The National Library of Australia.** Telnet to `janus.nla.gov.au`

Q 7.25. How do I access the Library of Congress?

Answered by Kathryn D. Ellis, Internet User's Group Coordinating Committee member at the Library of Congress

The Library of Congress has several online offerings at this time, including a Gopher server, an online catalog, and an FTP archive. Others (dependent on budgets, staff, and so on) are in the works. Possible additions include a World Wide Web server and publicly accessible WAIS databases.

The primary Net interface is the Library's Gopher LC MARVEL. MARVEL includes information about the Library and its hours, descriptions of its collections and services, employee information, and especially pointers to other information on the Net organized by subject. It includes Telnet connections to the Library's online catalog as well. Access MARVEL by Gophering to `marvel.loc.gov, port 70` or Telnet to `marvel.loc.gov`; login as `marvel`.

The online catalog is also available directly by using `telnet locis.loc.gov`, no login needed. This supports both VT100 and 3270 emulations, but works much better using TN3270 emulation. LOCIS, as the catalog and related files are called, contains all of the Library's public files. There are online help and instructions on FTPing a more detailed search guide. Unfortunately, it is open only during the hours during which the Library is open. For the exact hours, please Telnet to `locis.loc.gov` and check the information screens.

The Library also supports an FTP site, which was its first offering to the Net. To access it, anonymous FTP to `seq1.loc.gov`. The predecessor of LC MARVEL was the directory `/pub/Library.of.Congress`. This directory still exists, but has been largely superseded by MARVEL and is not necessarily up to date anymore.

7.26. Is the Library of Congress just books?

Answered by Kathryn D. Ellis, Internet User's Group Coordinating Committee member at the Library of Congress

Four online exhibits are currently to be found in the FTP site as well as through MARVEL. Each exhibit has its own directory under `/pub`. These are `/pub/soviet.archive`, `/pub/vatican.exhibit`, `/pub/1492.exhibit`, and `/pub/deadsea.scrolls.exhibit`. The same exhibits are found in MARVEL under

```
2. Library of Congress: Facilities, Activities, and Services
   2. Events and Exhibits
      4. Online Exhibits from LC (FTP ***site at seq1.loc.gov)***
```

and have also been picked up by various mirror sites. In particular, WWW versions of the exhibits can be viewed with Mosiac or another Web browser at the following: `*** http://sunsite.unc.edu/expo/ticket"office.html ***`. The exhibits will be up "indefinitely." If they are superseded by other types of technology, they may be removed or updated, but the intention is that they be available for the foreseeable future.

7.27. How can I access WAIS?

To use the Wide Area Information Server, use a local client program (like MacWAIS, HyperWAIS, or Xwais) or just Telnet to `quake.think.com` with the login `wais` or to `sunsite.unc.edu` with the login `swais`. Alternative WAIS sites are also available, as follows:

Hostname	*Login*	*Geographic Location*
`info.funet.fi`	`wais`	Finland
`cnidr.org`	`demo`	Eastern USA
`sunsite.unc.edu`	`swais`	North Carolina
`quake.think.com`	`wais`	Massachusetts

7.28. My son is writing a paper on Philoponus and his early criticisms of Aristotle and the Platonic ideals of philosophy. Is there any information on the Internet about this subject?

This is an ideal question to ask the Wide Area Information Service (WAIS) because it's very specific and there happens to be a public WAIS database that includes a considerable amount of information on philosophical issues of this nature.

There is actually some quite valuable information on this subject available in the WAIS system. Let's take a look. The first step is to search through the "directory-of-servers." I'll use the keywords `aristotle medieval philosophy` and see what I get.

```
#     Score     Source                    Title                            Lines
001:  [1000] (directory-of-se) bryn-mawr-medieval-review                    150
002:  [ 458] (directory-of-se) ANU-AustPhilosophyForum-L                     86
003:  [ 250] (directory-of-se) ANU-Asian-Religions                           93
004:  [ 250] (directory-of-se) ANU-Coombspapers-Index                        99
005:  [ 250] (directory-of-se) ANU-Taoism-Listserv                           69
006:  [ 250] (directory-of-se) ANU-Theses-Abstracts                          93
007:  [ 250] (directory-of-se) ANU-ZenBuddhism-Calendar                      81
008:  [ 250] (directory-of-se) ASK-SISY-Software-Information                 34
009:  [ 250] (directory-of-se) earlym-l                                      36
010:  [ 250] (directory-of-se) nonmono.bib                                   54
011:  [ 250] (directory-of-se) rec.music.early                               36
012:  [ 250] (directory-of-se) sci                                           17
```

The first source looks likely, so I'll choose it by typing `u` for *use it*, and `s` to go to the database sources page. I then use = to unmark all databases and then press the Spacebar to select the *Bryn Mawr Medieval Review.* I can now search for a more specific citation, `philoponus aristotle philosophy`, and here are the results:

```
#     Score    Source                       Title                          Lines
001:   [1000] (              bmmr)  93.10.5, Philoponus on Arist. Phys. II    118
002:   [ 212] (              bmmr)   93.8.6, O'Meara, Plotinus:  Introductio  95
003:   [  91] (              bmmr)  93.8.2:  Meynell, Grace, Politics and De  285
004:   [  91] (              bmmr)  94.1.5, Relihan, Ancient Menippean Satir  165
005:   [  75] (              bmmr)   93.8.8, Riddle, Contraception and Abort  180
006:   [  75] (              bmmr)   93.8.10, Moorhead, Theoderic in Italy    122
007:   [  75] (              bmmr)  93.10                                     136
008:   [  75] (              bmmr)  93.12.6, Walsh, ed., Love Lyrics from th  316
009:   [  75] (              bmmr)  94.4.2, Camille, Image on the Edge (II)   163
010:   [  75] (              bmmr)  94.4.4, Hamilton, Heresy and Mysticism    153
```

The first looks like it's a terrific match, so let's have a look by pressing Return. It is indeed excellent and right on target.

```
93.10.5, Philoponus on Arist. Phys. II

Philoponus, John  On Aristotle's Physics 2
Translated by A.R. Lacey. Ithaca, NY: Cornell University Press.
Pp. 241. $41.50 (hb.). ISBN 0-8014-2815-7.
     Reviewed by Patricia K. Curd — Purdue University

     Ancient commentaries provide modern readers with windows on both the
subject of the commentary and the philosophical world of the author. From
this commentary on Book 2 of the Physics we learn about Aristotle and about
the philosophical issues that exercised Philoponus himself. Thus we see
Philoponus comparing (and perhaps trying to reconcile) Plato and Aristotle,
we hear echoes of Stoicism, and we find the work as a whole suffused with
Philoponus' Neoplatonist arguments and assumptions. Internal evidence suggests
that Philoponus was at work on his commentary in 517; it has recently been
argued that the work was revised after 529, after Philoponus' conversion to
Christianity.<<1>> A.R. Lacey claims that there are no traces of Philoponus'
later views in the commentary on Book 2 (but note for instance, the comments
about Philoponus' use of the difficult KATADU/W  at 197,34 and 308,23), and he
remains agnostic about the exact date of composition.
```

The document continues, but this is enough for now.

Q 7.29. I have heard that gazpacho is really good, but I don't know where to find a recipe. Are there recipes on the Internet?

This is another job for WAIS. This time I'll start out by searching the directory-of-servers for keywords `cook recipe cookbook food`.

```
001:   [1000] (directory-of-se)  usenet-cookbook                         21
002:   [ 522] (directory-of-se)  recipes                                 15
003:   [ 304] (directory-of-se)  usdacris                                36
004:   [ 261] (directory-of-se)  ANU-Australia-NZ-History-L              71
005:   [ 261] (directory-of-se)  ANU-Tropical-Archaeobotany              86
006:   [ 261] (directory-of-se)  Omni-Cultural-Academic-Resource         31
007:   [ 261] (directory-of-se)  com-papers                              79
008:   [ 261] (directory-of-se)  cool                                   108
```

The first two look likely, so I'll `u` (use) them both and then use the `w` command to enter the keyword of `gazpacho`. The results of our search through these two recipe databases are as follows:

```
  #    Score      Source                          Title                          Lines
001:   [1000] (         recipes)  "J. F. 'Fr Re: Gazpacho                           61
002:   [ 750] (         recipes)  mblum@chao Re: Re: REQUEST: Gazpacho Sou          53
003:   [ 375] (         recipes)  natalie@me Re: REQUEST: Gazpacho Soup             25
004:   [ 375] (         recipes)  jjsulliv@C Re: Re: REQUEST: Gazpacho Sou          16
005:   [    1] (cmns-moon.think)  *** HELP for the Public CM WAIS Server *         351
```

Hmmm. Looks as though the `recipes` database was useful, so let's have a look at the first item on the list, #1.

```
Newsgroups: rec.food.recipes
From: "J. F. 'Fritz' Schwaller" <SCHWALLR@ACC.FAU.EDU>
Subject: Gazpacho
Organization: Taronga Park BBS
Date: Wed, 5 May 1993 08:25 EDT

    Please note that Gazpacho is a Spanish and not a Mexican dish. It is
especially popular in the southern part of Spain known as Andalucia, the
region where Cordoba, Granada, and Seville are located. Since nearly all of
the colonists of the Americas had to pass through Andalucia on their way to
the New World, they tended to pick up the regional dishes.
    When it reaches 44-46~ C in Ecija, in Andaluca, and maybe only 42~ in
Seville, in July, the population literally lives on gazpacho. For 12-14 hours
a day it is just too hot to eat, much less chew or cook. Between noon and 6 PM
you retreat to the privacy of your home, strip, lie on the cool floors to read
or nap, take cold showers or baths, and sip gazpacho straight from the frig to
keep up your strength. Maybe around midnight you'll quick fry a chop or fish
and eat cold potato salad for "cena," then go out for a constitutional stroll.
But thank God you had gazpacho for lunch and tea time. Out in the parks and
sidewalks of the city you'll find most of your neighbors at 1 or 2 AM doing
the same thing. By the way, we've never had the same gazpacho twice, each one
is slightly different. Don't bother to try for consistency, just enjoy each
for its uniqueness. One might be a little garlicky, another thinner, or more
peppery. They are all incredibly nutritious and refreshing.

Gazpacho

5-6 medium tomatoes, peeled, seeded, and diced
1/2 medium onion, diced
1 small clove garlic
1 medium cucumber, peeled and diced
1 small bell pepper, diced
```

```
1/2 cup bread crumbs
1/2 cup high quality olive oil
2 Tbs. wine vinegar
S & P to taste

     In a blender add all of the vegetables. Blend until fairly smooth. Add
the bread crumbs. If necessary add a small amount of tomato juice or cold
water to maintain the consistency. While the blender is running on medium
slow, slowly add the olive oil. Place the soup in a serving dish. Refrigerate
at this point until serving time. Prepare dishes of diced tomatoes, cucumbers,
pimiento or bell pepper, hard boiled egg, and crutons. Allow guests to garnish
their soup.

J. F. "Fritz" Schwaller, Associate Dean        schwallr@acc.fau.edu

The Schmidt College of Arts and Humanities     schwallr@fauvax
Florida Atlantic University                    (407) 367-3845
Boca Raton, FL  33431                          FAX (407) 367-2752
```

Great! You can see that this also includes some valuable and interesting information on the particular food as well as the recipe itself.

7.30. I'm shortly going to be traveling to Fiji. Any information about Fiji on the Internet?

This seems like a good question for WAIS, so let's search for keywords `country geographic political`. Here's the top few matches:

```
  #    Score     Source                        Title                         Lines
001:   [1000] (directory-of-se)  world-factbook93                               30
002:   [ 667] (directory-of-se)  USFWS_Region_9_Info_Res_Mgt_Data_Admin        147
003:   [ 556] (directory-of-se)  US-State-Department-Travel-Advisories          88
004:   [ 500] (directory-of-se)  Health-Security-Act                           296
```

Okay, both #1 and #3 look likely, so I'll `u` (use) them both, then search for the specific country I have in mind, Fiji. The results follow.

```
 #      Score      Source                    Title                                    Lines
001:   [1000] (world-factbook9)  Appendix C:International Organizations a   3693
002:   [1000] (US-State-Depart)  fiji    /var/spool/ftp/gopher/Internet Re    127
003:   [ 898] (world-factbook9)  Fiji  Geography    Location:     Oceania,    313
004:   [ 235] (US-State-Depart)  tonga    /var/spool/ftp/gopher/Internet R    113
005:   [ 206] (US-State-Depart)  french-polynesia-(tahiti)     /var/spool/f     65
006:   [ 206] (US-State-Depart)  nauru    /var/spool/ftp/gopher/Internet R    167
007:   [ 179] (world-factbook9)  Kiribati  Geography    Location:     Ocea    271
008:   [ 179] (world-factbook9)  Appendix E:Cross-Reference List of Geogr   3179
009:   [ 154] (world-factbook9)  Niue  Header     Affiliation:     (free as    251
010:   [ 154] (world-factbook9)  Tuvalu  Geography    Location:      Oceani    247
011:   [ 128] (world-factbook9)  American Samoa  Header    Affiliation:         277
012:   [ 128] (world-factbook9)  New Zealand  Geography    Location:     O     326
013:   [ 128] (world-factbook9)  Tonga  Geography    Location:     Oceania    256
014:   [ 128] (world-factbook9)  Vanuatu  Geography    Location:      Ocean    272
```

Source #2 and #3 look ideal. A closer look at each follows.

```
STATE DEPARTMENT TRAVEL INFORMATION - Fiji
============================================================
Fiji - Consular Information Sheet
 July 9, 1993

Country Description: Fiji recently returned to parliamentary government in
elections of May 1992. It has a developing economy. Tourist facilities are
available.

Immigration Requirements: Passport, proof of sufficient funds and an


onward/return ticket are required. A tourist visa is issued upon arrival for
an initial stay of up to four months. The tourist permit may be extended upon
application to the Fiji Immigration Department headquarters in Suva to allow a
total stay of six months. A visa is required for those entering Fiji to work,
study or reside. Information on specific requirements is available through the
Embassy of Fiji, 2233 Wisconsin Avenue, N.W., No. 240, Washington, D.C. 20007,
telephone (202) 337-8320 or the Fiji Mission to the U.N., New United Nations
Plaza, 26th Floor, New York, NY 10017, telephone (212) 355-7316.
```

That's great information (it continues for another 100 lines). Source #3 is equally valuable and is over 300 lines long.

```
Fiji
Geography

Location:
  Oceania, 2,500 km north of New Zealand in the South Pacific Ocean
Map references:
  Oceania, Standard Time Zones of the World
Area:
 total area:
  18,270 km2
 land area:
  18,270 km2
 comparative area:
  slightly smaller than New Jersey
Land boundaries:
  0 km
Coastline:
  1,129 km
Maritime claims:
  (measured from claimed archipelagic baselines)
 continental shelf:
  200 m depth or to depth of exploitation; rectilinear shelf claim added
 exclusive economic zone:
  200 nm
 territorial sea:
  12 nm
International disputes:
  none
Climate:
  tropical marine; only slight seasonal temperature variation
Terrain:
  mostly mountains of volcanic origin
Natural resources:
  timber, fish, gold, copper, offshore oil potential
```

7.31. I have heard a lot about the PowerPC Macintosh. Is there any information on this subject available through the Internet?

This is a job for the FAQ document! Indeed, it turns out that there's an FAQ database accessible within WAIS called `news.answers-faqs`. A search for `macintosh powerpc` revealed a number of matches, the very topmost being as follows:

```
001:   [1000] (            faqs)  PowerPC-FAQ    /
archive/doc/news/faqs/mac   589
```

A quick glance into the file shows that it's exactly what we want.

```
From: mac_ppc_faq@postbox.acs.ohio-state.edu
Subject: Macintosh PowerPC FAQ
Date: 13 Mar 1994 06:56:30 GMT

        answers about PowerPC and its relation to the Macintosh.
Archive-name: macintosh/PowerPC-FAQ
Last-modified: 1994/03/13
Version: 1.6

Finger-FAQ at - "finger sschecht@magnusug.acs.ohio-state.edu"
-----------------------------------------------
            Macintosh PowerPC Frequently Asked Questions
-----------------------------------------------

...

PURPOSE
   This FAQ was created in response to a request for a PowerPC FAQ in
comp.sys.mac.hardware. It exists to answer basic questions about the future
of Macintosh and its relation to the PowerPC series of microprocessors.
```

Q 7.32. Can I get FAQ documents through FTP?

Yes. There is an FAQ document server on the MIT computer system, `rtfm.mit.edu`. Use the FTP program to connect to the MIT computer system and then look in `/pub/usenet/news.answers`.

Q 7.33. Can I get FAQ documents through e-mail?

Yes. Send mail to the following:

```
To: mail-server@rtfm.mit.edu
Subject: <subject line is ignored>
Body: send <filename>
```

where `filename` is the name of the specific FAQ you seek. Almost all of them are in the directory `/pub/usenet/news.answers/`, so, for example, you could obtain the terrific Internet Services FAQ document by specifying `send usenet/news.answers/internet-services/faq`.

7.34. What magazines are available on the Internet?

Checking with Veronica reveals that there's information about a staggering number of magazines, but the strategy for finding them is a bit roundabout. I started out by searching for `computer magazine` but that revealed only two: *Computer Language* and *Computer World*. I cast my net a bit wider by searching for `magazine` and found a *lot* of matches—more than 600. Picking through it reveals quite a few that are of interest, including

American Quarterly Magazine
Artforum International Magazine
Arts Magazine
Billboard Magazine
Blue & Gold Illustrated Magazine — Notre Dame Football
Cadalyst Magazine (CADCAM)
Common Cause Magazine
Computer World Magazine
Consumers' Research Magazine
Cornell Magazine
Destination Discovery (Discovery Channel Magazine)
Discover: The World of Science Magazine
E, The Environmental Magazine
Economist, The (Magazine)
Financial World Magazine
Foreign Affairs Magazine
Growing Edge Magazine
Horticulture, The Magazine of American Gardening
Human Ecology Forum Magazine
IT Magazine
Inc Magazine
Internet World Magazine
Journal of NIH Research (Magazine)
Kennedy Journal of Ethics (Magazine)
LAN Magazine
Midrange Computing Magazine
Migration World Magazine

National Review (Magazine)
New Age Magazine
New Republic, The (Magazine)
New Yorker (Magazine)
OUT Magazine
Outside Magazine
Parent's Magazine
PC Magazine
Policy Review Magazine
Reason Magazine
Review in American History (Magazine)
Software Magazine
Tech Review (Magazine)
The Source (RapHip-hop Magazine)
TLC Monthly (The Learning Channel Magazine)
Today's Traveler Magazine
USA Today: The Magazine of the American Scene
World Politics Magazine
Worth Magazine
Yellow Silk, Journal of Erotica (Magazine)

To look at this another way, say that I'm interested in finding out whether *MacWeek* has any participation in the Internet. I can simply search for the magazine name in Veronica and see where I get: 100 matches, including a file that appears to contain a summary of all the reviews done in the magazine during 1993 and a survey from a *MacWeek* writer to Internet users.

NOTE If you have access to Gopher, you'll also want to check out the Electronic Newsstand, accessible by pointing your Gopher client to `gopher.internet.com`. There's all sorts of cool stuff there, including lots of actual articles from a variety of popular magazines.

Q 7.35. My daughter is learning the computer language LOGO in her fourth grade class. Is there information about LOGO on the Internet?

This one can have a number of facets, because you can find discussion groups about LOGO (on Usenet or a mailing list) and you can find specific items of information. I'll start by searching through the list of mailing lists that I've previously FTPed from MIT. A quick search with `grep -i logo part*` of the eight-part file reveals that there's a match in part five, which I can then find with a UNIX editor.

> **Logo**
>
> Contact: `logo-friends-request@aiai.ed.ac.uk`
>
> Purpose: Discussion of the Logo computer language.

Great. Now how about Usenet? I also have a copy of the newgroups list that I previously obtained, also from MIT, and `grep -i logo newsgroups` shows the following:

```
part1:comp.lang.logo        The Logo teaching
and learning language.
```

Not only is there a LOGO mailing list, there's also a Usenet group. How about using Veronica to see what we can find through that service? A quick search for `logo` reveals lots of matches (over 1,400) that are almost all actual graphics of a company, school, or organizational logo. I try again, narrowing the search to just directories with the word `logo` (Veronica search `logo -t1`) and find 135 matches, including some that have the name of the aforementioned Usenet group (`comp.lang.logo`). I choose one of the directories and it turns out that there's a version of LOGO for the Commodore Amiga just sitting there waiting to be downloaded!

Q 7.36. Can I find out about the weather in different areas of the world through the Internet?

That's one of the most interesting new features, and the answer is yes! To start, you can point your Gopher client at `wx.atmos.uiuc.edu` to talk to the University of Illinois weather server. For weather in England, try using FTP to look on host `cumulus.met.ed.ac.uk` for weather maps in the directory `/weather/gifs`. Other FTP sites worth checking are as follows:

Hostname	*FTP Directory*
`early-bird.think.com`	`pub/weather/maps`
`ftp.uwp.edu`	`pub/wx`
`kestrel.umd.edu`	`pub/wx (also see pub/wxsat)`
`wmaps.aoc.nrao.edu`	`pub/wx`
`wuarchive.wustl.edu`	`multimedia/images/wx`
`wx.research.att.com`	`wx`

A good source for information on weather maps is host `unidata.ucar.edu`. Login to the system with FTP and look in the directory `images` for information.

7.37. I have heard that there's weather information available through the "finger" service. What's out there and how can I find it?

The best place to find this information is by getting your own copy of the slick "fingerinfo" program that Scott Yanoff wrote. Use FTP to connect to the host `csd4.csd.uwm.edu`, and then get the file `/pub/fingerinfo`. When you run this script, here's what you see:

```
                    * Welcome to FingerInfo v2.6 *
                        (C) 1994 Scott Yanoff


[A] Auroral Activity                     [N] MnM/Coke Machine at CMU
[B] 3-Hour Solar and Geophysical Report  [O] Coke Machine in CS House at RIT
[C] Daily Solar and Geophysical Report   [P] Graph of soda at RIT
[D] List of Periodic Postings to Usenet  [Q] Cyber-Sleaze Daily Report
[E] Billboard Charts                     [R] Code of the Geeks
[F] DataBases via Finger                 [S] U.S. Weather Info Menu
[G] Earthquake Info Menu                 [T] Almanac Info/Sports Schedules
[H] NASA Headline News                   [U] Nova U's Grad. Catalog
[I] Nielsen TV Ratings                   [V] Baseball Scores/Standings
[J] Wisconsin Scores/Standings           [W] NFL Scores/Standings
[K] Tropical Storm Forecast              [X] NFL Line Spread
```

```
  [L] Remote Andrew Demo Service for X      [Y] Weekly Trivia
  [M] Cable Regulation Digest               [Z] Most Powerful Computing Sites
  [1] Seattle Radio News & Information      [2] Random talk.bizarre Stories
  [3] Paul's Hottub                         [4] ASCII Art FAQ

Please select one of the above (or return to quit): "
```


I choose s for weather and see

```
                       * Welcome to U.S. WeatherInfo *
                          (C) 1994 Scott A. Yanoff


 [A] Local Forecast (Milwaukee) - includes storm reports
 [B] Wisconsin State Forecast
 [C] Wisconsin Summary (statewide)
 [D] Climate Info for Today & Yesterday - hi/lo/normal, sunrise/sunset
 [E] Weather Info for Wisconsin Cities
 [F] Wisconsin Precipitation Map
 [G] Wisconsin Wind Map
 [H] Wisconsin Temperatures Map
 [I] Wisconsin Radar Map

 [J] Detroit Forecast
 [K] Colorado Forecast
 [L] Indiana Forecast/Bloomington Weather
 [M] Washington Forecast
 [N] Alabama/Auburn Forecast
 [O] Pensacola, FL Forecast
 [P] Youngstown, OH and Vicinity Forecast
 [Q] Oregon Forecast

Please select one of the above (or return to go back):
```

To see the weather forecast for Detroit, for example, I enter j and find out that it's cool, but not too bad.

```
SHORT TERM FORECAST FOR SOUTHEAST LOWER MICHIGAN
NATIONAL WEATHER SERVICE DETROIT MI
1025 PM EDT SUN APR 10 1994

SKIES WILL BE MOSTLY CLEAR OVERNIGHT WITH LOW TEMPERATURES FALLING TO AROUND
30 TO THE LOWER 30S. WINDS ALONG LAKE ERIE WILL BE LIGHT FROM THE
SOUTHEAST...
OTHERWISE WINDS WILL BECOME LIGHT NORTHEAST. SOME LOW TEMPERATURES WILL BE 29
AT PONTIAC AND PORT HURON...31 AT DETROIT AND ANN ARBOR...AND 33 AT ADRIAN.
```

7.38. What's the best source for weather information?

It's hard to identify the *best* source, but it's easy to identify a terrific service that you can always check: the Weather Underground, a service run by the University of Michigan. Simply type `telnet madlab.sprl.umich.edu 3000` to get there and then work through the menu system. To depress myself, I worked through the options to obtain current Caribbean weather data.

```
                   WEATHER        HIGH     LOW      PCPN   TIME
                                  F/C      F/C      IN     HR

ACAPULCO           FAIR          87 31    64 18
BARBADOS           FAIR          87 31    75 24
BERMUDA            CLOUDY        73 23    62 17
BOGOTA             PTCLDY        68 20    46  8
CURACAO            PTCLDY        89 32    78 26
FREEPORT           PTCLDY        82 28    66 19
GUADALAJARA        PTCLDY        89 32    54 12
GUADELOUPE         FAIR          89 32    71 22
HAVANA             PTCLDY        86 30    69 21
KINGSTON           FAIR          89 32    73 23
MONTEGO BAY        FAIR          87 31    75 24
```

7.39. What general reference works are available through the Internet?

This sounds like a job for Veronica, so I'll search for `general reference` and see what I find. Lots of great stuff. One of the best is the Gopher server at `rsl.ox.ac.uk`, but a quick compilation of a few different directories reveals the following:

```
Acronyms
Airlines Tollfree Phone Numbers
Airport Codes
American English Dictionary
CIA World Factbook 1991, 1992, and 1993
Daily Almanac
Dictionary of Computing
ISO Countries
```

```
Library Terminology (English)
Library Terminology (Spanish)
Local Times Around the World
Martini geography server (Info by city or area code)
New Hacker's Dictionary (Computer Jargon)
On-line Calendar for month/year
Periodic Table of Elements
Roget's Thesaurus (Published 1911)
U.S. Geographic Names Database
U.S. Telephone Area Codes
U.S. Zip Code Directory
Univ of Pennsylvania, Devils, and Jargon Dictionary
Weights & Measures.
World Phone Books
World Telephone Code Information
World Wide Area Codes
```


7.40. Is it possible to check for copyright information on the Internet?

The United States Copyright Office is on the Net through the Library of Congress! You can connect through Gopher to it (I learned this by using Veronica to search for `copyright`) directly by pointing your Gopher client to `marvel.loc.gov`. The introductory document explains what *copyright* is, for those of you who aren't sure.

```
Copyright is a form of protection provided by the laws of the
United States (title 17, U.S. Code) to the authors of "original
works of authorship" including literary, dramatic, musical,
artistic, and certain other intellectual works. This protection
is available to both published and unpublished works.
```

7.41. Is Microsoft on the Internet?

Questions of this nature hearken back to the `whois` command that we used earlier to look up a specific hostname to find out where it is and what it's all about. The same command can search by company name too, though the output is a bit more confusing! Here's what I found when I searched for Microsoft by typing `whois microsoft`.

```
Microsoft - Bldg 11 (NET-MSOFT-1) MSOFT-1                        198.105.232.0
Microsoft - Bldg 11 (NET-MSOFT-2) MSOFT-2                        198.105.233.0
Microsoft - Bldg 11 (NET-MSOFT-3) MSOFT-3                        198.105.234.0
Microsoft - Bldg 11 (NET-MSOFT-4) MSOFT-4                        198.105.235.0
Microsoft - Bldg 11 (NETBLK-MSOFT-NET) NETBLK-MSOFT-NET
                                                 198.105.232.0 - 198.105.235.0
Microsoft Corporation (NET-MICROSOFT) MICROSOFT                    131.107.0.0
Microsoft Corporation (MICROSOFT-DOM)                            MICROSOFT.COM
Microsoft Corporation (ATBD-HST)ATBD.MICROSOFT.COM                 131.107.1.7
Microsoft Workgroup Canada (NET-MGCNET) MGCNET                     199.60.28.0
Microsoft Workgroup Canada (GATEWAY17-HST) GATEWAY.MSWORKGROUP.BC.CA
                                                                 199.60.28.253
```

From here, I can see that their domain appears to be `microsoft.com`, so now I can search for `whois microsoft.com` to see what's recorded.

```
Microsoft Corporation (MICROSOFT-DOM)
   3635 157th Avenue
   Building 11
   Redmond, WA 98052

   Domain Name: MICROSOFT.COM

   Administrative Contact:
      Kearns, Paul  (PK47)  postmaster@MICROSOFT.COM
      (206) 882-8080
   Technical Contact, Zone Contact:
      NorthWestNet Network Operations Center  (NWNET-NOC)  noc@nwnet.net
      (206) 685-4444

   Record last updated on 11-Apr-94.

   Domain servers in listed order:

   DNS1.NWNET.NET              192.220.250.1
   DNS2.NWNET.NET              192.220.251.1
   NS1.BARRNET.NET             131.119.250.10
```

Here's another example: How about the National Broadcasting Company (NBC)? I'll try `whois NBC`. Bingo!

```
NBC News (NBCNEWS-DOM)
   30 Rockefeller Plaza
   New York, NY 10112

   Domain Name: NBCNEWS.COM

   Administrative Contact, Technical Contact, Zone Contact:
      Shearer, James C.  (JCS3)  shearer@THOMAS.GE.COM
      (609) 987-7611

   Record last updated on 04-Mar-94.

   Domain servers in listed order:

   NS.GE.COM                    192.35.39.24
   CRDNNS.GE.COM                192.35.44.6
```

Q 7.42. How do I access other systems from the Internet?

A variety of different services are now hooked up to the Internet, though you can't get to all of them directly. Here's a rundown:

> **AMERICA ONLINE.** You can't use AOL from the Internet due to AOL's special graphics software.
>
> **BIX.** `telnet x25.bix.com`. At the `username` prompt, enter `bix`.
>
> **COMPUSERVE.** CompuServe members can access CompuServe directly from the Internet. Members may access using the CompuServe Information Manager user interface or any general communications software. Telnet access will eliminate the need for a separate modem connection and, for some members, the need to dial long distance to reach CompuServe. CompuServe will provide free online membership sign-up for nonmembers who access via Telnet. Rates for accessing CompuServe through Telnet will be the same as dial-up rates via the CompuServe network.
>
> **DELPHI.** `telnet delphi.com`
>
> **DIALOG.** `telnet dialog.com`
>
> **GENIE.** `telnet hermes.merit.edu`. At the `Which host?` prompt, enter `sprintnet-313171`. SprintNet communica-

tion surcharges will apply. This is not guaranteed to work for file transfers or any other 8-bit transfers due to the nature of the Telnet protocol.

MCI MAIL. Cannot be accessed via the Internet.

NEXIS/LEXIS. `telnet lexis.meaddata.com` or `telnet 192.73.216.20` or `telnet 192.73.216.21`. When it asks for your terminal type, type `vt100a`. If characters do not echo back, set your terminal to "local" echo or "half duplex." You can also connect through Merit (see the CompuServe entry).

PC LINK. Can't be accessed due to the special graphics software.

PRODIGY. Can't be accessed due to the special graphics software.

QUANTUMLINK. Can't be accessed for technical reasons.

WELL. `telnet well.sf.ca.us`

Q 7.43. Okay. I'm looking for inner peace. Can I find it on the Internet?

That's an interesting question, actually. Let's look in Gopherspace with Veronica to see whether there are any suggestions about inner peace. Sad news: `Your search on 'inner peace' returned nothing`. The story of our times, undoubtedly.

Q 7.44. All right, so inner peace is out. How about a cheap, used Macintosh?

That's doubtless an easier question for anyone to answer. For this type of query, you want an information source that is updated very frequently, and that's where Usenet comes in handy. A quick search of the list of available newsgroups for `mac` reveals about forty newsgroups, one of which is `misc.forsale.computers.mac`. This is for buying, selling, and trading Apple Macintosh-related computer items.

A quick glance in that newsgroup for subjects shows that there are thirty matches to `mac` and `sale`. (You don't need to specify the word `used` because, by their very nature, the forsale newsgroups never have new products from vendors or distributors.)

Q 7.45. How can I keep up-to-date on nifty new Internet goings-on?

Here's information about some of the best places to find information about what's new on the Internet.

Net-Happenings Mailing List

The net-happenings mailing list is my favorite resource for finding out what's new — just about everything ends up in net-happenings, including various electronic newsletters, announcements of new Gopher servers, government agency databases, the Internet Hunt and much more.

Subscribe by sending e-mail

```
To: listserv@internic.net
Subject: <subject line is ignored>
Body: subscribe net-happenings Your Name
```

The Scout Report

The Scout Report is a weekly publication offered by InterNIC Information Services as a fast, convenient way to stay informed about what's new on the Net. It highlights new resources and offers news about the Internet. Some of what appears here parallels the Net happenings list, but the Scout Report is a lower-volume mailing list, published once a week.

To receive the Scout Report via electronic mail, send a message

```
To: majordomo@is.internic.net
Subject: <subject line is ignored>
Body: subscribe scout-report Your Name
```

Internet Monthly Report

The Internet Monthly Report announces the online accomplishments, milestones, and problems discovered by a variety of organizations in the Internet community. You can receive the report by e-mail by sending a message to `imr-request@isi.edu`. Your message will be read by a human, so ask nicely.

alt.internet.services

Another good place to look to stay updated on new Internet tools and toys is the Usenet newsgroup `alt.internet.services`. This newsgroup usually contains a selection of information about new resources, new user questions and an overwhelming number of questions asking, "Where can I find Internet access in Toledo?" If you manage to wade through these, you'll find some great Net info here.

Yanoff's Internet Services List

Also, read Scott Yanoff's Internet Services list. This list of resources is updated twice a month. If there's an database, game, or FTP site worth knowing about, it's probably listed in Yanoff's list. Finger `yanoff@csd4.csd.uwm.edu` to find ways to receive this list or check for it on `alt.internet.services`.

Q 7.46. What are some good places to continue learning about how to find information on the Internet?

I'm tempted to answer with a Zen koan, something about how the search for learning is a lifelong process, but that's probably not the best way to end this chapter! Instead, remember that there are a lot of different people out there who are also interested in the topics that interest you, and that the network is changing—and improving—daily. Start with the FAQ files if your topic is related to a Usenet group. Check Veronica to see whether there are any files in the vast reaches of Gopherspace, too. (And persevere. If you pick a busy time, you'll get lots of `too busy - try again soon` messages.) Check Archie if you're looking for specific files or documents. Build up a list of sites and files that you find particularly helpful; my Gopher bookmark list, for example, is up to 44 entries, and I constantly modify it to ensure that it lists the best places for the information I seek. If you use Mosaic, learn how to use the Hot Key feature to remember where you've been. Write it down. Ask your friends. And if you've exhausted all other channels, ask a brief question to the appropriate newsgroup or mailing list.

CHAPTER 8

Can I Do Business on the Internet?

The Internet is increasingly *the* place for business transactions, so this chapter focuses on doing business on the Net. The first section looks at how to find investment and stock information. The next section shows how to get a job and do a little online business research. The third section looks at the not-so-new practice of advertising and selling goods and services on the Net. Finally, a look at some of the products and services you can find online—with no obligation to buy, rock-bottom prices, and no finance charges until May! : -)

Finding Business and Investment Information

Q 8.1. Where can I find stock market and financial information online?

You won't be able to find current stock prices for the entire market on the Internet. If you're looking for a ticker of current stock prices or a complete list of closing quotes, you'll have to use a commercial online service like Prodigy or read the *Wall Street Journal.* However, there are a variety of places on the Internet where you can find good, albeit not complete, financial information.

Daily Stock Market Updates

If you're watching just about any financial market, listen up: Martin Wong provides Internet users with end-of-the-day stock reports along with other useful business information. These files are available via FTP from `dg-rtp.dg.com` and via e-mail.

If you would like to receive the daily quote mailings, send e-mail to `Martin.Wong@eng.sun.com`. Your e-mail will be read by a human, not a machine, so be nice. Wong requests "that people send me timely information on company earnings, products, or industry news for inclusion in the distribution. I also want to know if anyone gets rich from the information."

Here's a very abbreviated example of Mr. Wong's daily financial updates:

```
====Information deemed reliable, but never guaranteed=======================
— MARKET SUMMARY & NEWS (TWOCENTS or tosense) -[Your Nickel]————————
 Japan's market off sharply. DJIA opened up 10 and had a bullish bias all day
 for the start of April portfolio window dressing. Rallying to +16 and holding
 in the first hour, a small fade back to +8 and that was all the bears could
 do as the market moved ahead for the rest of the day, up 30 by midday, and
 finishing at the day's highs despite circuit breakers cutting off the computer
 buy programs at +50, the market finished up 57.10 points to a key level back
 above 3700, DJIA 3,705.78 on contracting, normally lighter Monday volume of
 262 million shares. Utilities up 1, Transports up 15, OTC up 8.25 points
 @730.81. Bonds up 3/4, $ lower, gold up 2.80, silver up .03 to $5.13.
 3-Month T-Bill rate at 3.85%, 6 month T bill at 4.25%, 30 year long bond yield
 dropped to 7.14%. Oscillator confirmed the buy signal and we should now have
 a 6-8 week buy cycle on the oscillator. Wall Street Week elves sell signal
 gone as the neutral elf moved to bullish, leaving 3 bulls, 7 bears and a -4
 reading. NYSE, ASE, and PSE all vote to close their markets for Nixon memorial
 services on Wed.

>                         I N D I C E S,    A V E R A G E S
>     Last  Change                                   Open      High     Low
>   136.46   +2.82  AMEX Computer Index             133.64    136.46   133.64
>   454.27   +5.04  AMEX Institution Index          449.23    454.27   449.12
>   373.51   +5.59  AMEX Major Market Index         367.92    373.51   367.75
>   435.97   +2.66  AMEX Market Value Index         433.31    435.99   433.29
>   264.54   +5.29  AMEX Oil Index                  259.25    264.64   259.07
>  3705.78  +57.10  Dow J Industrial Average       3648.68   3706.08  3648.68
```

```
>  1610.25  +15.23  Dow J Transportation Average  1594.58  1610.47  1593.25
>   200.17   +0.92  Dow J Utility Average          199.12   200.63   198.85
>   730.81   +8.25  NASDAQ Composite               723.65   731.22   722.56
>   899.40   +6.34  NASDAQ Financial Index         893.16   900.18   891.85
>   757.86   +6.15  NASDAQ Industrial Index        752.54   758.02   752.10
>   885.60   +5.12  NASDAQ Insurance Index         878.48   885.61   877.44
>   735.34   +5.37  NASDAQ Transp Index            731.57   736.08   731.11
>   250.47   +2.52  NYSE Composite                 247.95   250.47   247.92
>   209.36   +1.15  NYSE Finance                   208.21   209.37   208.09
>   306.90   +3.53  NYSE Industrials               303.37   306.90   303.37
>   251.03   +2.71  NYSE Transportation            248.32   251.08   247.80
>   216.06   +1.70  NYSE Utilities                 214.36   216.43   214.21
>   417.61   +5.26  Standard & Poors 100 Index     412.36   417.61   412.25
>   452.71   +5.08  Standard & Poors 500 Index     447.55   452.71   447.53

SYMB:TN PRICE-P CHANGE PCTCHG  HIGH    LOW      LAST  VOLUME-V P*V VALUE
  AA:S+ 68.625   0.875  1.29%  68.625  66.875   67.75    431.9K 29.6391M
AAPL:S* 31.000   1.250  4.20%  31.000  29.500   29.75   3207.5K 99.4325M
  ABF:S 32.875  -0.125 -0.38%  33.125  32.750   33.00    239.7K 7.8801M
 ABX:S+ 22.000   0.750  3.53%  22.000  21.375   21.25   1041.4K 22.9108M
 ACAD:S 55.375  -0.125 -0.23%  56.000  54.750   55.50    154.2K 8.5388M
 ACN:S+ 13.375   0.625  4.90%  13.375  12.625   12.75     69.7K 0.9322M
ADBE:S+ 26.000   1.000  4.00%  26.000  24.750   25.00    424.2K 11.0292M
ADCT:S+ 40.250   1.250  3.21%  40.250  39.000   39.00     49.6K 1.9964M
ADPT:S+ 17.875   1.375  8.33%  17.875  16.750   16.50    372.1K 6.6513M
  AGN:S 20.250  -0.250 -1.22%  20.500  20.125   20.50     66.9K 1.3547M
  AHP:S 59.250   0.250  0.42%  59.500  58.625   59.00    390.3K 23.1253M
 ALD:S* 35.500   0.375  1.07%  36.000  35.125   35.125   481.5K 17.0933M
ALDC:S+ 28.125   0.875  3.21%  28.125  27.250   27.25     90.3K 2.5397M
ALEX:S+ 25.000   0.500  2.04%  25.000  24.500   24.50     22.7K 0.5675M
```


Historical Stock Information

For historical stock information, FTP to

```
dg-rtp.dg.com:/pub/misc.invest
```

There's lots of good stuff there, including historical stock data, mutual fund information, and other useful facts and figures for investors. More complete information about this site (as well as listings of some other sites with financial information) is available from the `misc.invest` FAQ, which you can find on the Usenet. It's posted monthly to `misc.invest`, `misc.answers`, and `news.answers`. You can also get it via anonymous FTP,

```
rtfm.mit.edu:/pub/usenet/news.answers/investment-
faq/general/*
```

or by sending e-mail to

```
mail-server@rtfm.mit.edu
Subject: <subject line is ignored>
Body: send usenet/news.answers/investment-faq/general/*
```

Los Angeles Times Market Beat

As an experiment, the *Los Angeles Times* is offering Tom Petruno's "Market Beat" column online free of charge. "Market Beat" is a source of fresh, off-Wall Street perspective on investing and financial markets. It's written for the do-it-yourself investor in individual securities and mutual funds by a widely followed and market-savvy columnist who's been covering investing since 1979.

The electronic version of "Market Beat" is an experiment that may not last. Subscriptions are free at the time of this writing.

"Market Beat" is available on `misc.invest` and by electronic mail. To subscribe, send e-mail to

```
To: petruno@netcom.com
Subject: SUBSCRIBE
Body: <message body is ignored>
Questions and comments should also be sent to _petruno@netcom.com_.
```

Q 8.2. What's the Financial Economics Network?

Another source of stock and investment material is the Financial Economics Network. FEN is an e-mail discussion group where you can swap information on banking, accounting, options, stocks, bonds, small business issues, corporate finance, and emerging markets. FEN also delivers by e-mail to subscribers Holt's Stock Market Reports. The daily report provides a market summary of 29 indices and averages, including Standard & Poor's 500-stock index and the Dow Jones industrial average. It also lists the most actively traded stocks and foreign currency prices. For more information, contact Wayne Marr at `marrm@clemson.clemson.edu` or John Trimble at `trimble@vancouver.wsu.edu`.

8.3. The U.S. Government distributes the Commerce Business Daily. Can I access this document through the Internet?

The *Commerce Business Daily* is available free of charge via the CNS gopher server. Point your Gopher program at `cscns.com`. For more information, send e-mail to `info@cscns.com`.

8.4. Is EDGAR online?

The SEC's *Electronic Data Gathering, Analysis, and Retrieval System* (*EDGAR*) system is a database of SEC-required filings by publicly traded companies. The EDGAR Internet project is sponsored by the National Science Foundation and holds over 32,000 documents. Administrators of the system estimate that almost 14,000 megabytes of data are sent out each month. For more information, send e-mail

```
To: mail@town.hall.org
Subject: <subject line is ignored>
Body:  help
```

8.5. What other economics information is available?

To find out, I used Veronica to search Gopherspace for "economics." The search hit on more than 6500 matches, including a very promising article entitled "Gopher Servers for Economics and Management-Related Disciplines." I choose that and found

```
1.  Business Sources on the Net (Kent State U.)/
2.  CSF Conflict Resolution Consortium (Univ. of Colorado)/
3.  Economics Working Paper Archive (SHSU)/
4.  Harvard Business School Publishing Corporation/
5.  Institute of Economics, Zagreb/
```

```
6.  Murdoch Univ (Australia)/
7.  National Bureau of Economic Research/
8.  North Carolina State Economics Archive/
9.  ORSA/TIMS "INFORMS Online"/
10. Other Economics and Business Resources on the Net/
11. RESOURCES FOR ECONOMISTS ON THE INTERNET.
12. Rice University Economics Archive/
13. Technical Univ Berlin, Economics Gopher/
14. U.S. Commerce Business Daily [2003]/
15. UT Dallas Economics Archive/
```

Item #11 sounds most likely, so I typed `11` to see the file.

```
                RESOURCES FOR ECONOMISTS ON THE INTERNET

                                Bill Goffe

             Dept. of Economics and International Business
                    University of Southern Mississippi
                          Hattiesburg, MS 39406
                         bgoffe@whale.st.usm.edu

                             February 1, 1994

TABLE OF CONTENTS

*   1. INTRODUCTION
*   2. NEW IN THIS VERSION
    3. U.S. MACRO AND U.S. REGIONAL DATA
       A. Economic Bulletin Board (EBB)
       B. EconData
+      C. Bureau of Labor Statistics (LABSTAT)
+      D. Federal Reserve
       E. New England Electronic Economic Data Center (NEEEDc)
    4. OTHER DATA (INCLUDING NON-U.S.)
       A. Luxembourg Income Study (LIS)
       B. National Archives Center for Electronic Records
       C. Social Security Administration (OSS-IS)
       D. FedWorld
       E. Public Domain Financial Data
       F. Census
*      G. EDGAR
*      H. Vienna Stock Market
       I. Productivity Analysis Research Network (PARN)
+      J. U.S. Department of Agriculture Economic Research Service
+      K. World Bank Public Information Center (PIC)
+      L. Wall Street Journal and New York Times News Service
```

```
    5. WORKING PAPER ARCHIVES AND BIBLIOGRAPHICAL SERVICES
       A. NetEc (BibEc & WoPEc)
       B. Working Paper Archive (Wash. Univ., St. Louis)
       C. Feminist Economists Discussion Group Archive
    6. GOPHERS
       A. Economics Gopher at Sam Houston State University
       B. Computational Economics Gopher
       C. ClioNet (Cliometric Society)
*      D. National Bureau of Economic Research Gopher
       E. Academe This Week (Chronicle of Higher Education)
       F. Washington Univ. at St. Louis Econ. Dept.
       G. RiceInfo
*      H. University of Michigan Economics Department
       I. Communications for a Sustainable Future
       J. SunSITE
       K. RISKNet
       L. Florida State College of Business
    7. UNIVERSITY AND RESEARCH LIBRARY CARD CATALOGS
       A. Research Libraries in General
       B. Library of Congress
+      C. North Carolina State University's "Library Without Walls"
    8. PROGRAM LIBRARIES
       A. Netlib
       B. Statlib
       C. Univ. of Illinois at Chicago Statistical Library
    9. EDUCATIONAL SERVICES
       A. Iowa Electronic Markets
   10. USENET NEWSGROUPS
   11. MAILING LISTS
       A. Introduction
*      B. Single Topic Mailing Lists
+      C. Financial Economists Network (FEN)
   12. DATA RELATED TO THE ECONOMICS PROFESSION
       A. Graduate Programs
   13. WORD PROCESSING
       A. TeX References
       B. TeX Macros for Economics and TeX Sources
+  14. PROGRAMS FOR ECONOMISTS ON THE INTERNET
+      A. BCI Data Manager
   15. USEFUL BOOKS, PROGRAMS, AND RESOURCES ABOUT THE INTERNET
       A. Books
*      B. On-Line Guide
       C. Software
       D. Resources
   16. NON-INTERNET RESOURCES
       A. Introduction
       B. Federal Reserve Bank Bulletin Boards
       C. Electronic JEL Index
       D. On-Line Refereed Economics Journal
```

8

8.6. Hey, that looks useful! How do I get the *Resources for Economists on the Internet* document through electronic mail?

Send an electronic mail message to Bill Goffe of the Department of Economics and International Business at `bgoffe@whale.st.usm.edu`.

8.7. What about the *Internet Guide to Government, Business and Economics Resources*?

This guide is available through the Clearinghouse of Subject-Oriented Internet Resource Guides at the University of Michigan Libraries. (This is always a good place to check; point your Gopher to `lib.umich.edu` to see what's offered.) The document is about 50 pages at last count and can be obtained through gopher or anonymous FTP.

```
una.hh.lib.umich.edu:/inetdirsstacks/
govdocs:tsangaustin
```

To get this document via electronic mail, send a request to Kim Tsang of the School of Information and Library Studies of the University of Michigan: e-mail `kimtsang@sils.umich.edu`

8.8. What business-related newsgroups are on Usenet?

A quick search of the list of Usenet groups revealed these:

alt.business.multi-level	Multilevel (network) marketing businesses
bit.listserv.buslib-l	Business libraries list
clari.biz.courts	Lawsuits and business-related legal matters (moderated)
clari.biz.features	Business feature stories (moderated)

clari.biz.misc	Other business news (moderated)
clari.canada.biz	Canadian Business Summaries (moderated)
misc.entrepreneurs	Discussion on operating a business
soc.college.org.aiesec	The International Association of Business and Commerce Students

The most promising of the batch for business-related discussion is `misc.entrepreneurs`. Try asking there about the specific area of business or business-related information that you are interested in.

Q 8.9. What investment-related newsgroups are on Usenet?

Another quick look through the list of newsgroups revealed

clari.biz.finance.personal	Personal investing and finance (moderated)
clari.biz.invest	News for investors (moderated)
misc.invest	Investments and the handling of money
misc.invest.real-estate	Property investments

Take a closer look at `misc.invest` by hopping over to the MIT Usenet archive system `rtfm.mit.edu` and changing the directory to `/pub/usenet/misc.invest`. There are a bunch of curiously named files.

```
Pointer_to_misc.invest_general_FAQ_list
diffs_for_misc.invest_general_FAQ
m.i_F_o_g_i_t_(T_o_C)
m.i_F_o_g_i_t_(p_1_o_3)
m.i_F_o_g_i_t_(p_2_o_3)
m.i_F_o_g_i_t_(p_3_o_3)
misc.invest_FAQ_on_general_investment_topics_(Table_of_Contents)
misc.invest_FAQ_on_general_investment_topics_(part_1_of_3)
misc.invest_FAQ_on_general_investment_topics_(part_2_of_3)
misc.invest_FAQ_on_general_investment_topics_(part_3_of_3)
```

I'll use the `get` command to view the first file, which says (in a lot of words) that I need to look instead in the directory `/pub/usenet/news.answers/investment-faq/general`. I do so and find a table of contents (`toc`) document and three files called `part1`, `part2`, and `part3`. I opt to view the table of contents of the `misc.invest` FAQ document just to get an idea of what's inside.

```
Newsgroups: misc.invest,misc.answers,news.answers,misc.invest.stocks
From: lott@informatik.uni-kl.de (Christopher Lott)
Subject: misc.invest FAQ on general investment topics (Table of Contents)
Summary: Answers to frequently asked questions about investments.
        Should be read by anyone who wishes to post to misc.invest.
Organization: University of Kaiserslautern, Germany
Date: Sun, 27 Mar 1994 01:02:17 GMT

Archive-name: investment-faq/general/toc
Version: $Id: faq-toc,v 1.13 1994/03/23 06:56:18 lott Exp lott $
Compiler: Christopher Lott, lott@informatik.uni-kl.de

This is the table of contents for the general misc.invest FAQ.

Articles in this FAQ discusses issues pertaining to money and investment
instruments, specifically stocks, bonds, and things like options and life
insurance. Subjects more appropriate to misc.consumers are not included here.
For extensive information on mutual funds, see the mutual fund FAQ, which is
maintained by marks@ssdevo.enet.dec.com.

TABLE OF CONTENTS

    Sources for Current and Historical Market Data
    Beginning Investor's Advice
    Dave Rhodes and Other Chain Letters
    American Depository Receipts (ADR)
    Bankrupt Broker
    Beta
    Bonds
    Book-to-Bill Ratio
    Books About Investing (especially stocks)
    Bull and Bear Lore
    Buying and Selling Stock Without a Broker
    Computing the Rate of Return on Monthly Investments
    Computing Compound Return
    Derivatives
    Discount Brokers
    Dividends on Stock and Mutual Funds
    Dollar Cost and Value Averaging
    Dollar Bill Presidents
    Dramatic Stock Price Increases and Decreases
    Direct Investing and DRIPS
    Free Information
```

```
Future and Present Value of Money
Getting Rich Quickly
Charles Givens
Goodwill
Hedging
Instinet
Investment Associations (AAII and NAIC)
Initial Public Offering (IPO)
Investment Jargon
Life Insurance
Money-Supply Measures M1, M2, and M3
Market Makers and Specialists
NASD Public Disclosure Hotline
One-Letter Ticker Symbols
One-Line Wisdom
Option Symbols
Options on Stocks
P/E Ratio
Pink Sheet Stocks
Renting vs. Buying a Home
Retirement Plan - 401(k)
Round Lots of Shares
Savings Bonds (from US Treasury)
SEC Filings / Edgar
Shorting Stocks
Stock Basics
Stock Exchange Phone Numbers
Stock Index Types
Stock Index - The Dow
Stock Indexes - Others
Stock Splits
Technical Analysis
Ticker Tape Terminology
Treasury Debt Instruments
Treasury Direct
Uniform Gifts to Minors Act (UGMA)
Warrants
Wash Sale Rule (from U.S. IRS)
Zero-Coupon Bonds

------------------------------------------------------------

Compilation Copyright (c) 1994 by Christopher Lott, lott@informatik.uni-kl.de
—
"Christopher Lott / Email: lott@informatik.uni-kl.de / Tel: +49 (631) 205-
3334"
"Adresse: FB Informatik - Bau 57 / Universitaet KL / D—67653 Kaiserslautern"
```

It's clear that a tremendous amount of helpful information is available in this document, and it allows me to make a recommendation: if you're interested in any aspect of investing and would like to see what kind of services are available on the Internet, get a copy of this document from the MIT archive server.

8.10. So how do I get a copy of the *misc.invest* FAQ?

The best way is through anonymous FTP.

```
rtfm.mit.edu:/pub/usenet/news.answers/investment-
faq/general/*
```

It's also posted monthly to the Usenet groups `misc.invest`, `misc.answers`, and `news.answers`.

If you only have e-mail access, you can send electronic mail.

```
To: mail-server@rtfm.mit.edu
Subject: <subject line is ignored>
Body: send usenet/news.answers/investment-faq/general/*
```

Doing Business Research

This section answers some questions about doing business research: whether you're looking for a job or looking for ways to make the Internet work for you.

8.11. I also travel quite a bit on business, and it would be great if I could save some money on air fare (and learn more about my destination before I got there). What's available?

There are a couple of Usenet groups that discuss travel issues, but they're quite highly trafficked and can be difficult to read due to their volume. A better general resource for online travel information of any sort is to check the "Travel/Online-info FAQ" document. It lists a variety of interesting and useful online resources.

To obtain this FAQ, FTP to

```
rtfm.mit.edu:/pub/usenet/news.answers/travel/
online-info
```

You can also request this same file by electronic mail,

```
To: mail-server@rtfm.mit.edu
Subject: <subject line is ignored>
Body: send /pub/usenet/news.answers/travel/online-info
```

Another item of note is the desirably-named FAQ, "Airplane Tickets, Cheap," which is available via FTP,

```
rtfm.mit.edu/pub/usenet-by-group/news.answers/
travel/air/cheap-tickets
```

or by using your favorite World Wide Web browser at

```
http://www.cis.ohio-state.edu:80/hypertext/faq/
usenet/travel/air/cheap-tickets/top.html
```


8.12. I spent my last $25 on this book and I really need a job. There's gotta be job listings online, yes?

Certainly. If you have access to the Usenet, check out the `misc.jobs` set of newsgroups. Here you can find job listings, post your resume, or ask questions about the details of job hunting. (If you're already employed, don't let your boss find you reading these newsgroups!)

misc.jobs.misc	Random talk about employment
misc.jobs.offered	Many employment opportunities listed here
misc.jobs.offered.entry	Listings of entry-level employment opportunities
misc.jobs.resumes	Blindly post your resume here, along with thousands of other wishful thinkers

> **NOTE** If you're a computer person, electronics engineer, or other tech-head looking for gainful employment, you can't go wrong with misc.jobs.offered. Although these newsgroups are not dedicated to listing jobs in computing fields, the vast majority of the listings are computer-related. The simple reason is that companies need to be relatively technologically adept to be on the Internet. Who's more computer savvy than the computer firms themselves?

There are also a variety of "local" newsgroups devoted to finding and talking about jobs in specific areas. For instance, if you're looking for a job in the San Francisco Bay Area, you can read the newsgroup `ba.jobs.offered`. You won't see job listings from other, less interesting parts of the world. Here are a few local job newsgroups:

`ba.jobs.offered`	San Francisco Bay area
`ucb.jobs`	UC Berkeley
`atl.jobs`	Atlanta
`aus.jobs`	Australia
`can.jobs`	Canada
`tx.jobs`	Texas
`uk.jobs.offered`	United Kingdom

Q 8.13. I'm a contract computer programmer and there *must* be a lot of contract and consulting jobs offered through the Internet. Am I right? How do I find them?

Check out the newsgroup `misc.jobs.contract`.

The best place to start is the document "Frequently Asked Questions about contract jobs on Usenet." To obtain this FAQ, FTP to

```
rtfm.mit.edu:/pub/usenet/news.answers/contract-
jobs/faq
```

While you're there, you should grab a related file that serves as an introduction to the `misc.jobs.contract` newsgroup: to get it, FTP to

```
rtfm.mit.edu:/pub/usenet/news.answers/contract-
jobs/intro
```

If you want to receive these documents via electronic mail, you can send e-mail.

```
To: mail-server@rtfm.mit.edu
Subject: <subject line is ignored>
Body: send /pub/usenet/news.answers/contract-jobs/faq
      send /pub/usenet/news.answers/contract-jobs/intro
```


8.14. I'm a journalist. What's out there for me?

There's quite a bit for journalists on the Internet, actually. Your best place to start is (yet another) FAQs file available through MIT: the Net Resources for Journalists list.

You can obtain this journalism resources list via FTP from (where else?) `rtfm.mit.edu`.

```
rtfm.mit.edu:/pub/usenet/news.answers/journalism-
net-resources
```

You can also obtain this file through electronic mail by sending the message

```
To: mail-server@rtfm.mit.edu
Subject: <subject line is ignored>
body: send /pub/usenet/news. answers/journalism-net-resources
```

8.15. All right. I'm actually a lawyer and was just kidding about that journalism stuff. Is there anything on the Internet that I would be interested in?

You bet, although I'm not sure whether you have to know that a *tort* isn't something you find in a cookbook! There is an excellent document called "The Legal List, Law-related Resources on the Internet and Elsewhere" maintained by Erik J. Heels, with support from The University of Maine School of Law, The Maine Law and Technology Association, and Midnight Networks Inc. Obtain your own copy through anonymous FTP.

```
ftp.midnight.com:/pub/LegalList/legallist.txt
```

You can also get this list through electronic mail by sending a message

```
To: mail-server@rtfm.mit.edu
Subject: <subject line is ignored>
Body: send /pub/usenet/news.answers/law/*
```

Advertising and Selling on the Net

The questions that follow are among the most misunderstood and hotly debated issues about the Internet: commercial advertising and selling.

8.16. Commercial activity isn't allowed on the Internet, right? It's purely an academic and educational network, right? People who advertise and sell stuff on the Net should be flogged, right?

Yes and no. As mentioned earlier in this book, the Internet is composed of a variety of different networks. Each network has its own set of rules, called *acceptable use policies.* Certain networks (particularly the National Science Foundation network, the NSFnet) have strict acceptable use policies that ban most types of commercial use. On the other hand, another backbone network within the Internet world has been finding considerable interest among commercial Internet users—the Commercial Internet Exchange (CIX). The acceptable use policies of CIX are much more broad, and advertising and selling are both within its purview. So although commercial activity isn't allowed on certain parts of the Internet, it is allowed on others.

People who advertise on the Internet should only be flogged for heinous violations of Internet culture, such as sending unsolicited junk e-mail or posting commercial messages to Usenet groups that aren't supposed to be used for commercial messages.

8.17. How can I find out more about the Commercial Internet Exchange?

The best route is to contact to them directly. I use the Gopher service and point it at `cix.org`, but you can also FTP to the same site. Start with the files

```
cix.org:/CIX/press-release
cix.org:/CIX/README
```

The latter includes a list of commercial Internet service providers that are members of the CIX.

If you want info on CIX via e-mail, send your request

```
To: info@cix.org
Subject: <subject line is ignored>
Body: help
```

Q 8.18. Is advertising allowed on the Internet?

Answered by Michael Strangelove (`mstrange@fonorola.net`)

> **NOTE** Many of questions in this section are answered by Michael Strangelove (`mstrange@fonorola.net`), publisher of the *Internet Business Journal* and an expert on the commercialization of the Internet.

It is surprising how many people still see the Internet as a noncommercial, academic, purely technical environment. Not so: today, about fifty percent of the Internet is populated by commercial users. The commercial Internet is the fastest growing part of cyberspace, doubling in size every year.

Advertisers spend billions of dollars every year to communicate their message to potential consumers. Now businesses are discovering that they can advertise to the Internet community at a fraction of the cost of traditional methods. With tens of millions of electronic mail users out there in cyberspace today, Internet advertising is an intriguing opportunity not to be overlooked. When the turn of the century rolls around and there are one hundred million consumers on the Internet, we may see many ad agencies and advertising-supported magazines go under as businesses learn to communicate directly with consumers in cyberspace.

> **NOTE** Internet users who have accounts provided by their university or research institutions are the single major exception to the "Business on the Net is OK" rule. It is almost certain that if you have an academic Internet account, you are forbidden to engage in commercial activity over your university's Internet connection. This may also hold true for many Free-nets. If you are uncertain about local authorized use policy, ask your Internet provider or system postmaster.

As the Internet is not owned by any one company or nation, the only real restrictions placed on users are by the consensus of the virtual community itself. The key to effective Internet advertising is taking the time to learn what is and is not acceptable.

It should be noted that Usenet is no less commercial than the rest of the Internet. Gone forever are the days when the Internet was a private club for the techno-elite.

Potential advertisers take note: do your homework before blasting onto the Internet. This virtual community has some very strong feelings about inappropriate activity, and the penalties for incorrect advertising methods could be international hate mail to you, your boss, and your stockholders.

Q 8.19. Is advertising on the Internet new?

Answered by Michael Strangelove (`mstrange@fonorola.net`*)*

Even among many long-time Internet users, there is a perception that Internet advertising is a new phenomenon. It is not. In the mid 80s—when the Internet was largely an academic, scientific, and technical community—commercial activity was still allowed if it was in support of research efforts. This meant that right from the Internet's first days, there were software developers, publishers, consultants, and technicians hawking their wares to the academic community. Advertising has been taking place on the Internet since its beginning. The problem facing the Internet community is that the bigger the community gets (and it is going to be big enough to boggle any mind), the more it will attract the attention of advertisers and advertising agencies.

Q 8.20. Is the Internet a mass market?

Answered by Michael Strangelove (`mstrange@fonorola.net`*)*

For quite some time, the Internet won't represent a mass market, such as TV, where content is controlled, packaged, and distributed to a limited number of predefined and demographically homogenous audiences consisting of millions of viewers. There are no mass markets on the Internet—only micro communities with distinct histories, rules, and concerns. These communities are gathered into thousands of discussion forums ranging from hundreds to thousands of participants, but there are probably no groups of "millions." Internet-facilitated business must meet the challenge of reaching these virtual communities on their terms, respecting their local customs. The Internet is big, very big, but it is not a mass market that can be reached easily through mass mailing.

Q 8.21. Is unsolicited advertising permitted?

Answered by Michael Strangelove (`mstrange@fonorola.net`)

Unsolicited advertising does take place every day on the Net, and there even exists one company that sells access to over one million Internet addresses for direct e-mail advertising. Unsolicited advertising is a gray area of Internet culture and therefore requires careful planning and execution to avoid the wrath of an extremely vocal community.

Unsolicited advertising has been taking place on the Internet for quite some time, but it must be done with extreme caution. There is no one to force you not to send unsolicited commercial e-mail on the Internet, but if you send 10,000 annoying advertisements, be prepared to receive 10,000 complaints. Also, companies that disregard Internet users' wishes are likely to find that the Internet community has a long memory (as any "oral" culture does) and is quite capable of engaging in anti-advertising campaigns and boycotts.

In this new interactive, digital, wired-to-the-bellybutton world, bulk unsolicited advertising is unnecessary, bad netiquette, and simply lazy—particularly when there are so many creative alternatives. The author has no wish to support the rise of door-to-door salespeople in cyberspace and therefore is intentionally leaving out contact information for firms that sell Internet e-mail addresses and consult in bulk unsolicited e-mail advertising.

8.22. Can I send electronic mail advertisements to everyone on the Internet?

Answered by Michael Strangelove (`mstrange@fonorola.net`)

I always find it somewhat disturbing that there are companies that would want to do this. Fortunately for the Internet, it is not possible to send an "E-ad" to every person on the Internet.

Unfortunately for the Internet, it is probably only a matter of time before some sick mind figures out a method of simultaneously annoying every Internet user. For now at least, there is no way to post an e-mail message to every Internet user, nor in my opinion, should such a tool be developed.

8.23. How can I advertise my product on Usenet?

Announcements of professional products or services are allowed on Usenet; however, because someone else is paying the phone bills, the announcement should be of overall benefit to Usenet. Post to the appropriate newsgroup—such as `comp.newprod` to announce your new computer gizmo—but never to a general-purpose newsgroup such as `misc.misc` or `comp.sys.mac.games`. Clearly mark in the subject area of your article that it is a product announcement. At the most, post one article per product. If you're announcing multiple products, group them all into one article.

Advertising hype is especially frowned on. Stick to technical facts with a minimum of "pitch." Obnoxious or inappropriate announcements or articles that violate this policy will generally be rejected.

The Internet, when used properly, is a great way to find customers and sell your wares, whatever they may be. (Several examples of online products and services follow.) But beware: if you don't heed the Internet's culture, the masses will turn on you, doing your business more harm than good.

An excellent place to look for more information on Internet advertising is Michael Strangelove's "Advertising on the Internet" FAQ document. You can obtain this document by sending e-mail to Michael directly at `mstrange@fonorola.net`.

You can get the `comp.newprod` FAQ by FTP

```
rtfm.mit.edu:/pub/usenet/news.answers/newprod
```

A larger area for commercial postings is the `biz` news hierarchy. There's a FAQ for this group, too, available by FTP

```
rtfm.mit.edu:/pub/usenet/news.answers/biz-config-
faq
```

Here's the introduction to the newsgroups from that document:

```
"Biz" is a hierarchy of newsgroups that are carried and propagated by sites
interested in the world of business products around them — in particular,
computer products and services.  This includes product announcements,
announcements of fixes and enhancements, product reviews, and postings of
demo
software.
While not supporting the electronic equivalent of a newspaper ad, the "biz"
hierarchy is specifically intended to carry traffic of a commercial, factual,
and often technical nature. Thus, some sites that operate under restrictions
against carrying such traffic may not be able to carry the hierarchy.
```

8.24. I want my e-mail address to be *manager@furniture-mart* (or something). How can my business get its own domain name for e-mail?

To really be a part of the Internet you'll want your own domain name for your company. After all, `bill@pubnix11.com` is less informative and appealing to customers than `president@whitehouse.gov`, isn't it? Domains need to be registered with the Network Information Center: send a message with `index` or `help` to `MAILSERV@RS.INTERNIC.NET` for more information, or to save time, ask your service provider to set this up for you. (They'll most likely charge you a fee, of course, but it saves your learning about the incredibly weird internals of getting your own domain name.)

8.25. I want to show my technical prowess and global connectivity by putting my e-mail address on my business card. How should it look—all capitals? All lowercase?

It really doesn't matter how you express your e-mail address on your business cards. Internet e-mail is defined as being case-insensitive, so feel free to use whatever looks best on your card. You can use all uppercase: `SAVETZ@RAHUL.NET` (although I think that's a little loud), all lowercase: `savetz@rahul.net`, or mixed case: `Savetz@Rahul.Net`.

Being a Consumer on the Net

If you can sell stuff on the Net, it's logical that you can buy stuff there, too. Break out those credit cards and read these FAQs about being a consumer on the Net.

8.26. Can I buy stuff through the Internet?

Absolutely! Use Veronica to search for `Internet shopping -t0` and you'll find a variety of pointers to a document entitled "The Internet Mall: Shopping on the Information Highway."

```
The Internet Shopping Mall [dated 13 Feb, 94]

SunFLASH Vol 62 #32                                    February 1994
--------------------------------------------------------------------
62.32   The Internet Shopping Mall [dated 13 Feb, 94]
        From: taylor@netcom.com (Dave Taylor)

A monthly list of commercial services available via Internet
This listing is maintained by Dave Taylor, who is responsible for the specific
prose in each listing. If you disagree with anything stated, have good or bad
experiences with any of these services, or, most importantly, have additional
services to add to this list, please send electronic mail to taylor@netcom.com.
        (221 lines)
--------------------------------------------------------------------
```

8.27. How can I obtain a copy of the "Internet Mall: Shopping on the Information Highway"?

You can obtain the latest copy of this guide by using FTPing to

`ftp.netcom.com:/pub/Guides/Internet.Mall`

If you want a copy of the Internet Mall file e-mailed to you, send mail

```
To: mail-server@rtfm.mit.edu
Subject: <subject line is ignored>
Body: send usenet/alt.internet.services/Internet_Mall*
```

8.28. Can I buy books through the Internet?

From The Internet Mall

There are a lot of bookstores on the Internet:

Book Stacks Unlimited. A general subject bookstore in Cleveland, Ohio, can be connected through the Internet by using Telnet to connect to `books.com`.

Moe's Books. An excellent used bookstore in Berkeley, California, with over half a million titles and specializing in rare, antiquarian, remainders, and imported books. Available catalogs are photography, art monographs, fine press/ literature and illustrated children's books. Contact them through e-mail: `moesbooks@delphi.com`.

Future Fantasy. A bookstore of science fiction, fantasy, mystery, and horror, is now on the Net. You can browse their catalog and place orders through World Wide Web. Use the URL `http://www.commerce.digital.com/palo-alto/FutureFantasy/home.html`

United Techbook Company. Offers an online book service of more than a million titles. You can connect, search for titles, and order books from this company, located in Longmont, Colorado, by using the command `telnet utcbooks.com` with the account `utc` (the password is also `utc`).

You can contact a number of specialty bookstores through the Whole Earth 'Lectronic Link: type `gopher gopher.well.sf.ca.us` and choose `commercial services` to find

> **FringeWare, Extreme Books.** Catalog available via e-mail at catalog@mailer.extremebooks.com.
>
> **Nebula Books**. An online science fiction bookstore in Canada.
>
> **Powell's Technical.** Offers new, used, and antiquarian titles in fields including architecture, computing, communications, engineering, math, and physics. You can contact them in Portland, Oregon, through e-mail: `ping@technical.powells.portland.or.us`
>
> **Infinity Link Network Services.** Offers an online catalog of CDs, video tapes, books, and laserdisks, all by connecting via Telnet to `columbia.ilc.com`; log in as `cas` at the prompt. Alternatively, use Gopher to `columbia.ilc.com`

An interesting alternative to modern printed material is electronic books, which are available for purchase through the aptly named Online Bookstore. Connect with Gopher or WWW to `marketplace.com`.

Publications and related materials from Statistics Canada, the national statistical agency of Canada, are now available through its Talon service through Gopher, WAIS, e-mail, and anonymous FTP. Use your favorite connectivity package to connect with `talon.statcan.ca`

Q 8.29. Can I buy technical and computer books through the Internet?

From The Internet Mall

There are a bunch of possibilities.

> **SoftPro Books.** A small computer bookstore with shops in both Boston and Denver and an online catalog of more than 1,000 titles. SoftPro is also available on the `world.std.com` Gopher server (choose "Shops of the World"). You can also contact them through e-mail: `softpro@world.std.com`.

O'Reilly & Associates. Publishers of a wide variety of high quality books on UNIX and Internet topics offer their books directly through the Internet. Point your Gopher to `ora.com` (for example, `gopher ora.com`) or Telnet to `ora.com` with the login `gopher`.

High Mountain Press Direct. Offers books on UNIX, CAD, desktop publishing, and geographic information systems topics. You can request catalogs and order titles by sending mail to `info@bookstore.hmp.com`.

Artech House. A technical book and software publisher, offers hundreds of different technical titles—and some software and video tapes—via the Internet. Connect to `gopher world.std.com` and choose "Shops of the World."

Quantum Books. One of the larger technical bookstores accessible online is located Cambridge, Massachusetts, with 20,000 titles on-hand and a database of 65,000 titles. The focus is primarily computer science, math, and physics. Contact them by Gopher: look in "Shops of the World" after connecting with `gopher world.std.com`.

Roswell Computer Bookstore. If you're in Canada (Halifax, Nova Scotia, to be exact) and you're interested in computer and other technical books, this store has a catalog of more than 7,000 books available online. Use Gopher, connect to `nstn.ns.ca`, and choose items 8 and 4 to see what they have.

Computer Literacy Bookstore. Through the Internet, you can get to this store, located in Silicon Valley, by electronic mail. Send a message to `info@clbooks.com` to learn more about this service.

8.30. Can I buy music CDs and videotapes through the Internet?

From The Internet Mall

There are a couple of choices, with more coming online each month.

Infinity Link Network Services. Offers a catalog of video tapes, laserdisks, CDs, and books, accessible by connecting via Telnet to `columbia.ilc.com`. Log in as `cas` at the prompt.

Alternatively, point your Gopher there with `gopher columbia.ilc.com`.

Compact Disc Connection. Perhaps the best of the current bunch if you're looking for some specific music. This store has an online catalog of more than 80,000 titles. To visit, `telnet cdconnection.com` and log in as `cdc`.

The Virtual Record Store. Lists more than 3,500 CD titles and can be reached via Gopher: `gopher.nstn.ns.ca` or URL: `gopher://owl.nstn.ns.ca:70/11/e-mall`

8.31. Can I buy computer software through the Internet?

The Programmer's Shop is a ten-year-old company offering a wide selection of programming tools, with a catalog of thousands of different products. Also included in the list are applications, utilities, hardware, and more. Connect with them by `gopher world.std.com` and choose "Shops of the World" or through e-mail to `progshop@world.std.com`

8.32. I heard I can buy flowers on the Net. How?

From the Internet Mall

Here's the scoop: If you're perennially late with flowers and other gifts for your significant other, you'll be delighted to know that there's now a florist on the Internet. Grant's Florist and Greenhouse can be reached through World Wide Web (`http://florist.com:1080`) or Gopher to `gopher florist.com`.

8.33. Here's one for you: can I buy, um, adult toys through the Internet?

From the Internet Mall

You sure can! J.T. Toys has a mail-order service called The Stockroom that offers a wide variety of products befitting an electronic sex and adult toystore. It's accessible via Gopher: connect to `world.std.com` and look in "Shops of the World" or send electronic mail to `jttoys@world.std.com`.

CHAPTER 9

Is There Government Information Online?

The United States and Canadian governments are making information available to the masses via the Internet. There is almost no limit to the wealth of government information available online. There is, however, often too much information to sort through. Here I answer questions about some of the online services provided by the U.S. and Canadian governments.

United States

Q 9.1. How do I find online publications from the White House?

The White House has established an Internet address for retrieving White House publications via electronic mail.

With e-mail you can search White House documents for particular information and request the full texts of files that interest you. Following are the three most important commands for using the White House e-mail document server.

`topic` *`string`*—Will send you a list of files that contain the specified string in their title. Each file has a unique number, which becomes useful with the next command.

`send file` *`number`*—Will send you the specified file.

`send index`—Will send you the complete index of the documents available from the White House. It's pretty big, though; this file is approximately 400K.

To try this service, I sent a message with the body `topic health care` to `publications@whitehouse.gov`. About 20 seconds later, I received a 1,000-line message listing a ton of documents.

```
File-#  Name
25631   pub/political-science/US-Budget-1994-By-Section/FEDERAL-PROGRAMS-BY-
AGENCY-AND-ACCOUNT/Other-Independent-Agencies/Occupational-Safety-and-Health-
Review-Commission (402 bytes)
25678   pub/political-science/US-Budget-1994-By-Section/FEDERAL-PROGRAMS-BY-
AGENCY-AND-ACCOUNT/Other-Independent-Agencies/Federal-Mine-Safety-and-Health-
Review-Commission (402 bytes)
112657  pub/political-science/US-Budget-1994-By-Section/FEDERAL-PROGRAMS-BY-
AGENCY-AND-ACCOUNT/Department-of-Veterans-Affairs/Veterans-Health-
Administration (8379 bytes)
138456  pub/political-science/US-Budget-1994-By-Section/FEDERAL-PROGRAMS-BY-
AGENCY-AND-ACCOUNT/Department-of-Labor/Occupational-Safety-and-Health-
Administration (1209 bytes)
138458  pub/political-science/US-Budget-1994-By-Section/FEDERAL-PROGRAMS-BY-
AGENCY-AND-ACCOUNT/Department-of-Labor/Mine-Safety-and-Health-Administration
(488 bytes)
158922  pub/political-science/US-Budget-1994-By-Section/FEDERAL-PROGRAMS-BY-
AGENCY-AND-ACCOUNT/Department-of-Health-and-Human-Services,-except-Social-
Security/Summary (6504 bytes)
158924  pub/political-science/US-Budget-1994-By-Section/FEDERAL-PROGRAMS-BY-
AGENCY-AND-ACCOUNT/Department-of-Health-and-Human-Services,-except-Social-
Security/Social-Security-Administration (3724 bytes)
```

I requested a file from the server and received the following. What a treat!

```
## Regarding your request:
   send file 158923

Department-of-Health-and-Human-Services,-except-Social-Security Office-of-the-
Secretary
                                Federal funds
```

```
General and Special Funds:
  General departmental management:
      Appropriation, current          609 BA        196        90       94
      Spending authority from             BA         48        48       49
      offsetting collections
      Outlays (gross)                     0         136       243      142
                                               ----  ----  ----
      General departmental                BA        245       139      144
      management (gross)                  0         136       243      142
                                               ----  ----  ----
      Total, offsetting collections                 -48       -48      -49
                                               ----  ----  ----
      Total General departmental          BA        196        90       94
      management (net)                    0          88       195       93
```

By the way, in case you were wondering, you can also access the White House publications via FTP from `whitehouse.gov`, but you can't quickly search publication titles that way, so I suggest you stick with the electronic mail server.

To receive full instructions on using this server, send this message:


```
To: publications@whitehouse.gov
Subject: <subject line is ignored>
Body: send info


## Regarding your request:
topic Chelsea
No matching files found.
```

NOTE More White House information is available via FTP `sunsite.unc.edu/pub/academic/political-science/white-house-papers` or by Gopher `sunsite.unc.edu/sunsite.d/politics.d/white-house.d`.

Special legislative initiatives such as health care, NAFTA, National Performance Review, and the National Information Infrastructure are on the WWW.

```
http://sunsite.unc.edu/unchome.html
```

9.2. Can I get daily updates about White House publications?

The Extension Service of the U.S. Department of Agriculture provides a daily summary of White House electronic publications. These include press releases, transcripts of speeches, and other information from the White House.

To subscribe to the USDA Extension Service White House Summary service, send this message:

```
To: almanac@ESUSDA.GOV
Subject< <subject line is ignored>
Body: subscribe wh-summary
```

To "unsubscribe" from the USDA Extension Service White House Summary service, put the words `unsubscribe wh-summary` in the body of a message to the same place.

9.3. How can I search the White House documents at *esusda.gov*?

An easy-to-use search facility is available to search the White House documents archived at `esusda.gov`. To search, send an e-mail message

```
To: almanac@edusda.gov
Subject: <subject line is ignored>
body: search white-house keywords
```

I sent off a request to search the ever-popular catchphrase, *information superhighway*. Here's what I received.

```
## Regarding your request:
   search white-house information superhighway
```

```
Searching the following subject area:
    white-house
for ALL of the following terms:
    information   superhighway

1994-02-03 PRESIDENT'S REMARKS AT KRAMER JUNIOR HIGH SCHOOL
Request: send white-house 1378

1994-02-07 POTUS TO GREATER HOUSTON PARTNERSHIP
Request: send white-house 1399

1994-02-11 PRESIDENT'S REMARKS TO CALIFORNIA NEWSPAPER PUBLISHERS
Request: send white-house 1418

1994-03-12 PRESIDENT'S RADIO ADDRESS
Request: send white-house 1589

1994-03-15 PRESIDENT TO MARKHEM CORP. EMPLOYEES, KEENE, NH
Request: send white-house 1595

1994-03-14 PRESIDENT'S REMARKS AT THE G-7 JOBS CONFERENCE
Request: send white-house 1603

1994-03-16 PRESIDENT NAMES COWAN VOICE OF AMERICA DIRECTOR
Request: send white-house 1605

1994-04-13 REMARKS TO AMERICAN SOCIETY OF NEWSPAPER EDITORS
Request: send white-house 1772
```


To request a specific document from the daily summaries, send another message:

```
To: almanac@edusda.gov
Subject: <subject line is ignored>
Body: send white-house number
```

I requested President Clinton's radio address, file 1589. Here's some of what I got:

```
For Immediate Release                              March 12, 1994

                RADIO ADDRESS OF THE PRESIDENT
                       TO THE NATION

10:06 A.M. EST
```

```
            THE PRESIDENT: Good morning. This morning I want to
talk with you about what we're doing here at home and abroad to
create better jobs for our American workers, and about a breakthrough
we've had in our trade talks with Japan.

            Let me begin with this important news. Today we've
reached an agreement that will open up Japan's cellular telephone
market to high-technology products made here in America. This is a
big win for everyone. Workers in the United States will gain because
the agreement means more demand for cellular telephones and related
equipment made in America. Japanese consumers win because they'll
have access to better service and better technology at better prices.
Even Japanese manufacturers may win because of the increased demand
for cellular telephones.

            This agreement is designed to produce results; both
countries will be able to measure progress. And it demonstrates that
the United States and Japan can work together to open up jobs in
America by opening up markets in Japan in ways that help both
Americans and Japanese.
```

A complete catalog of the documents contained at `esusda.gov` can be retrieved through the almanac server. To get the summary catalog, send the message

```
To:    almanac@edusda.gov
Subject: <subject line is ignored>
Body: send wh-summary catalog
```

9.4. How do I send e-mail to Congress?

The U.S. House and Senate are conducting experimental electronic communications projects. One of these experiments is providing electronic mail to members of Congress. As of this writing, 23 members of the U.S. House of Representatives have been assigned public electronic mailboxes that may be accessed by their constituents. A number of House committees have also been assigned public electronic mailboxes.

For a current list of the representatives online, send e-mail to `congress@hr.whitehouse.gov` (any subject line and message body will do).

According to the document I received when I sent mail to the preceding address, "The results of the six-month public mail pilot have been very encouraging. The nature and character of the incoming electronic mail has demonstrated that this capability will be an invaluable source of information on constituent opinion. We are now in the process of expanding the project to other Members of Congress, as technical, budgetary, and staffing constraints allow."

Q 9.5. Does anyone use the White House's online services?

Apparently so. The following is from a White House press release issued in January of 1994, showing how its electronic offerings were used in the first six months since it went online.

Here is a brief outline of the principal first-year achievements of the White House Electronic Public Access Project.


```
1.  In the six months since June 1st, we have received over 100,000 e-mail
messages to the President & Vice President.
1a. This is the first Administration to accept e-mail from the public.
1b. President Clinton is the first sitting President to send e-mail to
citizens—5th graders in Oxford, Ohio, Spring, 1993.
2. This is the first administration to establish Internet addresses for
President & Vice President: president@whitehouse.gov
vice-president@whitehouse.gov
3. Over 220,000 requests for information have been processed
electronically since September 1, 1993.
4. In 1993 1,600 public documents were published electronically.
4a. This is the first administration to establish an electronic
self-service public document library: publications@whitehouse.gov.
The service opened experimentally in December, 1993.
5. The first ever live online computer conference by a sitting
Vice President was done by VP Gore on 1/13/94.  The VP took 10
questions in a 45-minute forum.
6.  We initiated the first White House forums on commercial networks:
America Online, CompuServe, GEnie, MCI Mail
7. Americans Communicating Electronically, an all-volunteer
organization, was started in Spring 1993. ACE represents the NII
in action. It aims to provide government services
electronically and enable interactive communications between
government agencies and the public, especially those citizens
without modem-equipped computers.
8. Starting in November, we became the first administration to
post audio files of the President's Saturday radio talks to the
Internet. This use of Internet radio is our latest experiment.
```

Q 9.6. Is there a central place in which I can look for information from U.S. Government agencies?

Yes! FedWorld offers Internet users access to more than 100 U.S. federal government Bulletin Board Systems. This project has been set up by the National Technical Information Service (NTIS) to provide access to federal government documents and files, national databases, and programs offered by the various participating agencies and departments. FedWorld is a gateway to an enormous repository of information from the U.S. Government.

To access FedWorld, Telnet to `fedworld.gov`. Due to a great interest in this service, FedWorld can be difficult to reach. Persistence, however, does pay as it opens the browser to such information sources as the National Agricultural Library BBS, the Federal Energy Regulatory Commission, The Bureau of Mines Bulletin Board Network, the NASA NODIS Locator System, Stat and Local FEMA user groups, DoD Export License Tracking System, DC Government Information, and much more.

Here's a sample of FedWorld:

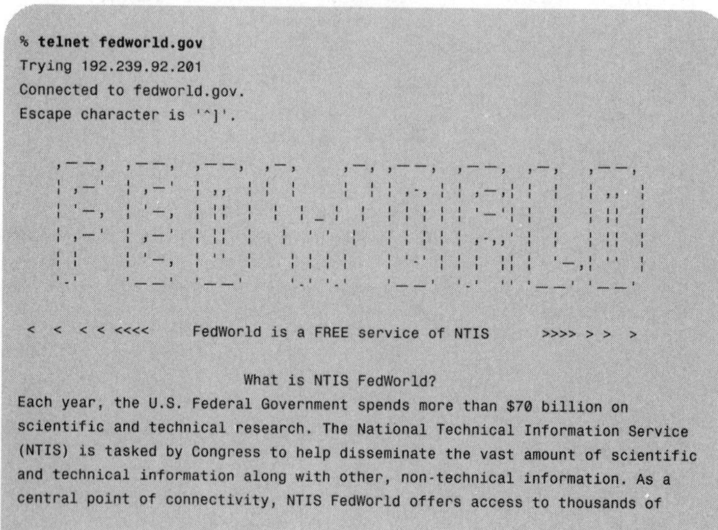

```
% telnet fedworld.gov
Trying 192.239.92.201
Connected to fedworld.gov.
Escape character is '^]'.

 < < < < <<<<     FedWorld is a FREE service of NTIS      >>>> > > >

                        What is NTIS FedWorld?
Each year, the U.S. Federal Government spends more than $70 billion on
scientific and technical research. The National Technical Information Service
(NTIS) is tasked by Congress to help disseminate the vast amount of scientific
and technical information along with other, non-technical information. As a
central point of connectivity, NTIS FedWorld offers access to thousands of
```

```
files across a wide range of subject areas. You can find information from
Environmental Protection to Small Business.
FedWorld Features include:
Marketplace: document ordering with popular DOWNLOADABLE products
Library of Files: collection of files/doc's on Govt info/other data
D'bases/Subsystems: DABATASES/SUBSYSTEMS of Govt information provided by other
agencies or info sources (Davis-Bacon, Patent Licenses, CALS ...)
FedWorld Gateway: a gateway connection to other Govt systems/databases.
Special Features: FTP of Library of Files (IP address FTP.FEDWORLD.GOV)
Public mail conferences; White House press release/doc's; Federal Jobs.

                          F e d W o r l d (R)
                  National Technical Information Service
  --------------------------------------------------------------------


      [B]  Help/Information Center          [E]  Public Mail/Forums
      [M]  FEDWORLD MARKETPLACE             [P]  Private Mail
      [D]  GateWay system                   [U]  Utilities
      [F]  Library of Files                 [W]  Who's on
      [O]  Subsystems/Databases             [G]  Goodbye (Logoff)
      [Q]  NTIS Quick Bulletins

                    [N]   FedWorld Newsroom
                    [J]   Federal Job Openings


                There are 21 other user(s) on-line now.

MENU=> MAIN
Please select (B,M,D,F,O,Q,E,P,R,U,W,G,N,J):o

                      Subsystems / Databases

      Follow each command with a "C" to bypass the splash screens.
 |------------------------------------------------------------------|

          A - Patent Licensing System (Patent Licensing Abstracts)
          B - Agency for Health Care Policy and Research (AHCPR)
          C - Computer Acquisition & Lifecycle Support (CALS)
          D - <reserved>
  NEW ->  E - Commerce Information Locator Service (CILS)
          F - U.S. Department of Labor Data (Wage determinations, etc...)
          G - National Health Security Act
  NEW ->  H - Government Grants (Catalog of Federal Domestic Assistance
  NEW ->  I - International Trade Administration Bibliography (ITA)
```

9

9.7. What is the Federal Information Exchange, Inc.?

Federal Information Exchange, Inc. (FIE) is an online information-services company offering database services, software development, and technical support to the government, private sector, and academic communities.

FIE provides a link between the federal government and educational institutions for the electronic transfer of information. In 1989, with a grant from the Department of Energy, FIE implemented DOEINFO system, converting and expanding it into the current FEDIX system with 11 participating agencies.

FEDIX provides instant access to federal agency information on research programs, contract information, educational programs and services, equipment grants, procurement notices, minority opportunities, and more.

FIE can be reached at `comments@fedix.fie.com`. Telnet: `fedix.fie.com` (port 23). Gopher: `fedix.fie.com`. URL: `http://fedix.fie.com`.

9.8. How do I find the U.S. Department of Agriculture on the Internet?

Gopher to `esusda.gov / usda and other federal agency information / usda`.

Here you will find agricultural statistics, agency directories, information about government assistance programs, full text of research reports, and more.

Cornell University has set up a Gopher site to provide statistics on a wide variety of agricultural topics—consumer food spending, milk and dairy sales, ozone levels, meat consumption, fertilizer use, and more. Most data can be downloaded in Lotus 1-2-3 format.

Gopher to

```
usda.mannlib.cornell.edu
```

or Telnet to

```
usda.mannlib.cornell.edu / login: usda
```

9.9. Is the Endangered Species Act on the Internet?

Yes, and it is available in full, as taken from the U.S. Code.

Gopher to

```
sunny.stat-usa.gov / economic conversion
information exchange / adjustment programs and
laws
```

9.10. Is there anything on the National Information Infrastructure on the Internet?

Oh, just a few things...: -)

High-Performance Computing and Communications

"Toward a National Information Infrastructure," the U.S. federal government's report on creating a National Information Infrastructure, is now available in full text.

Gopher to

```
gopher.hpcc.gov / hpcc-toward a national
information infrastructure
```

The Information Infrastructure Task Force has set up a Gopher site that provides access to task force directories, press releases, calendars, and committee reports as well as the full text of speeches, documents, and select legislation relevant to the National Information Infrastructure. Gopher to `iitf.doc.gov`.

The National Information Infrastructure Agenda

The full text of this Clinton-administration report describes the role of government in promoting the development of the telecommunications and information infrastructure by the private sector. The Agenda is available at

```
Gopher ace.esusda.gov / americans communicating electronically / national
policy issues
```

Making Government Work—Electronic Delivery of Federal Services

The full text of this Congressional Office of Technology Assessment report is about the use of computer and telecommunications technology in the delivery of government services. Gopher to

```
ace.esusda.gov / americans communicating electronically / office of technology
assessment
```

9.11. I feel like complaining about the government (anyone's!) and taking part in vicious political debate! Where on the Usenet can I do so?

Have fun on any or all of the following.

```
alt.activism
alt.impeach.clinton
alt.politics
alt.politics.british
alt.politics.bush
alt.politics.clinton
alt.politics.correct
alt.politics.datahighway
alt.politics.democrats
alt.politics.democrats.clinton
alt.politics.democrats.d
alt.politics.democrats.governors
alt.politics.drinking-age
alt.politics.economics
alt.politics.elections
alt.politics.equality
alt.politics.europe.misc
alt.politics.greens
alt.politics.homosexuality
alt.politics.india.communist
alt.politics.india.progressive
```

```
alt.politics.italy
alt.politics.libertarian
alt.politics.media
alt.politics.org.ccr
alt.politics.org.cia
alt.politics.org.covert
alt.politics.org.fbi
alt.politics.org.misc
alt.politics.org.nsa
alt.politics.org.suopo
alt.politics.org.un
alt.politics.perot
alt.politics.radical-left
alt.politics.reform
alt.politics.sex
alt.politics.socialism.trotsky
alt.politics.usa.constitution
alt.politics.usa.misc
alt.politics.usa.republican
alt.politics.vietnamese
misc.activism.progressive
soc.politics
soc.politics.arms-d
talk.politics.animals
talk.politics.china
talk.politics.crypto
talk.politics.drugs
talk.politics.guns
talk.politics.medicine
talk.politics.mideast
talk.politics.misc
talk.politics.misc
talk.politics.soviet
talk.politics.theory
talk.politics.tibet
```


Q 9.12. Where can I get more information about U.S. government resources on the Internet?

Read the FAQ "Internet Sources of Government Information," a lengthy listing of dozens of online government resources. To have a copy sent to you by e-mail, send a message

```
To: mail-server@rtfm.mit.edu.
Subject: <subject line is ignored>
Body: send usenet/news.answers/us-govt-net-pointers/*
```

O, Canada

by Natalie Strangelove. Ms. Strangelove is a partner in Strangelove Internet Enterprises Inc., Canada's foremost Internet publisher. Natalie is the author of The Directory of Networked Resources for Social Work Studies. *She is a regular contributor to* The Internet Business Journal *and is editor-in-chief of* Electropolis: Government Online, *a monthly newsletter devoted to government information on the Internet.*

9.13. Does the Canadian Government actively work with the Internet community?

Yes. The Open Government Pilot is a project developed by the Canadian Federal Department of Industry. It opens the Canadian federal government to all Internet users as a "one-stop shop" for government information. The project's aim is to provide Canadians wide access to government documents, databases, political parties, and elected officials, as well as Canadian legislative bodies such as the Senate of Canada and the House of Commons.

Information files also available through the project are contributed by the Supreme Court of Canada, government departments such as Industry Canada, Natural Resources Canada, Environment Canada, Department of Fisheries and Oceans, the National Research Council of Canada, National Library of Canada, and Health Canada. The Pilot also provides information from the Canadian provinces.

Important historical documents available via the Open Government Pilot include the Free Trade Agreement, North American Free Trade Agreement, GATT, as well as documents from NATO and the United Nations.

NOTE The project is still under development and the plan is to make available lists of e-mail addresses and biographies of Members of Parliament and Senators as well as historical information about the Parliament. Although the project is up and running, it has not yet been officially launched by the Canadian government.

The Pilot is available on WWW at the following:

```
http://debra.dgbt.doc.ca/opengov
```

or Gopher to

```
debra.dgbt.doc.ca/open government project
```

9.14. What is CANARIE?

No, it's not just a little yellow bird named Tweety. CANARIE Inc. (Canadian Network for the Advancement of Research, Industry, and Education) is the Canadian counterpart to the US National Research and Education Network (NREN).

CANARIE is a joint government- and private sector-funded project that began in 1988 under the initiative of Industry, Science, and Technology Canada to promote the development of new computer networking technologies and help facilitate their increased use and application by industry. The project is creating the foundation for a Canadian communications infrastructure.

For more information, Gopher to `muspin.gsfc.nasa.gov`.

9.15. Does Canada have an Information Highway Minister?

Yes. The Canadian prime minister has appointed a minister responsible for the construction of the Canadian Information Highway, the Honorable John Manley, Minister of Industry. You can send e-mail to Mr. Manley at `manley.john@istc.ca`.

9.16. Is Industry Canada on the Internet?

The Department has made available online documents in both of Canada's official languages (English and French). Documents online include the Canadian Information Highway directory and the Information Highway Advisory Council directory. A directory of Canadian companies and their services and products is also available at this site.

Industry Canada has also provided a listing of press releases, the Technology Networking Guide as well as a listing of the various publications available through the department.

Information is available for Industry Canada via The Open Government Pilot at the following:

```
http://debra.dgbt.doc.ca/opengov.
```

Industry Canada has also set up a listserver. To subscribe, send an e-mail message

```
To: listserv@debra.dgbt.doc.ca
```

9.17. Is the Department of Natural Resources Canada (formerly Energy, Mines, and Resources) on the Internet?

Natural Resources Canada has set up a Gopher site. It is still in the experimental stage; therefore, some of the documents are not yet accessible. The NRCan offers general information about the department, its mandate, and its various sectors. This site also offers Telnet access to four NRCan libraries.

Also included are an NRCan Internet Service, NRCan anonymous FTP public files and phone books, e-mail addresses, and other lookup services.

Gopher to

```
gopher.emr.ca
```

9.18. Can I get the Geological Survey of Canada on the Internet?

This service is available right from Natural Resources Canada Gopher. The Geological Survey of Canada, a division of NRC, offers information on earthquakes in Canada, listing seismic occurrences as far back 1918, across Canada from the Queen Charlotte Islands to the south of Newfoundland.

Gopher to

```
gopher.emr.ca/NRCan-Info-English/gsc
```

9.19. Is Statistics Canada on the Internet?

Yes it is. Statistics Canada is the country's national statistical agency. Under the Statistics Act, Statistics Canada is required to collect, compile, analyze, abstract, and publish statistical information on virtually every aspect of the nation's society and economy.

This Internet site gives general information about Statistics Canada, including press releases and a description of its services. It also points the visitor to other government Gophers and announces relevant conferences and workshops. It also points users toward other Internet Tools (other Gophers, Archie, Veronica, WAIS, WWW).

The service also offers StatsCan's publication, *The Daily*. It releases statistical data and publications produced by Statistics Canada and is a source guide for newly released data. Containing weekly and monthly schedules of upcoming major news releases, it announces the availability of electronic products and new services from Statistics Canada, as well. *The Daily* is published every business day in both official languages. This site also allows the user to search *The Daily* and provides an archive source for the publication.

Statistics Canada offers a listserver that automatically provides subscribers with up-to-date information. (A perfect Christmas idea for those number crunchers in the family!) To subscribe to Statistics Canada's listserver, send an e-mail message

```
To: listproc@statcan.ca
Subject: <leave subject line blank>
Body: subscribe statcan yourfirstname yourlastname
```

For interactive use, Gopher to `talon.statcan.ca` or FTP to `talon.statcan.ca/pub`.

Here's an example of some of the thrilling information available from Statistics Canada.

```
---------------------------------------------------------------------------
Apparent per capita consumption of red meats
1993

On a carcass-weight basis, the apparent per capita consumption of beef was 31.8
kg in 1993, compared to 32.3 kg in 1992. Veal consumption decreased to 1.4 kg
per capita, from 1.5 kg. But mutton and lamb consumption increased to 0.9 kg
per capita, from 0.8 kg. And pork consumption decreased to 27.5 kg per capita,
from 28.3 kg.
 On a retail weight basis, the apparent per capita consumption of beef was 23.2
kg in 1993, compared to 23.5 kg in 1992. Pork consumption decreased to 20.9 kg
per capita, from 21.5 kg.
 Estimates of the apparent per capita consumption of red meats have been
revised back to 1971, in order to reflect revisions to the estimates of Canada's
population.
---------------------------------------------------------------------------
Crushing statistics
March 1994

Oilseed processors crushed 190 thousand tonnes of canola in March 1994, a 14%
increase from February 1994 and an 8% increase from March 1993 (176 thousand
tonnes). Canola crushings for the current crop year (from August 1, 1993 to
July 31, 1994) continued at a record 1.5 million tonnes.
 Canola oil output totalled 79 thousand tonnes in March, while canola meal
production was 116 thousand tonnes. Oil stocks declined to 26 thousand tonnes
in March 1994, from 35 thousand in February. Canola meal stocks were 38
thousand tonnes in March.
```

9.20. What about Canadian Census and population information?

This site contains information on the 1991 Census. Also under construction is Census data for 1986. The list for 1991 Census Consortium member institutions and contact persons is also available.

Gopher to `gopher.epas.utoronto.ca/Data Library`.

9.21. I want Canadian Supreme Court rulings. Where can I find them?

As part of the Open Government Pilot, Supreme Court rulings have been made accessible via the Internet. Transcripts are available in both English and French.

You can access the information via WWW.

```
debra.dgbt.doc.ca/open government project/
supreme.court.rulings
```

Q 9.22. Can I get documents from the National Library of Canada on the Internet?

Yes and no. There is a Gopher site for the National Library, but as of this writing it is still being developed and the server is not yet registered with the University of Minnesota. As a result, many of the menu items that appear do not have links to other sites and may not contain any information yet. But do keep trying, as they are working on them.

The site does include a FAQ document about the Library, as well as information on their services and collections. Users are also able to access the Library's bibliographic database, DOBIS, via Telnet. The site also provides announcements, news releases, public programs and events, as well as a directory of NLC staff.

Gopher to `gopher.nlc-bnc.ca`.

Q 9.23. Is the National Research Council on the Internet?

Indeed. Visitors to this site can read general information on the NRC's Knowledge Systems Laboratory, the NRC itself, the Canadian Society for Computational Studies of Intelligence, as well as other related information.

It also includes a directory of NRC Phone and e-mail addresses, and home pages directing the users to the Canadian Astrophysical Data Center, the Canada-France-Hawaii Telescope, the Dominion Astrophysical Observatory, and the Joint Astronomy Center.

This WWW site is available at `http://ai.iit.nrc.ca/nrc_point.html`.

9.24. What about the National Archives Catalogue of Computer Files?

Researchers may browse through the catalog of computer files available from the National Archives from the comfort of their own PCs! What is the National Archives of Canada? Well, according to the system,

```
ABOUT NATIONAL ARCHIVES OF CANADA

    One of Canada's oldest cultural agencies, the National Archives of
    Canada was established in 1872, and serves as the collective memory
    of the nation. It does so by acquiring, describing, and preserving
    significant archival material relating to Canadian life - literally
    millions of manuscripts, photographs, films, maps, tapes, video
    recordings, books, paintings, drawings, prints, and electronic and
    other records.

    The Archives is responsible for conserving Canada's archival
    heritage and making it available to as wide an audience as
    possible. While most of the material is in traditional "hardcopy"
    form, the Archives has been collecting and preserving electronic
    records for about twenty years. We would like to make these
    computer files available to users of NCF.
```

Available online for your reading pleasure are such wonderful stories as "Borrowing microform from National Archives," "Tracing your ancestors," "Information on shipwrecks in Canada," and "Treaties with aboriginal peoples."

This site also provides a very useful guide to doing research at the National Archives in Ottawa.

Telnet to `freenet.carleton.ca` and login as `guest`. Choose the menu items: `Government Center/Federal Government/ National Archives of Canada`.

9.25. Is the federal budget online?

The full text of the 1994 federal budget is available online. The document was formatted by the staff of *The Mandarin*, the Senior

Executive Network's Electronic Journal, an electronic daily produced for senior federal bureaucrats.

Gopher to

```
debra.dgbt.doc.ca/industry canada documents/isc.news.releases/federal.budget.
1994
```

FTP to

```
debra.dgbt.doc.ca:/publ/isc/isc.news.releases/
federal.budget.1994
```

or WWW

```
http://debra.dgbt.doc.ca/isc/isc.html
```

9.26. I'm writing a paper about the political history of Canada. Where can I find Canadian historical documents online?

This site provides the complete documents of the Canada Constitution Act, 1867, the 1987 Canada Meech Lake Accord, and the Charlottown Constitutional Agreement. Also available are excerpts from Canada's Constitution Act, 1982, and Shaping Canada's Future Together (in both English and French).

Gopher to

```
wiretap.spies.com/government docs (US & the
World)/Canadian documents
```

9.27. What is Electronic Frontier Canada?

The EFC is a nongovernmental organization founded to ensure that the beliefs and tenets of the Canadian Charter of Rights and Freedoms remain intact with the sudden rise of new technologies and advancements in communications.

Their Internet site includes relevant court decisions, the Canadian Charter of Rights and Freedoms, and EFC Press Releases.

Gopher to

```
gopher.ee.mcgill.ca/Community Information/EFC-
Electronic Frontier Canada Gopher
```

NOTE If you live in Canada, check out the *Canadian Internet Handbook* by Jim Carroll and Rick Broadhead. This book tells Canadians everything they need to know about the Internet. It's a huge directory of Canadian Internet service providers, with a list of Gopher servers and campus-wide information systems in Canada, and lists of Canadian-based Usenet groups, WWW, Archie, IRC servers, and online catalogs. It's published by Prentice Hall Canada. (ISBN 0-13-304395-9. 414 pages. Price: $16.95.) For more information send e-mail to `handbook@uunet.ca` or call (800) 567-3800 (toll-free in Canada) or (416) 293-3621 (from elsewhere).

CHAPTER 10

Where Are All the Fun and Games?

Of course, the Internet is not all seriousness, business, and work. Far from it. From its beginnings, the Internet has been a haven for ways to relax, create, make friends, or just waste time. (After all, the Internet was built by the government and was used in its formative years mainly by educational institutions. If there's one thing the government and students know how to do, it's goof off!)

In this chapter we'll look at some ways to chat, play, and enjoy ourselves on the Internet. This chapter is divided into three sections: games; other diversions; and real-time chatting, MUDing, and pie-throwing.

Games

One of the Internet's most important, although often overlooked, uses is enabling people at different organizations and locations to engage in collaborative activity—to work together in a shared environment, collaboratively write a paper, or play together. It should come as no surprise that the Internet is home to a huge population of people who play games—and have found in the Internet a way to find and interact with fellow players.

Games on the Internet may not be as flashy as those on your Nintendo or Sega, but the Internet does offer the capability to play against other people—not just computerized opponents. As with the Internet's other tools, the people with whom you're communicating may be right down the hall or across the globe. Besides, it's certainly more satisfying to play (and beat) a human opponent than a digital one.

Q10.1. Is it OK to play games on the Internet?

Sure, it's OK to use your system and the Internet to play games, as long as it's not against the policies of your site. If you use the Internet from a school or business computer, ask the system administrators about your site's policy. (Then again, it may be easier to get forgiveness than permission. Use your own judgment.)

Q10.2. What kind of games are there?

The Internet is home to two styles of games—interactive and play-by-mail. In interactive games you can play and converse with your opponents in real time, whereas play-by-mail games take longer and are typically more involved. Unlike interactive games, play-by-mail games let people who have only e-mail access (folks on Bitnet, FidoNet, and Prodigy, for instance) join in the fun.

As you might expect, play-by-mail games on the Internet aren't far removed from play-by-mail games that have taken place by "snail mail" for decades, most notably chess.

Q10.3. How do interactive games work?

You become a participant (a player or observer) by utilizing a client program, which in turn accesses the appropriate game server. The client program handles your interaction with the game and your opponents. Its duties might include presenting your view of the game, keeping score, tallying your wins and losses, facilitating chatting with others, and so on.

Once connected to a server, you can play, watch, or kibitz with other users. A server usually has several games running simultaneously.

As with any Internet facility, there are usually public clients you can access via Telnet (the TCP/IP remote login facility) to check out a particular game. Your site may offer a local copy of the client program (this is likely if you use a public-access Internet provider rather than your school's or business' computer).

If you are likely to become a frequent player of any given game, you'll probably want to get a copy of the appropriate client program on your system, if it isn't already installed. There are several reasons for this, including not consuming someone else's resources unnecessarily, having better system response, and, most importantly to you, making it possible to take advantage of your local system's graphics, color, point-and-click tools, and other user interface features.

Q 10.4. Where can I find the game Go?

The game Go, a two-player strategy board game, is available by Telneting to one of several Go servers. These programs are home to informal games as well as international tournaments. (One such tourney had nearly 150 participants from twenty countries!)

Users in the United States can Telnet to the following:

```
bsdserver.ucsf.edu 6969
```

or

```
hellspark.wharton.upenn.edu 6969.
```

Users in France can Telnet to

```
flamingo.pasteur.fr 6969.
```

For more information about Go and online Go games, read the Go Frequently Asked Questions (FAQ) list. It is available via FTP as `rtfm.mit.edu:/pub/usenet/news.answers/games/go-faq`.

If you do not have FTP, you can request the Go FAQ using a mail server. Send e-mail

```
To: mail-server@rtfm.mit.edu
Subject: <subject line is ignored>
Body: send usenet/news.answers/games/go-faq
```

Here's an example of a game of Go in progress:

```
#> Game 3 (I): cfhopkins [10k ] vs xml [19k ]

     A B C D E F G H J K L M N O P Q R S T        H-cap 4 Komi  0.5
  19 ¦. # . . . . . . . . . . . . . . . . .¦ 19   Captured by #: 0
  18 ¦. 0 # . # 0 0 . . . . . . . . . . . .¦ 18   Captured by 0: 3
  17 ¦. . 0 # 0 . . 0 0 . 0 # . . . . . . .¦ 17
  16 ¦. 0 . # . 0 0 0 . 0 0 . . # . # . . .¦ 16   Wh Time 72:33
  15 ¦0 # # # # 0 0 # 0 # . . . . . . # # .¦ 15   Bl Time 62:03
  14 ¦# 0 0 0 # # # # . # . . . . . 0 0 0 .¦ 14
  13 ¦. 0 # # 0 0 0 # . . . . . . . . . . .¦ 13    Last Move: M6
  12 ¦0 # . . # . # 0 . . . . . . . . . . .¦ 12     #126 0 (White)
  11 ¦. . . # . # 0 . . . . . . . . . . . .¦ 11
  10 ¦. . . # . . # . . + . . . . . + 0 . .¦ 10       B #125 N6
   9 ¦. # # 0 0 . 0 . . . . . . . . . . . .¦  9       W #124 K7
   8 ¦. . 0 . . . . 0 . . . . . . . . # . .¦  8       B #123 J7
   7 ¦. # 0 0 0 0 0 # # 0 . . . . . . . . .¦  7       W #122 H8
   6>¦. 0 0 # # # # . . 0 .>0<# . . # . . .¦< 6       B #121 G6
   5 ¦# # # . . . . # # 0 . . 0 # . . . . .¦  5       W #120 G7
   4 ¦0 0 # # . . . . . # 0 . 0 # . # . . .¦  4       B #119 G10
   3 ¦. 0 0 0 # # . # # 0 0 . . 0 # . . . .¦  3       W #118 G16
   2 ¦. . . . 0 0 # . . # 0 . . 0 # . . . .¦  2       B #117 H13
   1 ¦. . . . . . . . . . . . . . . . . . .¦  1       W #116 H12
     A B C D E F G H J K L M N O P Q R S T
```

Q 10.5. How about backgammon?

Backgammon, another classic board game, is also available online. You can reach the First Internet Backgammon Server (FIBS) by Telneting to `fraggel65.mdstud.chalmers.se 4321`.

Those in the know tell me that several of the world's best backgammon players play on FIBS, including a two-time world champion and the developer of the strongest computer backgammon program.

10.6. What about Reversi (Othello)?

Fans of Reversi (also known by the commercial name Othello) can play with players or computerized opponents by Telneting to `faust.uni-paderborn.de 5000`.

10.7. Is there a chess server?

If you enjoy chess, you'll be grateful for the Internet's own chess server. To access it, Telnet to `ics.uoknor.edu 5000` or `rafael.metiu.ucsb.edu 5000`. For assistance once connected, type `help`.

Here's an example of a chess game in progress:

```
OBSERVATION REPORT : Game vancouver vs gsanchez [1]
      --------------------------------
   8 |   |   |   |   |   |   |   |   |     Move # : 48 (White)
     |---+---+---+---+---+---+---+---|
   7 |   |*P |   |   |   |*K |*P |   |     Black Moves : 'Bc2 (0:08)'
     |---+---+---+---+---+---+---+---|
   6 |*P |   |   |   |   |   |   |*P |
     |---+---+---+---+---+---+---+---|
   5 |   |   |   |   |   | P |   |   |     Black Clock : 5 : 35
     |---+---+---+---+---+---+---+---|
   4 |   |   |   |   |   |   | P |   |     White Clock : 4 : 13
     |---+---+---+---+---+---+---+---|
   3 | P | P | B |   |   |   |   | P |     Black Strength : 7
     |---+---+---+---+---+---+---+---|
   2 |   |   |*B |   |   | K |   |   |     White Strength : 8
     |---+---+---+---+---+---+---+---|
   1 |   |   |   |   |   |   |   |   |
      --------------------------------
       a   b   c   d   e   f   g   h
```

10.8. Is Chinese Chess online?

A Chinese Chess server is also available. From the United States, Telnet to `coolidge.harvard.edu 5555`.

Users in Sweden should use `hippolytos.ud.chalmers.se 5555`.

10

10.9. Can I play Bridge on the Internet?

Fans of Bridge aren't left out of the fun. OKbridge is a program that allows four people on the Internet to play the game of Bridge together. It provides a continuously running, 24-hour duplicate tournament that is open to anyone. The program supports exhibition games and partnership practice.

According to the administrators, OKbridge has about 2,000 users from some 20 countries. During the daytime in the US, there are typically 40 to 60 people playing at any one time at 8 to 15 tables.

From the OKbridge FAQ: "You are likely to meet a surprising range of talents at the OKbridge table. A number of today's top bridge players can be found regularly on OKbridge, including many members of the US Junior's team. At the other end of the spectrum, OKbridge is the first introduction to duplicate bridge for many people. Regardless of your playing level, it is likely that you can find challenging opponents here."

You'll need access to an OKbridge client in order to play. The OKbridge FAQ list and the client source code are available via FTP from the following:

```
cs.ucsd.edu:/pub/clegg/bridge
```

The FAQ gives information on how to have the client automatically compile on your system with a minimum of fuss.

If you're impatient and you want to play bridge right this minute, Telnet to `140.117.11.33` and login as `OKbridge`.

10.10. What is Netrek?

Board games are fine, but don't forget about the games that couldn't even exist without computers. Netrek, for example, is a 16-player, real-time battle simulation with a *Star Trek* theme. The game is divided into two teams of up to eight people, who dogfight and attempt to conquer each other's planets. There are several different types of ships, from fast, fragile scouts to big, slow battleships. This allows a great deal of variance in play styles.

What makes Netrek different from many other Internet games is that it features real graphics rather than dismal ASCII quasi-graphics. Because of this, you'll need special client software on your computer before you can play—along with a computer capable of supporting the graphics and a network connection with sufficient bandwidth.

If you're lucky, you have the right combination of hardware and Internet connection to do this. You'll need to be using a terminal that runs X Window. If you use the Internet from a command-line UNIX environment, Delphi or similar, you're out of luck. Sad, but true.

For more information, read the Netrek FAQ, available as follows:

```
rtfm.mit.edu:pub/usenet/games/netrek/faq
```

If you don't have FTP, send e-mail

```
To: mail-server@rtfm.mit.edu
Subject: <subject line is ignored>
Body: send usenet/news.answers/games/netrek/faq
```

Q 10.11. I like strategy games. How about Diplomacy?

As I mentioned earlier, a variety of play-by-mail games are available. Most play-by-mail games are strategy and war games, including Diplomacy.

For information on Diplomacy, send e-mail

```
To: judge@shrike.und.ac.za
```

or

```
To: judge@u.washington.edu
Subject: <subject line is ignored>
Body: help
```

Q 10.12. What is Core War?

Core War is a game in which players compete to write the most vicious computer program. The programs are written in an assembly language called *RedCode* and run in a simulated computer. The object of the game is to cause opposing programs to terminate, leaving your program in sole possession of the machine. This is pure hacker fun; it's sort of like writing your own virus without going to jail.

Core War has been around for many years and is available for dozens of computer systems. Not surprisingly, you can also play Core War versus other hackers via the Internet. The Internet's ongoing Core War tourney is called King of the Hill. Once you've written a nasty RedCode program, you can send it via electronic mail to the King of the Hill server, which pits your program against 20 others on "the hill." Replies via electronic mail indicate how your program fares.

Core War is only for true hackers. If the following example program doesn't frighten you,

```
;redcode
;name Dwarf
;author A. K. Dewdney
;strategy Throw DAT bombs around memory, hitting every 4th memory cell.
bomb  DAT   #0
dwarf ADD   #4,    bomb
      MOV   bomb, @bomb
      JMP   dwarf
      END   dwarf ; Programs start at the first line unless
                  ; an "END start" pseudo-op appears to indicate
                  ; the first logical instruction.
```

find out more about Core War and King of the Hill by getting the Core War FAQ via FTP as follows:

```
rtfm.mit.edu:/pub/usenet/news.answers/games/
corewar-faq
```

10.13. What other play-by-mail games are available on the Internet?

For complete information on play-by-mail games (both traditional ones and Internet-based games), read the play-by-mail FAQ, available via FTP.

```
rtfm.mit.edu:/pub/usenet/news.answers/games/play-by-mail
```

A list of commercial and free play-by-mail games, including information about play-by-e-mail games, is available via FTP at the following:

```
ftp.erg.sri.com:/pub/pbm/PBM_List.Z
```

10.14. How can I find out about other games?

But wait, there's more! Other games are available on the Internet for your pleasure. Internet services come and go daily—it's probable that a new game has popped up somewhere, or one mentioned here has disappeared.

First, check your system's own menus and Gopher to find out what game clients and servers might be running locally. Next, check Scott Yanoff's list of Internet services for an up-to-date look at games (and lots of other stuff to do) on the Internet. (Finger `yanoff@csd4.csd.uwm.edu` to find out how to receive this list.)

The Usenet is rife with discussion about games of all sorts, in play-by-mail, online, and traditional formats.

```
Abstract games        :     rec.games.abstract
Backgammon            :     rec.games.backgammon
Battletech et al      :     rec.games.mecha
Bridge                :     rec.games.bridge
Board games           :     rec.games.board
Chess                 :     rec.games.chess
Cosmic Encounter      :     rec.games.board.ce
Diplomacy             :     rec.games.diplomacy
General game design   :     rec.games.design
Go                    :     rec.games.go
```

```
Miniatures              :       rec.games.miniatures
Multi-User Dungeons     :       rec.games.mud.announce
Play-by-Mail games      :       rec.games.pbm
Role-Playing Games      :       rec.games.frp
Trivia games            :       rec.games.trivia
Video games             :       rec.games.video
```

Other Diversions

The questions in this section cover fun things that aren't games in the traditional sense, but are entertaining.

Q 10.15. What is the Internet Hunt?

What's the capital of Liechtenstein? What are the top ten U.S. television programs according to the most recent Nielson ratings? Can you get AIDS from kissing? What was the total amount of sales in liquor stores in the United States last September?

Rick Gates (`rgates@nic.cic.net`) is asking questions like these in a monthly contest dubbed "the Internet Hunt." Participants in the Hunt score points for finding the answers to Gates' questions—but not using traditional reference material like encyclopedias and almanacs. Instead, hunters must find the answers online, using information sources on the net.

Individuals and teams compete to find the answers to Gates' questions. All the answers are to be found online using the Internet, Usenet, and other linked services. The winner is the person who answers the questions first. The true purpose of the Hunt is not to find the answers but to learn how to find them. It is a sly maneuver to make people dive in and make networked information resources work for them. The best way to learn, Gates says, is by "getting your hands dirty." Each Hunt is a set of 12 questions, ranging from one to ten points based on difficulty.

The first Hunt took place in September, 1992. The contest has spawned a loyal following, with about 20 entries in any given month. The coveted answers, however, enjoy a much larger readership. "Based on responses I get from people around Netland,

I'd say there are from 200 to 500 users working through the answers that get posted," Gates says.

Gates' idea for the Hunt was based on the typical library search assignment from school: "Here's a set of questions, here's the Library's reference collection. Answer these questions. You have one hour." Some of us enjoyed this type of challenge. We called it "The Thrill of the Hunt." I thought, "Why not try doing something similar with the Net?"

"I have a fondness for exploring the Net, traversing little-known routes, and discovering valuable information resources. I suspected that others might as well," says Gates. "The Hunt was an immediate small success. There were a few individuals who enjoyed the challenge, but most Net users were interested in getting their hands on the answers. They wanted to see how the explorers found their way around."

Gates says the Internet Hunt has accomplished three things: it helps Net users realize the enormous amount of information on the Net, and it helps novices—whom he calls "settlers"—understand how to move around the "trails" that more experienced users have blazed. It also provides training in context, which works better for most of us than learning from a book or a chalkboard.

Here's a sample Hunt. This is one of my favorite old Hunts, from way back in January of 1993. I like it because it shows a nice slice of the variety of information that is scattered on the Internet. And, in the spirit of the Hunt, I'm not going to tell you how to find the answers to these questions. : -)]

1. (5 points) How does one say "Merry Christmas and a Happy New Year" in Czech?
2. (6 points) Is the Toyota Motor Corporation connected to the Internet?
3. (3 points) Hi! I have a new account on a UNIX machine here, and I HATE the editor I have for my mail. It's called *vi.* So I found another editor that I can use called *emacs.* Emacs is supposed to be customizable, but I've managed to screw things up a little. Can you tell me where I can get some advice from more experienced emacs users?
4. (5 points) Can you get AIDS from kissing?

5. (3 points) I read in an electronic journal somewhere that a conference was held in Padova, Italy, on models of musical signals. I wrote down the name of a contact, 'Giovanni De Poli.' Can you find his e-mail address for me?
6. (2 points) What is the primary religion in Somalia?
7. (4 points) I understand that the Net is being put to use distributing information and pictures of missing children. Where can I find out more, and where can I find the pictures?
8. (4 points) Where can I find tables listing the nutritive values of different foods?
9. (3 points) What is the text of the First Amendment to the Constitution of the United States?
10. (5 points) You know, I've gotten a lot of good network information by FTPing files from `nnsc.nsf.net`. What kind of computer and operating system is `nnsc.nsf.net`?

10.16. Where can I find the Internet Hunt?

Lots of places.

Via Gopher

```
CICNet Gopher
   Host=gopher.cic.net
   Name=The Internet Hunt
   Type=1
   Port=70
   Path=1/hunt
```

```
CNI Gopher
   Host=gopher.cni.org
   Name=i-hunt
   Type=1
   Port=70
   Path=1/Coalition FTP Archives/public/net-guides/i-hunt
```

or via FTP

```
ftp.cni.org:/pub/net-guides/i-hunt/*
ftp.cic.net pub/internet-hunt/*
ftp.nic.surfnet.nl mirror-archive/resources/
internet-hunt/*
```

or on the Usenet

```
alt.internet.services
alt.bbs.internet
```

> **NOTE** A new Hunt is released once a month. If you're looking forward to competing in the next one, keep an eye out for an announcement on the newsgroups `alt.internet.services` or `alt.bbs.internet`. The Gopher and FTP sites also have archives of past Hunts—and although you can't compete for prizes and glory with old Hunts, you can learn a whole lot about how to find what you're looking for on the Net.

10

10.17. I keep hearing that there's a radio station on the Internet. What is Internet Talk Radio?

From the depths of cyberspace, a new medium has emerged. Internet Talk Radio (ITR) is a new information service that is blurring the line between the online world and traditional media.

ITR distributes weekly "radio shows" via the Internet's anonymous FTP service. Each show—a half hour or an hour long—can be downloaded to a workstation or home computer and played using audio playback software. Unlike a myriad of other Internet newsletters and journals, Internet Talk Radio is the only one that actually speaks. And unlike the stations on your FM dial, you won't hear most of ITR's programs live. You can hear the prerecorded shows any time you like.

Each show is composed of several `.au` format sounds that can be played on a Sun or NeXT workstation, among other machines. Personal computer users can also listen in, but (depending on the computer) you may need to convert the `.au` sounds into a format more familiar to your hardware.

NOTE All this talk comes at a price, however. A typical hour-long radio show consumes a whopping 30 megabytes of disk space. Despite its relatively slow sampling rate of 8kHz (that's 8 kilobytes per second of sound), ITR is a memory hog.

Carl Malamud, the founder of ITR, explained how he got into the business. "The idea for ITR came from my frustration with the trade press. I knew they weren't providing the information I wanted and was looking for an alternative." He notes that the trade press focuses on marketing and reviews, leaving a gap for a general-interest, technically-oriented publication for Internet users. "I couldn't start a magazine because it takes money to print and distribute a magazine," he said. Malamud turned to the Internet as a general-purpose distribution method. "I looked at the trends in multimedia support on the Internet, at the number of users with more and more bandwidth and bigger disk drives, and decided to give 'radio' a try," he said.

Some Net users have criticized the talk radio concept as a grandiose waste of network bandwidth, given the fact that the same information in text format could fit into only a few kilobytes. "The reason you get audio information from a $3,000 (or $30,000) computer," Malamud said, "is because ultimately this gives you a very new medium. We're not trying to replace radio, just as the trucks didn't replace the railroads and the telephone didn't replace the telegraph. There are things we can do that you can't do on a radio, like go interactive or add WAIS databases to support a program, or use general-purpose languages like PERL to make an audio-on-demand server...." It is the versatility of ITR that is its selling point.

ITR is free for the listening. To pay the rent, each program carries sponsors, and a minute of each program is given to acknowledge the supporting vendors. The blurbs aren't quite commercials; they resemble public TV's post-show sponsor messages. ("Brought to you by a grant from Frobnitz Corporation and viewers like you!")

For the most part, ITR consists of interviews. Whether they're talking with the "Geek of the Week" (a featured member of the technical community) or focusing on "the new American reality" during the "Tech Nation" show, it all boils down to people conversing with each other. As the name says, Internet Talk Radio parallels its mainstream counterpart. Except that ITR is a lot more nerdy.

"Geek of the Week" is a weekly interview with prominent members of the technical community. The show focuses on "sophisticated discussions of issues facing the Internet, networking, and computing," Malamud said, calling it "the intelligent alternative to today's trade press." "Tech Nation" is a weekly radio show that focuses on "the new American reality"—that the U.S. has become the "tech" nation. The premise is that this new reality is causing introspection: "Americans are looking at who they are and where they are going," according to Malamud.

There is also ITR's sister service, called "Internet Town Hall," which includes audio recordings of speeches. In the first week they released speeches by the Dalai Lama, Bob Dole, Hershel Shanks on the Dead Sea Scrolls, and the hearings by Congressman Markey on encryption and privacy.

"Internet Town Hall" programs are good to pick and choose from. Unlike ITR, "Town Hall" doesn't necessarily focus on computers and technology. One program consisted of Secretary Bruce Babbit presenting President Clinton's environmental program to the National Press Club. This sort of archival sound information could prove useful for those who don't want to watch C-SPAN all day. If you find that you need information from a speech given last month, "Town Hall" might be the forum in which to find it.

The programs sound good, considering that the medium is in its infancy. After a snazzy musical introduction, Malamud announces (in his best DJ voice), "This is Internet Talk Radio, flame of the Internet." Sound quality isn't wonderful, but has been improving as the creators get the hang of the medium. Malamud said the sound quality is improving "as we learn how to use our equipment and adapt it to the realities of this rather strange publishing platform."

Q10.18. How can I listen to Internet Talk Radio?

Once you've downloaded some Talk Radio files to your computer, you'll need the right program to listen to them. If you use a Sun workstation (you lucky devil) you need only the system's `audiotool` program to listen in.

Listening on a PC requires SoundBlaster or some other audio gadgetry, plus a program that plays `.au` files or converts them to Windows' own `.wav` files. I don't use an IBM-PC compatible, so I'll steal from the FAQ: If you use SOX, you can easily convert the files to a `.wav` file and play them using any of your standard sound utilities. Another approach is to bring the native files straight down (no conversion) and use PLANY. This clever little program will handle pretty much any sound format on a SoundBlaster card. The software is widely mirrored, but one source is the following:

```
ftp.uga.edu:/pub/msdos/mirror/sound/plany12.zip
```

Macintosh users need a program to convert `.au` to "audio IFF" format or a program that can play ITR's native `.au` files. As a Mac person myself, I highly recommend Sound Machine, a great freeware program that I grabbed using anonymous FTP.

```
sumex-aim.stanford.edu:/info-mac/snd/util/sound-
machine-10.hqx
```

No matter what computer you use, you will need enough disk space and memory to hold the five- to ten-megabyte chunks of the programs.

> **NOTE** As compression technology advances, ITR (and its eventual copycats) will be able to stuff longer programs into less space. This may be essential to the proliferation of the medium. At about half a minute of sound per megabyte, ITR doesn't have time to waste.

For more information on the service and listening to the programs on your particular machine, send electronic mail to `info@radio.com`. You'll automatically receive the Internet Talk Radio FAQ list, which explains all the interesting bits about ITR and the Internet Multicasting Service. For a list of FTP sites that carry ITR shows, send e-mail to `sites@radio.com`.

The latest information, including program schedules, questions, and answers is available on the Usenet group `alt.internet.talk-radio`.

10.19. What's the Usenet Oracle?

The Internet abounds with documents answering your FAQs, on everything from astrology to electrical engineering. But we all have questions so personal and unique that there is no place to go for a ready-made answer. When this happens, does the Internet have a place to go? You bet: The Usenet Oracle.

The Oracle can answer all your important questions: "What's the meaning of life?" "Where does the dryer put the socks it steals from the wash?" and "How much wood could a woodchuck chuck if a woodchuck could chuck wood?" Or he could <ZOT> you into a smoldering pile of ashes. Either way, he's a great guy.

The Usenet Oracle isn't really a person. It's an electronic mail service run by Steve Kinzler (`kinzler@cs.indiana.edu`), a systems administrator at Indiana University. Send the Oracle your question, and within a few hours, you'll receive an answer from the all-knowing one.

The Oracle is a cooperative effort for creative humor. When you send a question to the Oracle server, your message is actually forwarded to someone else who uses the program. She or he mails a (preferably witty) answer back to the Oracle server, which forwards it to you. Thanks to the server program, all this is done anonymously—the questioner (or "supplicant") and the answerer (that is, the Oracle incarnate) never know who the other is.

The Oracle started as a program running on an Indiana University computer system. The program became popular, so Kinzler, with the help of hacker Ray Moody, created a network version of the service that went online in October of 1989. The best questions and answers—as selected by volunteer "priests"—are distributed in "Oracularity digests" on the Usenet group `rec.humor.oracle`.

> **NOTE** Ocularities on `rec.humor.oracle` are read by an estimated 57,000 people. Over 1,300 additional readers (who presumably cannot access the Usenet) subscribe to the Oracle mailing list, receiving the Oracularities via e-mail. As of the beginning of 1994, over 15,000 people have participated by sending in a question or an answer, with 82,000 questions answered.

Over time, the Usenet Oracle has developed its own personality. Writers incarnated as the Oracle often blend in known aspects of the persona: an inflated ego, a sense of humor, a girlfriend named Lisa, and the propensity to <ZOT> less fortunate supplicants.

Why did Kinzler start the Oracle? “Well, it was fun most of the time. Challenging frequently from a programming and system design perspective. But mostly it was that typical hacker’s motivation: When a great idea comes along, it just deserves to be done. I thought an e-mail Oracle was a great idea, had the resources and desire to do it, and so I did it. Part of my interest in the Oracle was experimental; I wanted to see what would come of it, what people would do with an interactive, anonymous system like this.”

Kinzler calls the anonymous mail aspect of the Oracle server a crucial aspect of its popularity. “Anonymity gives more people the security to try to be witty or funny in their creative writing. I hope to include people who discover through the Oracle they can and can enjoy writing creatively. And the Oracle gives them a guaranteed audience of two, and, if they’re lucky, maybe tens of thousands.”

For more information about the Usenet Oracle, send electronic mail to `oracle@cs.indiana.edu` with a subject line of `help`. To ask a question, the subject line should include the words `tell me`, and the body of the message should contain your question. (If you don’t grovel to the sometimes-egotistic Oracle, you may find that you’ve been <ZOT>ted to oblivion, so you may want to pander to his ego!) You should receive an answer in a day or two, probably much sooner.

NOTE A German Oracle (dubbed, appropriately enough, *Orakel*) is also up and running. A Finnish Oracle is also in the works.

Once you ask a question, the Oracle may ask you to answer somebody else's question, as a sort of payment for services. You should respond with the most witty answer possible so that the supplicant feels gratified in his or her quest for knowledge. If you can't think of a worthy reply, do nothing and the question will be sent to someone else. If you wish to answer a question without asking one, just send a message to the Oracle server with a subject line of `ask me`.

If you don't have access to `rec.humor.oracle` and would like to receive the Oracularities, send mail to `oracle-request@cs.indiana.edu`. To get on the distribution list, include a subject line of `subscribe`; to remove yourself from the list of recipients, put `unsubscribe` in the subject line.

Here are some sample questions and answers from the Usenet Oracle.

```
The Usenet Oracle has pondered your question deeply.
Your question was:
> Oh mighty Oracle, whose greatness and glory yada yada yada:
> Is it possible to get charged with assault for shooting the breeze?
And in response, thus spake the Oracle:
} No, but it's possible to get charged with battery if you have a D cell
} in your pocket while being hit by lightning.

The Usenet Oracle has pondered your question deeply.
Your question was:
> O Masterful Oracle, please answer your humble suppliant this question:
> How do I invent the world's best compression algorithm?
And in response, thus spake the Oracle:
} .

The Usenet Oracle has pondered your question deeply.
Your question was:
> Oh great and powerful Oz....oops, wrong super power...
> ...great and powerful Oracle,
```

```
>    who knows more about Athlete's Foot
>    than Dr. Scholls.  Please tell me,
>    Exactly how young of a woman is it acceptable
>    for me to date, I'm almost 24  ???
And in response, thus spake the Oracle:
} If you love someone, set her free.
}    If she comes back, she's yours.
} If she toddles away or crawls, definitely too young.
```

Q 10.20. Are there any comic strips online?

Yes indeed, check out Dr. Fun, a cartoon published on the Net daily. Use Mosaic (or your favorite graphical World Wide Web browser) to connect to

```
http://sunsite.unc.edu/Dave/drfun.html
```

Q 10.21. Where can I find conversation of a prurient nature?

Oh, just about everywhere. The Internet is awash with erotica, dirty talk, sexy pictures, and fetishists of every type. Sorry, kids, no screenshots for this question; this is a family book.

> **NOTE** Not surprisingly, some of the following newsgroups may not be available at your site. Your system administrator may have explicitly refused entry of the newsgroups that don't, well, focus on traditional scientific, literary, or artistic expressions. Also notice that most of these newsgroups are in the `alt` domain, which isn't available at some sites.

Okay, ahem. On the Usenet, you can find a myriad of prurient newsgroups, including

`alt.sex`

`alt.sex.beastiality`

```
alt.sex.bondage
alt.sex.boredom
alt.sex.exhibitionism
alt.sex.fetish.fashion
alt.sex.fetish.feet
alt.sex.fetish.hair
alt.sex.fetish.orientals
alt.sex.fetish.waifs
alt.sex.fetish.watersports
alt.sex.homosexual
alt.sex.masturbation
alt.sex.motss
alt.sex.movies
alt.sex.spanking
alt.sex.stories
alt.sex.stories.d
alt.sex.trans
alt.sex.voyeurism
alt.sex.wanted
alt.sex.watersports
alt.sex.wizards
alt.magick.sex
gay-net.erotic-storys
rec.arts.erotica
```


NOTE Sex, an inherently silly thing, has spawned quite a few silly newsgroups. (Actually, it can be pretty hard to tell the ones that are meant to be silly from some of the ones that aren't.) Among the truly silly are `alt.sex.bondage.particle.physics`, `alt.sex.nfs` (which stands for Network File System), `alt.sex.NOT` and `alt.sex.aluminum.baseball.bat`.

Dirty pictures are available, too, on the following:

```
alt.sex.pictures
alt.sex.pictures.d
alt.sex.pictures.female
alt.sex.pictures.male
alt.sex.pictures.misc
alt.binaries.erotica.male
alt.binaries.pictures.erotica
alt.binaries.pictures.erotica.blondes
alt.binaries.pictures.erotica.cartoons
alt.binaries.pictures.erotica.d
alt.binaries.pictures.erotica.female
alt.binaries.pictures.erotica.furry
alt.binaries.pictures.erotica.male
alt.binaries.pictures.erotica.orientals
alt.binaries.pictures.erotica.redheads
alt.binaries.sounds.erotica
```

True multimedia mavens might venture to check out `alt.sex.sounds`.

As usual, some of these newsgroups have FAQ lists associated with them. The `alt.sex` FAQ is available from

```
rtfm.mit.edu:/pub/usenet/alt.sex/*
```

For real-time dirty talk, check out the Internet Relay chat and Multi-User Dungeons (both are covered later). Erotic talk is appropriate on *some* channels on IRC and *some* locations on some MUDs. Use your best judgment and don't offend people.

Real-Time Chatting, MUDing, and Pie-Throwing

The Internet also offers a variety of real-time, conversational modes of communication. Among them are talk, multi-user dungeons, and the Internet Relay Chat.

Q 10.22. How can I chat with someone else on the Internet?

If you want to have a real-time, one-on-one conversation with someone and you know that person's e-mail address, you can use the `talk` program to type "live" messages to each other. `talk` is a very simple program that two people can use to converse; you'll see a split screen with your words on one half and your friend's on the other. As you type, your friend sees what you have to say immediately—typos and all. It's basic, interactive, two-way communication that works between many Internet sites.

> **NOTE** Because there are so many kinds of computers on the Internet, not all of them support `talk`. Even worse, the ones that do don't necessarily have talk programs that can talk to each other. A variety of alternate talk programs are available, like `ytalk` and `ntalk`. Check with your system administrator to see which one will work for you.

To make a talk request, simply type

```
talk user@domain.com
```


If the person you wish to communicate with is online and willing to receive messages, he or she will see an invitation to talk.

```
Message from Talk_Daemon@jive at 23:29 ...
talk: connection requested by waffle@bolero.rahul.net.
talk: respond with:  talk waffle@bolero.rahul.net
```

If he or she isn't available, you'll see a message like this. Pretty simple.

```
[Your party is not logged on.]
```

> **NOTE** Most talk programs will send a zillion or so talk requests at regular intervals until they are answered. Each request dumps a few lines of text to the recipient's screen, which will annoy the heck out of someone who is, say, in the middle of composing an e-mail message or trying to use a database. When making a talk request, let it "ring through" once and then type control-c to stop the annoying messages. Wait to see whether the recipient "returns your call."

Here's a sample talk session:

```
[Ringing your party]
[Ringing your party again]
[Connected]
hey, how's it going?

Yum. Dill pickles?

----------------------------------------------------------------------
Hi.
fine. I'm hungry and could really go for a nice pickle pizza
right about now.
```

Q 10.23. How about chatting with lots of people at once?

Check out IRC—the Internet Relay Chat. This is the Citizen's Band of the Net, where the inhabitants of Cyberspace come to chat.

IRC was originally designed as a replacement for the talk program but has become much more than that. IRC is a multiuser chat system, where people convene on "channels" (discussion group, akin to a citizen's band radio channel) to talk publicly or in private.

On a busy IRC server at any given time, you can find thousands of users chatting on hundreds of topic channels. Most of the time people gather to simply chew the rag, make friends, or talk dirty. IRC isn't just frivolous fun, though; according to the IRC FAQ list,

"IRC gained international fame during the 1991 Persian Gulf War, where updates from around the world came across the wire, and most IRC users who were online at the time gathered on a single channel to hear these reports. IRC had similar uses during the coup against Boris Yeltsin in September, 1993, where IRC users from Moscow were giving live reports about the unstable situation there."

NOTE Maybe, but IRC has never done anything for me. The concept is neat—type to hundreds of people all over the world on any topic you can dream of. The reality, for me anyway, is that IRC is more like a large, loud room filled with horny, bored, or angst-ridden individuals. I prefer a nice MUD (covered next) to IRC any day. (I have just set myself up for lots and lots of hate mail from lovers of IRC. Sigh.)

Here's the obligatory sample session. I usually try to find something interesting to show in these examples, but in my experience, IRC just doesn't get interesting. Maybe I don't hang out on the right channels.


```
$ irc
*** Connecting to port 6667 of server w6yx.stanford.edu
*** Welcome to the Internet Relay Network waffle
*** You have new email.
*** If you have not already done so, please read the new user information
with
    +/HELP NEWUSER
*** Your host is w6yx.stanford.edu, running version 2.8.16
*** This server was created Wed Nov 10 1993 at 19: 45:15 PST
*** umodes available oiws, channel modes available biklmnopstv
*** There are 2171 users and 1413 invisible on 116 servers
*** There are 80 operators online
*** 1 : unknown connection(s)
*** 1213 channels have been formed
*** This server has 41 clients and 10 servers connected
*** - w6yx.stanford.edu Message of the Day -
*** - Welcome to w6yx.stanford.edu (BARRNet Hub Server)
*** - Please report problems to techie (irc@w6yx.stanford.edu)
*** -
```

```
*** - This server is running version 2.8.16
*** - You will need to use a client version  ircII2.2.6 or later to interface
*** - properly with this server.  ircII2.2.9 is recomended.
*** - ***************************************************************
*** - Do not run Bots on this server. If you must run a bot, use B-w6yx.
*** - This also means that you should restrict yourselves to one (1)
*** - client on this server. Additional clients should be run on B-w6yx.
*** - Please do not idle on this server for more than 15 minutes.
*** - Idle clients that auto-reconnect will be considered bots, and will
*** - be banned from the server.
*** - ***************************************************************
*** - Absolutely NO floodbots or tsunami bots on any Stanford server.
*** - Violation of this rule may lead to loss of access for your entire
*** - site or domain. Don't spoil it for others.
*** - ***************************************************************
*** -
*** - If you are at a site that has a local server, you are requested
*** - to use the local server if it is up. This includes UCDavis,
*** - CalPoly, and Portal. If your local server is down, please use
*** - B-w6yx.
*** -
*** - Enjoy!
/chan #hottub
*** waffle (waffle@bolero.rahul.net) has joined channel #Hottub
*** Topic for #Hottub: *** Welcome to #hottub's UP ALL NITE viewing...
*** Users on #hottub: waffle @TBA @Jasmine @Bloodshot @WintrHawk CtChocula
+@beeblebro Grendal @boomboom @Rikitiki @Chweryl @Sorcery @Dark-Elf @Murkyl
+@Xbot
<Rikitiki> Well.. Kristin?
<boomboom> TJ wants to know how tall i am...
<boomboom> rich..the hot guy
* Bloodshot is tall
<boomboom> what was his name?
<Bloodshot> bb you are just my size :)
*** Skyraider has joined channel #hottub
* CtChocula is 8' tall
<boomboom> estrada?
<Bloodshot> hmm
* Bloodshot isnt that tall
<boomboom> blood...am i?
<Jasmine> TBA!!
<beeblebro> boomboom <-- amazon  (which of course i find extremely attractive
* Bloodshot is 6 ft
<Rikitiki> Bruce Jenner.
<beeblebro> )
<boomboom> BEEBS!
*** Signoff: Bloodshot (Leaving)
<boomboom> NO!
<boomboom> I AM NOT!
*** scooter has joined channel #hottub
*** Prothan has joined channel #hottub
```

```
*** Xney has joined channel #hottub
* Rikitiki drools over Kristin just to be like everyone else.
<boomboom> YOU ARE THE *SECOND* PERSON TO CALL ME THAT TONIGHT!!!!
<beeblebro> boomboom:  you are only an inch shorter than I am!
<boomboom> rich...f*** you
<boomboom> :)
<Prothan> Hi everyone!
*** Mode change "+o Xney" on channel #hottub by Xbot
* CtChocula doesnt drool
<Prothan> What's up?
* Rikitiki figures he's still in deep trouble for calling her a
+fundamentalist.
<scooter> howdy
<Chweryl> well I do  gotta get going
<Xney> who's a fundamentalist?
<Rikitiki> I apologize for that too.
<Chweryl> I have to work to day
*** WintrHawk has changed the topic on channel #hottub to Amazon boombooms
+from the moon
<boomboom> *sixx* hmm im afraid thats no good
<CtChocula> hahahahaha
<Rikitiki> You can kick my ass when you meet me or something.
<Prothan> CtChocula: not even over chocalatey Count Chocula cereal?!
<beeblebro> <-- is suffering from the libido that often accompanies
+drunkeness, please excuse him.  :)
<Chweryl> CtChoc.... Night *hugs*
<boomboom> that was his response to my 5'10 answer :)
<Rikitiki> Whoa.. Chuck.. wanna f*** my couch?
*** scooter has left channel #hottub
<Xney> beeb; you're excused
<Xney> boom's not 5'10
<Murkyl> riki...
<Rikitiki> :)
<CtChocula> chweryl nite! *HUGS* :)
<Chweryl> Bloodshot .. Sweet dreams *hugs&kisses*
<boomboom> rich...it 's not the fundamentalist thing...
<Rikitiki> Yes, Murk?
<boomboom> xney..i'm not?
<Murkyl> not the couch, riki...
<beeblebro> Rich:  um, not tonight.
<Chweryl> Murkyl: Night sweetie *hug*
<Xney> No.. I'm 6'2 and you're way smaller than me
<Rikitiki> I met a girl tonight.. who told me.. "When I get drunk, I get so
+horny, I'd f*** furniture."
* Murkyl huggers chweryl.
```

10.24. How do I access IRC?

You may have an IRC client running on your system. Check with other users or the system administrator to find out. Try typing `irc` or `ircii` to see whether anything extraordinary happens. If so, chances are you've found your system's IRC client.

If you are use the emacs environment, try typing `M-x irc`.

If not, you can use one of the Internet's public IRC systems. Instead of running the client on your own machine, you can Telnet to another system that has it.

```
telnet sci.dixie.edu 6677
telnet exuokmax.ecn.uoknor.edu 6677
telnet caen.fr.eu.undernet.org 6677
telnet caen.fr.eu.undernet.org 7766
telnet obelix.wu-wien.ac.at 6996
telnet ircclient.itc.univie.ac.at 6668
telnet irc.tuzvo.sk 6668
telnet irc.nsysu.edu.tw (Login: irc)
```

When you connect to many of these systems you'll see a message announcing that you should use public IRC clients only as a last resort. If you can, compile an IRC client for your system.

10.25. How can I compile my own IRC client?

They're available via anonymous FTP.

```
cs.bu.edu/irc/clients
```

Or you can try this: the following command will automatically get and compile and IRC client on your system, if you use UNIX.

```
telnet sci.dixie.edu 1 ¦ sh
```

10.26. Where can I learn more about IRC?

There are several Usenet newsgroups specifically devoted to talking about the IRC program, its users and its features, including

alt.irc	For general talk about Internet Relay Chat
alt.irc.bot	For discussion of creating IRC "bots"
alt.irc.ircii	For discussion of the IRC II client program
alt.irc.recovery	For those recovering from IRC addiction

For more information, including a complete tutorial, primer, and the `alt.irc` FAQ, anonymous FTP to the following:

cs.bu.edu:/irc/support/IRCprimer1.1.txt

cs.bu.edu:/irc/support/alt-irc-faq

cs.bu.edu:/irc/support/tutorial.*

Q 10.27. Pray tell, what is a Multi-User Dungeon (MUD)?

One of the more popular leisure activities on the Internet is "MUDing, use of a form of "shared-world role-playing." MUDs—Multi-User Dungeons—are the basis for games and role playing as well as educational services and even serious collaborative research.

MUDs are among the most popular online diversions today. MUDs are programs that allow you to interact in real-time with other people in a virtual environment. Just as the Internet Relay Chat (IRC) lets people at different Internet sites share ASCII conversations in real-time, the Internet also lets users at different locations play together in MUDs.

Historically, MUDs have been "ASCII-based shared virtual reality," with conversations and descriptions consisting of ASCII text and possibly ASCII graphic displays. You give commands through ASCII, cursor or Control-key sequences. This isn't as complicated as it sounds; if you've ever played a computer game such as Adventure or Zork, you are already familiar with it. For example,

```
You are in the Living Room. You see a cherry pie and Fred.
Throw cherry pie at Fred
You throw the pie at Fred. SPLAT!
Fred says, "Hey! Stop that."
```

Your electronic world surroundings might include any combination of characters, creatures, rooms, and objects. Users in the world of a MUD can converse, move around, affect the environment, play games, program, hunt for treasure, and fight vile beasties.

MUDs usually have various "locations" through which players can move by typing the compass directions. Objects can be manipulated with commands such as GET, LOOK, EAT, and THROW. Conversation with other users (and sometimes intelligent programs) is done using the SAY command, for speaking "aloud," and EMOTE, to show actions. (For instance, "waffle looks at you cross-eyed.")

Like board and book-oriented role-playing games (RPGs), most MUDs start with specific rules and contents. In D&D (Dungeons & Dragons) type RPGs, a person who creates, runs, or helps keep control of the games is often called the *dungeon master.* In MUDs, these people are often known as the *wizards.*

MUDs incorporate ideas from "real life," affectionately known as *RL* to mudders. On some MUDs, elements pilfered from RL include economic systems, household appliances, magic, and weddings. I'd tell you that MUDs can have "everything but the kitchen sink," but I know of one that has one of those, too.

There are over 500 *MUD sites* on the Internet, meaning computers that are running a MUD server program. Depending on its popularity and the time of day, any MUD might have just a few or hundreds of users simultaneously.

Here's what it looks like:

```
look
misty blue room
A small, misty blue room. There is new misty blue carpet on the floor. The
west, north and east walls are freshly painted misty blue; the west half of
the south wall is misty blue brick. The ceiling is also misty blue, with blue
waffle-iron circle patterns. Small incandescent ceiling lights bathe the room
in a diffuse light. There isn't any furniture.
You see vent, old cabinet, Heroes, and new-help-wizards here.
Gru (dozing) is here.
emote waves
Gru says, "WAFFLE!"
waffle waves
```

```
Gru pours maple syrup ALL OVER you!
emote is getting a transscript for his book. Wave to the readers, Grump.
waffle is getting a transscript for his book. Wave to the readers, Grump.
Gru says, "you misspelled transcript, you better fix it before you publish
it,
or they'll know you're a d00f"
say OK! :-) Gotta go.
You say, "OK! :-) Gotta go."
@go pizza parlor
The Pizza Parlor
This is a fine eatery, owned by Mama Bungweisi, a kindly but strange Italian
woman. The restaurant is furnished as any restaurant should be: with tables
and chairs, lots of customers mulling loudly about, and sticky spots on the
shabby green carpet. A jukebox sits quietly in the corner. Near the front of
the restaurant is a pizza counter. Sadly, there are no pizzas on it. Above
the
counter is a sign: "To order a pizza, type 'order <size> pizza with
<toppings>'." A smaller sign reads: "We deliver! `@addfeature #15229' &
'deliver <size> <toppings>'!"
You see a change machine, the pizza counter, jukebox, and drink dispenser
here.
look juke
This worn-out jukebox has seen better days, but it is still in working
condition. There is a slot to insert quarters, a list of songs, and a lot
of dust on this jukebox. A display on it reads:   CREDITS: 0
look changer
This is an enormous, circa-1970 machine that looks as if it once made change
from one's dollar bill. However, the machine is now very dented and surely
does not work properly.
kick changer
You kick a change machine, denting it slightly.
A quarter drops from a change machine into your hands.
put quarter in juke
You put a quarter in the slot. It disappears with a >Clink!<
The display now reads:   CREDITS: 1
play 150 on juke
You enter the number 150 into the keypad.
The jukebox goes >Klunk!< and the display changes to   CREDITS: 0
The jukebox makes grinding sounds as it seems to come to life.
The jukebox begins whirring.
The jukebox begins playing Freewill by Rush.
A guy walks in, sings a bar of 'Alice's Restaurant' and walks out.
order small pizza with pickles
You place the order. That'll be just a few minutes.
Mama Bungweisi rearranges the furniture a bit.
The jukebox continues playing Freewill by Rush
A man tries to attach a fake cyberspace deck to an electrical socket.
There is a horrible screeching from the loudspeaker: Hey! Iw this thing
on? Er, piwza for wafwle.
get pizza from counter
You remove a small pickles pizza from the pizza counter.
```

```
look pizza
This is a piping hot tray of small pickles pizza. The small pizza has 4
slices
left. waffle ordered it.
eat pizza
waffle ingests a slice of a small pickles pizza.
drop pizza
You drop a small pickles pizza.
share pizza with everyone
waffle offers to share his pizza with everyone here! Dig in!
```

10.28. Are all MUDs text only? I want graphics!

Most MUDs are text only. Although graphics-oriented MUDs exist, they have drawbacks. First, they are usually slower than text-only MUDs.

Second, using a graphical MUD requires special "client" software that interprets the graphics data and displays it on your screen. Because there are so many computer systems—from Atari ST to Macintosh and from Sun to Z80s—it's not always possible to get the right client software for your machine. So, for now, text-based MUDs are the norm.

Most mudders don't consider this a drawback, however. MUDs are quite like Zork and other text adventure games: The graphics are unnecessary when there are detailed and imaginative descriptions of players and objects.

10.29. So MUDs are just fancy games, right?

That depends on who you ask. One "wizard" I know vehemently proclaims that his MUD is a "social experiment in a text-based virtual reality." Maybe, but to most of his users, it's a game.

Each MUD has a theme. Connect to any given MUD, and you might find yourself on a drifting space station, in medieval England, in a sprawling Northern California mansion, or in any other of a million scenarios.

Because many MUDs differ in theme, scope, and goals, each one attracts different sorts of users. In some MUDs, users can cast spells, chase dragons, and frolic in a virtual wilderness with electronic gnomes. I think it would be safe to call this type of MUD a game. Then again, some MUDs are used mainly for programming, conversation, and information exchange between professionals. Obviously, these aren't being used for gaming.

NOTE Some Multi-User Dungeons contain more traditional games within the game. For instance, if you wander into the Dining Room on LambdaMOO, you'll find a huge pile of games, including Mastermind Board, poker, Connect Four, "MOOnopoly," Twister, Go, and chess. Granted, playing Twister with people ten thousand miles away using a computer that doesn't even have graphics may not have been an obvious choice; you can try it if it suits you. LambdaMOO is available by Telneting to `lambda.parc.xerox.com 8888`.

In many MUDs, users do what they will; if you're in the mood to be dragon bait, fine; if you would rather converse with users on the other side of the globe, that's fine, too.

Q 10.30. Can MUDs actually be useful for real-life activities?

Answered by Dave Van Buren (`dave@ipac.caltech.edu`), Infrared Processing and Analysis Center, Institute of Technology and Jet Propulsion Laboratory. Supported by NASA under contract to the Jet Propulsion Laboratory.

MUD servers' functionality, which provides such a rich gaming and social environment, is a missing component of current "useful" network resources (such as bibliographic databases and tools for access and analysis of data.)

In a small project here at Caltech we have been merging MUD technologies with tools to access remote information servers with the goal of providing a virtual space for collaborators to do astronomical research. Our system, dubbed *AstroVR* and based on the LambdaMOO server from Xerox, is a place where astronomers can jointly peek into large astronomical databases, launch queries into the cyberspace representing those services, hold small group meetings, sketch ideas on virtual whiteboards and shared plotters, conduct seminars, and be apprised instantly of new comets, supernova, and other cosmic events.

Several enhancements to gaming MUDs are keys to our project. First, the newer versions of MOO provide tools for importing data to and from remote servers. Thus, programs written inside AstroVR can directly call a bibliographic service and ask to be shown a particular journal article. Second, the program used to access AstroVR (the client) is able to interpret certain messages coming from AstroVR in special ways. For example, the client can automatically transfer a galaxy image file from a distant collection to the user and show it on the screen, making the task of fetching information from the Net trivial. Third, we are using the new multicast technology to provide audio and even video channels for users, removing the tedium of typing all conversation.

A number of other real-life MUD projects are being undertaken elsewhere. MediaMOO at MIT's Media Lab seeks to bring media researchers together to explore the uses of this new technology. The Global Network Academy is the first "virtual" corporation and has as a goal the creation of an accredited online university. Several small companies are leasing virtual space on MUDs to provide simple conferencing with customers. A project at the University of Dublin is to build an AstroVR-like system for mathematics, and the Jupiter project at Xerox Palo Alto Research Center aims to explore the potential for a hardware-rich system, including ubiquitous video and audio pickups in a large research facility where there is significant telecommuting.

Q 10.31. Where did MUDs come from?

According to the *New Hacker's Dictionary* (a wholly nifty book, edited by Eric Raymond and published by the MIT Press), MUD derives from an artificial intelligence experiment at the University of Essex in the early 1980s. Students on the European academic networks liberated the idea, creating a slew of derivatives with names like AberMUD, VaxMUD and LPMUD.

MUDs crossed the Atlantic around 1988 and gained popularity in the United States. As the New Hacker's Dictionary says, "[The] second wave of MUDs emphasized social interaction, puzzles, and cooperative world-building as opposed to combat and competition."

In 1992, more than 50 percent of MUD sites were of a third major variety, LPMUD, which combines the combat and puzzle aspects of AberMUD with extensibility. The trend toward greater programmability and flexibility has continued.

As programmers create new types of MUDs, new names appear for the environments. These include TinyMud, DUM, MOO, MUCK, MUG, and a plethora of others. Although some types of systems are generally used for a certain type of game, the best way to find out what a certain MUD is like is to connect to it.

Q 10.32. How do I connect to a MUD?

Most MUDs are open to the public. The first time you enter, you are asked for a name and a password. Then you are dropped into the virtual reality to fend for yourself. What you do then is up to you.

NOTE Be aware, however, that some MUDs are closed to the Internet public. Some are reserved for students at a specific college, educators, or just the friends of the wizard who runs the place.

Like Gopher, Telnet, FTP, WWW, the IRC—indeed, like just about every facility you use on the Internet—MUDs are client-server programs.

The server is the program that's the heart of the simulated environment. It is in charge of receiving user commands, relaying and broadcasting messages among players, maintaining information such as player locations, room, and object definitions, help text, and so on.

You can generally use Telnet as the client program. Typically, you'd access a MUD game via Telnet by giving the Telnet command along with the server's Internet address and the port number for the game. For example,

```
telnet lambda.parc.xerox.com 8888
```

Telnet is usually all you need to access a MUD, but Telnet is less than elegant. Some users connect to MUDs with "client" programs that make the MUD experience that much nicer. Typical features in MUD clients include scrollback (for reviewing a conversation that's gone off the screen), fancy word-wrapping, and a Rolodex of favorite MUDs. Some clients are stand-alone programs that run on your Internet host; others work alongside other programs (for instance, MUD.EL, a client that works from within EMACS).

NOTE MUDs come and go daily. Hourly. So I'm not including a list of MUDs here. For a possibly complete and potentially up-to-date listing, read "The Totally Unofficial List of Internet Muds" compiled by Scott Goehring. Goehring's list is posted to the Usenet `rec.games.mud.misc` and `rec.games.mud.announce` newsgroups. You may also get it via anonymous-FTP from

```
rtfm.mit.edu:/pub/usenet/
rec.games.mud.announce
```

You might be interested in taking a look at the Internet Gopher Automatic MUD Registry, available at

```
gopher.tc.umn.edu (under Fun&Games/Games/MUDs)
```

It is a jumping-off point for accessing MUDs. New ones are added weekly. It's a great way to discover interesting new MUDs without bothering with the MUD list.

There are several very good FAQ files available online that detail MUDs, MUD clients and servers, and a complete, current

MUD-list. The most recent versions of the MUD FAQs are available by anonymous-FTP sites including

ftp.math.okstate.edu:/pub/muds/misc/mud-faq

rtfm.mit.edu:/pub/usenet/alt.mud/*

In addition, there are a variety of Usenet newsgroups related to MUDs.

rec.games.mud.announce	Informational articles about MUDs
rec.games.mud.diku	All about DikuMuds
rec.games.mud.lp	Discussions of LPMUD
rec.games.mud.moo	Discussion about MOO (Object Oriented MUD)
rec.games.mud.misc	Various aspects of multiuser computer games
rec.games.mud.tiny	Discussion of Tiny MUDs, IE MUSH, MUSE, and MOO
rec.games.mud.admin	Administrative issues of Multi-User dungeons
alt.mud.german	For German-speaking mudders

CHAPTER 11

What Do I Need to Know About Internet Culture and Lore?

The Internet is its own society—a world that shares a lot with the outside world (Real Life) but has a variety of unique elements: its own jargon, legends, and culture. Those elements are as important—perhaps more important—than the networking technology itself. A sampling of those elements is presented in this chapter.

Q 11.1. What's :-) mean?

Ah, this is the dreaded "smiley," or "emoticon." Tilt your head 90 degrees to the left and that random jumble of punctuation will look like a smiling face. Isn't that cuuute? Smileys in all shapes and sizes are frequently used to denote a variety of emotions. Here are just a few. Rest assured that there are thousands of other possibilities.

```
:-)  your basic smile, denoting happiness or sarcasm
:)   also a smile
;-)  wink
:-D  laughing
:-P  plbbbt!
:-}  grin
:-(  frown
8-)  wide-eyed
B-)  wearing glasses
:-X  close mouthed
```

NOTE O'Reilly & Associates has published an entire book of smileys, entitled (appropriately enough) *Smileys*. If you need such a book to be a complete person, you can find it listed in the book list in Appendix C, "The Internet Offline: Books and Magazines."

Q 11.2. What does that acronym stand for?

The online world is filled with cryptic abbreviations and acronyms. Many of these arise out of a need to save time, a desire to type fewer characters, or laziness or pure silliness. Below is a partial list of acronyms you'll see on the Internet (especially on the Usenet, MUDs, and IRC) and their translations. Of course, you'll also find terms such as RAM, CD-ROM, and SCSI, but these computer terms were born in laboratory test tubes, not in cyberspace.

While researching this answer, I ran across a posting by Dan Hofferth, who sums up the acronym problem nicely: "BTW, FWIW, I once saw an amusing (IMHO) summary of common e-mail abbreviations somewhere on Internet. Apparently, it has been long forgotten or nobody RTFM. IAE, I kept thinking that I'd repost it again, RSN, to cut down on these FAQ's re: TLAs. Guess I could summarize now. If, after reading it, you find that you are SITD, remember that TANSTAAFL."

AFK	Away from keyboard
b4	Before
BAK	Back at keyboard (used on MUDs and talk sessions)
BBL	Be back later
BCNU	Be seeing you
BRB	Be right back
BTSOOM	Beats the s*** out of me
BTW	By the way
BYOH	Bat you onna head
CFV	Call for votes
CU	See you
CUL	See you later
CUL8R	See you later
DYJHIW	Don't you just hate it when…
F2F	Face-to-face, or meeting in person
FAQ	Frequently asked question or frequently asked questions list
FUBAR	Fouled up beyond all recognition
FWIW	For what it's worth
FYA	For your amusement
FYI	For your information
GA	Go ahead
GR&D	Grinning, running, & ducking
HHOJ	Ha ha only joking
HHOK	Ha ha only kidding
HHOS	Ha ha only serious
IAE	In any event
IANAL	I am not a lawyer
IMHO	In my humble opinion
IMO	In my opinion
IOW	In other words
IRL	In real life

JASE	Just another system error
L8R	Later
LOL	Laughing out loud
MORF	Male or female?
MOTAS	Member of the appropriate sex
MOTOS	Member of the opposite sex
MOTSS	Member of the same sex
NFW	No f*** ing way
NRN	No reply necessary
OBTW	Oh, by the way
OIC	Oh, I see
OTOH	On the other hand
PD	Public domain
PITA	Pain in the ass
rehi	Hello again
RFD	Request for discussion
ROFL	Rolling on floor laughing
ROTFL	Rolling on the floor laughing
RSN	Real soon now
RTFM	Read the fine manual (except the *f* doesn't stand for *fine*)
SITD	Still in the dark
SNAFU	Situation normal, all fouled up
SO	Significant other
SOL	S*** outta luck
SW	Shareware
TANSTAAFL	There ain't no such thing as a free lunch
TIA	Thanks in advance
TIC	Tongue in cheek
TLA	Three-letter acronym (also ETLA, extended three-letter acronym)

TNX 1.0E6	Thanks a million
TNX	Thanks
TTFN	Ta-ta for now
TTYL	Talk to you later
WRT	With regard to, or with respect to
WTF	What the f *** or who the f ***
WTH	What the hell?!
YKYBHTLW	You know you've been hacking too long when…
.oO ()	This is a thought bubble, like in the cartoons. .oO (See?)
<g>	Grin
<gr&d>	Grinning, running, and ducking

Q 11.3. What's a flame? A flame war?

A flame is a posting or e-mail message that's intended to insult, provoke, and otherwise irritate the recipient. We're not talking little annoying comments and innuendo; we're talking flaming missives—nastygrams. When a flame message elicits equally fiery replies, a flamewar has begun. It isn't pretty. There's a whole newsgroup, `alt.flame`, devoted to this high art. I was going to include an example…but this is a family book. Better not.

Q 11.4. What's the Jargon File?

The Jargon File is a comprehensive compendium of hacker slang illuminating many aspects of hackish tradition, folklore, and humor. In it are definitions of all that funky slang that computer hackers (including Internet users) tend to use. The Jargon File is a common heritage of the hacker culture. I highly recommended reading this file—it's educational and has high giggle value.

It is available online in many places, among them

```
quartz.rutgers.edu:/etext/jargon/jarg300.txt.gz
```

NOTE You can also get the Jargon File in book form. It's called the *New Hacker's Dictionary* and it contains the full text of the Jargon File (plus cartoons that aren't available in the online version). I recommend shelling out the big bucks for the book version because 1) it takes up less disk space; 2) it's easier to read in the bathroom; and 3) it looks mighty impressive on a bookshelf or coffee table. *The New Hacker's Dictionary*, Second Edition (ISBN 0-262-68079-3) is available from MIT Press. You should be able to find it at any major bookstore, or you can order by phone at (800) 356-0343 or (617) 625-8481.

Q 11.5. How can I fall in love over the Internet?

Very carefully. I don't suggest trying it, although thousands of people have tried. There are plenty of online places to meet people and make friends, but trust me here–don't start a long-distance romance over the Internet. I'll give you two reasons. 1) Long-distance relationships are always difficult. Chances are, whomever you meet on the Internet will indeed be a long distance from you. 2) Things and people may not be what they seem. Beware of people who claim to be something they're not. It's easy to be deceptive on the Net. Cross-gender masquerading, for instance, is a favorite pastime of some folks.

Ask around—you'll hear about only a few happy relationships that started on the Net, but lots of horror stories. Disclaimers aside, here's how to fall in love on the Internet.

If you like to place or read personal ads (just like the ones in your local newspaper), check out the following Usenet groups.

```
alt.personals
alt.personals.ads
alt.personals.misc
alt.personals.poly
```

```
alt.personals.bi
alt.personals.spanking
alt.personals.bondage
alt.sex.wanted
```

NOTE There are also a few "local" personals newsgroups, such as `austin.personals` and `aus.personals`, if you want a remote chance at finding a friend in your geographic area.

Q 11.6. I heard someone hooked a toaster to the Internet?! Really?

Answered by Daniel Dern (`ddern@world.srd.com`)

In 1990, the toast of INTEROP (an annual networking show and exhibition) was a Sunbeam Deluxe Automatic Radiant Control Toaster, connected to INTEROPnet (an annual networking show and exhibition), the network deployed for the duration of the show, via a SLIP connection and controlled via Simple Network Management Protocol (NSMP).

The Internet Toaster was the creation of John Romkey, whose credits include coding the first version of TCP/IP for DOS, co-founding FTP Software and a few other companies specializing in TCP/IP technologies, and being a leading developer of many of the things Internet users rely on daily.

At the October, 1989 INTEROP conference in San Jose, California, Dan Lynch, President of the Interop Company (then Internet Inc.), promised Romkey that, if Romkey was able to "bring up his toaster on the Net," the appliance would be given star placement in the floor-wide internetwork to which all INTEROP exhibitors are required to link, at INTEROP '90.

Romkey did and it was.

The Sunbeam toaster, according to Romkey, had one real control: power on and off. When the power goes off, it automatically pops the toast.

"We found we could calibrate the 'degree of doneness' in software by controlling how long the power was on," says Romkey.

To save time and effort, Romkey joined forces with fellow Internet appliance networkers. "Team Toaster" included Simon Hackett, an Australian networking engineer whose company, Pnakotic Software (Adelaide, South Australia), does computer-controlled technology for audio/video applications.

The final toaster was a gleaming triumph of technology, both as "a good hack" and a demonstration that Internet technology could be made to do real-world tasks.

The Internet Toaster began a multiyear INTEROP tradition for funky networked devices. Subsequent years have seen the "Lego Loader" (an SNMP-controlled loader and remover for toast built of Legos), the SNMP weather bear, the SNMP tabletop electric train, and the giant mouse (big enough to sit on).

Consider it an example of bread-and-butter networking.

Q 11.7. I read somewhere that someone has connected their Coke machine to the Internet. Is that true?

Actually, folks at several schools, research labs, and other institutions have connected their cola machines to the Internet. The idea is that during a hot afternoon hacking away in the computer lab, the last thing you want is to trudge all the way down the hall just to find out that there's no more Coke/Jolt/root beer/or whatever your beverage of choice is. So clever hackers have connected their drink machines to the network so that they can avoid unsuccessful trips down the hall. Of course, because this is the Internet, we can all eyeball their colas, even if we're half a world away.

Here's a list of a few cola machines that are online. Some of these may not work for you (these things tend to come and go frequently…):

```
drink@drink.csh.rit.edu
graph@drink.csh.rit.edu
bargraph@coke.elab.cs.cmu.edu
```

```
mnm@coke.elab.cs.cmu.edu
coke@cs.wisc.edu
cocacola@columbia.edu
pepsi@columbia.edu
```

Let's check the cola inventory at the Rochester Institute of Technology. (The RIT motto is "We do more after 2 AM than most people do all day!")

```
$ finger drink@drink.csh.rit.edu
[drink.csh.rit.edu]
CSH Drink Finger Information Server, V0.99 Fri Oct 29 16:32:58 EDT 1993
WARNING: This software doesn't contain any bugs!

MOTD:
------------------------------------------------------------------------
Helpful Hints:
                finger info@drink.csh.rit.edu for 'help' type action.

Tue May 18 14:31:46 EDT 1993
        X client support finally added.  To check out 'xdrink' do a
        'finger displayname:0@drink.csh.rit.edu'.  Soon, (if everything goes
        well (as in, if you give drink.csh.rit.edu permission to use your
        x server (as in xhost +drink.csh.rit.edu))) xdrink will pop up.

        Hopefully, the balance will be $0.00 so that you can't drop
        any drinks, but if it happens not to be, then go ahead and drop
        something... unfortunately, unless you know where the coke machine
        is, it will just end up being a free drink for someone who is around
        when it drops.
                                        -Enjoy
                                                CSH Drink Admin
------------------------------------------------------------------------
                        Balance:  $  0.00

                        1) JOLT!!           $ 0.50  Full   (28/44)
                        2) Mountain Dew     $ 0.50  Empty  (0/44)
                        3) Mystery Slot?!   $ 0.50  Empty  (0/44)
                        4) Diet Stuff       $ 0.50  Full   (12/44)
                        5) Coke Classic     $ 0.50  Empty  (0/44)

          Drink   3+ hrs        1-3 hrs        0-1 hrs           Total
          :::::   ::::::        :::::::        :::::::           :::::
         JOLT!!       28              0              0              28
   Mountain Dew        0              0              0               0
 Mystery Slot?!        0              0              0               0
     Diet Stuff       12              0              0              12
   Coke Classic        0              0              0               0
```

```
+-----------------------+
| Computer Science House |
|     Drink Machine      |
+----+----+----+----+----+
| JO | Mo | My | Di | Co |
| 28 |  0 |  0 | 12 |  0 |
|$.50|$.50|$.50|$.50|$.50|
+-----------------------+
|       +----+   +        |
|       |+--+'   |        |
|       ||   |   |        |
|       |   ||   |        |
|       |+--+.   |        |
|       +----+   +        |
+-----------------------+
```

NOTE The truly interested will want to read the RIT Coke Machine FAQ, which is posted monthly to `alt.folklore.computers` and `alt.internet.services`. You can also get it via FTP from

`ftp.csh.rit.edu:/pub/drink/FAQ`

11.8. Well, that's cute, but I'm a coffee drinker myself. Is there a coffee pot on the Net?

There is indeed. Use your favorite graphical WWW browser (such as Mosaic) to connect to the following:

```
http://www.cl.cam.ac.uk
```

and you'll see a realtime image (well, it's updated once a second. That's almost realtime!) of someone's coffee pot. (See Figure 11.1.)

11.9. Wow, people sure hook weird things up to the Net. What other funky gadgets have been plugged in?

Let's see, there's a hot tub.

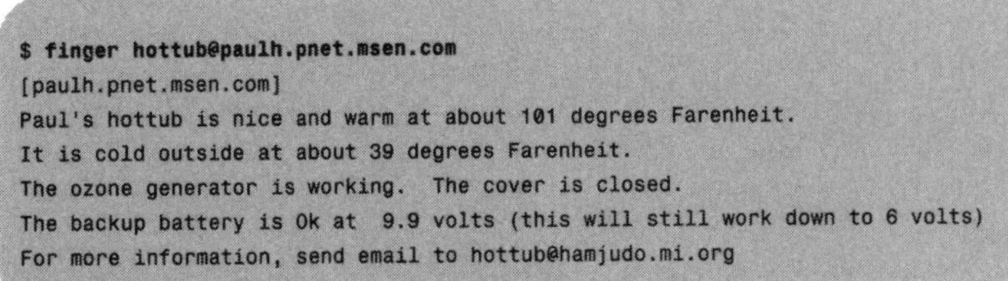

```
$ finger hottub@paulh.pnet.msen.com
[paulh.pnet.msen.com]
Paul's hottub is nice and warm at about 101 degrees Farenheit.
It is cold outside at about 39 degrees Farenheit.
The ozone generator is working.  The cover is closed.
The backup battery is Ok at  9.9 volts (this will still work down to 6 volts)
For more information, send email to hottub@hamjudo.mi.org
```

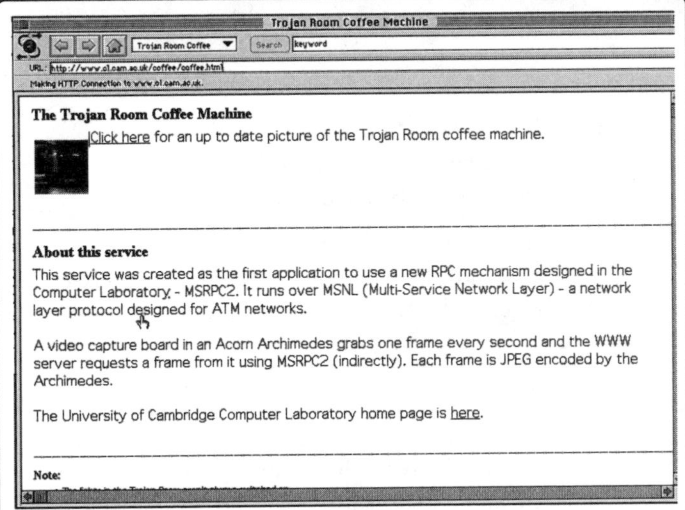

Figure 11.1. *Half empty or half full?*

Not long after I discovered that, I found this post on `news.misc`:

```
From: Andrew K Sheaff <IO92384@MAINE.MAINE.EDU>
Subject: In the spirit of coke@cmu
```



```
In the spirit of the monitored coke machine at CMU, I've set up a system
that will give users all over the world the temperature in my office.
To get the info just 'telnet small.eece.maine.edu 9876'.  If you have
any ideas to expand this send me some mail.

                                Andy
```

```
----------------------------------------------------------------------
Andrew K. Sheaff                    Bitnet:  I092384@Maine
Univeristy of Maine               Internet:  I092384@Maine.Maine.EDU
Orono, Maine                           DEC:  Sheaff@Bunter.EECE.Maine.EDU

Sure enough, it's a crisp 68 degrees in his lab, somewhere in Maine...
Welcome to the Small Temperature system!
The current temperature in Eric's and Andy's lab,
Room 220, Barrows Hall, UMaine, Orono, Maine, USA
is: 76.17 degrees Fahrenheit
is: 24.54 degrees Celsius
```

11.10. That's cool! How do I put my refrigerator, television, porch lights, cat, whatever on the Internet?

I have no idea at all. And, sadly, as far as I know there isn't a FAQ document that tells how. I asked Andrew Sheaff (who hooked his office thermometer to the Net) whether he intended to write some documentation divulging the tricks of the trade. He replied, "Kevin, I unfortunately have no intention of documenting how to connect things to the Internet. This was quite an involved project, which included writing assembly on a 68HC11, writing C code on a DEC3100, and a little bit of hardware construction." So for now, the rest of us remain uninformed.

11.11. People on the Internet certainly are fond of the word *foo* as a sort of filler word. Where does the word *foo* come from?

The most common story is that *foo* comes from *fubar*, an acronym for *fouled up beyond all recognition* (except the *f* "don't" usually stand for *fouled*).

11.12. What was the Great Renaming?

The Great Renaming is the day (Flag Day of 1985, if you must know) on which all of the nonlocal groups on the Usenet had their names changed from the `net.` format to the current hierarchical naming system. For instance, the newsgroup `net.sources` became `comp.sources.misc`.

11.13. What's an *obhack*? An *obquestion*? An *objoke*?

Ob stands for *obligatory*. When someone posts a message to a newsgroup or mailing list that is not particularly on the topic of that forum, they sometimes will include an obligatory statement that *is* on topic. For example, I might post a message about transcendental signifiers in `alt.internet.services`, but end with the line:

```
ObInternet: Like Trivia?
finger cyndiw@magnus1.com !!
```

thereby absolving me of my sin of rambling off-topic.

11.14. How many people on the Internet know you're a dog?

According to a mildly famous cartoon in the *New Yorker* magazine, no one on the Internet knows you're a dog.

11.15. Who posts more to the Internet's Usenet, women or men?

Research has shown that although the average woman and man post a similar number of articles to the Usenet, only seven percent of articles are submitted by women. Why? Because there are fewer women on the network and using the Usenet. Once they're talking, though, men and women use the system in similar ways: the average woman and man post articles of similar length. The amount of "follow-up" discussion does not seem to correlate with the gender of the topic initiator.

11.16. How can I find out what someone on the Internet looks like?

Answered by Steve Kinzler (`kinzler@cs.indiana.edu`)

There are a few online ways that you might be able to view an image of a particular Internet user, if you're lucky.

First, if both your site and the site for the user in question are running a special version of `finger` that supports face images and if a face image is available for that user, you can use `finger` to view the person's face along with his or her ordinary `finger` information. Such special versions of `finger` are GNU `finger` and its derivatives. GNU `finger` is available from most GNU software archives, such as

```
ftp.gnu.ai.mit.edu:/pub/gnu/finger*
```

A recommended derivative is ICSI's version, available in `ftp.icsi.berkeley.edu:/pub/stolcke/icsi-finger*`

One GNU finger server with lots of face images available is `cs.indiana.edu`. Finger `help@cs.indiana.edu` for details.

Second, if you can expect that the person you're interested in has ever attended a Usenix conference, that person might have had his or her photo digitized as part of Usenix's FaceSaver project. These images and further information are available in `ftp.uu.net:/published/usenix/faces`. This archive is updated after each Usenix conference with a FaceSaver room.

Third, there exists a collection of small bitmaps of Internet users in `cs.indiana.edu:/pub/faces/facedir*`.

The FaceSaver images are also available in this archive in a smaller, monochrome format as `facesaver*`. Also, in `logos*`, there's a collection of bitmaps representing various Internet domains using the appropriate company or organization logo. See the `README*` files in these collections for information about submitting bitmaps to them. They're updated on a frequent basis as new submissions come in. They're also mirrored in `ftp.uu.net:/published/usenix/faces/bundled`, where they're available for uucp.

If you use a Web browser, a convenient way to reference these collections for a particular user is to access the "WWW to Finger Gateway" at the URL `http://cs.indiana.edu/finger/gateway`. When fingering via this gateway, any face and logo bitmaps available are displayed along with any finger information.

Software is available that can take advantage of these bitmap collections. "faces" is available in `cs.indiana.edu:/pub/faces`, runs under X11, NeWS, SunView, and XView windowing systems, and can be used to monitor one's mailbox, jobs in a print queue, users on a system, unread newsgroups, weather forecasts, users on IRC channels, and other such things using displays of faces and logos for the items monitored. The exmh interface to the MH mail system can use these collections to display the face or logo for the mail messages it processes. It's available in `parcftp.xerox.com:/pub/exmh`. "Meuf" (mail enhanced using faces) is available in `ftp.enst.fr:/pub/mail/meuf*` and can serve as an X11 graphical interface to mail using face or logo bitmaps to represent messages in the mailbox. All these programs can recognize a special item in a mail header labeled X-Face as a compressed and encoded face bitmap for the sender of the mail message.

Other software that can deal with face images in some manner is as follows:

```
xfaces        ftp.x.org:/contrib/xfaces*            mailbox monitor
xwafemail     ftp.wu-wien.ac.at:/pub/src/X11/wafe   mail interface
quipu/X.500   ISO Development Environment           user directory server
vismon        AT&T Version 8 Unix                   visual monitor
```

GIF archives of some regulars on Internet Relay Chat are available from

```
ftp.informatik.tu-muenchen.de:/pub/comp/
networking/irc/RP
```

Q 11.17. What is *alt.best.of.internet*?

The newsgroup `alt.best.of.internet` contains articles that people have read in other newsgroups and that could be of interest to other people who don't have time to read *every* newsgroup. This group is (supposed to be) only for copies of especially interesting posts elsewhere on Usenet. It's worth a look.

You can get the `alt.best.of.internet` FAQ via FTP.

```
rtfm.mit.edu:/pub/usenet/alt.best.of.internet/
ABOI_Frequently_Answered_Questions
```

11.18. What Usenet groups should I read for more insight into the culture o' the Internet?

My favorite newsgroup for killing time reading about computers, hackers, and the Internet is `alt.folklore.computers`. The group `alt.culture.internet` is also sometimes interesting, but (despite its name) is mostly just a clearinghouse for random chatter, announcements about new Internet services, and the like.

11.19. What organizations exist that protect the Internet and its users?

Here's a listing of the biggies. Join one of them (or join them all!).

Electronic Frontier Foundation

The Electronic Frontier Foundation is a nonprofit public-interest membership organization working to protect individual rights in the information age. The EFF was founded in July of 1990 to ensure that the principles embodied in the Constitution and the Bill of Rights are protected as new communications technologies emerge.

Here's the EFF's mission, in the organization's own words:

```
From the beginning, EFF has worked to shape our nation's communications
infrastructure and the policies that govern it in order to maintain and
enhance First Amendment, privacy and other democratic values.  We believe
that our overriding public goal must be the creation of Electronic
Democracy, so our work focuses on the establishment of:

o       new laws that protect citizens' basic Constitutional rights as they
use new communications technologies,

o       a policy of common carriage requirements for all network providers
so that all speech, no matter how controversial, will be carried without
discrimination,

o       a National Public Network where voice, data and video services are
accessible to all citizens on an equitable and affordable basis, and

o       a diversity of communities that enable all citizens to have a voice
in the information age.
```

EFF supports legal and legislative action to protect the civil liberties of online users and hosts, and participates in related conferences and projects. It works to educate the online community about its legal rights and responsibilities. It also publishes the Big Dummy's Guide to the Internet, an online guide to navigating the Internet.

EFF members receive online bulletins about the critical issues and debates affecting computer-mediated communications; members also participate in online political activism.

For information, send e-mail to `info@eff.org`.

Lots of great information from the EFF is available via FTP from `ftp.eff.org`.

Electronic Frontier Foundation
1001 G St. NW, Suite 950 E
Washington DC 20001, USA
voice: (202) 347-5400
fax: (202) 393-5509

Internet Society

The Internet Society (which I talked a bit about in Chapter 1, "Just What Is This Internet?") is a professional, not-for-profit organization with the goal of fostering the well being, interest in, and evolution of the Internet. The following goals of the Society are taken from its charter:

```
    A.  To facilitate and support the technical evolution of
the Internet as a research and education infrastructure, and to
stimulate the involvement of the scientific community,
industry, government and others in the evolution of the
Internet;

    B.  To educate the scientific community, industry and the
public at large concerning the technology, use and application
of the Internet;

    C.  To promote educational applications of Internet
technology for the benefit of government, colleges and
universities, industry, and the public at large;

    D.  To provide a forum for exploration of new Internet
applications, and to stimulate collaboration among
organizations in their operational use of the global Internet.
```

More information about the Internet Society is available via anonymous FTP from the following:

```
nnsc.nsf.net:/isoc.
```

Center for Civic Networking

The Center for Civic Networking is a nonprofit organization that promotes broad public benefits of the emerging national information infrastructure. The Center brings together expertise in large-scale computer and network systems, community-based applications of computing, nonprofit management, community development, architecture, public policy, and democratic participation. The Center's programs focus on framing a national vision for civic networking, developing a policy framework that supports civic networking, developing and supporting model civic networking projects, and assisting in the technology transfer needed to achieve the broad-based benefits of civic networking.

For information, send e-mail to `mfidelman@world.std.com`.

Info is also available via FTP.

```
ftp.eff.org:/pub/Groups/CCN
world.std.com, ftp/amo/civicnet
```

or you can pick up the phone and call (202) 362-3831.

Computer Professionals for Social Responsibility

CPSR is a national membership organization that conducts a variety of activities to protect privacy and civil liberties. According to the CPSR boilerplate, "CPSR's mission is to provide the public and policymakers with realistic assessments of the power, promise, and problems of information technology. As concerned citizens, CPSR members work to direct public attention to critical choices concerning the applications of information technology and how those choices affect society."

Founded in 1981 by a group of computer scientists concerned about the use of computers in nuclear weapons systems, CPSR has grown into a national public-interest alliance of information-technology professionals and others. CPSR has 22 chapters in the US and affiliations with similar groups worldwide. CPSR is based in Palo Alto, California, and maintains an office in Washington, D.C., which is home to our Civil Liberties and Computing program.

CPSR membership is open to everyone who uses or is concerned about the role of information technology in our society. For information, send e-mail to `cpsr@csli.stanford.edu`.

You can get CSPR information via FTP from `ftp.cpsr.org` or via Gopher from `gopher.cpsr.org`.

CPSR National Office
P.O. Box 717
Palo Alto, CA 94302 USA
Voice: (415) 322-3778
Fax: (415) 322-3798

National Public Telecomputing Network

The National Public Telecomputing Network, the folks who bring us Free-nets, exists to help people establish free, open-access, community computer systems.

For information, FTP to

```
ftp.eff.org:/pub/Groups/NPTN-Freenet/login.info
```

For more information, send e-mail to `info@nptn.org` (where your mail will be read by a human, so ask nicely).

National Public Telecomputing Network
P.O. Box 1987
Cleveland, OH 44106
Voice: (216) 247-5800
Fax: (216) 247-3328

NOTE Check out "Outposts on the Electronic Frontier," a great online resource listing dozens of international, national, and regional organizations supporting the online community. This list is available via FTP from

```
rtfm.mit.edu:/pub/usenet/news.answers/net-
```

```
community/orgs-list
```

It's also available via e-mail:

```
To: mail-server@rtfm.mit.edu
Subject: <subject line is ignored>
Body: send
```

CHAPTER 12

How Can I Keep My Privacy and Stay Secure?

Although many of us in our day-to-day activities take our right to privacy and safety for granted, users on the Internet cannot. This chapter answers important questions that affect everyone who uses the Internet, including how to protect your data from prying eyes, keep your private information truly private, and veil your identity by using anonymous mail servers.

Q 12.1. Should I worry about security?

Answered by Dave Taylor (`taylor@netcom.com`)

The answer to this thorny question really depends on what you're using the Internet for and how private you want your files and electronic mail to remain. Perhaps the best way to answer this question is to talk about my own perspective on privacy and the Internet. Right up front, it's important to remember that if you're on the Internet, you're probably using a machine that other people are using, too. Certainly when you send electronic mail, your message will travel through other systems in route to your correspondent.

Security therefore encompasses a variety of aspects, including account security, file security and electronic mail security. Despite what you will read in this chapter (believe it or not) I really don't think you need to worry much about security at all.

The main reason is that most systems are set up to be "pretty secure"; that is, secure enough so that casual interlopers won't be able to wander through your files or e-mail. Combine that with the tremendous traffic rate on the network, and you can see that so much is going on that you and I are safely just part of the crowd. Don't ignore security issues entirely. Take the simple precautions outlined here and you'll be fine.

12.2. How can I keep my password secure?

On any networked computer system, your password is the only thing standing between you and disaster. Anyone guessing your password will be able to read your electronic mail, snoop in your files, delete your work, and post electronic mail or Usenet news that appears to come from you. Each of these things can be embarrassing, annoying, and dangerous.

Ensuring your account's security is relatively easy: make sure your password is something that's impossible for anyone to guess. If a password is particularly easy for you to remember or type, chances are it is a bad choice because its also easy to guess. Here is a partial list of passwords not to use:

- `password`
- `opensaysme`
- `letmein`
- **`qwerty`, `asdfghjkl`, or any other combination of neighborly letters on the keyboard**
- **your initials**
- **Your login name (this is very common and stupid.** Trivia buffs might care to know that an account with the same login and password is called a *Joe*.)

- Your cat's name or your spouse's name, your phone number, your Social Security number, or any other information that can be found by *fingering* your account or going through your wallet.
- Any word that's in the dictionary.
- Any common name (Steve, Quinn, Smith, Rover, and so on).

To be as safe as possible, make your password a bunch of unrelated characters, such as `K#*2ww>`. Use a combination of upper- and lowercase letters, punctuation, and numbers and make sure your password is six characters or longer. If you find this type of password too hard to remember, try using two unrelated words separated by a punctuation mark, like *explore*grasshopper* or *get*A*life*. Finally, don't feel secure just because your password is long; many systems check only the first eight characters of your password!

Q 12.3. Is it possible for my system administrator to see my password?

On most large-scale computer systems, system administrators cannot find out your password. However, this should be of little comfort to you because if administrators want to snoop in your files, they don't even need your password. System administrators, or anyone with superuser power, can nonchalantly check your files, make copies of them, delete them, whatever. That's the number one reason that you need to use a service provider you can trust.

> **NOTE** Some systems on the Internet—especially certain types of bulletin board systems—do not shield your password from the system administrator's eyes. For that reason, you should never use the same password on more than one system. If you have multiple accounts, you need multiple passwords. It's a drag, I know, but it protects you.

UNIX systems (among others) use a tricky feature called *one-way password encryption*. When you first choose a new password (for instance, with the UNIX `passwd` command) the computer encrypts your password so thoroughly that it can never be decrypted and only stores the encrypted version. Later, when you type your password while logging in, the computer encrypts your guess using the same method and compares the encrypted version of your guess to the encrypted version of your actual password. If they match, you're allowed in.

Following are a few lines from the UNIX file `/etc/passwd`, where users' passwords are stored. Notice that the second field, right after the username, is gibberish. That's the user's encrypted password. Don't bother trying to decode them, you can't.

```
waffle:VHqgnuFKk.BC2:579:20:Kevin Savetz:/files/home/waffle:/local/bin/tcsh
rayfox:eF/gtVIB9JhOY:1122:20:Raymond D. Fox:/i/home/rayfox:/local/bin/tcsh
mramesh:qupwsgBxxneqs:1123:20:Ramesh Meyyappan:/i/home/mramesh:/local/bin/tcsh
onethumb:ohki3YdLQFQLg:1124:20:Don MacAskill:/i/home/onethumb:/local/bin/tcsh
lorna:mx8YsCiZmYzuQ:1125:20:Lorna Overby:/i/home/lorna:/local/bin/tcsh
tersa:kD83hHLlIv59Y:1126:20:Tersa Lewandowski:/i/home/tersa:/local/bin/tcsh
mmaniar:lUQ.4QyZXBb9k:1127:20:Mihir Maniar:/i/home/mmaniar:/local/bin/tcsh
usha:z4SJ0J1F89/rQ:1128:20:Usha Ramaswamy:/i/home/usha:/local/bin/tcsh
bgregory:6Avv92pPO5rHs:1129:20:Brian Gregory:/i/home/bgregory:/bin/csh
forte:gqvOnATmb8jWs:1130:20:Forte Systems:/i/home/forte:/local/bin/tcsh
shannah:md9JGo3Do5V3c:1131:20:Teri Miller:/i/home/shannah:/local/bin/tcsh
robot:s4AsiqzcZmPk6:1132:20:Robert Kennedy:/i/home/robot:/local/bin/tcsh
gwenaver:pbHienGd4bWAs:1133:20:Gwenaver:/i/home/gwenaver:/local/bin/tcsh
shatter:mEpqGznkx7EAM:1134:20:Jay Srinivasan:/i/home/shatter:/local/bin/tcsh
eliu:dn63y4ScGA2z6:1135:20:Elaine Liu:/i/home/eliu:/local/bin/tcsh
```

NOTE Although your password can't be decrypted, you're never perfectly safe. Unscrupulous crackers can use the same encryption routine to stab guesses at your password. Several computer programs are available that can quickly and silently encrypt every word in the dictionary and compare them to the list of encrypted passwords on your system. Therefore, if your password is in the dictionary, is a common name, and so on, you can get zapped.

Q 12.4. Is my electronic mail private?

Although electronic mail is useful, quick, and easy to use, it is not necessarily private. In the best of all worlds (and the vast majority of the time), no one will read your electronic messages except you and the intended recipients. But because electronic mail is made up of plain old easy-to-read ASCII text and because your e-mail message can be passed through any number of strangers' computers on the way to its destination, an e-mail message is the electronic equivalent of a postcard.

It's as if you dropped your letter in the postal service mailbox and knew it would get to the other side, but really had no way to ascertain what would happen in route. Would it be popped open and read out loud to the mailroom at an intermediate stop? Federal law prohibits U.S. Postal workers from doing that, and they're more likely to get caught than electronic mail pirates who can effortlessly make a duplicate of your message without leaving a trace. For that reason, here's my advice: never say anything in electronic mail that you wouldn't want your boss, your competition, your mom, or the government to know.

Q 12.5. Who could be reading my e-mail?

Answered by Dave Taylor (`taylor@netcom.com`)

Anyone between your host computer and your message's destination can intercept your e-mail. Your system administrator or the administrator at the receiving end could read it. For that matter, a clever cracker or sysadmin anywhere along your mail's path can easily intercept and read your message.

The good news, before you get too paranoid, is that there is a *lot* of information traveling through the wires, and there's precious little reason for anyone to intercept your mail. How much information? Late in 1993, the National Science Foundation calculated that over 500 megabytes of information travel through the network backbone per hour, and 17 percent of that traffic was electronic mail. If we assume that the average e-mail message is about 1,000 bytes (10–15 lines), about 8,800 e-mail messages go through the network each second. If you are a rabid e-mail user and send a message every ten minutes, you're still less than a teeny drop in the bucket.

As a result, although I know that there's a chance that my e-mail could be monitored en-route, the odds of it happening are infinitesimal, and I certainly don't average one e-mail message every ten minutes, either!

> **NOTE** Here are some UNIX-centric notes from Dave Taylor on keeping your incoming mail files free from prying eyes:
>
> One of the few files that contains information you'll doubtless want to keep private is your incoming mailbox. Stored, typically, in either a shared directory called `/usr/spool/mail` or `/usr/mail`, mailbox files share the name of their associated account. My account is `taylor`, so my mailbox is `/usr/spool/mail/taylor`, and Kevin goes by `waffle` on one machine, so his mailbox is doubtless `/usr/spool/mail/waffle` on that machine. The good news is that most systems have things set up exactly as you would want: your mailbox can be read and written by you and by the program that delivers mail but by no one else. You can check the permissions of your mail file by typing `ls -l /usr/spool/mail/$LOGNAME`. The permissions should be `rw----` or `rw-rw--`. If they are something different, ask your system administrator to ensure that things are configured correctly; in this situation a quick e-mail message to your administrator can save some unpleasant situations later.
>
> Even with this security, however, a directory and file that's beyond your control is a potential problem, so a good strategy if you receive sensitive electronic mail is to immediately save it in a mailbox file in your home directory. I must

admit that I don't do this because I end up forgetting about saved mail messages (I receive so much electronic mail each day; about 100 messages or so arrive on a daily basis and the volume is gradually increasing!). A bit of self-discipline on your part, however, and you should be able to use this strategy with nary a problem. An even better solution is to download confidential mail to your local computer. Anytime that I receive a mail message that must remain private, I make a copy of it on my Macintosh and delete the original on my UNIX host.

Q 12.6. What about Pretty Good Privacy as a way to protect my e-mail?

Pretty Good Privacy, commonly known as *PGP*, is an encryption program that gives your electronic mail something it otherwise would not have: privacy. It can ensure that any text messages—e-mail files, letters to Grandma, whatever, can be read only by their intended recipients.

PGP uses a technique called *public key encryption* in which a message's sender and recipient hold two keys: a public key and a private key. When you want to send an encrypted message to someone, you encrypt it using their public key. Then only their private key can unlock the message.

Example: When encrypted, a message looks like a meaningless jumble of random characters. Here's an unencrypted message:

```
Your Internet Consultant - the FAQs of Life Online
by Kevin M. Savetz ... ISBN 0-672-30520-8
Buy as many as you can afford! Makes a great stocking stuffer!
```

Here's an encrypted version. Only the person for whom it is intended will be able to decode it. It works wonderfully, but it won't sell a lot of books.

```
--BEGIN PGP MESSAGE--
Version: 2.3

pgAAAKku9D8whJCJZN8jx9Am4xKDrg8UrjHPhA5FF1EtxOWFXw+nltb+Ar52FMEr
eLs2kYg8PJdxfAN1F2dIJbGSE01a7NT4gOBINfBFG+iG4DEd/Vbgs7A/S9wB8K1Y
GUSY4gNZXQIKMKGMK4vRxbkMCS9OdSpUdb2JhL1PHwlQuK9TEBZLygDkRi2diDgi
+c3Bt4kTfNbg11auJtK+SfY5ENunsEhsdMrqT2oi
=1xYk
--END PGP MESSAGE--
```


PGP is very controversial, both legally (because of patent rights and export laws) and politically (because it gives individuals the power to ensure their own right of privacy). PGP is contraband: if you live in the USA, and you are not a federal agency, you shouldn't actually run PGP on your computer. Still, it is freely available and is the most powerful encryption tool available to the masses.

I highly recommend that you grab and read the `alt.security.pgp` FAQ list. It does a great job of answering many questions about PGP and certainly covers PGP in more depth than I can here. It is available via anonymous FTP from

```
rtfm.mit.edu:/pub/usenet/alt.security.pgp/
alt.security.pgp_FAQ*
```

Here's some of the information you'll find there:

```
What is PGP?
Why should I encrypt my mail? I'm not doing anything illegal!
What are public keys and private keys?
How much does PGP cost?
Is encryption legal?
Is PGP legal?
Is there an archive site for alt.security.pgp?
Is there a commercial version of PGP available?
What platforms has PGP been ported to?
Where can I obtain PGP?
Why does it take so long to encrypt/decrypt messages?
How does PGP handle multiple addresses?
How can I use PGP to create a return receipt for a message?
Where can I obtain scripts to integrate pgp with my email or news reading system?
Can I be forced to reveal my pass phrase in any legal proceedings?
What are the Public Key Servers?
What public key servers are available?
What is the syntax of the key server commands?
Glossary of Cryptographic Terms
United States Congress Phone and FAX List
```

Macintosh users should get the "How to MacPGP" guide, which is available via e-mail.

```
To: qwerty@netcom.com
Subject: Bomb me!
Body: <message body is ignored>
```

NOTE For more general information about cryptography, read the "Cryptography" FAQ. This huge FAQ list is posted to the newsgroups `sci.crypt`, `talk.politics.crypto`, `sci.answers`, and `news.answers` every three weeks. It is also available via anonymous FTP.

```
rtfm.mit.edu:/pub/usenet/news.answers/
cryptography-faq/*
```

Q12.7. Where can I get PGP?

Send e-mail with any message body and subject line

```
To: info-pgp-request@lucpul.it.luc.edu
```

for an up-to-date list of where to find PGP. Another PGP FTP site list is available by sending e-mail (again, with any message body and subject line)

```
To: pgpinfo@mantis.co.uk
```

PGP is free. In the United States, the free version may be a violation of a patent held by Public Key Partners. There is a commercial product called ViaCrypt that is definitely legal to use.

NOTE When cryptography is outlawed, bayl bhgynjf jvyy unir cevinpl.

12.8. What is privacy enhanced mail?

Privacy enhanced mail (*PEM*) is a new standard for transferring encrypted electronic mail. Like PGP, it allows you to encrypt your mail before sending it and ensures that your message can only be decrypted by its intended recipient. PEM works differently than PGP and isn't embroiled by the legal battles that have troubled PGP. PEM is just beginning to catch on in the Internet community; it certainly hasn't received the recognition or media play that PGP has.

For more information, get the PEM FAQ list from

```
ftp.tis.com:/pub/PIM/FAQ
```

NOTE To join the PEM electronic mailing list, send a request to `pem-dev-request@tis.com`. If you like gory technical details, you should know that PEM is described in Request For Comment documents (RFCs) 1421 though 1424.

12.9. What is Riordan's Internet privacy enhanced mail?

Riordan's Internet privacy enhanced mail (*RIPEM*) is one implementation of privacy enhanced mail. As of this writing, RIPEM isn't complete but is still said to be useful. It hasn't been around as long as PGP, and the two work differently. Their encrypted texts are not compatible.

For more information, check the "RIPEM Frequently Asked Questions" file, which is posted monthly in the newsgroup `alt.security.ripem`. It's also available via FTP from

```
rtfm.mit.edu:/pub/usenet/alt.security/
RIPEM_Frequently_Asked_Questions
```

12.10. How can I keep my files private?

Answered by Dave Taylor (`taylor@netcom.com`)

File security is subtle if you're using a UNIX-based Internet host, because each file and directory can have its own access permissions, independent of the security of any other files or directories. In other words, if you set up your home directory to have minimal access permission, files within your account still have the potential of being read by others if their permission is set incorrectly.

There are two steps to solving this: I recommend typing `chmod 711 $HOME` to allow the system to access files such as `.forward` and `.plan` without problems but prevent people from using `ls` to list the contents of your home directory. Further, if you're prepared to work with your `.login` or `.profile` account customization file, type `umask 077` so that any files you create are, by default, set up so that you can read and write them but no one else can do anything with them. You can always type `chmod +r filename` to add read capability later if needed. If you're not sure what your account security is, ask your system administrator for assistance and be sure to indicate the results of the command `ls -ld $HOME`, too.

If you're not on a UNIX system, your files are probably local to your personal computer, and much of this is less of an issue. Nonetheless, remember that people can still flip on your computer and look through your files, so private data should be kept encrypted or on a floppy disk that you keep in your office desk or your briefcase. An ounce of prevention can save a lot of embarrassment later.

12.11. What newsgroups should I read for more information about privacy and security on the Internet?

Try these:

alt.privacy	General discussion about privacy issues
alt.privacy.clipper	Discussion of the U.S. Government's Clipper Chip

`alt.security`	General security discussions
`alt.security.index`	Index to `alt.security`
`alt.security.pgp`	Discussion of Pretty Good Privacy
`alt.security.ripem`	Discussion of RIPEM
`alt.society.civil-liberty`	General civil liberties, including privacy issues
`comp.org.eff.news`	News reports from the Electronic Frontier Foundation
`comp.org.eff.talk`	Discussion of EFF-related issues
`comp.security.misc`	Random discussions about computer security
`comp.security.unix`	Security on UNIX systems
`comp.society.privacy`	General privacy issues
`sci.crypt`	Cryptography discussions

Q 12.12. Is it safe to send credit card information over the Internet?

The answer to this question depends on whom you ask. Some folks will tell you that you should never, ever, give anyone your credit card number via the Internet. Others will say that using a credit card over the Internet is no more dangerous than forking over your plastic in an unfamiliar restaurant.

The more paranoid folks say that it would be a simple task for some Internet cracker to write a "network sniffer" program to scan for credit card numbers as packets fly through the Internet. Such a program could watch, for example, an online bookstore for folks placing orders. Said evil user could then, armed with dozens of names, credit card numbers, and expiration dates, go on a shopping spree.

Well, I suppose it could happen (and it probably will eventually). Then again, I've taken my chances by ordering stuff online using a credit card (some compact discs and a magazine subscription to be exact). It seems more likely to me that a waiter in a restaurant or a salesperson in a department store will get my credit card number by saving carbons than a network cracker. You take your chances both ways, but the odds are usually stacked in your favor.

So the piece of advice I can give is this: use your best judgment and trust your gut feelings. If you connect to an online store that seems reputable, go ahead and order something from them. If you have any doubts, jot down their telephone number and place your order over the phone (assuming you don't think your phone is bugged, too!). Make sure you're in control: if you ever get an unsolicited electronic mail message or telephone call asking for your credit card number, don't give it out. Kapiche?

Q 12.13. How do I send e-mail anonymously? How can I post to the Usenet anonymously?

If you've read the chapters on electronic mail and the Usenet, you know that every e-mail message has an envelope of sorts, which tells who it is to, what it is about, and who it is from. What if you don't want the world to know that you sent that e-mail or Usenet news post? Can you prowl around the Internet incognito? The answer is yes. Using a tool called an *anonymous mail server* (*remailer*) you can hide your identity when sending e-mail and Usenet messages.

How do anonymous remailers work? Instead of sending your message directly to its destination, you send it to the remailer. The server will strip off your message's headers and signature, tack on a unique (but anonymous) identification code, and mail it to your intended recipient. Although the recipient will see the message is from an anonymous remailer, he can't know the sender's true identity. If the recipient replies, his message will go to the anonymous mail server, which will redirect the message to you while protecting the sender's identity.

There is an server at `anon.penet.fi` that can help you anonymously send e-mail and post to the Usenet. Other anonymous mail servers exist, and they all tend to come and go frequently. I have a list of others here, but many of these services are experimental, unstable, or won't exist any longer by the time this book hits your hot hands. However, the `anon.penet.fi` server has been operational and stable for several months.

anon.penet.fi's anonymous Usenet posting service works in a similar way; sending mail to alt.sex@anon.penet.fi will post your message to the Usenet group alt.sex *sans* your name and e-mail address. It will include your own anonymous alias, however, which people can use to reply to you.

For complete information on using the anonymous mail and Usenet posting service, send a message to help@anon.penet.fi. You will receive a document via electronic mail explaining the details. (Incidentally, you can also send mail to deutsch@anon.penet.fi or italiano@anon.penet.fi if you want your help in German or Italian.) Be prepared to wait as long as 24 hours to receive a reply. One of penet's failings, because it's one of the few stable anonymous remailers, is that it's heavily overloaded.

Matthew Ghio maintains a FAQ on the anonymous remailers, which lists over a dozen alternative anonymous services. He says that many of them are much faster than anon.penet.fi because they do not have such a heavy load. You can get the information by sending mail (any subject line/any message body) to

```
To: mg5n+remailers@andrew.cmu.edu
```

Take care when posting anonymously. Your anonymity and privacy can never be guaranteed. Anonymous services have their pros and cons, but like them or not, they're here to stay.

Also, read the "Anonymity on the Internet" FAQ. This is a lengthy FAQ list—nearly 100 printed pages—rife with information, lore, and opinions about anonymous mailing services. The first thing covered in this FAQ is a current list of operational anonymous mail services. The document is available via anonymous FTP,

```
rtfm.mit.edu:/pub/usenet/news.answers/net-
anonymity/*
```

and on the Usenet newsgroups alt.privacy and news.answers.

Q12.14. Why would someone want to post anonymously?

There are a variety of reasons folks might need or want anonymous access to the Usenet and e-mail. It is understandable that the participants on newsgroups such as `alt.sex.beastiality`, `alt.sexual.abuse.recovery`, or `alt.whistleblowing` may want to participate incognito (although likely for different reasons). "Serious" uses such as sexual abuse counseling in Usenet newsgroups have increased dramatically since the dawn of anonymous mailers, as have the number of posts to groups such as `alt.personals` and `alt.sex`. Occurrences of harassing messages have also increased with the introduction of networked anonymity. Again, for a detailed look at the reasons behind anonymity on the Internet, read the "Anonymity on the Internet" FAQ.

NOTE Services through which users send anonymous e-mail and Usenet postings—and the people who use them—are extremely disliked in some circles. Critics say that anonymous remailers are used to distribute child pornography, harass innocent people with impunity, and lots of other nasty things. Maybe so, but it's clear that anonymous remailers are here to stay.

It doesn't take much programming savvy to set up a remailer for the public. In fact, many remailers have been run out of student accounts without the knowledge or permission of the system administrators. (That's one reason that the Internet's anonymity services are notoriously unstable.)

Dozens of remailers have come and gone over time. Whenever one goes away for some reason, another one pops up somewhere. You don't have to like them, but you do have to get used to them.

Q12.15. What are the responsibilities associated with anonymity?

Answered by L. Detweiler
(`ld231782@longs.lance.colostate.edu`)

Responsibilities for users of anonymous mail/post services:

- **Use anonymity only if you have to.** Frivolous uses weaken the seriousness and usefulness of the capability for others.
- **Do not use anonymity to provoke, harass, or threaten others.**
- **Do not hide behind anonymity to evade established conventions on Usenet, such as posting binary pictures to regular newsgroups.**
- **If posting large files, be attentive to bandwidth considerations.** Remember, simply sending the posting to the service increases network traffic.
- **Avoid posting anonymously to the regular hierarchy of Usenet;** this is the mostly likely place to alienate readers. The `alt` hierarchy is preferred.
- **Give as much information as possible in the posting (that is, references and so on).** Remember that content is the only means by which readers can judge the truth of the message and that any inaccuracies will tend to discredit the entire message and even future ones under the same handle.
- **Be careful not to include information that will reveal your identity or enable someone to deduce it.** Test the system by sending anonymous mail to yourself.
- **Be aware of the policies of the anonymous site and respect them.**
- **Be prepared to forfeit your anonymity if you abuse the privilege.**
- **Make sure you can trust the system operator.**
- **Be considerate and respectful of other's objections to anonymity.**
- **"Hit-and-run" anonymity should be used with utmost reservation.** Use services that provide anonymous return addresses instead.

- **Be courteous to system operators, who may have invested large amounts of time, be personally risking their accounts, or dedicating their hardware, all for your convenience.**

Responsibilities of those who read anonymous postings:

- **Do not complain, attack, or discredit posters for the sole reason that they are posting anonymously, make blanket condemnations that equate anonymity with cowardice and criminality, or assail anonymous traffic in general for mostly neutral reasons (for example, its volume is heavy or increasing).**
- **React to the anonymous information unemotionally.** Abusive posters will be encouraged further if they get irrationally irate responses. Sometimes the most effective response is silence.
- **Notify operators if severe abuses occur, such as piracy, harassment, extortion, and so on.**
- **Do not complain about postings being inappropriate because they offend you personally.**
- **Use kill files to screen anonymous postings if you object to the idea of anonymity itself.**
- **Avoid the temptation to proclaim that all anonymous postings should be barred from particular groups because no possible or conceivable need exists.**

Q 12.16. Where can I find more information about privacy and anonymity on the Net?

The two best resources are the "Anonymity on the Internet" FAQ (which I mentioned earlier) and the "Privacy and Anonymity FAQ." Despite their similar names, these two documents are very different and are both worthwhile reading.

The Anonymity on the Internet FAQ is filled with information, primarily about anonymous remailers. It is available via anonymous FTP.

```
rtfm.mit.edu:/pub/usenet/news.answers/net-
anonymity/*
```

The Privacy & Anonymity FAQ is a lengthy document (weighing in at about 60 printed pages) covering broader aspects of privacy in Cyberspace. This one should he required reading, right up there with "1984." Topics include

What is "identity" on the Internet?

Why is identity important on the Internet?

What is "privacy" on the internet?

How secure is my account?

What is the future of privacy on the Internet?

How can anonymity be protected on the Internet?

What was "Operation Sundevil" and the Steve Jackson Game case?

What is the Clipper Chip Initiative?

What are compliments/criticisms of the Clipper Initiative?

It can be obtained via anonymous FTP from

```
rtfm.mit.edu:/pub/usenet/news.answers/net-
privacy/*
```

It is also posted to the Usenet newsgroups `news.answers`, `sci.answers`, and `alt.answers` every 21 days.

APPENDIX A

Internet Access Providers

This appendix lists companies and organizations that provide dial-up access to Internet services for individuals. For more information on how to choose an Internet access provider, see Chapter 2, "How Do I Get Connected to the Internet?"

Area Code Summary—US/Canadian Providers

This is a listing of North American provider names arranged by telephone area code. Details and contact information for each provider follow in the next section.

202	CAPCON Library Network Clarknet
204	MBnet
205	Nuance Network Service

206	Eskimo North
	Netcom
	Olympus
	Teleport
212	Echo
	Maestro Information Service
	Mindvox
	Netcom
	Panix
	Pipeline
213	CRL
214	Netcom
	Texas Metronet
301	CAPCON Library Network
	ClarkNet
	Digital Express Group (Digex)
303	CNS
	Colorado SuperNet
	Netcom
305	CyberGate
	Gateway to the World
310	CERFnet
	CRL
	Netcom
312	CICNet
	InterAccess Co.
	Netcom
313	Msen
314	Neosoft
403	Alberta SuperNet Inc.
	CCI Networks
404	CRL
	Netcom
408	a2i Communications
	Netcom
	Portal

410	CAPCON Library Network ClarkNet Digital Express Group (Digex)
412	Telerama
415	CERFnet CRL Institute for Global Communications (IGC) Netcom The WELL
416	Internet Online Inc. UUNorth Incorporated
503	Agora Netcom Teleport
504	Neosoft
508	The World
510	CCnet Communications CERFnet CRL HoloNet Netcom
512	Netcom
513	Freelance Systems Programming
514	Communications Accessibles Montreal, Inc.
516	Panix
519	Data Tech Canada Hookup Communication Corporation
602	CRL Data Basix Evergreen Internet
603	MV Communications, Inc.
604	Cyberstore Systems Inc. DataFlux Systems Limited Wimsey Information Services
609	Digital Express Group (Digex) Global Enterprise Services, Inc.
614	OARNet

617	Delphi Netcom North Shore Access The World
619	CERFnet CTS Network Services Netcom
702	Evergreen Internet
703	CAPCON Library Network ClarkNet Digital Express Group (Digex) Meta Network Netcom
704	Interpath VNet Internet Access, Inc.
707	CRL
708	CICNet InterAccess Co. XNet Information Systems
713	Neosoft
714	CERFnet Digital Express Group (Digex) Netcom
718	Echo Mindvox
719	CNS Colorado SuperNet
800	CERFnet CICNet CNS CRL Global Enterprise Services, Inc. Msen Neosoft
801	Evergreen Internet
810	Msen
815	InterAccess Co.

817	Texas Metronet
818	CERFnet Netcom
908	Digital Express Group (Digex)
909	Digital Express Group (Digex)
910	Interpath
916	Netcom
919	Interpath
CompuServe Packet Network	The WELL The World
PSINet	HoloNet
SprintNet	Delphi Meta Network Neosoft Portal
Tymnet	Delphi Holonet

Providers in United States and Canada

a2i Communications

Area code(s)	408
Voice phone	(408) 293-8078
E-mail address	`info@rahul.net`
Dialup number	(408) 293-9010, login as `guest`
Services provided	Shell, Usenet, e-mail, Internet access, including Telnet and FTP

Agora

Area code(s)	503
E-mail address	`info@agora.rain.com`
Dialup number	(503) 293-1772
Services provided	Shell, Usenet, FTP, Telnet, Gopher, Lynx, IRC, mail; SLIP/PPP coming

Alberta SuperNet Inc.

Area code(s)	403
Voice phone	(403) 441-3663
E-mail address	`info@supernet.ab.ca`
Services provided	Shell, e-mail, Usenet, FTP, Telnet, Gopher, SLIP/PPP

CAPCON Library Network

Area code(s)	202, 301, 410, 703
Voice phone	(202) 331-5771
E-mail address	`capcon@capcon.net`
Services provided	Menu, FTP, Archie, e-mail, FTP, Gopher, Telnet, WAIS, Whois, training

CCI Networks

Area code(s)	403
Voice phone	(403) 450-6787
E-mail address	`info@ccinet.ab.ca`
Services provided	Shell, e-mail, Usenet, FTP, Telnet, Gopher, WAIS, WWW, IRC, Hytelnet, SLIP/PPP

CCnet Communications

Area code(s)	510
Voice phone	(510) 988-0680
E-mail address	`info@ccnet.com`
Dialup number	(510) 988-7140, login as `guest`
Services provided	Shell, SLIP/PPP, Telnet, e-mail, FTP, Usenet, IRC, WWW

CERFnet

Area code(s)	619, 510, 415, 818, 714, 310, 800
Voice phone	(800) 876-2373
E-mail address	`sales@cerf.net`
Services provided	Full range of Internet services

CICNet

Area code(s)	312, 708, 800
Voice phone	(800) 947-4754 or (313) 998-6703
E-mail address	`info@cic.net`
Services provided	SLIP, FTP, Telnet, Gopher, e-mail, Usenet

ClarkNet (Clark Internet Services, Inc.)

Area code(s)	410, 301, 202, 703
Voice phone	(800) 735-2258, ask for extension (410) 730-9764
E-mail address	`info@clark.net`
Dialup number	(301) 596-1626, login as `guest`, no password
Services provided	Shell/optional menu, FTP, Gopher, Telnet, IRC, news, Mosaic, Lynx. MUD, SLIP/PPP/CSLIP, and much more

CNS

Area code(s)	303, 719, 800
Voice phone	(800) 748-1200
E-mail address	`service@cscns.com`
Dialup number	(719) 520-1700, (303) 758-2656
Services provided	Shell/menu, e-mail, FTP, Telnet, all newsgroups, IRC, 4m, Gopher, WAIS, SLIP, and more

Colorado SuperNet

Area code(s)	303, 719
Voice phone	(303) 273-3471
E-mail address	`info@csn.org` or `help@csn.org`
Services provided	Shell, e-mail, Usenet news, Telnet, FTP, SLIP/PPP, and other Internet tools

Communications Accessibles Montreal, Inc.

Area code(s)	514
Voice phone	(514) 931-0749
E-mail address	`info@cam.org`
Dialup number	(514) 596-2255
Services provided	Shell, FTP, Telnet, Gopher, WAIS, WWW, IRC, Hytelnet, SLIP/CSLIP/PPP, news

CRL

Area code(s)	213, 310, 404, 415, 510, 602, 707, 800

Voice phone	(415) 837-5300
E-mail address	`support@crl.com`
Dialup number	(415) 705-6060, login as `newuser`, no password
Services provided	Shell, e-mail, Usenet, UUCP, FTP, Telnet, SLIP/PPP, and more

CTS Network Services (CTSnet)

Area code(s)	619
Voice phone	(619) 637-3737
E-mail address	`support@cts.com`
Dialup number	(619) 637-3660
Services provided	Shell, e-mail, Usenet, FTP, Telnet, Gopher, IRC, MUD, SLIP/PPP, and more

CyberGate

Area code(s)	305
Voice phone	(305) 428-4283
E-mail address	`sales@gate.net`
Services provided	Shell, e-mail, Usenet, FTP, Telnet, Gopher, Lynx, IRC, SLIP/PPP

Cyberstore Systems Inc.

Area code(s)	604
Voice phone	(604) 526-3373
E-mail address	`info@cyberstore.ca`
Dialup number	(604) 526-3676, login as `guest`
Services provided	E-mail, Usenet, FTP, Telnet, Gopher, WAIS, WWW, IRC, SLIP/PPP

DataFlux Systems Limited

Area code(s)	604
Voice phone	(604) 744-4553
E-mail address	`info@dataflux.bc.ca`
Services provided	Shell, e-mail, Usenet, FTP, Telnet, Gopher, WAIS, WWW, IRC, SLIP/PPP

Data Basix

Area code(s)	602
Voice phone	(602) 721-1988
E-mail address	`info@data.basix.com`
Services provided	Shell, Usenet, FTP, Telnet

Data Tech Canada

Area code(s)	519
Voice phone	(519) 473-5694
E-mail address	`info@dt-can.com`
Dialup number	(519) 473-7685
Services provided	Shell, e-mail, Usenet, FTP, Telnet, Gopher, WAIS, WWW

Delphi

Area code(s)	617, SprintNet, Tymnet
Voice phone	(617) 491-3393
E-mail address	`info@delphi.com`
Dialup number	(617) 492-9600
Services provided	Gopher, FTP, e-mail, Usenet, Telnet

Digital Express Group (Digex)

Area code(s)	301, 410, 609, 703, 714, 908, 909
Voice phone	(800) 969-9090
E-mail address	`info@digex.net`
Dialup number	(301) 220-0258, (410) 605-2700, (609) 348-6203, (703) 281-7997, (714) 261-5201, (908) 937-9481, (909) 222-2204, login as `new`
Services provided	Shell, SLIP/PPP, e-mail, newsgroups, Telnet, FTP, IRC, Gopher, WAIS, and more

Echo

Area code(s)	212, 718
Voice phone	(212) 255-3839
E-mail address	`info@echonyc.com`
Dialup number	(212) 989-3382
Services provided	Conferencing, e-mail, shell, complete Internet access including Telnet, FTP, SLIP/PPP

Eskimo North

Area code(s)	206
E-mail address	`nanook@eskimo.com`
Dialup number	(206) 367-3837
Services provided	Shell, Telnet, FTP, IRC, Archie, Gopher, Hytelnet, WWW, Lynx, and more

Evergreen Internet

Area code(s)	602, 702, 801
Voice phone	(602) 230-9339
E-mail address	`evergreen@libre.com`
Services provided	Shell, FTP, Telnet, SLIP, PPP, others

Freelance Systems Programming

Area code(s)	513
Voice phone	(513) 254-7246
E-mail address	`fsp@dayton.fsp.com`
Dialup number	(513) 258-7745
Services provided	Telnet, FTP, FSP, Lynx, WWW, Archie, Gopher, Usenet, e-mail, and more

Gateway to the World

Area code(s)	305
Voice phone	(305) 670-2930
E-mail address	`m.jansen@gate.com`
Dialup number	(305) 670-2929
Services provided	Dial-up Internet access

Global Enterprise Services, Inc.

Area code(s)	609, 800
Voice phone	(800) 358-4437
E-mail address	`market@jvnc.net`
Services provided	Dial-up Internet access

HoloNet

Area code(s)	510, PSINet, Tymnet
Voice phone	(510) 704-0160
E-mail address	`support@holonet.net`

Dialup number	(510) 704-1058
Services provided	Complete Internet access

Hookup Communication Corporation

Area code(s)	519, Canada-wide
Voice phone	(800) 363-0400
E-mail address	`info@hookup.net`
Services provided	Shell, e-mail, Usenet, FTP, Telnet, Gopher, WAIS, WWW, IRC, Hytelnet, Archie, SLIP/PPP

Institute for Global Communications (IGC)

Area code(s)	415
Voice phone	(415) 442-0220
E-mail address	`support@igc.apc.org`
Dialup number	(415) 322-0284
Services provided	E-mail, Telnet, FTP, Gopher, Archie, Veronica, WAIS, SLIP/PPP

InterAccess Co.

Area code(s)	312, 708, 815
Voice phone	(800) 967-1580
E-mail address	`info@interaccess.com`
Dialup number	(708) 671-0237
Services provided	Shell, FTP, Telnet, SLIP/PPP, and more

Internet Online Inc.

Area code(s)	416
Voice phone	(416) 363-8676

E-mail address	`vid@io.org`
Dialup number	(416) 363-3783, login as `new`
Services provided	Shell, e-mail, Usenet, FTP, Telnet, Gopher, IRC, Archie, Hytelnet

Interpath

Area code(s)	919, 910, 704
Voice phone	(800) 849-6305
E-mail address	`info@infopath.net`
Services provided	Full shell for UNIX, SLIP/PPP

Maestro Information Service

Area code(s)	212
Voice phone	(212) 240-9600
E-mail address	`info@maestro.com`
Dialup number	(212) 240-9700, login as `newuser`
Services provided	Shell, e-mail, Usenet, Telnet, FTP, Archie, IRC

MBnet

Area code(s)	204
Voice phone	(204) 474-9590
E-mail address	`info@mbnet.mb.ca`
Dialup number	(204) 275-6132, login as `mbnet` with password `guest`
Services provided	Shell, e-mail, Usenet, FTP, Telnet, Gopher, WAIS, WWW, IRC, Archie, Hytelnet, SLIP/PPP

Meta Network

Area code(s)	703, SprintNet
Voice phone	(703) 243-6622
E-mail address	`info@tmn.com`
Services provided	Shell, e-mail, FTP, Telnet, conferencing

Mindvox

Area code(s)	212, 718
Voice phone	(212) 989-2418
E-mail address	`info@phantom.com`
Dialup number	(212) 989-1550
Services provided	Shell, e-mail, Usenet, FTP, Telnet, Gopher, Archie, IRC, conferencing

Msen

Area code(s)	313, 810, 800
Voice phone	(313) 998-4562
E-mail address	`info-request@msen.com`
Services provided	Shell, e-mail, Telnet, FTP, Usenet, Gopher, IRC, WAIS, SLIP/PPP

MV Communications, Inc.

Area code(s)	603
Voice phone	(603) 429-2223
E-mail address	`info@mv.mv.com`
Dialup number	(603) 424-7428
Services provided	Shell, Usenet, FTP, Telnet, Gopher, WAIS, SLIP/PPP

Neosoft

Area code(s)	713, 504, 314, 800, SprintNet
Voice phone	(713) 684-5969
E-mail address	`info@neosoft.com`
Services provided	Shell, Usenet, FTP, Telnet, Gopher, SLIP/PPP, and others

Netcom On-Line Communications Services

Area code(s)	206, 212, 214, 303, 310, 312, 404, 408, 415, 503, 510, 512, 617, 619, 703, 714, 818, 916
Voice phone	(800) 501-8649
E-mail address	`info@netcom.com`
Dialup number	(206) 547-5992, (212) 354-3870, (214) 753-0045, (303) 758-0101, (310) 842-8835, (312) 380-0340, (404) 303-9765, (408) 261-4700, (408) 459-9851, (415) 328-9940, (415) 985-5650, (503) 626-6833, (510) 274-2900, (510) 426-6610, (510) 865-9004, (512) 206-4950, (617) 237-8600, (619) 234-0524, (703) 255-5951, (714) 708-3800, (818) 585-3400, (916) 965-1371; login as `guest`
Services provided	Shell, e-mail, Usenet, FTP, Telnet, Gopher, IRC, WAIS, SLIP/PPP

North Shore Access

Area code(s)	617
Voice phone	(617) 593-3110
E-mail address	`info@shore.net`

Dialup number	(617) 593-4557, login as `new`
Services provided	Shell, FTP, Telnet, Gopher, Archie, SLIP/PPP

Nuance Network Services

Area code(s)	205
Voice phone	(205) 533-4296
E-mail address	`info@nuance.com`
Services provided	Shell, Usenet, FTP, Telnet, Gopher, SLIP/PPP

OARNet

Area code(s)	614
Voice phone	(800) 627-8101
E-mail address	`info@oar.net`
Services provided	Shell, SLIP/PPP

Olympus

Area code(s)	206
Voice phone	(206) 385-0464
E-mail address	`info@olympus.net`
Services provided	Shell, FTP, Telnet, Gopher

Panix Public Access UNIX and Internet

Area code(s)	212, 516
Voice phone	(212) 787-6160
E-mail address	`info@panix.com`
Dialup number	(212) 787-3100, (516) 626-7863, login as `newuser`
Services provided	Shell, Usenet, FTP, Telnet, Gopher, Archie, WWW, WAIS, SLIP/PPP

Pipeline

Area code(s)	212
Voice phone	(212) 267-3636
E-mail address	`infobot@pipeline.com`
Dialup number	(212) 267-6432, login as `guest`
Services provided	Pipeline for Windows software, e-mail, Usenet, Gopher, Telnet, Archie, FTP, WAIS

Portal Communications Company

Area code(s)	408, SprintNet
Voice phone	(408) 973-9111
E-mail address	`info@portal.com`
Services provided	Shell, e-mail, Usenet, FTP, Telnet, Gopher, IRC, SLIP/PPP

PSI

Area code(s)	North America, Europe, and Pacific Basin; send e-mail to `numbers-info@psi.com` for list
Voice phone	(703) 709-0300
E-mail address	`all-info@psi.com`
Services provided	Complete Internet services

Teleport

Area code(s)	503, 206
Voice phone	(503) 223-4245
E-mail address	`info@teleport.com`
Dialup number	(503) 220-1016
Services provided	Shell, e-mail, Usenet, FTP, Telnet, Gopher, SLIP/PPP

Telerama

Area code(s)	412
Voice phone	(412) 481-3505
E-mail address	`sysop@telerama.lm.com`
Dialup number	(412) 481-4644
Services provided	Shell, e-mail, Telnet, Usenet, FTP, Telnet, Gopher, IRC, SLIP/PPP

Texas Metronet

Area code(s)	214, 817
Voice phone	(214) 705-2900
E-mail address	`info@metronet.com`
Dialup number	(214) 705-2901, (817) 261-1127; login as `info`, with password `info`
Services provided	Shell, e-mail, Usenet, FTP, Telnet, Gopher, IRC, SLIP/PPP

UUNorth Incorporated

Area code(s)	416
Voice phone	(416) 225-8649
E-mail address	`uunorth@north.net`
Dialup number	(416) 221-0200, login as `new`
Services provided	E-mail, Usenet, FTP, Telnet, Gopher, WAIS, WWW, IRC, Archie, SLIP/PPP

VNet Internet Access, Inc.

Area code(s)	704, public data network
Voice phone	(800) 377-3282
E-mail address	`info@vnet.net`

Dialup number	(704) 347-8839, login as `new`
Services provided	Shell, e-mail, Usenet, FTP, Telnet, Gopher, IRC, SLIP/PPP, UUCP

The WELL

Area code(s)	415, CompuServe Packet Network
Voice phone	(415) 332-4335
E-mail address	`info@well.sf.ca.us`
Dialup number	(415) 332-6106, login as `newuser`
Services provided	Shell, e-mail, Usenet, FTP, Telnet, conferencing

Wimsey Information Services

Area code(s)	604
Voice phone	(604) 936-8649
E-mail address	`admin@wimsey.com`
Services provided	Shell, e-mail, Usenet, FTP, Telnet, Gopher, WAIS, WWW, IRC, Archie, SLIP/PPP

The World

Area code(s)	508, 617, CompuServe Packet Network
Voice phone	(617) 739-0202
E-mail address	`office@world.std.com`
Dialup number	(617) 739-9753, login as `new`
Services provided	Shell, e-mail, Usenet, FTP, Telnet, Gopher, WAIS, WWW, IRC

XNet Information Systems

Area code(s)	708
Voice phone	(708) 983-6064
E-mail address	`info@xnet.com`
Dialup number	(708) 983-6435, (708) 882-1101
Services provided	Shell, e-mail, Usenet, FTP, Telnet, Gopher, Archie, IRC, SLIP/PPP, UUCP

A

Australia

Aarnet

Voice phone	+61 6-249-3385
E-mail address	`aarnet@aarnet.edu.au`

Connect.com.au

Area code(s)	02, 03, 06, 07, 08, 09
Voice phone	+61 3-528-2239
E-mail address	`info@interconnect.com.au`
Services provided	Shell, FTP, Telnet, PPP, Gopher, WAIS

Germany

Contributed Software

Voice phone	+49 30-694-69-07
E-mail address	`info@contrib.de`
Dialup number	+49 30-694-60-55, login as `guest` or `gast`

Individual Network

Voice phone	+49 2131 64190
E-mail address	`in-info@individual.net`

Inter Networking System (INS)

Voice phone	+49 2305 356505
E-mail address	`info@ins.net`

Netherlands

Knoware

E-mail address	`info@knoware.nl`
Dialup number	030 896775

NetLand

Voice phone	020 6943664
E-mail address	`info@netland.nl`
Dialup number	020 6940350, login as `new` or `info`

Simplex

E-mail address	`simplex@simplex.nl`
Dialup number	020 6653388, login as `new` or `info`

New Zealand

Actrix

Voice phone	(04) 389-6316
E-mail address	`john@actrix.gen.nz`

Switzerland

SWITCH—Swiss Academic and Research Network

Voice phone	+41 1 268 1515
E-mail address	`postmaster@switch.ch`

United Kingdom

Almac

Voice phone	+44 0324-665371
E-mail	address`alastair.mcintyre@almac.co.uk`

Cix

Voice phone	+44 49 2641 961
E-mail address	`cixadmin@cix.compulink.co.uk`

Demon Internet Limited

Voice phone	081-349-0063 (London) 031-552-0344 (Edinburgh)
E-mail address	`internet@demon.net`
Services provided	SLIP/PPP accounts

The Direct Connection (UK)

Voice phone	+44 (0)81 317 0100
E-mail address	`helpdesk@dircon.cu.uk`
Dialup number	+44 (0)81 317 2222

APPENDIX B

Information About the Internet, on the Internet

You will find information about the Internet and its services in just about every online nook and cranny imaginable. This appendix lists several hundred (but certainly not all) Internet documents, services, and archives; it should give you a taste of the kinds of worthwhile information that are available on the Net.

The information in this appendix is adapted from the document "Information Sources: The Internet and Computer-Mediated Communication," by John December (`decemj@rpi.edu`). The complete document (which is over 50 single-spaced, typewritten pages and is too long to reproduce here) lists pointers to information describing the Internet, computer networks, and issues related to computer-mediated communication. It is available by anonymous FTP.

```
ftp.rpi.edu:/pub/communications/internet-cmc.txt
```

Here is the first section, "The Internet and its Services," from December's document. This section lists information about the

Internet, the services available on it, and topics related to computer networking.

All of the following items are listed in the form

Item Name
Access_Method Parameters

The Item Name is a short name describing the information or service. Access Method describes how you can access the document or service by one of the following methods: e-mail, finger, FTP, Gopher, http, Telnet, Usenet news, or WAIS. Parameters as follows give further access information depending on the access method:

e-mail address. "message body"

finger address. *:port#*

FTP. *host:/path-to-directory/filename*
(All FTP access uses the login name anonymous unless stated otherwise.)

Gopher. *host*

http. *host :port /path-to-directory/filename*

Usenet news. *newsgroup-name*

Telnet. *host port# login-name*

WAIS. *host:/path*

Internet Descriptions

New User Introduction/Motivation

Gold in Networks!
`ftp nic.merit.edu:/documents/fyi/fyi_10.txt`

Hitchhiker's Guide
`ftp nic.merit.edu:/documents/rfc/rfc1118.txt`

Internet
`http www.lysator.liu.se`
`:7500/ etexts/the_internet.html`

Internet Index
`ftp crl.dec.com:/pub/misc/internet-index.txt`

New User's Questions
`ftp nic.merit.edu:/documents/fyi/fyi_04.txt`

Surfing the Internet
ftp nysernet.org:/pub/resources/guides/surfing.2.0.3.txt

What Is the Internet?
ftp nic.merit.edu:/documents/fyi/fyi_20.txt

Internet Services FAQ
ftp rtfm.mit.edu:/pub/usenet/news.answers/internet-services/faq

Comprehensive Guides

AARnet Guide
ftp aarnet.edu.au:/pub/resource-guide/

AARnet User Guide
ftp aarnet.edu.au:/pub/user-guide/

Big Dummy's Guide
ftp ftp.eff.org:/pub/Net_info/Big_Dummy/

Big Dummy Web
http www.eff.org:/papers/bdgtti/bdgtti.html

Big Dummy Search
http alpha.acast.nova.edu:/cgi-bin/srch.cgi/search/bigdummy/mylist

CERFnet Guide
ftp nic.cerf.net:/cerfnet/cerfnet_info/

Desktop Internet
ftp ftp.uwp.edu:/pub/msdos/dir/

De Presno Guide Gopher
gopher wuecon.wustl.edu:10672/ 11/online

De Presno Guide via FTP
ftp ftp.eunet.no:/pub/text/

De Presno Guide E-mail
mail LISTSERV@vm1.nodak.edu
"get to where"

DDN New User Guide
ftp nic.ddn.mil:/netinfo/nug.doc

InfoPop
ftp ftp.gmu.edu:/library/

Internet Companion (parts)
`ftp ftp.std.com:/OBS/The.Internet.Companion/`

Internet Guide
`ftp sunsite.unc.edu:/pub/docs/about-the-net/libsoft/guide1.txt`

Meng's
`http ccat.sas.upenn.edu:/mengwong/guide.html`

Neophyte
`ftp hydra.uwo.ca:/pub/libsoft/NETWORK_KNOWLEDGE_for_the_NEOPH.TXT`

NSF Resource Guide
`ftp ds.internic.net:/resource-guide/overview`

NWNet Internet Guide
`ftp ftphost.nwnet.net:/user-docs/nusirg/README.nusirg`

NYSERnet Internet Guide
`ftp nysernet.org:/pub/guides/Guide.V.2.2.text`

SURAnet Internet Guide
`ftp ftp.sura.net:/pub/nic/`

SURFnet Guide
`ftp ftp.nic.surfnet.nl:/surfnet/user-support/docs/training/`

Zen/Art of Internet
`ftp csn.org:/pub/net/zen/`

Zen Web
`http sundance.cso.uiuc.edu:/Publications/Other/Zen/zen-1.0_toc.html`

Specialized Guides of General Interest

Agricultural Guide
`ftp sunsite.unc.edu:/pub/docs/about-the-net/libsoft/agguide.dos`

Electric Mystics Guide
`ftp panda1.uottawa.ca:/pub/religion/`

Library Resources
`ftp dla.ucop.edu:/pub/internet/libcat-guide`

BUBL
`gopher bubl.bath.ac.uk`

BUBL Web
`http bubl.bath.ac.uk:/BUBLHOME.html`

Exploring

DOS Internet Kit
`ftp tbone.biol.scarolina.edu:/pub/kit/`

DOS Internet Kit Web
`http tbone.biol.scarolina.edu:/~dean2/kit/kit.html`

Internet Beginner
`ftp oak.oakland.edu:/pub/msdos/info/bgi13.zip`

Internet Cruise
`ftp nic.merit.edu:/resources/`

Internet Explorer's Kit
`ftp sunsite.unc.edu:/pub/docs/about-the-net/libsoft/explorer.doc`

Internet Hunt
`ftp ftp.cni.org:/pub/net-guides/i-hunt/`

Internet Hunt Gopher
`gopher gopher.cic.net`

Internet Navigating
`ftp ubvm.cc.buffalo.edu:/navigate/`

Internet Mining
`ftp ftp.ucdavis.edu:/ucd.netdocs/mining/mining_readme`

Training

Ackerman Tutorial
`ftp s850.mwc.edu:/pub/tutorial`

CBL
`http cbl.leeds.ac.uk`

Compass in Cyberspace
`http www.clark.net:/pub/journalism/brochure.html`

Competencies
`mail listserv@uhupvm1.uh.edu`
`"GET CORBIN PRV4N6"`

DELTA
`http gozer.idbsu.edu:/business/nethome.html`

Discussion Help
`mail rre-request@weber.ucsd.edu`
`Subject`
`archive send courtesy`

Gopherin
`ftp ubvm.cc.buffalo.edu:/gophern/`

Gopherin Course
`gopher wealaka.okgeosurvey1.gov:/11/K12/GOPHERN`

HTML Assistant
`ftp ftp.cs.dal.ca:/htmlasst/`

HTML Developer's
`http oneworld.wa.com:/htmldev/devpage/`
`dev-page.html`

HTML FAQ
`http www.umcc.umich.edu:/~ec/www/html_faq.html`

HTML Guide
`http www.ncsa.uiuc.edu:/demoweb/html-primer.html`

HTML Guide/Flynn
`http www.ucc.ie:/info/net/htmldoc.html`

HTML Tutorial
`http fire.clarkson.edu:/doc/html/htut.html`

HWGUIDE
`ftp sunsite.unc.edu:/pub/docs/about-the-net/`
`libsoft/hwguide.txt`

Intro/Internet
`http uu-gna.mit.edu`
`:8001/ uu-gna/text/internet/index.html`

ITTI
`http info.mcc.ac.uk:/CGU/ITTI/ITTI.html`

LeJeune Course
`ftp pilot.njin.net:/pub/Internet-course/`

Milles
`ftp sluaxa.slu.edu:/pub/millesjg/interlaw.txt`

Mining
`mail 34mjkeq@cmuvm.csv.cmich.edu`

Monsarrat
`ftp wilma.cs.brown.edu:/pub/internet_course.tar.Z`

MOREnet
`ftp ftp.more.net:/pub/nic/training`

Navigating
`ftp ftp.sura.net:/pub/nic/training/`

Navigating
`gopher jake.esu.edu:/11/Help/net_stuff/training`

Net Workbook
`mail listserv@bingvmb.bitnet`
`"GET NETKNOW NEOPHYTE BI-L"`

Newcastle/Tyne
`ftp mailbase.ac.uk:/pub/lists/itti-networks/`
`files/tms-list.txt`

Schneider Bib
`ftp alexia.lis.uiuc.edu:/pub/training.bib`

Start
`ftp sluaxa.slu.edu:/pub/millesjg/newusers.faq`

Syracuse Courses
`http eryx.syr.edu:/bmis/bmis.html`

Trainmat
`gopher trainmat.ncl.ac.uk`

Trainpack
`ftp ftp.ncl.ac.uk:/pub/network-training/README`

Tutorial Gateway
`http www.civeng.carleton.ca:/~nholtz/tut/doc/`
`doc.html`

Wheeler
`ftp s850.mwc.edu:/nettrain/nettrain.00readme`

UNIX tutorials
`gopher jake.esu.edu:/11/Help/Tutorials`

UNIX Help
`http alpha.acast.nova.edu:/Unixhelp/TOP_.html`

UNIX Man Pages
`http nmt.edu:/bin/man`

URL
`gopher gopher.well.sf.ca.us:/00/matrix/internet/curling.up.02`

URL guide
`http www.ncsa.uiuc.edu:/demoweb/url-primer.html`

Usenet and trn
`ftp cs1.presby.edu:/pub/trn-intro/`

UT-Austin
`http rowan.lib.utexas.edu:/handouts/etc/InternetGuides.html`

VAX/VMS Networking
`ftp ftp.temple.edu:/pub/info/help-net/vms-mail.guide`

Windows-Based
`ftp WinFtp.CICA.Indiana.edu`

World/Desktop
`http http1.brunel.ac.uk :8080/ world-on-your-desktop/title.html`

WWW Talk
`http www.cs.princeton.edu:/grad/Dan_Wallach/www-talk/talk0.html`

Administrative/Technical/History

Internet Growth
`ftp tic.com:/matrix/growth/internet/`

Internet Growth/Lottor
`ftp nic.merit.edu:/documents/rfc/rfc1296.txt`

Internet History/ISOC
`gopher gopher.isoc.org:/11/internet/history`

Internet History
`ftp umcc.umich.edu:/pub/users/seraphim/doc/nethist8.txt`

Internet History Collection
`http www.cedar.buffalo.edu:/~kapis-p/Inter.html`

Internet History
`ftp cs.beloit.edu:/Public/Internet/History/`

Internet History Line
`mail timeline@hobbes.mitre.org`

Internet Monthly Report

`ftp nic.merit.edu:/internet/newsletters/internet.monthly.report/`

Internet Maps (Europe)

`ftp eunet.fi:/nic/pub/netinfo/maps/`

Internet Maps (many)

`ftp ftp.uu.net:/inet/maps/`

Internet Maps (NSFNET)

`ftp nic.merit.edu:/maps/`

Internet Maps (SURAnet)

`ftp ftp.sura.net:/pub/maps/`

Internet Size

`ftp ftp.nisc.sri.com:/pub/zone/`

Internet Statistics

`ftp nic.merit.edu:/nsfnet/statistics/`

Web Country Maps

`http www.tue.nl:/maps.html`

Information Repositories

Comprehensive Collections

Merit

`ftp nic.merit.edu:/READ.ME`

Merit Gopher

`gopher nic.merit.edu`

NIC/DDN

`ftp nic.ddn.mil`

Network Information Centers

InterNIC Telnet

`telnet ds.internic.net`

`"guest"`

InterNIC FTP

`ftp ds.internic.net:/pub/InterNIC-info/internic.info`

InterNIC via E-mail

`mail mailserv@internic.net "help"`

InterNIC Gopher

`gopher rs.internic.net`

InterNIC Home Page

`http www.internic.net:/internic.html`

InterNIC DS Web

`http ds.internic.net`

InterNIC Database Services

`ftp ds.internic.net`

InterNIC Reg Services

`ftp rs.internic.net:/netinfo/`

InterNIC Information Sources

`ftp is.internic.net:/infosource/infosource-contents`

Document Series

FYI

`ftp nic.merit.edu:/documents/fyi/`

Internet Drafts

`ftp nic.merit.edu:/documents/internet-drafts/`

Internet Standards

`ftp nic.merit.edu:/documents/std/`

RFC

`ftp nic.merit.edu:/documents/rfc/`

RFC Web

`http www.cis.ohio-state.edu:/hypertext/information/rfc.html`

Internet Home Pages

Duke's NetCom

`http porter.netcom.duke.edu`

EIT

`http www.eit.com:/web/web.html`

Notre Dame

`http www.nd.edu:/NDHomePage/Exploring.html`

Internet Tour
`http www.kei.com:/internet-tour.html`

Internet Web Text
`http www.rpi.edu:/Internet/Guides/decemj/`
`text.html`

Italian Net Tools
`http www.mi.cnr.it:/NIR-IT/NIR-map.html`

GNN's Internet
`http nearnet.gnn.com:/wic/internet.toc.html`

GNN's Internet Center
`http nearnet.gnn.com:/gnn/meta/internet/`
`index.html`

ISOC's Internet Information
`gopher ietf.cnri.reston.va.us:/11/internet`

Naval Research Lab
`http netlab.itd.nrl.navy.mil`

Netlink
`http honor.uc.wlu.edu`
`:1020/`

Nova Links
`http alpha.acast.nova.edu:/start.html`

SLAC
`http slacvm.slac.stanford.edu:/FIND/internet.html`

Stanford
`http med-www.stanford.edu:/hypertext/net/Net.html`

The Net
`http www.ai.mit.edu:/the-net/overview.html`

NCIH
`http www.cnidr.org`
`:5050/ welcome.html`

NMIS
`http nmis03.mit.edu`
`:8001/`

NOSC Page
`http white.nosc.mil:/internet.html`

Tractatus CyberNauticus
`http kaml1.csi.uottawa.ca`
`:3000/ tractatus.html`

Yale

`http www.cs.yale.edu:/HTML/WorldWideWebTop.html`

University of Texas

`http fiat.gslis.utexas.edu:/internet/`
`internet.html`

WWW World Maps

`http wings.buffalo.edu:/world`

WWW European Maps

`http www.tue.nl:/maps.html`

ZGDV

`http zgdv.igd.fhg.de`

Sources of Networking, Computing, and Related Information

ACM Gopher

`gopher acm.org`

ACM WWW Home Page

`http info.acm.org`

ALAWON Archive

`mail listserv@uicvm.uic.edu`
`"send ala-wo filelist"`

ARPA

`http ftp.arpa.mil`

ATP at LLNL

`http www-atp.llnl.gov`

ATM Information

`ftp datanet.tele.fi:/atm`

BITNET Address

`mail listserv@ubvm.bitnet`
`"SHOW ALIAS UBVM"`

BITNET Nodes

`gopher nak.berkeley.edu`
`:4303/ 11/bitnet`

CCAE

`http www.inesc.pt:/inesc/centros/ccae.html`

Cell Relay

`gopher cell-relay.indiana.edu`

CIT
`http logic.stanford.edu:/cit/cit.html`

CMD
`http www.cmd.uu.se`

CNI Gopher
`gopher gopher.cni.org`

CNI Search
`telnet gopher.cni.org`
`"brsuser"`

Cognitive
`http www.gatech.edu:/cogsci/cogsci.html`

CPSR Gopher
`gopher gopher.cpsr.org`

CRG at Nottingham
`http web.cs.nott.ac.uk`

CTR/Columbia
`http www.ctr.columbia.edu:/CUCTR_Home.html`

Communications Res Cen
`http debra.dgbt.doc.ca:/index.html`

CERN
`http www1.cern.ch`

CWI
`http buizerd.cwi.nl:/default.html`

Dern's Information
`gopher gopher.internet.com`
`:2200/ 11/`

EARN Gopher
`gopher gopher.earn.net`

EFF Gopher
`gopher gopher.eff.org`

French INT
`http arctique.int-evry.fr`

Hacking and Phreaking
`http www.ugcs.caltech.edu:/~phd`

HelpNet Archives
`ftp ftp.temple.edu:/pub/info/help-net`

HCI FTP Site
`ftp archive.cis.ohio-state.edu:/pub/hcibib/`

HCI Index/deGraaff
`http www.twi.tudelft.nl:/Local/HCI/HCI-Index.html`

HCI Launching Pad
`http hydra.bgsu.edu:/HCI/`

HPC Centre
`http cs1.soton.ac.uk`

HPCC Office Web Page
`http www.hpcc.gov`

HPCC Gopher
`gopher gopher.hpcc.gov`
`:70/`

HPCWire
`telnet hpcwire.ans.net`

ICBL
`http www.icbl.hw.ac.uk`

IIASA
`gopher /gopher.iiasa.ac.at`

ICSI
`http http://http.icsi.berkeley.edu`

IEEE Gopher
`gopher info.ieee.org`

IEEE Tech
`mail info.new.tech@ieee.org`
`"anything"`

INRIA
`http zenon.inria.fr`
`:8003/`

IRIS
`http www.iris.brown.edu:/iris`

ISOC Gopher
`gopher gopher.isoc.org`

ISI at USC
`http www.isi.edu`

ISS
`http www.iss.nus.sg`

ISRI
`http www.isri.unlv.edu`

Introducing the Internet
`ftp nic.merit.edu:/introducing.the.internet/`

Library of Congress
`ftp ftp.loc.gov:/pub/iug/`

LIT
`http litsun.epfl.ch`
`:80/`

Mem U of Newfoundland
`gopher cwis.ucs.mun.ca:/11/`
`Venturing%20into%20the%20Internet`

MetaCenter
`http www.ncsa.uiuc.edu:/General/MetaCenter/`
`MetaCenterHome.html`

Meta Net Gopher
`gopher tmn.com`

MSU Net and DB
`gopher burrow.cl.msu.edu`

MSEN Gopher
`gopher gopher.msen.com`

NEARnet
`ftp nic.near.net:/docs/`

NECTEC
`http www.nectec.or.th:/nectec.html`

NCHPC
`http www.ncsa.uiuc.edu:/General/NCHPCHome.html`

NCSA
`http www.ncsa.uiuc.edu:/General/NCSAHome.html`

NIST Web Page
`http www.nist.gov:/welcome.html`

NIST Gopher
`gopher gopher-server.nist.gov`

NPAC
`http minerva.npac.syr.edu:/home.html`

NRL AITB
`http www.ait.nrl.navy.mil:/home.html`

NSF Gopher
`gopher stis.nsf.gov`
`:70/ 11`

NTTC
`http iridium.nttc.edu:/nttc.html`

NYSERnet
`ftp nysernet.org:/pub/resources/guides/`

Ohio Supercomputer
`http www.osc.edu:/welcome.html`

OPTOLINK
`ftp mom.spie.org`

OSS
`gopher gopher.oss.net`

Pitt SC
`http pscinfo.psc.edu`

PSGnet/RAInet
`gopher gopher.psg.com`

RICIS
`http http://rbse.jsc.nasa.gov`

RIPE Gopher
`gopher gopher.ripe.net`

RIPE Web
`http www.ripe.net`

Sandia
`http www.cs.sandia.gov:/pub/WWW/`
`Sandia_directory.html`

SDSC
`http gopher.sdsc.edu:/Home.html`

SFI
`http santafe.edu`

Singapore DMC
`http king.ncb.gov.sg`

Software Tool and Die
`gopher ftp.std.com`

SRI's Network Information
`ftp sri.com:/netinfo/`

SURAnet
`ftp ftp.sura.net:/pub/README`

SWITCH Information
`ftp nic.switch.ch:/info_service/`

Telecomm Archives
`ftp lcs.mit.edu:/telecom-archives/`

Telecom Information
`gopher unix5.nysed.gov:/11/TelecommInfo`

Telecomm Research
`ftp ftp.ctr.columbia.edu:/CTR-Research/`

TMN
`gopher tmn.com`

UNC's Sunsite
`ftp sunsite.unc.edu:/pub/docs/about-the-net/`

UniForum
`http www.uniforum.org`

USENET Repository
`ftp rtfm.mit.edu:/pub/usenet/`

USENET Periodic Postings
`ftp rtfm.mit.edu:/pub/usenet/news.answers/`
`periodic-postings/`

UUCP
`gopher agate.berkeley.edu`
`:4324/ 1uumaps`

UUNET Archive
`ftp ftp.uu.net:/uunet-info/`

UWO's NIC
`ftp julian.uwo.ca:/nic/`

Washington and Lee
`gopher liberty.uc.wlu.edu`

WATERS
`http www.cs.odu.edu:/WATERS/WATERS-GS.html`

WELL Matrix
`gopher gopher.well.sf.ca.us:/11/matrix`

Services and Tools

Information and Services Lists

Cyberpoet Guide
ftp ftp.eff.org:/pub/Net_info/Cyber/cyberpoet.gvc

Cyberspace Points
ftp netcom10.netcom.com:/pub/consensus/www/CyberStart_TOC.html

Electronic Information
http cbl.leeds.ac.uk:/nikos/doc/repository.html

Fishnet
http www.cs.washington.edu:/homes/pauld/fishnet/

Freeside FAQ
http www.seas.upenn.edu:/~mengwong/fsfaq.html

Gopher Jewels
gopher cwis.usc.edu:/11/Other_Gophers_and_Information_Resources/Gophers_by_Subject/Gopher_Jewels

Gopher Jewels Web
http galaxy.einet.net:/GJ/index.html

Gopher Jewels
ftp usc.edu:/pub/gopher/

Gopher Jewels
http galaxy.einet.net:/GJ/index.html

Gopher Jewels Information
mail listproc@einet.net
"get gopher-lists.txt"

Hot/Cool List
http 141.214.4.176:/uwi/reviews.html

Houh's People
http tns-www.lcs.mit.edu:/people/hhh/people.html

Internet Handbook
ftp sri.com:/netinfo/internet-technology-handbook-contents

Internet/Disk
http www.eff.org:/pub/Publications/CuD/Internet_on_a_Disk

Information Sources
`ftp ftp.rpi.edu:/pub/communications/internet-cmc.readme`

Internet Meta-Index
`http www.ncsa.uiuc.edu:/SDG/Software/Mosaic/MetaIndex.html`

Internet Reviews
`gopher jupiter.willamette.edu:/11/library/reviews`

Joel's List
`http www.cen.uiuc.edu:/~jj9544/index.html`

MaasInfo Indexes
`ftp ftp.unt.edu:/pub/articles/maas/maasinfo.files`

May List
`ftp aug3.augsburg.edu:/files/bbs_lists/nal006.txt`

Must Have List
`ftp pilot.njin.net:/pub/Internet-course/musthave-list.txt`

Networking Overview
`http web.doc.ic.ac.uk:80/ bySubject/Networking.html`

Planet Earth
`http white.nosc.mil:/info.html`

Pop FTP
`gopher gopher.tc.umn.edu:70/ 11/FTP`

Smith's BigFun List
`ftp owl.nstn.ns.ca:/pub/netinfo/bigfun.txt`

Stanford WWW Links
`http www.stanford.edu:/otherLinks.html`

ThesisNet FAQ
`http www.seas.upenn.edu:/~mengwong/thesisfaq.html#ftp`

Thousand/Sites
`http legendre.ucsd.edu:/Research/Fisher/Home/randomjump.html`

Tong's Collection
http www.ugcs.caltech.edu:/~werdna/info.html

Yale Overview
http www.cs.yale.edu:/HTML/WorldWideWebTop.html

Yanoff's Services List
ftp csd4.csd.uwm.edu:/pub/inet.services.txt

Yanoff List HTML
ftp csd4.csd.uwm.edu:/pub/inet.services.html

What's New Gopher
gopher liberty.uc.wlu.edu:/11/internet/new_internet

Lists of Tools

Best of Web
http wings.buffalo.edu:/contest

GNN's Tools
http nearnet.gnn.com:/gnn/meta/internet/res/tools/index.html

Internet Browsers
http life.anu.edu.au:/links/syslib.html

Internet Tools EARN
ftp ns.ripe.net:/earn/earn-resource-tool-guide.txt

Internet Tools/EARN HTML
http www.huji.ac.il:/www_help/earn.html

Internet Tools NIR
ftp mailbase.ac.uk:/pub/lists/nir/files/nir.status.report

Internet Tools/December HTML
http www.rpi.edu:/Internet/Guides/internet-tools.html

Internet Tools/December
ftp ftp.rpi.edu:/pub/communications/internet-tools

Internet Systems UNITE
ftp mailbase.ac.uk:/pub/lists/unite/files/systems-list.txt

Web-Searching Tools

Archie via Web
`http hoohoo.ncsa.uiuc.edu:/archie.html`

Gopher Jewels Search
`http galaxy.einet.net:/gopher/gopher.html`

GNA Meta-Library
`http uu-nna.mit.edu`
`:8001/ uu-nna/meta-library/index.html`

Hyper-Index
`http flick.lerc.nasa.gov:/cgi-bin/h-index/`
`query-index-form`

HTML Analyzer
`http www.gatech.edu:/pitkow/html_analyzer/`
`README.html`

JumpStation
`http www.stir.ac.uk:/jsbin/js`

NorthStar
`http comics.scs.unr.edu`
`:7000/ top.html?`

SUSI
`http web.nexor.co.uk:/susi/susi.html`

WWW Catalog
`http cui_www.unige.ch:/w3catalog`

WWW Nomad
`http www.rns.com:/www_index/intro.html`

WWW Search Engines
`http cui_www.unige.ch:/meta-index.html`

WWW Worm
`http www.cs.colorado.edu:/home/mcbryan/WWWW.html`

WWW Wanderers
`http web.nexor.co.uk:/mak/doc/robots/robots.html`

Services

Anonymous Post
`mail anonymus+ping@tygra.michigan.com`
`"help"`

Anonymous Post

```
mail help@anon.penet.fi
"help"
```

Anonymous Remail

```
mail remail@tamsun.tamu.edu
Subject
remail help
```

BITFTP

```
mail Bitftp@PUCC.Princeton.edu
"help 13-Dec-93"
```

CARL Systems

```
telnet database.carl.org
```

Correct Time/NBS

```
telnet india.colorado.edu
13
```

ENewsstand

```
telnet enews.com
"enews"
```

ENewsstand Gopher

```
gopher gopher.internet.com
```

E-mail FTP

```
mail ftpmail@decwrl.dec.com
"help"
```

E-mail Gopher

```
mail gophermail@ncc.go.jp
"help"
```

E-mail Gopher

```
mail gophermail@calvin.edu
"help"
```

E-mail WWW

```
mail listserv@info.cern.ch
"www URL"
```

E-mail Usenet

```
mail hierarchy-group-name@cs.utexas.edu
Subject
Your Subject "Your Contents"
```

FAXNET

```
mail info@awa.com
"help"
```

FAX FAQ

`ftp rtfm.mit.edu:/pub/usenet/news.answers/`
`internet-services/fax-faq`

Finger Database

`finger help@dir.su.oz.au`

Hytelnet

`telnet telnet "hytelnet"`

Internet Marketing

`mail market@internet.com`
`"send market info""`

Knowbot

`telnet info.cnri.reston.va.us`
`185`

Mail Name Server

`mail dns@grasp.insa-lyon.fr`
`"help"`

Softlock

`mail Info@SoftLock.com`
`"send info"`

WorldWindow

`telnet library.wustl.edu`

Networking

Amateur Radio Packet

`ftp ftp.std.com:/pub/hamradio/faq/packet.faq`

Andrew Consortium

`http www.cs.cmu.edu`
`:8001/ afs/cs.cmu.edu/project/atk-ftp/web/`
`andrew-home.html`

ATM Research

`http netlab.itd.nrl.navy.mil:/ATM.html`

BITNET Introduction

`mail listserv@bitnic.educom.edu`
`"send BITNET INTRO"`

BITNET Nodes with Internet Addresses

`mail listserv@bitnic.educom.edu`
`"get internet listing"`

CERT
`ftp cert.org:/pub/`

DoD Security
`ftp asc.dtic.dla.mil:/pub/tafim/`

FidoNet Guide
`gopher digital.cosn.org:/11/Networking%20Information/Reference/The%20BIG`

Ethernet Page
`http mojo.ots.utexas.edu:/ethernet/ethernet-home.html`

FidoNet News
`ftp rtfm.mit.edu:/pub/usenet/comp.org.fidonet/`

FidoNet Nodes
`ftp genome.wi.mit.edu:/wais-sources/fidonet-nodelist.src`

FidoNet Gateway
`ftp csn.org:/pub/mail/internet.fidonet`

Hypercard TCP/IP
`http ericmorgan.lib.ncsu.edu:/staff/morgan/papers/tcp-communications/tcp-communications.html`

INET 93
`ftp mordor.stanford.edu:/pub/inet93/`

International Connect
`ftp ftp.cs.wisc.edu:/connectivity_table/`

Internet Country Codes
`ftp rtfm.mit.edu:/pub/usenet/news.answers/mail/country-codes`

Internet Domain Names
`ftp nic.merit.edu:/documents/rfc/rfc1394.txt`

Internet/Networking EINet
`http galaxy.einet.net:/Reference-and-Interdisciplinary-Information/Internet-and-Networking.html`

Internet Root Domain
`ftp ftp.rs.internic.net:/domain/`

Internet Security
`ftp nic.merit.edu:/cise/gao8957.txt`

InterNetwork Mail
`ftp csd4.csd.uwm.edu:/pub/internetwork-mail-guide`

Intro TCP/IP
`ftp nic.merit.edu:/introducing.the.internet/`
`intro.to.ip`

ISDN Information
`ftp info.bellcore.com:/pub/ISDN/`

JANET
`http gala.jnt.ac.uk`

List of FTP Sites
`ftp ftp.gsfc.nasa.gov:/pub/ftp-list`

Networking EInet
`http galaxy.einet.net:/galaxy/Engineering-and-`
`Technology/Computer-Technology/Networking.html`

PSGnet/RAInet Information
`gopher rain.psg.com`

NREN Information
`ftp nic.merit.edu:/nren/INDEX.nren`

NREN Recompetition
`ftp nic.merit.edu:/cise/recompete/INDEX.recompete`

N+I 94
`http programs.interop.com`

RSA Information
`ftp rsa.com`

SDSC Appl Net Res Group
`ftp ftp.sdsc.edu:/pub/sdsc/anr/README`

Sprintlink
`ftp ftp.sprintlink.net`

Sprintlink Gopher
`gopher ftp.sprintlink.net`

USENET Maps
`ftp gatekeeper.dec.com:/pub/maps/`

WWIV
`gopher gopher.technet.sg`
`:2100/ 11/pub/msdos/wwiv`

Accessing Networks

BBS Internet List

ftp sunsite.unc.edu:/pub/docs/about-the-net/libsoft/internet_bbs.txt

Community Networks

ftp ftp.netcom.com:/pub/amcgee/community/communet.msg

Connecting to Internet

ftp nic.merit.edu:/documents/fyi/fyi_16.txt

DLIST

mail dlist@ora.com

"Please send DLIST"

Freenet Papers

ftp alfred.carleton.ca:/pub/freenet/working.papers/

FSLIST

ftp freedom.nmsu.edu:/pub/docs/fslist/

GNET Archive

ftp dhvx20.csudh.edu:/global_net/

Internet Access Guide

ftp nic.merit.edu:/introducing.the.internet/access.guide

Internet Access

ftp sluaxa.slu.edu:/pub/millesjg/internet.access

Internet Modem

ftp dla.ucop.edu:/pub/internet/dial-access

Internet Providers

ftp sri.com:/netinfo/internet-access-providers-alphabetical-listing.txt

Internet Providers Non-US

ftp sri.com:/netinfo/internet-access-providers-non-us.txt

K12 Access

ftp ftp.cc.berkeley.edu:/k12/README

K12 Gopher

gopher gopher.cic.net:/11/cicnet-gophers/k12-gopher

NII
http sunsite.unc.edu:/nii

Network Startup
ftp ftp.psg.com:/README

PDIAL
ftp rtfm.mit.edu:/pub/usenet/news.answers/pdial

PDIAL Search
http www.commerce.net:/directories/news/
inet.prov.dir.html

NIXPUB
ftp rtfm.mit.edu:/pub/usenet/alt.bbs/
Nixpub_Posting_(Long)

Registering on the Net
ftp nic.merit.edu:/documents/rfc/rfc1400.txt

Rural Nets/GAIN Report
ftp nysernet.org:/pub/gain/final_report

Rural Nets
mail rjacot@cic.net

Rural Datafication Gopher
gopher gopher.cic.net:/11/cicnet-gophers/
ruraldata-project

Rural Datafication Web
http www.cic.net:/rd-home.html

SEA Community Network
ftp atlas.ce.washington.edu:/pub/seattle-
community-network/

Information Retrieval and Dissemination

Advertising
ftp ftp.cni.org:/CNI/wg.docs/modernization/
adpaper-draft.txt

Bibl-Mode
ftp ftp.maths.tcd.ie:/pub/bosullvn/elisp/

Carl/Uncover
telnet database.carl.org

Cataloging Internet Res

`mail listserv@uhupvm1.uh.edu`
`"get caplan prv4n2"`

CGI

`http hoohoo.ncsa.uiuc.edu:/cgi/overview.html`

CHAT

`ftp debra.dgbt.doc.ca:/pub/chat/`

CHAT

`telnet debra.doc.ca`

CIIR

`http ciir.cs.umass.edu`

CNI

`ftp ftp.cni.org:/CNI/`

DIMUND FTP

`ftp dimund.umd.edu:/pub/`

CNI TopNode Project

`ftp ftp.cni.org:/CNI/projects/topnode/`

CNI Gopher

`gopher gopher.cni.org`

CNIDR Gopher

`gopher gopher.cnidr.org`

CNIDR Web Page

`http cnidr.org:/welcome.html`

Doc Center

`http doccenter.com:/doccenter/home.html`

DA-CLOD

`http schiller.wustl.edu:/DACLOD/daclod`

DIMUND

`gopher dimund.umd.edu`

IAFA

`ftp archive.cc.mcgill.ca:/pub/Network/iafa/`
`charter`

Information Provider

`http info.cern.ch:/hypertext/WWW/Provider/`
`Overview.html`

Integrated Information

`ftp venera.isi.edu:/internet-drafts/draft-ietf-`
`iiir-vision-01.txt`

Interpedia

`http www.hmc.edu:/www/interpedia/index.html`

IRLP

`http www.cs.colorado.edu:/home/gc/cs/genbbb_wwww.html`

Library Special

`ftp vm1.nodak.edu:/nnews/nnews.1993-10`

Mailbase

`http mailbase.ac.uk:/welcome.html`

NIR Archives

`ftp mailbase.ac.uk:/pub/lists/nir/`

NIR Gopher

`gopher mailbase.ac.uk`

OCLC Research

`ftp ftp.rsch.oclc.org:/pub/internet_resources_project/report/`

PCP

`http pespmc1.vub.ac.be:/RELATED.html`

Publishing

`http www.ifi.uio.no:/~terjen/WWWauthoring/abstract.html`

Resource Transponders

`ftp venera.isi.edu:/internet-drafts/draft-ietf-iiir-transponders-01.txt`

Retrieval Success

`ftp mailbase.ac.uk:/pub/lists/unite/files/internet-stories.txt`

Riddle

`ftp ftp.cwi.nl:/pub/RIDDLE/`

Standards + Z39.50

`http cnidr.org:/cnidr_papers/info.html`

Uniform Resources

`ftp info.cern.ch:/pub/ietf/url3.txt`

UNITE Archive

`ftp mailbase.ac.uk:/pub/lists/unite/`

URN

`ftp venera.isi.edu:/internet-drafts/draft-ietf-uri-resource-names-01.txt`

URI Archive
ftp archives.cc.mcgill.ca:/pub/mailing-lists/
uri-archive

URL
ftp info.cern.ch:/pub/www/doc/url-spec.txt

UWI
http zapruder.pds.med.umich.edu:/uwi/
uwi-info.html

WISE
http zgdv.igd.fhg.de:/zgdv/Dept.uig/
research.html#WISE

WWW 94
http www1.cern.ch:/WWW94/Welcome.html

Directories

Commercial List
http tns-www.lcs.mit.edu:/commerce.html

CSOIRG Home Page
http http2.sils.umich.edu:/~lou/chome.html

Dartmouth Merged SIGL
ftp dartcms1.dartmouth.edu:/siglists/

Electronic Conferences
ftp ksuvxa.kent.edu:/library/acadlist.readme

Electronic Conferences
http www.austin.unimelb.edu.au
:800/ 1s/acad

Electronic Conferences
gopher info.monash.edu.au:/11/Other/lists

Electronic Zines/Jrl
http www.acns.nwu.edu:/ezines

Electronic Journals
ftp ftp.cni.org:/pub/net-guides/strangelove/

Electronic Magazines
ftp etext.archive.umich.edu:/pub/Zines/

Electronic Resources
gopher watserv2.uwaterloo.ca:/11/servers

EZines List
`ftp netcom.com:/pub/johnl/zines/e-zine-list`

EZines Web
`ftp netcom.com:/pub/johnl/zines/e-zine-list.html`

EInet Galaxy
`http galaxy.einet.net:/galaxy.html`

Finding Lists
`mail listserv@vm1.nodak.edu`
`"get NEW-LIST wouters"`

Free-Nets Home Page
`http jester.usask.ca:/~scottp/free.html`

Free Databases
`ftp idiom.berkeley.ca.us:/pub/free-databases`

Interactive Yellow Pages
`mail tuna@netcom.com`
`Subject`
`yellow pages "YOUR EMAIL ADDRESS"`

IYP
`ftp ftp.netcom.com://pub/tuna/`

Internet Trainers/Consultants
`gopher gopher.fonorola.net:/00/`
`Internet%20Business%20Journal/`
`Directory_of_Trainers_and_Consultants`

Interest Groups List
`ftp ftp.nisc.sri.com:/netinfo/interest-groups.txt`

Japanese
`http fuji.stanford.edu:/japan_information/`
`japan_information_guide.html`

Library Access Script
`ftp sonoma.edu:/pub/libs.tar`

Library Guide
`ftp ftp.utdallas.edu:/pub/staff/billy/libguide`

Library Catalogs Noonan
`ftp sunsite.unc.edu:/pub/docs/about-the-net/`
`libsoft/guide2.txt`

Library Catalogs St Geo
`ftp nic.cerf.net:/internet/resources/`
`library_catalog/`

Nonprofits
`http www.ai.mit.edu:/people/ellens/non.html`

Online Books
`http www.cs.cmu.edu`
`:8001/ Web/books.html`

Online Bibs
`http www.cs.cmu.edu`
`:8001/ Web/bibliographies.html`

Online Journals
`http www.cs.cmu.edu`
`:8001/ Web/journals.html`

Online Libraries
`http www.cs.cmu.edu`
`:8001/ Web/e-libraries.html`

PAML
`http www.ii.uib.no:/~magnus/paml.html`

Publisher's Catalogs
`http jester.usask.ca:/~scottp/publish.html`

Reference Sources
`gopher nfo.lib.uh.edu`

Scholarly Societies Gophers
`gopher watserv2.uwaterloo.ca:/11/servers/campus/`
`scholars`

Subject Guides
`ftp una.hh.lib.umich.edu:/inetdirs/`

Subject Guides
`gopher una.hh.lib.umich.edu:/11/inetdirs`

Subject Guides
`http www.lib.umich.edu:/chhome.html`

Subject Lists
`gopher info.anu.edu.au`
`:70/ 11/elibrary/lc`

Technical Reports
`ftp daneel.rdt.monash.edu.au:/pub/techreports/`

Virtual Tourist
`http wings.buffalo.edu:/world`

WAIS Sources
ftp kirk.bond.edu.au:/pub/Bond_Uni/doc/wais/readme

WAIS Directory of Servers
wais cnidr.org:/210 directory-of-servers?

WAIS Databases
http kaml1.csi.uottawa.ca:3000/ wais.html

WWW Catalogues
http www.cs.colorado.edu:/homes/mcbryan/public_html/bb/summary.html

WWW Sites
http www.mit.edu:8001/ afs/sipb/user/mkgray/ht/compre3.html

Communication

Audio

Berklee
gopher gopher.berklee.edu

CERL
http datura.cerl.uiuc.edu

Clips
http www.eecs.nwu.edu:/~jmyers/other-sounds.html

Internet Sound
ftp ftp.cwi.nl:/pub/audio/INDEX

Internet Talk Radio
ftp sunsite.unc.edu:/pub/talk-radio/ITRintro.readme

Internet Multicasting FAQ
mail info@radio.com
"send FAQ"

Internet Multicasting WWW
http www.cmf.nrl.navy.mil:/radio/radio.html

Internet Talk Radio Sites
mail sites@radio.com
"send SITES"

Leeds/Music
http www.leeds.ac.uk:/music/Man/c_front.html
MIDI
http www.eeb.ele.tue.nl:/midi/index.html
Multicast Backbone
ftp venera.isi.edu:/mbone/faq.txt
Mbone FAQ Web
http www.research.att.com:/mbone-faq.html
Music Resources
http www.music.indiana.edu:/misc/
music_resources.html
Say
http utis179.cs.utwente.nl
:8001/ say/form/
IUMA
http sunsite.unc.edu:/ianc/index.html

Hyper/Virtual/Multimedia

ANIMA
http wimsey.com:/anima/ANIMAwelcome.html
Beyond Gutenberg
http www.cis.yale.edu:/htxt-conf/index.html
Bush, Vannevar
http www.csi.uottawa.ca:/~dduchier/misc/vbush/as-
we-may-think.html
CGU (Manchester, UK)
http info.mcc.ac.uk:/CGU/CGU-research.html
Comparisons
mail asmith@mammoth.chem.washington.edu
"Please send comparisons table"
Cyber Art
http www.rpi.edu:/~daniek2
Digital World
http www.interop.com
:80/ digitalworld/
File Formats
ftp ftp.ncsa.uiuc.edu:/misc/file.formats/

GA Tech Graphics
`http www.gatech.edu:/gvu/gvutop.html`

H Hyperbook
`http siva.cshl.org:/h/h.body.html`

HTML Guide
`http www.ucc.ie:/info/net/htmldoc.html`

HTML Guide/Tilton
`http www.willamette.edu:/html-composition/strict-html.html`

HTML Information
`http info.cern.ch:/hypertext/WWW/MarkUp/MarkUp.html`

HTML+ DTD
`ftp nic.merit.edu:/documents/internet-drafts/draft-raggett-www-html-00.txt`

Hypermedia/Internet
`http life.anu.edu.au:/education/hypermedia.html`

Hypermedia Review
`http www.csi.uottawa.ca:/~dduchier/misc/hypertext_review/`

Hypertext Terms
`http info.cern.ch:/hypertext/WWW/Terms.html`

Images
`http midget.towson.edu:8000/ home.html`

Interactive Media Festival
`mail inquire@media.festival.com`

MediaMOO
`telnet purple-crayon.media.mit.edu 8888`

Meta VE
`http www.gatech.edu:/gvu/people/Masters/Rob.Kooper/Meta.VR.html`

MICE
`http www.cs.ucl.ac.uk:/mice/mice.html`

MPEG
`http www.eeb.ele.tue.nl:/mpeg/index.html`

Multimedia Index
`http cui_www.unige.ch:/OSG/MultimediaInfo`

Multimedia Survey
`ftp ftp.ed.ac.uk:/pub/mmsurvey/mmsurvey.txt`

Multimedia Lab BU
`http spiderman.bu.edu`

MIT Media Lab
`ftp media-lab.media.mit.edu:/access/`

MIT Media Lab—How To
`http cs.indiana.edu:/docproject/`
`mit.research.how.to/mit.research.how.to.html`

MIT Telemedia
`http tns-www.lcs.mit.edu:/tns-www-home.html`

Rob's Multimedia Lab
`http www.acm.uiuc.edu`
`:80/ rml`

Scientific Visualization
`http www.nas.nasa.gov:/RNR/Visualization/`
`annotatedURLs.html`

SUD
`gopher actlab.rtf.utexas.edu:/11/SUD`

Sunsite Multimedia
`http sunsite.unc.edu:/exhibits/exex.html`

TX A+M Media Lab
`ftp bush.cs.tamu.edu:/pub/home.html`

Video
`http tns-www.lcs.mit.edu:/cgi-bin/vs/vsbrowser`

VR Page/Cardiff
`http www.cm.cf.ac.uk:/AndysTestMenu/moo.html`

VR Page/Chris Hand
`http www.cms.dmu.ac.uk`
`:9999/ People/cph/vrstuff.html`

VR Page/Luke Sheneman
`http www.cs.uidaho.edu:/lal/cyberspace/VR/VR.html`

VR Web
`http guinan.gsfc.nasa.gov:/W3/VR.html`

VR Archive
`ftp sunsite.unc.edu:/pub/academic/computer-science/virtual-reality/`

VSR
`http nfhsg3.rus.uni-stuttgart.de:/virtual/index.html`

Group Communication

CCCC
`http it.njit.edu:/njIT/Department/CCCC/default.html`

CoMMedia
`http www.ludvigsen.dhhalden.no:/webdoc/this_server.html#commedia`

Communication Archive
`ftp sunsite.unc.edu:/pub/academic/communications/`

Communication Archive Web
`http sunsite.unc.edu:/pub/academic/communications/communications.html`

Computer Network Conf
`ftp nic.merit.edu:/documents/rfc/rfc1324.txt`

Hypermedia/Internet
`http life.anu.edu.au:/education/hypermedia.html`

HyperNews
`http ginko.cecer.army.mil:8000/ ~liberte/hypernews.html`

Interactive Geo
`http www.hcc.hawaii.edu:/htbin/plotd`

Internet Relay Chat (IRC)
`ftp cs.bu.edu:/irc/support/`

IRC FAQ
`http www.kei.com:/irc.html`

ISO/IEC STDS
`gopher mars.dsv.su.se:70/ 0/iso-mess/gc/X.acc-First_CD.TXT`

Free for All
`http south.ncsa.uiuc.edu:/Free.html`

Multiple User Dialogue (MUD)

`ftp ftp.math.okstate.edu:/pub/muds/misc/mud-faq/`

MUD Lists

`ftp caisr2.caisr.cwru.edu:/pub/mud/`

MUD Page

`http math.okstate.edu`
`:8001/ mud.html`

LISTSERV Managing

`mail listserv@uhupvm1.uh.edu`
`"get kovacs prv2n1"`

LISTSERV Searching

`mail listserv@ulkyvm.bitnet`
`"get database search"`

LISTSERV Tips

`mail listserv@bitnic.bitnet`
`"get listserv tips"`

NCW

`gopher uclink.berkeley.edu`
`:3030/ 1`

SHARE

`http gummo.stanford.edu:/html/SHARE/share.html`

Organizational Communication

Campus Net

`ftp gandalf.iat.unc.edu:/technote/teknote4.txt`

Campus Net Bib

`ftp gandalf.iat.unc.edu:/guides/irg-15.txt`

E-Mail

E-mail Services

`ftp sunsite.unc.edu:/pub/docs/about-the-net/`
`libsoft/email_services.txt`

E-mail Understanding

`ftp ftp.cso.uiuc.edu:/doc/net/uiucnet/vol3no2.txt`

E-mail 101

`ftp mrcnext.cso.uiuc.edu:/etext/etext93/`
`email025.txt`

College E-mail Addresses

`ftp rtfm.mit.edu:/pub/usenet/soc.college/`

Finding E-mail Addresses

`ftp sunsite.unc.edu:/pub/docs/about-the-net/libsoft/email_address.txt`

IBM

`mail whois@ibmmail.com`

`"HELP"`

Mail2Html

`http neptune.corp.harris.com:/mail2html.html`

MetaMail

`ftp thumper.bellcore.com:/pub/nsb/README`

MIME

`ftp nic.merit.edu:/documents/rfc/rfc1341.txt`

MIME Overview

`ftp thumper.bellcore.com:/pub/nsb/MIME-overview.txt`

MIME Information

`ftp ftp.uu.net:/networking/mail/mime/`

Pine E-mail

`ftp ftp.cac.washington.edu:/pine/pine.blurb`

PGP Mail

`ftp ftp.uu.net:/pub/security/pgp/`

PGP/PEM

`http hoohoo.ncsa.uiuc.edu:/docs/PEMPGP.html`

PEM

`ftp ftp.tis.com:/pub/PEM/FAQ`

RIPEM

`http cs.indiana.edu:/ripem/dir.html`

RSAREF(TM)

`mail rsaref@rsa.com`

Language/Culture/Community/Society

Activism

`ftp ftp.netcom.com:/pub/amcgee/activism`

ACW
mail twbatson@gallua.gallaudet.edu

Anonymity FAQ
ftp rtfm.mit.edu:/pub/usenet/news.answers/net-anonymity/

African
ftp ftp.netcom.com:/pub/amcgee/african

ANIMA
http wimsey.com:/anima/ANIMAhomeF.html

APC
ftp igc.apc.org:/pub/orgs-on-igc

April Fools
ftp sunsite.unc.edu:/pub/academic/communications/april-fools/

Art/Images
gopher cs4sun.cs.ttu.edu://11/Art%20and%20Images

ArtSource
http www.uky.edu:/Artsource/artsourcehome.html

Artwork
ftp sunsite.unc.edu:/pub/multimedia/pictures/OTIS/

ASCII Art
ftp genesis.mcs.com:/mcsnet.users/jorn/asciifaq.us

ASCII Art Collection
ftp ftp.cs.ttu.edu:/pub/asciiart/

ATLAS
http wimsey.com:/anima/ATLAShome.html

BABEL 94
ftp ftp.temple.edu:/pub/info/help-net/babel94a.txt

Baylor Etexts
ftp ftp.byu.edu:/pub/next/Literature/

Book Information Center
http sunsite.unc.edu:/ibic/IBIC-homepage.html

Bordeaux and Prague
http mailbox.cdtl.umn.edu

Cirque de la Mama

`http lancet.mit.edu:/cirque/cirque.html`

CIS-AH

`http web.cal.msu.edu`

CTI

`mail ctitext@vax.ox.ac.uk`

Code of the Geeks

`http www.cs.odu.edu:/~mark/geek.html`

Coke Machines

`http www.cs.cmu.edu`
`:8001/ afs/cs.cmu.edu/user/bsy/www/coke.html`

Community Nets Surveys

`http www.cs.washington.edu`
`:80/ research/community-networks/`

Community Nets

`ftp ftp.apple.com:/alug/`

Community Nets

`gopher gopher.well.sf.ca.us`
`:70/ 11s/Community/communets/net.com`

Computer Jargon Search

`http web.cnam.fr:/bin.html/`
`By_Searchable_Index?Jargon_File.html`

Computer Jargon

`ftp aeneas.mit.edu:/pub/gnu/jargon-README`

CMC Glossary

`gopher sjumusic.stjohns.edu`
`:1070/ 11/%40uni%3acmc.glossary`

Computer Underground

`ftp ftp.eff.org:/pub/Publications/CuD/Papers/`
`meyer`

Computing Dictionary

`gopher wombat.doc.ic.ac.uk`

Computing Dictionary

`http wombat.doc.ic.ac.uk`

Coombs Papers

`gopher coombs.anu.edu.au`

CPET
`ftp guvax.georgetown.edu:/cpet_projects_in_electronic_text/`

Culture/Tech
`http english-server.hss.cmu.edu:/Cyber.html`

CyberCafe
`http cybercafe.demon.co.uk`

Cyber Papers
`ftp ftp.eff.org:/pub/Net_info/Cyber/`

Cyberspace
`http www.cs.uidaho.edu:/lal/cyberspace/cyberspace.html`

Cyberspace/Law
`ftp ftp.eff.org:/pub/Publications/CuD/Papers/cyberspace`

Cyberpunk FAQ
`ftp rtfm.mit.edu:/pub/usenet/news.answers/cyberpunk-faq`

Cyberspace/Language
`http nearnet.gnn.com:/gnn/news/archives/94.01.31/MLA.html`

Cypherpunk Topics
`ftp ftp.u.washington.edu:/public/phantom/cpunk/README.html`

Cypherpunks Gopher
`gopher chaos.bsu.edu`

Cypherpunks Home Page
`ftp soda.berkeley.edu:/pub/cypherpunks/Home.html`

Digital Co-op
`http www.wimsey.com:/~jmax/DCO.html`

Digital Gallery
`http ziris.syr.edu:/home.html`

Encyclopedia Britannica
`ftp eb.com:/pub/`

EStyle
`ftp aultnis.rutgers.edu:/litext`

Electronic Text Archive
`gopher fir.cic.net:/00/0-README`

Electronic Text
`ftp guvax.georgetown.edu:/cpet_projects_in_electronic_text/`

ETC
`http www.lib.virginia.edu:/etext/ETC.html`

Electronic Word
`ftp press-gopher.uchicago.edu:/pub/Excerpts/lanham.txt`

English Server
`http english-server.hss.cmu.edu`

FineArt Forum
`ftp ra.msstate.edu:/pub/archives/fineart_online`

FineArt Forum
`http www.willamette.edu:/~jpatters/art-resources.html`

Friends + Partners
`http solar.rtd.utk.edu:/friends/home.html`

FreeNet93
`ftp alfred.carleton.ca:/pub/freenet/93conference/`

Future Culture
```
mail future-request@nyx.cs.du.edu
Subject
send faq
```

Future Culture
`http www.ifi.uio.no:/~mariusw/futurec/index.html`

Gender
`ftp ftp.netcom.com:/pub/amcgee/gender/`

Gender Issues
`ftp alfred.carleton.ca:/pub/freenet/93conference/leslie_regan_shade.txt`

Gender/Spertus
`http www.ai.mit.edu:/people/ellens/gender.html`

Global/Women
`http www.ai.mit.edu:/people/ellens/gfw.html`

Gutenberg Project Texts
`ftp quake.think.com:/pub/etext/`

Gutenberg Web Page
`http med-amsa.bu.edu:/Gutenberg/Welcome.html`

Hacker Crackdown

`http www.scrg.cs.tcd.ie:/scrg/u/bos/hacker/hacker.html`

Hacker's Dictionary

`http iicm.tu-graz.ac.at:/Cjargon`

Humanities

`mail rre-request@weber.ucsd.edu`
`Subject`
`archive send humanities`

CCH

`gopher alpha.epas.utoronto.ca:/11/cch`

Humanities/Computing

`http nearnet.gnn.com:/wic/hum.05.html`

Hypertext/Rhetoric

`http fire.clarkson.edu:/horn/proposal-mla.html`

Indigenous

`ftp ftp.netcom.com:/pub/amcgee/indigenous/`

Interactive Games

`http www.cs.cmu.edu`
`:8001/ afs/cs.cmu.edu/user/zarf/www/games.html`

Internet Demographics

`ftp ftp.tic.com:/survey/`

Internet Glossary

`wais pinus.slu.se:/210 Internet-user-glossary?`

Internet Glossary

`ftp nic.merit.edu:/documents/fyi/fyi_18.txt`

Internet Town Hall

`http www.town.hall.org`

Internet Town Hall

`ftp town.hall.org`

Internet Town Hall

`gopher town.hall.org`
`:70/`

Internet Wiretap

`ftp wiretap.spies.com:/About/FEATURES`

Internet Wiretap Gopher

`gopher wiretap.Spies.com`

IRC Community
`ftp ftp.eff.org:/pub/Publications/CuD/Papers/electropolis`

ISEA
`http www.uiah.fi:/isea/index.html`

ITK
`http itkwww.kub.nl:2080/ itk/itkhome.html`

Latin
`ftp ftp.netcom.com:/pub/amcgee/latin/`

LETRS
`gopher gopher.indiana.edu:1067/ 11/letrs/gopher`

LUX LOGIS
`http www.contrib.de:/Art/LuxLogis/luxlogis_intro_dt.html`

MLA93 Forum
`ftp epas.utoronto.ca:/pub/cch/mla/`

MTV
`http mtv.com`

MUSE
`http muse.mse.jhu.edu`

Net Behavior
`http www.iss.nus.sg:/public/Internet_Links/Internet_Behavior.html`

Net Rights
`ftp ftp.american.edu:/au/brrec.text`

Net Ethics
`ftp nic.merit.edu:/documents/rfc/rfc1087.txt`

Net Etiquette Guide
`ftp ftp.sura.net:/pub/nic/internet.literature/netiquette.txt`

Net Orgs
`ftp rtfm.mit.edu:/pub/usenet/news.answers/net-community/orgs-list`

Netizen Anthology
`ftp wuarchive.wustl.edu:/doc/misc/acn/netbook`

B

Netizen Paper

`ftp wuarchive.wustl.edu:/doc/misc/acn/papers/netizens.Z`

Networking

`mail rre-request@weber.ucsd.edu`
`Subject`
`archive send network`

NWHQ

`http www.wimsey.com:/~jmax/index.html`

Off the Wall

`http nearnet.gnn.com:/gnn/arcade/gallery/art.html`

Online Book Initiative

`ftp ftp.std.com:/obi/README`

OWL

`mail owl@sage.cc.purdue.edu`
`Subject`
`owl-request`

Oxford Archive

`ftp black.ox.ac.uk:/ota/`

Post-Gutenberg Galaxy

`ftp infolib.murdoch.edu.au:/pub/jnl/harnad.jnl`

Privacy

`ftp rtfm.mit.edu:/pub/usenet/alt.privacy/`

Privacy Forum

`gopher vortex.com:/11/privacy`

Reasons for NII

`ftp ftp.cni.org:/CNI/documents/farnet/README`

SeniorNet Profile

`http nearnet.gnn.com:/gnn/meta/internet/mkt/seniorNet/center.html`

Smileys (all)

`gopher gopher.ora.com:/00/feature_articles/universe.smiley`

Smiley Dictionary

`ftp ftp.gsfc.nasa.gov:/pub/smiley-dictionary`

Smileys

`ftp ftp.uu.net:/usenet/comp.sources.misc/volume23/smiley/part01.Z`

Togethernet
`gopher gopher.together.uvm.edu`

Tribe
`mail listserv@lists.colorado.edu`
`"info tribe"`

Usenet
`ftp ftp.eff.org:/pub/Publications/CuD/Papers/`
`leviathan`

Virtual Community
`ftp ra.msstate.edu:/pub/docs/words-l/Net-Stuff/`
`slice.of.life`

Women
`http www.mit.edu`
`:8001/ people/sorokin/women/index.html`

Taking/Web
`http minnie.cs.su.oz.au:/writ/start.html`

The WELL
`ftp ftp.eff.org:/pub/Net_info/Cyber/town-on-`
`internet-highway`

UWI Cultural Play
`http zapruder.pds.med.umich.edu:/uwi.html`

ReWIRED
`http www.clas.ufl.edu:/CLAS/Departments/Rewired/`
`Re-WIRED.html`

Virtual City
`http riceinfo.rice.edu:/ES/Architecture/RDA/VC/`
`VirtualCity.html`

Writer's Resources
`ftp rtfm.mit.edu:/pub/usenet/news.answers/`
`writing/resources`

Education/Academia

AskERIC
`ftp ericir.syr.edu:/pub/`

AskERIC Web
`http eryx.syr.edu:/Main.html`

AskERIC Gopher
`gopher ericir.syr.edu`

AskERIC Cows
`http eryx.syr.edu:/COWSHome.html`

BBN NSN
`gopher copernicus.bbn.com`

CAF FTP Archive
`ftp ftp.eff.org:/pub/caf`

CAF Web Page
`http www.eff.org:/CAF/cafhome.html`

CALICO
`mail CALICO@Dukemvs.ac.duke.edu`

CAUSE Gopher
`gopher cause-gopher.Colorado.edu`

CELIA
`ftp archive.umich.edu:/celia-ftp/`

Cisco
`http sunsite.unc.edu:/cisco/edu-arch.html`

CoVis
`http www.covis.nwu.edu`

CWIS List
`ftp sunsite.unc.edu:/pub/docs/about-the-net/cwis/cwis-l`

CWIS Paper
`ftp sunsite.unc.edu:/pub/docs/about-the-net/cwis/hallman.txt`

Cyberion City
`telnet michael.ai.mit.edu`
`"guest"`

DeweyWeb
`http ics.soe.umich.edu`

Distance Ed
`ftp una.hh.lib.umich.edu:/inetdirsstacks/disted:ellsworth`

NDLC
`telnet ndlc.occ.uky.edu`
`"ndlc"`

Distance Ed DB
mail n.ismail@open.ac.uk

Distance Ed DB
telnet acsvax.open.ac.uk
"icdl"

Diversity U
telnet erau.db.erau.edu
8888

Diversity U Web
http pass.wayne.edu:/DU.html

Education Gopher
gopher sci-ed.fit.edu

EOS
ftp home.geo.brown.edu:/pub/eos1/

EOS
http home.geo.brown.edu:/eos1/

Educational Technology
http tecfa.unige.ch:/info-edu-comp.html

Educator's E-mail
ftp nic.umass.edu:/pub/ednet/educatrs.lst

Educator's USENET
ftp nic.umass.edu:/pub/ednet/edusenet.gde

Empire Schoolhouse
telnet nysernet.org
"empire"

Electronic Academic Village
http jefferson.village.virginia.edu:/iath/iath_pamphlet.html

ETB/NLM
http wwwetb.nlm.nih.gov

Exploratorium
http www.exploratorium.edu

High School/Internet
ftp sci-ed.fit.edu:/pub/Internet/study/

IAT
mail INFO.IAT@mhs.unc.edu
"send help"

IAT Archive

`ftp gandalf.iat.unc.edu:/user/home/anonftp/guides/`

IKE

`gopher ike.engr.washington.edu`

IKE Web

`http ike.engr.washington.edu:/ike.html`

Incomplete Guide K12

`ftp ftp.ncsa.uiuc.edu:/Education/Education_Resources/Incomplete_Guide/`

Internet and Ed

`ftp ftp.msu.edu:/pub/education/`

IRD/Educators

`ftp tcet.unt.edu:/pub/user-supported/horsehorse/K-12NREN1.1 pub/telecomputing-info/IRD`

JASON

`telnet topcat.bsc.mass.edu`

JASON Project Web

`http seawifs.gsfc.nasa.gov:/JASON/JASON.html`

KidLink

`gopher kids.ccit.duq.edu`

K-12 Info/CNIDR

`http k12.cnidr.org`

K-12 Briarwood

`gopher gopher.briarwood.com`

K-12 Essays

`gopher quest.arc.nasa.gov:/00/essay`

K-12 NASA

`http k12mac.larc.nasa.gov:/hpcck12home.html`

K-12 NREN

`ftp ftp.u.washington.edu:/pub/user-supported/horsehorse/K-12NREN1.1`

Learning V

`mail tmg@nptn.org`

Maricopa

`http hakatai.mcli.dist.maricopa.edu`

MEU BBS

`telnet bbs.meu.edu`

Networking
mail comserve@vm.its.rpi.edu
"send Profess Network"

NCET
http datasun.ncet.org.uk

NPTN
ftp nptn.org:/pub/info.nptn/basic.guide.txt

Novalink's Education Collection
http alpha.acast.nova.edu:/education.html

OISE Gopher
gopher porpoise.oise.on.ca
:70/

Online LC
gopher pringle.mta.ca

Primary/Sec
ftp nic.merit.edu:/documents/fyi/fyi_22.txt

Scholarly Communication
ftp borg.lib.vt.edu:/pub/vpiej-l/reports

Scholary Comm Project
http borg.lib.vt.edu
:80/ z-borg/www/scholar.html

Scholarly Comm/Libraries
ftp ftp.cni.org:/ARL/mellon/

Scholarly Communication
http www.lib.virginia.edu:/mellon/mellon.html

Scholarly Publishing
http info.anu.edu.au

Scholarly Publishing
ftp sunsite.unc.edu:/pub/docs/about-the-net/
trln-copyright-paper

Scholarly Societies
gopher watserv2.uwaterloo.ca:/11/servers/campus/
scholars

SME
mail jbharris@tenet.edu
"Please send Subject Matter Experts info"

SUMMIT

`http summit.stanford.edu:/welcome.html`

TECFA

`http tecfa.unige.ch:/tecfa-overview.html`

Tech/Schools

`ftp ftp.u.washington.edu:/pub/user-supported/horsehorse/refuse_1.4`

US Department of Education

`gopher gopher.ed.gov`

US Department of Education Web

`http www.ed.gov`

USENET University

`ftp nic.funet.fi:/pub/doc/uu/FAQ`

Willow

`http shebute.com:/Projects/Willow/Willow.HTML`

Government/Public Policy

ACE

`gopher cyfer.esusda.gov:/11/ace`

Clinton Information

`ftp ftp.cpsr.org:/cpsr/clinton/`

Clipper

`ftp ftp.eff.org:/pub/EFF/Policy/Clipper/`

Copyright FAQ

`ftp rtfm.mit.edu:/pub/usenet/news.answers/law/Copyright-FAQ/`

DIIG

`gopher farnsworth.mit.edu:/11/.1/DIIG`

FCC FTP

`ftp ftp.fcc.gov`

FCC Gopher

`gopher gopher.fcc.gov`

Federal Information Resources

`ftp nic.merit.edu:/omb/INDEX.omb`

Federal Information

`ftp ftp.nwnet.net:/user-docs/government/keller-gov-guide.txt`

FNC

`gopher fncac.fnc.gov`
`1`

Fedworld

`telnet fedworld.doc.gov`

Fedworld Feasibility

`ftp ftp.nwnet.net:/user-docs/government/`
`fedline.txt`

GILS

`ftp ftp.cni.org:/pub/docs/gils/`

Government/Citizenship Information

`gopher eryx.syr.edu`

Government Agencies

`ftp is.internic.net:/infosource/internet-info-`
`for-everybody/government-agencies`

Government Gophers

`gopher peg.cwis.uci.edu`
`:7000/ 11/gopher.welcome/peg/GOPHERS/gov`

Government Information

`ftp ftp.nwnet.net:/user-docs/government/`
`gumprecht-guide.txt`

Economic BB

`telnet ebb.stat-usa.gov`
`"trial"`

Electronic Records

`ftp ftp.cu.nih.gov:/nara_electronic/`

Humanities Initiative

`mail chhenry@vassar.edu`

Information Policy

`mail listserv@uhupvm1.uh.edu`
`"GET GOODYEAR PRV4N6"`

Information Superhighway

`http ai.iit.nrc.ca:/superhighway.html`

Internet Accounting

`ftp ftp.sdsc.edu:/pub/sdsc/anr/papers/`
`accting.sg.ps.Z`

Internet Economics
ftp gopher.econ.lsa.umich.edu:/pub/Papers/
Economics_of_Internet.txt

Internet Economics Collection
http gopher.econ.lsa.umich.edu:/EconInternet.html

Internet Policy
ftp nic.merit.edu:/documents/rfc/rfc1527.txt

Internet Pricing
ftp gopher.econ.lsa.umich.edu:/pub/Papers/
Pricing_the_Internet.txt

Internet Public Subsidy
ftp ssugopher.sonoma.edu:/pub/schickele.txt

LC-MARVEL
gopher gopher.loc.gov

Library of Congress
telnet marvel.loc.gov
"marvel"

MIT
http farnsworth.mit.edu

NII FTP
ftp ftp.ntia.doc.gov:/pub/niiagenda.asc

NII BBS
telnet iitf.doc.gov
"gopher"

NII Gopher
gopher iitf.doc.gov

NII Web
http iitf.doc.gov

NTIA
telnet ntiabbs.ntia.doc.gov

NTTC
telnet iron.nttc.edu

Open Platform
ftp ftp.eff.org:/pub/EFF/papers/Open_Platform/

Politics
gopher fir.cic.net:/11/Politics

Scholarly Comm
`ftp ftp.cni.org:/CNI/projects/Harvard.scp/kahin.txt`

Tap Information
`ftp ftp.cpsr.org:/taxpayer_assets`

Telecom Comments
`ftp ftp.govt.washington.edu:/wutc/`

Telecom Legislation
`ftp ftp.govt.washington.edu:/legislation.telecom/`

US Federal Government
`ftp nevada.edu:/liaison/`

US Government Hypertexts
`http sunsite.unc.edu:/govdocs.html`

US Patents and Trademarks
`http www.uspto.gov`

US House of Representatives
`gopher gopher.house.gov:70/`

US Senate
`gopher gopher.senate.gov:70/`

APPENDIX C

The Internet Offline: Books and Magazines

Magazines

3W. A global networking newsletter. *3W* is published bimonthly. For all European countries, the *3W* costs UK Sterling £24 for an annual subscription and UK Sterling £4 for an individual copy, including postage. Outside Europe, *3W* costs UK Sterling £30 (US $45) for an annual subscription, including airmail postage. Individual issues cost UK Sterling £5 (US$7.50), including airmail postage. For more information, contact `3W@ukartnet.demon.co.uk`.

Boardwatch. $36 for 12 monthly issues. (800) 933-6038. E-mail: `jack.rickard@boardwatch.com`. Focus includes bulletin board systems, legal aspects of the online world, and the Internet.

Internet Business Journal. Strangelove Press. E-mail: `mstrange@fonorola.net` or phone: (613) 565-0982. $149 ($179 Canadian) 12 issues annually; $75 ($89 Canadian) for educational institutions and small businesses. Sample copies are available on request or by Gopher to `gopher.fonorola.net`.

Internet World. Meckler Corp. E-mail: `meckler@jvnc.net`. Phone: (800) MECKLER. A monthly magazine covering all aspects of the Internet. Features are geared toward the beginner to intermediate-level user. The cost for a one-year subscription is $24.95. A two-year subscription is $37.00. Outside the US, add $18.00.

Matrix News. Matrix Information and Directory Services. E-mail: `mids@tic.com`. Published in online and paper editions. Online edition is $25 for 12 monthly issues ($15 for students.)

Online Access. (Chicago Fine Print.) E-mail: `70324.343@compuserve.com`. Subscription is $19.80 for 8 issues. Topics of this monthly magazine include national online services, the Internet, and bulletin board systems. Internet topics tend to best suit beginning users.

Books

Publishers are churning out Internet books like mad, quelling any notion that the Internet is moving us toward a "paperless" world. Here is the Unofficial Internet booklist, a periodic posting that I publish, well, periodically.

NOTE You can find the most recent version of this file online. It is posted twice monthly (on the 5th and 19th of each month) to the Usenet newsgroups `alt.internet.services`, `alt.online-service`, `alt.books.technical`, `misc.books.technical`, `alt.bbs.internet`, `misc.answers`, `alt.answers`, and `news.answers`.

You can receive it via anonymous FTP

```
rtfm.mit.edu:/pub/usenet/news.answers/internet-
services/internet-booklist
```

or by electronic mail

```
To: mail-server@rtfm.mit.edu
Subject: <subject line is ignored>
Body: send usenet/news.answers/internet-services/internet-booklist
```

Title: *All About Internet FTP: Learning and Teaching to Transfer Files on the Internet*
Author: David Robinson
Publisher: Library Solutions Press
ISBN: 1-882208-06-4
Price: $30 ($45 with disk)
Pages: 90
Published: 1994
Notes: For use by Internet trainers or for self-study.

Title: *The Big Dummy's Guide to the Internet*
Author: Adam Gaffin
Publisher: M.I.T. Press
ISBN: 0-262-57105-6
Price: $14.95
Pages: about 260
Published: July, 1994
Thanks for the information: Adam Gaffin (`adamg@world.std.com`)
Notes: This is basically a printed version of version 2.2 of the EFF's online guide of the same name, plus an index.

Title: *Canadian Internet Handbook*
Authors: Jim Carroll and Rick Broadhead
Publisher: Prentice Hall Canada
ISBN: 0-13-304395-9
Price: $16.95
Pages: 414
Published: 1994
For more information: `handbook@uunet.ca`.

Notes: If you live in Canada, get this book. It contains sections about getting Internet access in Canada; growth of Net use there; short basic sections about how to use some of the most popular Internet tools; a huge directory of Canadian Internet service providers; an even larger list of Gopher servers and campus-wide information systems in Canada; and to top it off, lists of Canadian-based Usenet groups, WWW, Archie, IRC servers, and online catalogs. I wish I lived in Canada just so I could make more use of this book.

Title: *The Complete Idiot's Guide to the Internet*
Author: Peter Kent
Publisher: Alpha Books
ISBN: 1-56761-414-0
Price: $19.95
Pages: 386
Goodies: DOS disk
Published: 1994
For more information: (800) 428-5331 or (317) 581-3500

Title: *The Complete Internet Directory*
Author: Eric Braun
Publisher: Fawcett
Price: $25
Pages: 325
Published: 1993
Notes: A directory of newsgroups, discussion lists, FTP sites, and so on, with just a few pages on how to use these resources.

Title: *Computers Under Attack: Intruders, Worms, and Viruses*
Author: Peter Denning
Publisher: ACM Press/Addison-Wesley
ISBN: 0-201-53067-8
Price: $23.95
Pages: 574
Published: 1990
Thanks for the information: John Quarterman in RFC 1432
Notes: Details of celebrated network security cases. Includes Stoll's original article about the Wiley Hacker and responses and articles by others on the same subject. Has extensive coverage of the 1988 Internet Worm. Also includes information on viruses. Has quite a bit of material on the cultures of the networks and on social, legal,

and ethical matters. Starts with the standard historical network papers, including "Notable Computer Networks" by Quarterman and Hoskins.

Title: *Connecting to the Internet*
Author: Susan Estrada
Publisher: O'Reilly and Associates
ISBN: 1-56592-061-9
Price: $15.95
Pages: 170
Published: 1993
Notes: This small book focuses on choosing the best type of network connection for your personal, school, or business needs, and how to get the best price for the type of access you require. Explains the differences between SLIP, PPP, ISDN, X.25, and other options. Includes an extensive list of Internet service providers. The first edition (August, 1993) has more than its fair share of typos.

Title: *Crossing the Internet Threshold: an Instructional Handbook*
Authors: Roy Tennant, John Ober, and Anne Lipow
Publisher: Library Solutions Press
ISBN: 1-883308-01-3
Price: $45
Pages: 134
Published: 1993
For more information: (510) 841-2636. FTP `simsc.si.edu:/networks/crossing.ad`
Notes: An instructional package for librarians teaching Internet basics.

Title: *The Cuckoo's Egg: Tracking a Spy Through the Maze of Computer Espionage*
Author: Clifford Stoll
Publisher: Doubleday
ISBN: 0-385-24946-2
Price: $5.95
Pages: 332
Published: 1989
Notes: A spy novel, except it's true. A first-person account by a down-on-his-luck Berkeley astronomer who with others tracked down a KGB network spy. Contains a very good recipe for chocolate chip cookies, too!

Title: *Cyberpunk*
Authors: Katie Hafner and John Markoff
Publisher: Simon and Schuster
ISBN: 0-671-68322-5
Price: $22.95
Pages: 368
Published: 1991
Thanks for the information: John Quarterman in RFC 1432
Notes: Interviews with some of the crackers who have appeared conspicuously in the press in the past few years. One of the coauthors is the New York Times reporter who broke the Stoll story to the public. Very readable.

Title: *Directory of Directories on the Internet: A Guide to Information Sources*
Author: Gregory B. Newby
Publisher: Meckler
ISBN: 0-88736-768-2
Price: $29.50
Pages: 153
Published: 1993
For more information: `gbnewby@uiuc.edu`
Notes: Intended for those who need to identify Internet information resources that point to other resources.

Title: *Doing Business on the Internet*
Author: Mary Cronin
Publisher: Van Nostrand Reinhold
ISBN: 0-442-01770-7
Price: $29.95
Pages: 308
Published: 1994
Notes: One view of how the Internet has changed the way some companies are doing business. Must reading for anyone looking at the impact of the Internet on commerce and why Internet access is becoming critical for businesses.

Title: *DOS User's Guide to the Internet*
Author: James Gardner
Publisher: Prentice Hall
ISBN: 0-13-106873-3
Price: $34.95

Pages: 308
Goodies: DOS disk
Published: 1993

Title: *The Easy Internet Handbook*
Authors: Javed Mostafa, Thomas Newell, Richard Trenthem
Publisher: Hi Willow Research and Publishing
ISBN: 0-931510-50-3
Price: $20
Pages: 150
Published: 1994
For more information: `tnewell@fiat.gslis.utexas.edu` or (800) 237-6124

Title: *Electronic Style: A Guide to Citing Electronic Information*
Authors: Xia Li and Nancy Crane
Publisher: Meckler
ISBN: 0-88736-909-X
Price: $15
Pages: 80
Published: 1993
Notes: Here you can find out how to cite, in bibliographies, references found on the Internet, on CD-ROMs, and during online database searches.

Title: *The Electronic Traveller: Exploring Alternative Online Systems*
Author: Elizabeth Powell Crowe
Publisher: Windcrest/McGraw-Hill
ISBN: 0-8306-4498-9
Price: $16.95

Title: *The Elements of E-Mail Style*
Authors: Brent Heslop and David Angell
Publisher: Addison-Wesley
ISBN: 0-201-62709-4
Price: $12.95
Pages: 157
Published: March, 1994
For more information: `dangell@shell.portal.com`
Thanks for the information: David F. Angell (`dangell@shell.portal.com`)

Notes: How to write effective e-mail. Simplifies and summarizes essential writing techniques so that users can upgrade their writing skills and see their e-mail make maximum impact in minimal time.

Title: *Everyone's Guide to Online Environmental Information*
Author: Don Rittner
Publisher: Peachpit Press
Published: 1992
Notes: Directed at concerned citizens, environmentalists, and scientists interested in sharing ideas and research on environmental issues. Covers resources on Fidonet, Bitnet, Internet, Usenet, local bulletin boards, America Online, CompuServe, EcoNet, GEnie, WELL.

Title: *Exploring the Internet: A Technical Travelogue*
Author: Carl Malamud
Publisher: Prentice Hall
ISBN: 0-13-296898-3
Price: $26.95
Pages: 379
Published: 1992
For more information: (515) 284-6751
Notes: A look at the Internet and the emerging global village in 21 countries and 56 cities.

Title: *From A to Z39.50: A Network Primer*
Authors: James Michael and Mark Hinnebusch
Publisher: Meckler
ISBN: 0-88736-766-6
Price: $25
Pages: 225
Published: March, 1994
Notes: Introduction to and discussion about the issues and standards involved in electronic telecommunications.

Title: *A Guide for Accessing California Legislative Information over Internet*
Author: Legislative Counsel Bureau, State of California
Publisher: State of California
Price: free to California residents
Pages: 30
Published: 1994

For more information: `comments@leginfo.public.ca.gov`
Thanks for the information: Mike Quinn
Notes: This pamphlet tells how you can find California legislative information online. Explains what legislation information is available, what assistance is available, and how the information is organized. The majority of the book is spent explaining the Internet, how to get access, how to use electronic mail, and where to go for more detailed information. There's also a simple glossary of legislative terms. This pamphlet is also available online, in PostScript format. Send e-mail to

```
To: ftpmail@leginfo.public.ca.gov
Body: connect leginfo.public.ca.gov
      get README_public_access_guide_ps
      quit
```

Title: *The Hacker Crackdown: Law and Disorder on the Electronic Frontier*
Author: Bruce Sterling
Publisher: Bantam
ISBN: 0-553-08058-X
Price: $23
Pages: 352
Published: 1992
Thanks for the information: John Quarterman in RFC 1432
Notes: An in-depth examination of the forces of law that try to deal with computer crime, and of the issues involved, written by one of the science fiction writers who invented cyberpunk. The real story behind Operation Sundevil and the Legion of Doom. Readable, informative, amusing, and necessary.

Title: *Hackers: Heroes of the Computer Revolution*
Author: Steven Levy
Publisher: Anchor Press/Doubleday
ISBN: 0-385-19195-2 (hard) 0-440-13405-6 (paper)
Price: $17.95/$4.95
Pages: 458
Published: 1984
Notes: Describes the early culture and ethos of hackers and computer homebrewers, the culture that ultimately resulted in the Internet and Usenet.

Title: *Hands-On Internet: A Beginning Guide for PC Users*
Authors: David Sachs and Henry Stair
Publisher: Prentice Hall
ISBN: 0-13-056392-7
Price: $29.95
Pages: 274
Goodies: DOS disk
Published: 1994

Title: *In acht Sekunden um die Welt (In eight seconds around the world)* Second Edition
Language: German
Authors: Gunther Maier and Andreas Wildberger
Publisher: Addison-Wesley
ISBN: 3-89319-701-X
Price: DM 39.90/oeS 311,00
Pages: 160
Published: 1994
For more information: `wildberg@nestroy.wu.wien.ac.at`
Thanks for the information: Lutz Lademann, `pcsaal15@fub46.zedat.fu-berlin.de`
Notes: It's a quite comprehensive introduction to the Internet, its history, and the services available (Mail, News, Gopher, FTP, Telnet, WWW, and more). Three chapters of this book are available via WWW: URL: `http://rektorat.wu-wien.ac.at/stuff/netzbuch.html`

Title: *The Instant Internet Guide*
Authors: Brent Heslop and David Angell
Publisher: Addison-Wesley
ISBN: 0-201-62707-8
Price: $14.95
Pages: 209
Published: 3rd printing
For more information: `dangell@shell.portal.com`
Thanks for the information: `dangell@shell.portal.com`
Notes: A hands-on beginners guide that covers pine, tin, FTP, Telnet, Gopher, and more.

Title: *Internet Access Providers: An International Resource Directory*
Author: Greg Notess
Publisher: Meckler
ISBN: 0-88736-933-2

Price: $30
Pages: 330
Published: March, 1994
Notes: This directory provides descriptive information on more than 100 companies and networks that offer dial-up Internet access. Aimed at those without current access, looking for personal access.

Title: *The Internet and Special Librarians: Use, Training, and the Future*
Author: Sharyn Lander Hope Tillman
Publisher: Special Libraries Association
Published: 1993
Notes: Implications of a study of special librarians' use of the Internet and the future of librarianship. Includes a glossary, primer on Internet basics, resources, and how to get connected.

Title: *The Internet at a Glance*
Author: Susan E. Feldman
Publisher: Datasearch
ISBN: None listed
Price: $7
Pages: 10
Published: 1994
For more information: Susan Feldman (`suef@TC.Cornell.EDU`)
Thanks for the information: Susan Feldman (`suef@TC.Cornell.EDU`)
Notes: A collection of "cheatsheets" for the Net. It's short (only 10 thin pages), but it covers the basics for using the Internet and UNIX. Topics include finding resources on the Internet, tools, electronic mail, anonymous FTP, Telnet, mailing lists and newsgroups, plus basic UNIX commands and the vi editor.

Title: *Internet Basics*
Authors: Steve Lambert and Walt Howe
Publisher: Random House
ISBN: 0-679-75023-1
Price: $27.00
Pages: 495
Published: 1993
Thanks for the information: Gayle Keresey (`aflgayle@aol.com`)
Notes: General book on the Internet with a slight slant toward Delphi. (Howe is Delphi's Internet SIG Manager.)

Title: *The Internet Companion, A Beginner's Guide to Global Networking*
Author: Tracy LaQuey with Jeanne C. Ryer
Publisher: Addison-Wesley
ISBN: 0-201-62224-6
Price: $10.95
Pages: 196
Published: 1993
Notes: The Companion includes a detailed history of the Internet, a discussion on "netiquette" (network etiquette), and how to find resources on the Net. Useful for the computer-literate Internet novice.

Title: *The Internet Companion Plus*
Authors: Tracy LaQuey and Jeanne Ryer
Publisher: Addison-Wesley
ISBN: 0-201-62719-1
Price: $19.95
Goodies: DOS disk
Published: 1993

Title: *The Internet Complete Reference*
Authors: Harley Hahn and Rick Stout
Publisher: Osborne McGraw-Hill
ISBN: 0-07-881980-6
Price: $29.95
Pages: 818

Title: *The Internet Connection: System Connectivity and Configuration*
Authors: John S. Quarterman and Smoot Carl-Mitchell
Publisher: Addison-Wesley
ISBN: 0-201-54237-4
Price: $32.25
Pages: 271
Published: 1994
For more information: `awbook@aw.com`
Notes: According to the publisher, this book gives step-by-step instruction on connection to the Internet for system designers, system administrators, and their managers; offers assistance in setting up naming and mail and news systems; and explains the use of common Internet services such as Archie, WAIS, and Gopher.

Title: *Internet Connections: A Librarian's Guide to Dial-Up Access and Use*
Authors: Mary E. Engle, *et al.*
Publisher: American Library Association
ISBN: 0-8389-7677-8
Price: $22.00
Pages: 166
Published: 1993

Title: *The Internet Directory*
Author: Eric Braun
Publisher: Fawcett Columbine
ISBN: 0-449-90898-4
Price: $25.00
Pages: 704
Published: 1994
Thanks for the information: Gayle Keresey (`aflgayle@aol.com`)
Notes: Each chapter in this book covers a particular information service or resource type, including mailing lists, newsgroups, FTP archives, Gophers, WAIS, WWW, and so on. All sources have been verified. Extensive index. A must have for Internet surfers.

Title: *The Internet for Dummies*
Authors: John Levine and Carol Baroudi
Publisher: IDG Books
ISBN: 1-56884-024-1
Price: $19.95
Pages: 355
Published: 1993
Thanks for the information: Graham Keith Rogers (`scgkr@mucc.mahidol.ac.th`)
Notes: Intended as a beginner's guide to the Internet; includes useful sections on mail, Gopher, news, FTP, and so on. All in a fairly light-hearted style intended to set novices at ease. At more than 350 pages, there is much information and the book is well indexed. For those who have a direct connection, for example, SLIP or PPP.

Title: *Internet: Getting Started*
Authors: April Marine, Susan Kirkpatrick, Vivian Neou, and Carol Ward
Publisher: Prentice Hall
ISBN: 0-13-327933-2

Price: $28.00
Pages: 360
Published: 1993
Notes: Explains how to join the Internet, the various types of Internet access, and procedures for obtaining a unique IP address and domain name. An extensive list of Internet access providers of all types is provided, including access outside of the United States. The guide explains many concepts essential to the Internet, such as the domain name system, IP addressing, protocols, and electronic mail.

Title: *The Internet Guide for New Users*
Author: Daniel P. Dern
Publisher: McGraw-Hill
ISBN: Paperback 0-07-016511, Hardcover 0-07-016510-6
Price: Paperback $27.95, Hardcover $40.00
Pages: 570
Published: 1993
For more information: `ddern@world.std.com`
Notes: A complete introduction to the world of the Internet. Along with the obligatory topics, such as Telnet, FTP, and Archie, the book suggests how to get an Internet account and teaches enough UNIX to survive on the Net.

Title: *Internet Instant Reference*
Author: Paul E. Hoffman
Publisher: Sybex
ISBN: 0-7821-1512-8
Price: $12.99
Pages: 317
Published: 1994
Notes: This book is part quick reference, part lexicon, and part Internet tutorial. Arranged in dictionary format, it defines Internet jargon, such as *shareware* and *hypertext*, gives brief descriptions of tools, such as Knowbot and Listserv, includes short command summaries for using popular programs, such as FTP, emacs, and elm, and describes various Net organizations and policies. This book contains a variety of information, but is rather unevenly edited and contains some factual errors that might not be clear to newbies. For instance, in one section it confuses the terms *upload* and *download*.

Title: *The Internet Library: Case Studies of Library Internet Management and Use*
Editor: Julie Still
Publisher: Meckler
ISBN: 0-88736-965-0
Price: $37.50
Pages: 200
Published: June, 1994
Notes: The case studies in this volume focus on how electronic resources have changed relationships with the library and also focus on the way libraries relate to the larger world.

Title: *Internet: Mailing Lists*
Authors: Edward Hardie and Vivian Neou
Publisher: Prentice Hall
ISBN: 0-13-289661-3
Price: $26.00
Pages: 356
Published: 1993
Notes: A list of Internet mailing lists. Note that a current "list of lists" is available online for free, both via Usenet and FTP.

Title: *The Internet Message: Closing the Book with Electronic Mail*
Author: Marshall Rose
Publisher: Prentice Hall
ISBN: 0-13-092941-7
Price: $44.00

Title: *The Internet Navigator*
Author: Paul Gilster
Publisher: John Wiley and Sons, Inc.
ISBN: 0-471-59782-1
Price: $24.95
Pages: 470
Published: August, 1993
Thanks for the information: Gayle Keresey (`aflgayle@aol.com`)
Notes: Information for the dial-up Internet user. Includes Internet history, signing on to the Net, UNIX commands, getting files, Telnet, electronic mail, Bitnet, electronic journals, Usenet, Gophers, and Internet resources.

Title: *The Internet Passport: NorthWestNet's Guide to Our World Online,* Fourth Edition
Author: Jonathan Kochmer
Publisher: NorthWestNet and the Northwest Academic Computing Consortium
ISBN: 0-9635281-0-6
Price: $29.95
Pages: 516
For more information: e-mail `passport@nwnet.net`. Order forms can be obtained via FTP at `ftp.nwnet.net/user-docs/passport/nonmem-order-form.txt`
Notes: Covers everything from Net etiquette to supercomputers; very comprehensive.

Title: *Internet Primer for Information Professionals: A Basic Guide to Internet Networking Technology*
Authors: Elizabeth Lane and Craig Summerhill
Publisher: Meckler
ISBN: 0-88736-831-X
Price: $37.50
Pages: 175
Published: 1993
Notes: Description of the current state of the Internet, the proposed NREN, and basic information on network usage and concepts.

Title: *Internet Public Access Guide*
Author: Phil Hughes
Publisher: SSC Publications
ISBN: 0-916151-70-0
Price: $2.95
Pages: 64
Published: 1994
For more information: `sales@ssc.com` or (206) 527-3385.
Thanks for the information: Graham Keith Rogers (`scgkr@mucc.mahidol.ac.th`)
Notes: Graham Rogers says: "64-page guide to Internet basics. Very easy-to-follow instructions, clearly set out. With the small size not everything can be included, but the price represents good value. The paper cover deteriorates with use." I say, "A whole lot of information for the money. Well presented, simple, and above all, short. Covers 'What is the Internet?', terms, UNIX basics, e-mail, Usenet,

FTP, rlogin and Telnet, finger, Archie, Gopher, and Veronica. Easy-to-follow examples." They'll sell you just one copy, but the book is primarily intended for sale to service providers and distribution to their users.

Title: *Internet Quickstart*
Authors: Mary Ann Pike and Tod G. Pike
Publisher: Que
ISBN: 1-56529-658-3
Price: $21.99
Pages: 387
Published: March, 1994
For more information: (800) 428-5331 or (317) 581-3500
Thanks for the information: Connie Marijs
(`otsgroup@pop.knoware.nl`)
Notes: A series of quick tutorials, this book explains Internet basics to absolute beginners. Lots of extras—such as buzzword definitions, tips, and warnings. Helps users get more from this premier online service. Task-oriented skill sessions cover topics such as login, e-mail, database searches, Internet news, and more.

Title: *The Internet Resource Quick Reference*
Author: William Tolhurst
Publisher: Que
Published: 1994
Notes: Contains a list of Usenet news groups, a list of publicly accessible mailing lists, Scott Yanoff's list of online resources and the Inter-Network Mail Guide. All of this information is available online.

Title: *The Internet Roadmap*
Author: Bennett Falk
Publisher: Sybex
ISBN: 0-7821-1365-6
Price: $12.99
Pages: 263
Published: 1994
Thanks for the information: David M. Stevenson
(`david@dms.muc.de`)
Notes: David M. Stevenson says, "This book is written by someone who is concerned that the reader get a good grasp of the Internet system quickly. In my case he succeeded; and what he can do for

me, he can do for you!" I say, "This book is a winner. It explains the basics of the Internet in a clear and concise style. Covers the tools for reading Usenet news, doing e-mail, using FTP, Gopher, and World Wide Web. Doesn't get into the newer, funkier tools too much. It's an easy read and doesn't get bogged down in esoteric, dull stuff. I even like the cover."

Title: *The Internet Starter Kit for the Macintosh*
Author: Adam Engst
Publisher: Hayden Books
ISBN: 1-56830-064-6
Price: $29.95
Pages: 640
Goodies: Mac floppy disk filled with great software
Published: 1993
For more information: `ace@tidbits.com`
Notes: This terrific book (with a floppy disk) gives Macintosh users the complete scoop on getting connected to the Internet using PPP, SLIP, and so on. This is one of my favorite Internet books because it's so readable. It's definitely the best one dedicated to Mac users.

Title: *Internet System Handbook*
Authors: Daniel Lynch and Marshall Rose
Publisher: Addison-Wesley
ISBN: 0-201-56741-5
Price: $54.95
Published: 1993

Title: *The Internet Unleashed*
Authors: Steve Bang, *et al.*
Publisher: Sams Publishing
ISBN: 0-672-30466-X
Price: $44.95
Pages: 1,380
Goodies: 1 PC-format HD disk. (Macintosh users can mail an enclosed coupon to receive a disk with similar Mac software for a nominal shipping and handling fee.)
Published: April, 1994
Notes: This book is a huge tome, weighing in with 62 chapters plus 7 appendixes. It is cowritten by a zillion authors and falls in the "everything you could possibly want to know about the Internet" category, with blanket coverage of accessing the Net from different

types of home computers and networks and with high-speed connections. This book covers just about every Internet topic you can think of—from security to MUDs and from doing business on the Net to copyright issues and problems.

Title: *1994 Internet White Pages*
Authors: Seth Godin and James S. McBride
Publisher: IDG Books
ISBN: 1-56884-300-3
Price: $29.95
Published: 1994
Notes: A thick book listing thousands of e-mail addresses. Addresses are listed by last name and are also indexed by Internet domain name. This book may be useful for finding associate's e-mail addresses, but is probably no more useful than using one of the many Net-based e-mail-address search utilities. The book is unevenly edited (I'm in there three times!) and was woefully out-of-date before the ink was dry.

Title: *The Internet Yellow Pages*
Authors: Harley Hahn and Rick Stout
Publisher: Osborne Publishing (McGraw Hill)
ISBN: 0-07-882023-5
Price: $27.95
Pages: 447
Published: 1994
Thanks for the information: `jeynes@adobe.com`
Notes: This is a summary book that is laid out like the phone book yellow pages and includes descriptions of various services available on the Internet. Most of these services are Usenet newsgroups, established mailing lists, or FTP site/directory listings. It's an interesting, readable, and unique way to present a catalog of stuff on the Net.

Title: *Mac Internet Tour Guide*
Authors: Michael Fraase
Publisher: Ventana Press
ISBN: 1-56604-062-0
Price: $27.95
Pages: 286
Goodies: Mac floppy disk with a bit of useful software. Periodic updates via e-mail. One month of free online time from MRNet.
Published: 1993

For more information: `dilennox@aol.com` or FTP to `ftp.farces.com`
Notes: This book (with floppy disk) for Macintosh users helps newcomers get online and get acquainted with graphical Internet software "Fetch" and "Eudora."

Title: *Introducing the Internet: A Trainer's Workshop*
Authors: Lee David Jaffe
Publisher: Library Solutions Press
ISBN: 1-882208-05-6
Price: $30.00 ($45.00 with diskette)
Pages: 92
Published: 1994
Notes: The first in a series of supplements to *Crossing the Internet Threshold.* Based on a trainer's handouts and script. May be used as a self-instruction workbook.

Title: *Libraries and the Internet/NRED: Perspectives, Issues and Challenges*
Authors: Charles McClure *et al.*
Publisher: Meckler
ISBN: 0-88736-824-7
Price: $25
Pages: 500
Published: March, 1994
Notes: This major study identifies key factors within the library and larger environments that will affect libraries' involvement in national networking policies.

Title: *The Matrix: Computer Networks and Conferencing Systems Worldwide*
Author: John S. Quarterman
Publisher: Digital Press
ISBN: 0-13-565607-9
Price: $50.00
Published: 1990

Title: *Navigating the Internet*
Authors: Mark Gibbs and Richard Smith
Publisher: Sams Publishing
ISBN: 0-672-30362-0
Price: $24.95

Pages: 500
Published: 1993
For more information: (800) 428-5331 or (317) 581-3500

Title: *Navigating the Internet, Deluxe Edition*
Authors: Richard Smith and Mark Gibbs
Publisher: Sams Publishing
ISBN: 0-672-30485-6
Price: $29.95
Pages: 640
Goodies: 1 PC-format HD disk. (Macintosh users can mail a coupon for a Mac disk with similar software for a nominal shipping and handling fee.)
Published: April, 1994
For more information: (800) 428-5331 or (317) 581-3500

Title: *Netguide*
Authors: Peter Rutten, Albert Bayers III, and Kelly Moloni
Publisher: Random House
ISBN: 0-679-75106-8
Price: $19.00
Published: 1994
Thanks for the information: Educom newsletter
Notes: As the "TV Guide of Cyberspace," this book provides pointers by subjects to various topics including Internet sites, Usenet newsgroups, and commercial resources (CompuServe, American Online, and so on). It proves that there's something for everyone somewhere out in the electronic world.

Title: *NetPower: Resource Guide to Online Computer Services*
Author: Eric Persson
Publisher: Fox Chapel Publishing
ISBN: 1-56523-031-0
Price: $39.95 + $3.00 shipping
Pages: 774
Published: 1993
For more information: `netpower1@aol.com`, (800) 457-9112
Notes: All I know is what their catalog says: "The most exciting section of this guide is devoted to the Internet. Netpower includes a primer and tutorial on using the network, information on getting started and navigating with Internet tools, and hundreds of Internet-accessible resources with contact information and

C

descriptions. The guide will point you in the direction of millions of megabytes of information, all yours free for the downloading around the Internet."

Title: *The New Hacker's Dictionary,* Second Edition,
Editors: Eric Raymond and Guy L. Steele
Publisher: MIT Press
ISBN: 0-262-68079-3 (hard) 0-262-18154-1 (paper)
Price: $10.95
Pages: 453
Published: 1994
Thanks for the information: Petrea Mitchell (`ravn@mvp.rain.com`)
Notes: *The New Hacker's Dictionary* is a great book for learning about the slang, jargon, customs, and folklore of the Net (as well as other lairs of the hacker). Very silly and highly recommended. An FTPable version, called the *Jargon File,* is available from `rtfm.mit.edu`, but the bound book makes great bathroom reading and contains silly cartoons and stuff.

Title: O*n INTERNET 94: An International Title and Subject Guide to Electronic Journals, Newsletters, Texts, Discussion Lists, and Other Resources on the Internet*
Author: Internet World Magazine
Publisher: Meckler
ISBN: 0-88736-929-4
Price: $45.00
Pages: 500
Published: 1994
Notes: "Your guide to the full range of Internet-accessible data files—from artificial intelligence to women's studies, from space exploration to rock music, from environment studies to AIDS research." Nearly 6,000 mailing lists, electronic journals, archives, and so on.

Title: *The Online User's Encyclopedia: Bulletin Boards and Beyond, Second Edition*
Author: Bernard Aboba
Publisher: Addison-Wesley
ISBN: 0-201-62214-9
Price: $32.95
Pages: 806
Published: 1993

Thanks for the information: Gayle Keresey (`aflgayle@aol.com`)
Notes: Comprehensive compendium of information and a guide to bulletin boards and the computer networks they are connected to. First edition of this book was a manual for the BMUG BBS. Indispensable guide to connecting your modem to the world.

Title: *OPAC Directory 1994*
Author: Mecklermedia
Publisher: Meckler
ISBN: 0-88736-962-6
Price: $70
Pages: 500
Published: May, 1994
Notes: A detailed listing of dial-in, online, and public-access catalogs and databases. Includes *Accessing Online Bibliographic Databases,* the annotated list of 700+ Internet-accessible OPACs.

Title: *PC Internet Tour Guide*
Author: Michael Fraase
Publisher: Ventana Press
ISBN: 1-56604-084-1
Price: $24.95
Pages: 284
Goodies: PC floppy disk with useful software. Two periodic updates via e-mail. One month of free online time from MRnet.
Published: 1994
For more information: `dilennox@aol.com`
Notes: This book (with floppy disk) for MS-DOS users helps newcomers get online.

Title: *Pocket Guides to the Internet: Volume 1—Telnetting*
Authors: Mark Veljkov and George Hartnell
Publisher: Meckler
ISBN: 0-88736-943-X
Price: $9.95
Pages: 64
Published: 1994

Title: *Pocket Guides to the Internet: Volume 2—Transferring Files with File Transfer Protocol (FTP)*
Authors: Mark Veljkov and George Hartnell
Publisher: Meckler
ISBN: 0-88736-944-8

Price: $9.95
Pages: 64
Published: 1994

Title: *Pocket Guides to the Internet: Volume 3—Using and Navigating Usenet*
Authors: Mark Veljkov and George Hartnell
Publisher: Meckler
ISBN: 0-88736-945-6
Price: $9.95
Pages: 64
Published: 1994

Title: *Pocket Guides to the Internet: Volume 4—The Internet E-Mail System*
Authors: Mark Veljkov and George Hartnell
Publisher: Meckler
ISBN: 0-88736-946-4
Price: $9.95
Pages: 64
Published: 1994

Title: *Pocket Guides to the Internet: Volume 5—Basic Internet Utilities*
Authors: Mark Veljkov and George Hartnell
Publisher: Meckler
ISBN: 0-88736-947-2
Price: $9.95
Pages: 64
Published: 1994

Title: *Pocket Guides to the Internet: Volume 6—Terminal Connections*
Authors: Mark Veljkov and George Hartnell
Publisher: Meckler
ISBN: 0-88736-948-0
Price: $9.95
Pages: 64
Published: 1994

Title: *Riding the Internet Highway*
Author: Sharon Fisher
Publisher: New Riders Publishing
ISBN: 1-56205-192-X

Price: $16.95
Pages: 266
Published: 1993

Title: *sendmail*
Author: Bryan Costales
Publisher: O'Reilly and Associates
ISBN: 1-56592-056-2
Price: $32.95
Pages: 830
Published: 1993
Notes: Although not strictly an Internet book, this tome focuses on one thing: the UNIX program sendmail, which is a huge part of how electronic mail moves around on the Internet. Mainly for system administrators, the book shows how to use every function, mode, and mood of sendmail to get your e-mail where it's going. A great, if single-minded, book.

Title: *smileys*
Author: Lesley Strother
Publisher: O'Reilly and Associates
ISBN: 1-56592-041-4
Pages: 595
Published: 1993
Notes: A collection of 650 "smileys." Although not an Internet book *per se*, smileys are certainly used enough on the Internet to warrant an entry here. : -)

Title: *TCP/IP Illustrated, Volume 1, The Protocols*
Author: W. Richard Stevens
Publisher: Addison-Wesley
ISBN: 0-201-63346-9
Pages: 576
Published: 1994
Thanks for the information: Bob Stein (`stein@gcomm.com`)
Notes: This textbook is the best way to understand the nuts and bolts of TCP/IP, the Internet's networking protocols. Great figures, diagrams, tables, and other references. (No Volume 2 yet.)

Title: *Teach Yourself the Internet: Around the World in 21 Days*
Author: Neil Randall
Publisher: Sams Publishing
ISBN: 0-672-30519-4

Price: $25.00
Pages: 700
Published: June, 1994
For more information: (800) 428-5331 or (317) 581-3500
Thanks for the information: Connie Marijs (`otsgroup@knoware.nl`)
Notes: This well-organized tutorial can be used by individuals and in seminars, training sessions, and classrooms. It takes readers on a global learning expedition of the Internet in just 21 fun-filled lessons.

Title: *Using the Internet*
Authors: William A. Tolhurst, Mary Ann Pike, and Keith A. Blanton
Publisher: Que
ISBN: 1-56529-353-3
Price: $39.95
Pages: 1188
Goodies: DOS disk
Published: January, 1994
For more information: `tpike@pittslug.sug.org`
Thanks for the information: Gayle Keresey (`aflgayle@aol.com`)
Notes: Introduction to, structure of, and history of the Internet. Finding and using resources, legal considerations, features and services, and tools and technology.

Title: *Using UUCP and Usenet*
Authors: Grade Todino and Dale Dougherty
Publisher: O'Reilly and Associates
Pages: 194
Published: 1991

Title: *WAIS and Gopher Servers: A Guide for Librarians and Internet End-Users*
Author: Eric Lease Morgan
Publisher: Meckler
ISBN: 0-88736-932-4
Price: $30.00
Pages: 150
Published: March, 1994
Notes: The first book-length treatment of WAIS and Gopher servers.

Title: *Welcome to...Internet from Mystery to Mastery*
Authors Tom Badgett and Corey Sandler
Publisher: MIS Press
ISBN: 1-55828-308-0
Price: $19.95
Pages: 324
Published: 1993
Thanks for the information: Gayle Keresey (`aflgayle@aol.com`)
Notes: Introduction to the Internet and its resources and navigational tools. The strength of this book is the chapter entitled "Collecting Souvenirs on the Internet," which details subjects and tells exactly where and how to find information about those subjects on the Net.

Title: *The Whole Earth Online Almanac*
Author: Don Rittner
Publisher: Brady Books
ISBN: 1-56686-090-3
Price: $32.95
Pages: 540
Published: 1993
Notes: Covers America Online, CompuServe, GEnie, The WELL, FidoNet, the Internet, and CD-ROMs. Each subject area includes applicable forums and databases, network discussion lists, and other online sources and CD-ROMs.

Title: *The Whole Internet User's Guide and Catalog, Second Edition*
Author: Ed Krol
Publisher: O'Reilly and Associates
ISBN: 1-56592-063-5
Price: $24.95
Pages: 572
Published: April, 1994
For more information: `info@ora.com`
Notes: This book covers the basic utilities used to access the Net and then guides users through the Internet's "databases of databases" to access the millions of files and thousands of archives available. It includes a resource index that covers a broad selection of approximately 300 important resources available on the Internet. The second edition has been completely updated to reflect the development of new Internet tools, including Mosaic, MIME, tin, pine, xarchie, and a greatly expanded resource catalog. Highly recommended.

C

Title: *Windows Internet Tour Guide*
Author: Michael Frasse
Publisher: Ventana Press
ISBN: 1-56604-081-7
Price: $24.95
Pages: 344
Goodies: Windows disk. Two free electronic updates via e-mail. One month of free online time from MRnet.
Published: 1994
For more information: `dilennox@aol.com`

Title: *Zen and the Art of Internet, Third Edition*
Author: Brendan Kehoe
Publisher: Prentice Hall
ISBN: 0-13-121492-6
Price: $23.95
Pages: 193
Published: January, 1994
Notes: This guide should give you a reference to consult if you're curious about what can be done with the Internet. It also presents the fundamental topics that are all too often assumed and considered trivial by many network users. It covers the basic utilities and information reaching other networks. An earlier, much less comprehensive version is available via FTP.

Title: *!%@:: A Directory of Electronic Mail Addressing and Networks*
Authors: Donnalyn Frey and Rick Adams
Publisher: O'Reilly and Associates
ISBN: 1-56592-031-7
Price: $24.95
Pages: 458
Published: 1993

New Internet Books: Online Updates

The Top Ten Internet Book List is a weekly list that lists the top ten Internet books sold in Europe. The list represents the ten most popular titles of Prentice Hall, Sams Publishing, Que, and other publishers, based on weekly sales. It also announces new Internet books to be released. To subscribe, send e-mail to: `otsgroup@pop.knoware.nl`.

Contact the Addison-Wesley information server for periodic updates on new titles from this publisher. Send e-mail to

```
To: awbook@aw.com
Subject: information
Body: send information
```

Contact the O'Reilly and Associates information server for periodic updates on new titles from this publisher. Send e-mail to

```
To: listproc@online.ora.com
Subject: <leave blank>
Body: subscribe ora-news "Your name" of "Your Company"
```

Information about retrieving the Unofficial Internet Booklist is included at the beginning of this appendix.

INDEX

Symbols

A

E

F

G

H

I

J-K

L

N

O

P

Q-R

S

T

U

X-Y-Z

Book ISBN 0-672-30520-8